W9-BEG-378

WORLD IN MY EYES

RICHARD BLADE
THE AUTOBIOGRAPHY

WORLD IN MY EYES

RICHARD BLADE
THE AUTOBIOGRAPHY

Copyright © 2017 BladeRocker Entertainment Inc.

All rights reserved. No portion of this publication may be reproduced, stored in a re-
trieval system, or transmitted by any means—electronic, mechanical, photocopying, recording, or any other—except for brief quotations in printed reviews, without the prior
written permission of the publisher.

All photographs, news clippings, and transcripts of news articles are the property of
their respective owners and publications unless otherwise noted. Used with permission.

Cover Design: Firelight Interactive LLC

Interior Design: 3SIXTY Marketing Studio

Indigo River Publishing
3 West Garden Street Ste. 352
Pensacola, FL 32502
www.indigoriverpublishing.com

Ordering Information:

Quantity sales: Special discounts are available on quantity purchases by corporations,
associations, and others. For details, contact the publisher at the address above.

Orders by U.S. trade bookstores and wholesalers: Please contact the publisher at the
address above.

Printed in the United States of America

Library of Congress Control Number: 2017957646
ISBN: 978-1-948080-50-7

First Edition

With Indigo River Publishing, you can always expect great books, strong voices, and
meaningful messages. Most importantly, you'll always find...words worth reading.

———⟍◇⟍———

To Mum and Dad,
the beginning, middle and end of
everything, this all happened
because of you.

To my beloved Krista,
for allowing me to have a history.

———⟍◇⟍———

TABLE OF CONTENTS

Part Two: A.D.

THE PROLOGUE

TO CUT A LONG STORY SHORT

For more than a decade people have come up to me at my live shows and asked the same three questions, "Who is your favorite group?", "When are you going to write a book about your experiences?" and "With everything you've done what are you most proud of?"

I can answer two of those questions right now. My favorite group, Depeche Mode, and as to when I'm going to write a book, well, you are holding it.

I wrote every word of my autobiography. I didn't want a "ghost writer," they weren't there, I was. When I finally sat down to write I explained to my beautiful wife, Krista, that I had to be completely open about everything and that meant it would be uncensored and perhaps a little shocking including some revelations that I have never told anyone, not even her! She laughed and said, "Honey, everyone's got a past." Then she read some of the book and I watched as her eyes opened wide and she stared across the room and simply stated, "Wow, you were a man-whore!"

I was and that is a big part of the story and the reason that one of my three great loves ended. Hopefully I've grown up a little by now. I think I have but my story is in your hands now so that's up to you to decide.

This book also names names. Everything that is between these covers happened with very real people, many of whom you will be familiar with. Only three names have been changed for legal reasons, the rest are who they are.

And talking of names, the origin of how Richard Blade came about is spelled out, but that wasn't my first name change, hopefully your new favorite superhero alias will be Dick Sheppard, but his costume wasn't tights and a cape; Disco Dick was outfitted in platform heels and twenty-four inch flared pants and instead of battling super villains he toured Scandinavia and Europe packing the dance floors from Oslo to Vienna.

A lot of people thought I would just write about the eighties but I didn't want to start my story in the middle; so much came before that amazing decade and I think you'll enjoy the early years as much or maybe even more than the KROQ, MV3 and Video One days.

As the pages of the book fleshed themselves out I was asked by the publisher to come up with a title and I wanted to stay with the theme I was using for each chapter – and that's naming each one after a song (there is a single exception, one chapter is named after an album title rather than a specific song. See if you can spot which one that is, there's five Blade points up for grabs). For me it was a no-brainer what to call the book, after all I wanted to take the reader on a trip around the world and back and they wouldn't have to do a thing, just sit there. And my travels would take them to the highest mountains (of Norway), to the depths of the deep blue sea (as we get into the world of SCUBA) and the islands in the ocean (say hello to St. Maarten). To encompass all that there was only one song that fit the bill and it just happened to be from my favorite group (see above if you've forgotten already!) I emailed Martin Gore who had written that brilliant track and I was told he would be thrilled for me to use its title so World In My Eyes took shape with MLG's blessing.

But now I'd better get going, there's a lot of people lined up within these pages for you to read about and discover the untold stories of my time with them and I wouldn't want to keep Depeche Mode, Michael Jackson, Morrissey, Barbra Streisand, Duran Duran, George Michael, Pet Shop Boys, Larry Hagman, Spandau Ballet, Donna Summer, Michael Hutchence, Terri Nunn, Judas Priest, Boy George and Ted Nugent waiting, would you?

Oh, and as to the final question, "What are you most proud of?" I promise it will be answered and I think it will surprise most of you. It certainly surprised me when I came to that realization. You'll find out when you get to it, no spoilers here. Be prepared to laugh out loud, to gasp in surprise and to shed a tear – you might want to grab a hankie or two – and most of all I really hope you enjoy seeing the World In My Eyes.

KID

Mary Sheppard's anguished screams echoed down the long, damp corridors of the former sanitarium. Two nurses hurrying to attend to the needs of another patient paused for a second at the sound of the suffering and turned in concern.

The elder of the two shook her head and sighed, "If anyone can ease her pain, Doctor Sunderland can."

Doctor Sunderland was already doing everything he could to help Mary. He had cancelled his weekend plans to be there with her that Friday night. He had promised his wife and family that he would finally take a few days off from work so they could enjoy a short break together in North Cornwall away from the grime and the soot that Bristol's factories spewed into the air but all that was forgotten when he received the urgent call that Mrs. Sheppard needed him.

He'd almost lost her nearly seven years before. He remembered it vividly. It was November 1945 and Frenchay hospital was slowly moving from being a wartime treatment facility run by the US Army Medical Corps under the control of the 117th General Hospitals division, back to becoming a strictly civilian hospital governed by the Bristol Corporation.

As a young doctor, the war had forced him to specialize in dealing with horrific injuries caused by the foulest engines of battle; bombs, guns, shrapnel. From 1942 onwards he and his team had worked on more than 4,000 American GIs who had sailed across the Atlantic and risked their all to save the world. He was shocked when he was asked on that night in November to bring his experience in dealing with combat wounds to assist a woman enduring a prolonged labor.

Mary Sheppard had been struggling to give birth for more than twenty-eight hours when he was called in. She had refused a C-section and now with the baby having moved position within her womb it was too late to attempt one successfully. She was hemorrhaging and the attending physician was worried that he was about to lose both mother and child. Doctor Sunderland was the most knowledgeable person in the hospital in dealing with internal injuries; perhaps his expertise could save at least one of the patients.

As soon as Doctor Sunderland saw Mary Sheppard's rapidly deteriorating condition he realized the seriousness of the situation and assumed control of the operating room, calling for fluids and blood.

He took the hand of the exhausted woman on the operating table and spoke softly and reassuringly to her, "Don't worry, Mrs. Sheppard, I'm going to take care of this. You have my word that you will both be fine."

Two hours later he kept his promise and delivered a healthy baby. After a silent prayer of gratitude he told his exhausted patient she could breathe normally now.

"It's over, Mrs. Sheppard. You've got a baby waiting for you. Your husband's here. He's been outside the whole time."

Reg Sheppard stepped forward, his six-foot frame towering over his still shaking wife. He looked to the doctor.

"Can I . . .?" he asked.

"Yes," replied Doctor Sunderland. "And not to worry, she's going to make a full recovery."

Reg took his wife's hand and smiled at her, "You did it, Mary. You did it, my love."

Mary Sheppard looked up at her devoted husband but the pain was too recent and intense to be forgotten. The only words she uttered were a straightforward but firm statement.

"Never again, Reg. I can't ever do this again."

"I know. And I will never ask you to."

Mary had spoken those words almost seven years before and she had been determined to stick to them. One child would be enough for them, it would have to be. Let others have the big families; hers might be small but it would be full of love.

There's an old Greek saying "If you want to hear God laugh, tell him you made a plan." In late October 1951 the heavens exploded with mirth when Mary went to visit her GP to pick up medication to help soothe her stomach. He broke it to her with a smile, hoping she would embrace the news.

"Really, Mrs. Sheppard, I thought a woman of your age would know the difference between an upset tummy and a pregnancy!"

Mary was in a daze as she walked the half mile back to her house on Vassell Road. She sat motionless in the front room waiting for her husband to return home from his teaching post at Staple Hill Secondary School. When Reg arrived two hours later he saw this beautiful, petite woman sitting there, hunched up, her hands clutched tightly in her lap, her face white as a ghost.

"What is it, Mary?"

She tried to speak but all that came out were tears.

Doctor Sunderland knew her history well. When he received the call that Mary Sheppard was in labor he dropped all his plans and raced to the hospital that warm night in late May. He'd saved her once, he'd not risk letting some hack make an error and have to hear about "that unfortunate incident" when he returned from a long weekend break.

Now this patient that he had so much invested in was again in his hands, and he was well-prepared for what was ahead. This time he was not being called to take over at the last moment; he was the supervising physician, and tonight her delivery would be different.

She had been screaming in agony for almost five minutes and he could tell by her dilation that she was already past the active-labor phase. He squeezed her arm lightly to give her comfort.

"I know it hurts but you are almost there, Mary. I need you to be quiet for just a moment and only think about breathing. If you do that the pain will fade away. And I want you to push hard now, very hard. Do this and I promise you it will be over," He glanced at the large, round clock on the wall; it was 10:30 at night. "By eleven. We'll have that baby in your arms in less than thirty minutes. Will you push for me?"

At that moment Mary trusted him more than any other person on the planet. Her screams stopped and she pushed. Fifteen minutes later, at 10:45pm, May 23, 1952, Mary Sheppard gave birth to her second and final child.

Reg was hurried into the room and his eyes welled with tears as he saw his beloved wife cradling the newborn infant in her arms. Mary managed to smile.

"It's a boy, Reg, it's a boy."

Doctor Sunderland smiled, "Ten fingers, ten toes. It's all there. He's a healthy little son of a gun and after the last time I'm pleased to say this one couldn't wait to get out into the world. The big question is, have you picked a name for him yet?"

My mother managed to nod, "We have. I told Reg that if it was a boy we'd call him after his grandfather."

Dad took me in his arms and beamed at the doctor. "His name is Richard."

CITIES IN DUST

In the early 1950s, Bristol was not a great place to grow up. A decade earlier the city had been targeted repeatedly by the Luftwaffe during the air raids of World War II and more than 100,000 buildings had been damaged or destroyed. Rebuilding had not started in earnest because of the government's financial crisis; Britain's economy was in a shambles and before any funds could be freed up and sent to Bristol, the country needed to pull itself out of the malaise caused by the lingering effects of the war and the ruling party's ongoing battle with the trade unions. As a result the evidence of the devastation caused by the German bombs remained everywhere throughout the city.

But wartime carnage and burned-out shells of houses weren't my first memory. The earliest thing I can recall is a kiss.

I had just turned two years old. My parents had taken us to Nana McCann's house on Grove Park Terrace to celebrate my birthday and Nana was proudly throwing a little party for her newest grandson. My brother, Stephen, who was nearly seven years older than me, was out front playing football in the street with the other children. I was in Nana's tiny back garden being pushed on a swing and as I soared back and forth through the air I could feel the sensation of the breeze blowing through my hair, the warm sun on my skin and hear the sound of birds singing to welcome the coming of an early summer.

The person doing the pushing was the next-door neighbor's daughter, Rebecca Bailey. She was much older than me, almost three, and after a few minutes she stopped the swing and walked around to face me. She stood there in the sunshine, just looking at me with a strange expression on her face; then she smiled and leaned in, kissing me squarely on the lips. I liked it.

A second later the garden erupted with the sound of clapping and laughter from the grownups who were standing, watching, from the open kitchen doorway. I didn't mind the laughter or the applause; the kiss had been nice and it made me feel good.

That kiss is my fondest recollection of Bristol. The only other things I can remember from the next four years are lying down for my afternoon naps at the infant school, running through the wooded parkland overlooking the venerable Clifton suspension bridge and one morning sneaking into the front bedroom of my Auntie Grace's house to wake up Nanny Sheppard but instead of her stirring from her slumbers and greeting me with a smile and a hug, I found her lying there, still.

I was confused as to why she wasn't waking up; I thought she might be playing a game with me and that I should join in so I snuck around the bed and then jumped up and cried *Boo!* but she still didn't move.

I gave her a little poke with my finger but she just lay there, not even turning her head to look and see who was causing all the noise and trouble. I knew something was wrong but I didn't know what. I ran out of the room and into the lounge where the rest of the family was gathered for their morning cup of tea and biscuits.

"There's something wrong with Nanny," I cried, "She won't wake up."

The next few minutes at Number 10, Clifford Road were chaos. It was all movement, uproar and crying. Stephen, our beloved cousin Christine and I were quickly herded out of the house by Uncle Jim and taken to a neighbor who offered us lemonade and cake to take our minds off of what was happening just next door.

A few days later my parents were all dressed in black and waiting for a car to pick them up. When Christine and I asked where they were going we were told not to concern ourselves with that; they would be back soon and we should just stay home with the babysitter and finish our jigsaw puzzle.

In England at that time, death was yet another thing you didn't talk about in public, lest you reveal your weakness dealing with sadness and loss. Heaven forbid that anyone should see your real emotions and know how much you were suffering with grief.

With his mother gone and realizing what a bleak place Bristol had become to raise two young boys, my father decided that we should all move away to a smaller town with a healthier environment and cleaner air. I can only imagine the explanations and pleading that must have gone on between Dad and Mum to convince my mother to leave the city that she had so many roots in. But somehow he pulled it off and after one final Christmas in Bristol they packed everything up and we headed south one hundred miles to a coastal town called Torquay.

It was the first week of January 1959 when we arrived at 52 Davis Avenue in a downpour that would have had Noah rounding up the animals. Stephen's cough had turned into influenza midway on our journey down the A38 and he had become so weak that my father had to pick him up in his arms out of the back seat and carry the trembling thirteen-year-old boy through the torrential rain into the dark, cold house. My mother was traumatized and refused to get out of the car. She sat there, rocking back and forth, crying hysterically.

"I want to go back. I want to go back, Reg, I don't want to be here," she wailed.

My father, always the rock, stood there in the driving rain taking the brunt of the storm and kept calm, speaking softly to Mum.

"It won't stay like this much longer, Mary. We have to go in. Stephen needs us and we can't leave little Rich sitting out here in the damp."

The three of us sprinted through the deluge and spent our first few minutes in the town that's famed to be one of England's sunniest spots towel-drying each other and attempting to get warm.

TORQUAY

My father's decision to move was absolutely right. Torquay was everything that Bristol was not. It had beautiful clean beaches, rolling hills, endless countryside and a quaint town center that bustled with tourists in the summer months.

I found myself at Sherwell Valley Junior School where I excelled in looking out of the window and imagining far-off places. Even in my pre-teen days I wanted to travel, to explore, to get out into the world and have adventures. I read incessantly; books such as *Tarzan of the Apes, Around the World in Eighty Days, Huckleberry Finn,* and *Treasure Island,* and longed to experience for myself the thrill of discovery and the unknown vistas that waited around the next bend, but until I was old enough to actually go out and do that then Torquay with its sea to swim in, its trees to climb and its fields to hike was more than enough to suffice.

My teachers would see me lost in thought and call me a dreamer. I didn't mind the label. I was dreaming, dreaming of unfamiliar countries and distant shores. Of being the first to lay down my footprints on a sandy

At Sherwell Valley Junior School

beach instead of gazing out of a grimy school window at threatening skies and inclement weather.

One of my favorite television shows when I was a young boy was *Blue Peter*. It was on every Monday, right after school and was made for kids. There was always a feature on science, a story about traveling, an animal segment, often with their resident dog, Petra, and a piece on how to be better at something, like how to keep fit, the best way not to get winded when running cross-country or how to dribble a soccer ball. I took their advice to heart and would inevitably attempt all the things they put before me.

I was ten when I watched Christopher Trace tell me that I should set goals in life and make a list of the ten things I wanted to do then check them off as I achieved them. He gave examples like make the bed every day, do your homework before going out to play and to one day get a respectable job. This seemed a good idea, but I didn't like his examples. I already made my bed and mostly did my homework and as for a job, I had no idea what I wanted to do and *respectable* did sound a little boring; after all, not many explorers were "respectable." So I decided to make a different kind of list of goals.

The wind was howling outside as I went up to my room and the rain crashed against the window with such force it seemed as if the glass would inevitably shatter under the onslaught. In that cold, hostile environment I found a pen and paper and started to write my list.

1. I want to live somewhere sunny
2. I want to swim with the fish in warm water like Jacques Cousteau
3. I want to travel the world
4. I want to be famous
5. I want to be on television like Blue Peter
6. I want to meet my favourite singers
7. I want a beautiful girlfriend
8. I want to be in a movie
9. I want to write a book

The first nine items came easily; they were all things that I dreamed about doing every day at school when I should have been studying essential subjects like algebra instead. But what should be number ten? Christopher Trace had said the list wouldn't be complete unless it was ten things.

Outside the storm intensified as the wind turned to a roar and shadows flashed across the curtains as the branches of the trees flailed and whipped in the winter gale. To me those rapidly moving silhouettes became dinosaurs pacing back and forth outside my window, just waiting for me to fall asleep when they would smash through the glass and devour me.

I loved to read about dinosaurs and study them, and I would watch any movie that came on the telly that had a dinosaur in it, my favorites being *King Kong* and *Dinosaurus!* But at night, when the lights were out and the house creaked as it settled, that prehistoric love turned to fear as I felt that inevitable certainty that I was to be the next victim of a ravenous T. rex. Those horrific thoughts would drive me deep under the covers where I would remain, awake and unmoving, hoping against hope that those waiting monsters would think that my room was empty and there would be no delicious morsel for them that night.

The winter storms with their wailing winds only served to make my night terrors worse and even at ten years old I knew in my heart that this fear was irrational but I still suffered through it every evening as I lay there alone in the dark. I needed this to end; I didn't want to be afraid anymore. That's when it came to me what number ten on my list should be. I picked up my pen and wrote,

10.   I want to be brave

Just writing those words seemed to make the winds outside diminish and the dinosaurs scatter. Tonight, at least, I would be safe.

I read and re-read the list to make sure I was happy with it then folded it carefully and put it in the top drawer of my little dresser. My last thoughts as I fell into a blissful sleep were of wondering just how many of the ten items I would be able to check off one day.

In 1962 my school held a year-long fundraiser to build a swimming pool. For twelve months all of the children pestered our parents for tin cans and newspapers to recycle, to bake cookies and cakes for us to sell and to sponsor us in long-distance runs, anything to get the funds necessary for the pool. When the money was finally raised and the pool put in, swimming became my favorite competitive sport. To my delight my father had taught me to swim off the beach at Torre Abbey during our first summer in Torquay. Mum was worried sick as I bobbed around in the deep water but Dad wasn't concerned, "He's a little fish, Mary. And if there's any trouble I'll be in there in a flash."

The next year I left junior school and it was time for blazers, badges and long pants as secondary school beckoned. Torquay Boys Grammar School was an institution with its origins in the Victorian days and many of the teachers acted as if Victoria Regina were still on the Empire's throne.

"Neddy Kneebone," who taught history, would ride to work on his gun-metal-grey moped, pedaling furiously to conquer the final steep hill that led to the school. Instead of a crash helmet he strapped on his World War I Brodie helmet as if to ward off shrapnel from the cars that sped past the struggling teacher, leaving him in a cloud of exhaust fumes.

Mr. Kneebone had been shipped off to Europe in 1917 and fought in the trenches during the apocalyptic battles in France and Belgium. Two decades later when WWII shook the planet he found himself too old to enlist so he volunteered to serve as an air-raid warden in the West Country. He loved to wear parts of his various uniforms to school. One day it would be his combat boots, the next his midnight-blue warden's jacket and on rainy days he would retrieve his full-length wool trench coat from his closet and bundle up in that to fight his way through the downpour.

His favorite day of the year was November 11, Armistice Day. That's when this seasoned veteran of two tragic global conflicts was allowed to come to school and teach in his full military uniform complete with medals and insignia. We were sure that should World War III break out he would be the first to report to the recruiting office before the missiles were launched.

All that service had definitely biased Neddy Kneebone's version of history. His viewpoint was simple; Great Britain was always right.

"Of course we had to defeat the Zulu tribes. We knew best what was good for them."

"And the Aborigine?" we would ask, knowing we were winding him up.

"Yes, them too. Wandering around in that hot Australian Outback under the blazing sun with no clothes and no shoes. Not right at all. They're much happier now under British rule."

"And the American Indians?"

"Don't get me started on the Indians!" he would yell. "All that war paint and bows and arrows. Now they've got real houses to live in instead of bloody wigwams!"

That attitude ran through every subject taught at school. In Religious Knowledge I dared question "Bummer" Stokes, a teacher who acquired his nickname by boring every class half to death. He was rattling on during a comparative religions lesson whose sole purpose seemed to be to demean every belief that wasn't strictly Church of England.

"All the other religions might be well-meaning but they have a lot of mumbo-jumbo nonsense in them; the Catholics mask everything with all that smoke and incense, Hindus have a god with so many arms he looks like an octopus and the Jews stand there and chant at a wall. We (Church of England) stick to the basics because that is our direct path to God."

I raised my hand and asked a question that was innocent and simple,

"But wasn't the Church of England started by Henry VIII so he could get a divorce?"

"Don't be stupid, boy. Of course it wasn't. It was inspired by divine guidance."

"But I thought that the Pope wouldn't let Henry divorce Catherine of Aragon and so the King forced England to split from the Catholic Church just so he could remarry?"

"And you were there to see that with your own eyes?" He turned mockingly to the class. "It seems that Sheppard either has his own personal time machine or is a lot older than he looks. How was it back in King Henry's time? Did he tell you anything interesting, boy?"

I smiled, "As a matter of fact he did, sir. He said that once a king, always a king, but once a night's enough."

The class burst into laughter and the enraged Bummer Stokes spun around to the chalkboard, grabbed the wood-reinforced eraser and hurled it at me.

Unfortunately his aim was a lot better than his teaching ability and the eraser hit me squarely in my left eye.

"Now get out of my classroom and stand by the door, you idiot," he screamed.

I obeyed and thirty minutes later when the class let out I had the most awesome shiner that looked like I'd stepped into the ring and gone two rounds with that new, young American fighter Cassius Clay.

My father was not amused and left that night to confront Mr. Stokes at his house. I'm not sure what happened between the malicious teacher and the furious deputy headmaster but it was the last time I ever had to step foot in that small-minded bigot's class and yet I still received an A from him at the end of the year.

My favorite teacher was Mr. Roper, "String." From his Adolph Hitler mustache to his affinity for wearing corduroy hunting jackets with leather patches on the sleeves and elbows, he was unique. He taught art and was great at what he did, not only in his instruction but also as an artist and painter in his own right. He encouraged the students and made us want to learn and improve.

My one problem was that even though I was decent at drawing, painting and design, I wasn't my brother.

Stephen was a prodigy when it came to art. He could do it all—watercolor, oils, scraperboard—if it was in the curriculum he would not only master it but improve upon the course. He was so exceptional that at the age of seventeen the town held a painting exhibition to showcase his works at Torre Abbey and a year later he won a full scholarship to Dartington College of Arts. Stephen was a hard act to follow.

Mr. Roper was proud of my brother and understandably so; the more acclaim Stephen received for his work the more it correctly reflected on his school and his mentor, String. He liked me but I was no Stephen.

String had many endearing qualities and two terrifying ones—the twist and the strap! If he caught you talking in class he would sneak up behind you, grab a handful of hair from the base of your skull and lean in and say in a loud stage whisper, "Talking, boy?"

"No, sir!" would immediately be the reply.

"Oh, then I must be hearing things, is that what you're saying?"

"No, sir, I didn't mean that."

String was now readying his *piece de resistance*, "So you are or you're not saying that? Make up your mind; it sounds like you are getting . . . TWISTED!"

And with that high-pitched cry he would pull and twist your hair and yank you up onto your toes.

"That's the twist, boy!"

We all felt the pain of the twist but we welcomed that agony compared to what was feared most; the strap.

String had a series of sayings that he would recite like poetry. Every year winter rolled around and the cold season that bore down on the students turned Torquay Boys Grammar School into a petri dish. If you dared sniffle or cough in String's class he would instantly stop what he was doing and serenade us in his sing-along voice:

"Coughs and sneezes spread diseases,

If you fail to use your hankie, you will surely get a spanky!"

When he returned to the blackboard and had his back to us we would chant:

"If your hanky you forget to bring,

You will get the strap from String."

He would whirl around, pretending to be annoyed. "Who said that?" We would shake our heads. We didn't know.

The strap was the nuclear option for String and a real threat that he used at least once or twice a month. One lunch time I returned to the art room to finish an architectural project I was working on. This was common practice, but officially you had to ask permission every single time before you came inside and started. However few pupils ever did that and most teachers were flattered that their students were putting in the extra work. But not that day.

I was working on a detailed scale line drawing of the incredible dome that Sir Christopher Wren had designed and built for St Paul's Cathedral in the late 1600s, when String walked into the classroom and saw me there.

"Just what do you think you are doing, Sheppard?"

"I'm working on our architecture project for the class, sir."

"And who said you could be in here now?"

"No one, sir, I just thought—"

"No you didn't!" he cut me off. "You didn't think. That's your problem, boy." He drew himself up to his full five foot eight inches. "There will be a reckoning for you during our lesson this afternoon."

Two hours later I found myself called out to the front of the class. String had me push forward a sketching desk then retrieve the strap from his drawer. I had to hand it to him, then in front of the class, bend over the desk, pull down my trousers and underpants and take "six of the best" from String.

His strap was made of leather, twenty-four-inches long and had a flex on it like a whip. It was the kind of strap that's found in an old-time barber shop. But this strap's purpose was not for polishing straight-edged razors but for punishing wayward students.

String's technique for corporal punishment was simple and devastating. The first four swings would land on your naked butt. Just as you fought through the pain and hoped you could handle the final two blows he would lower the strap and whip it across the top of your thighs right below your ass cheeks. These were the two killers. The impact from the burning leather lashing your exposed legs would race through every atom of your body causing you to jerk upright and gasp out loud in pain.

It was a lesson for the observers too; they could see welts instantly appear where the strap had landed and they turned a nasty purple highlighted by flecks of red from broken blood vessels trying to push through your skin. But you couldn't cry, not if you wanted to keep the respect of your friends. String would then step away.

"Put your trousers back on, Sheppard. We don't need to see any more of that."

He then finished the ritual in his usual way by making you push the desk back into its place, handing you the strap to return to the drawer you'd taken it from and then having you stand in front of him and say the magic words, "Thank you, sir. I won't do that again."

"Okay, class," said String, "Now we have that unfortunate incident out of the way let's get back to work." He turned to me and said, with a sympathetic smile, "You can do this standing if it's more comfortable for you, Sheppard."

In January 1964 we moved about a mile across Torquay to the house that I will always consider my home, 22 Drake Avenue. Do you have a place that is close to your heart, which always says "home" to you? That was number 22 for me. It was never just a house; it was always the Sheppard's home.

It was in a brand-new development that Mum and Dad had learned about before anybody else from a friend at their school. They went up to the fields where the new homes were to be built and had the first choice of all the lots there. They picked out their favorite. It sat on the crest of the hill and had a view that encompassed Torquay's Victorian harbor and from there out across Torbay.

The developer allowed them to customize the design to their tastes, but being English they stuck fairly closely to the architect's plans. "After all we didn't want to upset him," said Dad.

They took me up there to see the site when I was eleven years old. It had rained non-stop for the previous three days and everything was so wet that Mum opted to stay in the car. My father led Stephen and me to a muddy patch of ground that clawed at our Wellington boots like quicksand.

"This is where we are going to be living," he proudly announced.

Stephen and I looked at each other and at the marsh that was threatening to suck us down and engulf us and we didn't quite get it; were we going to set up a tent in this open swampland and cook around a camping stove?

Dad sensed our apprehension and laughed as he tousled my hair, "Don't you worry, boys, I promise it'll all be fine."

Dad was right. Eight months later the drainage had been put in, the roads laid and the house built. It was everything Mum and Dad had wanted and more. We all loved number 22, especially Dad, and every spare moment that he had, my dad tended the garden, planted trees, dug out and poured concrete for pathways and was up on a ladder pruning hedges. If a reporter from *Architectural Digest* had shown up then my parents' garden would have been ready for the cover.

HALCYON

When I turned thirteen Mum and Dad bought me a transistor radio for my birthday. This small plastic battery-powered device changed my world. Suddenly I could tune in and hear records that I related to, music that was made for teenagers. No more Perry Como, Bing Crosby and Ray Conniff. Now I could hear The Beatles and The Monkees on the radio. But only at night.

The problem was that in Britain in 1965 there was no pop music radio. None. The BBC had a total monopoly on the airwaves and had no interest in playing anything remotely interesting to kids. Even though John, Paul, George and Ringo were number one on the sales charts they were considered unsuitable for broadcast by the BBC. To hear songs from the pop charts you either had to buy the record or go over to a friend's house who already had a copy. But that changed when the pirates arrived.

Strictly speaking Radio Luxembourg wasn't a pirate station. It had been granted a license by the country that gave the station its name and allowed it to operate a massive 100,000-watt transmitter at 208 on the AM dial. *Two-Oh-Eight*, as it was affectionately called, would start its pop music shows around seven at night after the sun went down and its signal could then blast unencumbered across Europe and the UK. The British government frowned upon this intrusion into its airwaves but could do nothing as suddenly every kid in the UK was listening to 208 and buying the songs they heard on the station. The DJs became massive stars and Tony Prince and Kid Jensen were as famous as Mick Jagger or Keith Moon.

With 208 having such a huge audience other entrepreneurs had the idea to follow their act, but if they couldn't convince another country to grant them a license to broadcast as Luxembourg had done then where would they put their transmitters? The answer was floating in front of them. On a boat!

Radio Caroline became the first of the pirate stations whose signal came screaming in from a ship anchored in the North Sea in international waters barely three miles off of the English coast. No longer did we teenagers have to bow down to the Beeb and put up with Henry Mancini's greatest hits night after night, now we had options for our music.

Most evenings, after I fibbed to my parents that I had finished my homework, I would leave the house clutching my beloved transistor radio and join my buddies Mike Frost, John Bennett, Ian Acton, Malcolm Alsop and Steven Easterbrook at Kitson Park where we would huddle together for warmth as we tuned into Radio Caroline to hear the world of music revealed to us. It was there that I heard what I consider to be arguably the very first punk song, "My Generation" from The Who, and was introduced to musical geniuses like Roy Wood and Brian Wilson.

Those nights at Kitson Park, waiting breathlessly for "this week's pick of the pops" or "something brand-new from the U.S. of A!" created a love in me for music and the pioneering DJs who brought it to us. As I listened, hour after hour, that portable transistor was shaping my musical tastes forever.

I made a point to thank my parents for the little radio that had become my gateway to a new dimension. They were happy their gift was appreciated and they knew that it hardly ever left my side. But there was one thing I wanted to know that had me puzzled. The brand name of the model of that tiny portal to the world of music was a word I had never heard. It was called Halcyon.

"What does halcyon mean, Dad?" I asked.

"It means happy times that were in the past. Long departed days that you think of often and wish they would come again," he explained.

There was no irony in his answer but what an appropriate name for that little radio and the joy that it brought me. To this day when a song comes on that I first heard on that tiny transistor those moments that come flooding back and I return to that time of innocence and discovery, those halcyon days.

LOVE ME DO

Girls were always an attraction for me as a boy. I never went through that period of "girls are gross." Gross? Hell, no. Having a girlfriend and making out was something you aspired to even before you hit your teens.

Every Saturday someone would have a party in their parents' front room, preferably when their mum and dad were out of the house, at "the pictures" or the pub. The routine was simple and excitedly anticipated by all. After about thirty minutes of small talk everyone who didn't already have a current boyfriend or girlfriend would pair off and the lights would be turned all the way down. This was the cue for the make-out session to start and the host would put Simon & Garfunkel or The Beatles on the record player to create the mood. The object for the boys was to find out how far they could go; for the girls it was to get the most from the boys without "going all the way."

For three hours your lips were locked together as hands fumbled in the dark for bra straps and zippers.

Sadly there were always one or two unfortunates who didn't get paired up or failed to hit it off and you could hear them munching sadly on their crisps and noisily drinking their Coca-Cola through straws as "Sound of Silence" played.

Until I was fifteen all of my girlfriends were local; they lived close by and would hang out with us at the bowling alley or the park. But then in the summer of 1967 I started noticing the Scandinavian girls that flooded into town for eight weeks during the summer.

These were tall, lean, flaxen-haired exotic beauties with rocking accents and no local ties to worry about. They were away from their families and boyfriends and in Torquay to learn English and have a good time.

I tried hard that summer to "get off" with one of those blond babes but I was too young; their ages ranged from sixteen to twenty, so that would be impossible, right? But I still persevered to no avail.

It was late August and I was at St Luke's Church's dance. Reverend Ryder-Jones held the disco for teens every Friday in the church hall and it was something that every kid who was too young to go to a pub or a real club looked forward to. That Friday I was shocked that a half-dozen Swedish girls were there. One was stunning with golden hair and a short, pink dress. My favorite song at the time, "Gimme Some Lovin'" by Spencer Davis, came blaring over the speakers and I plucked up enough courage to ask her to dance.

Her name was Elizabeth and she was from the east coast of Sweden where she lived in a town I couldn't pronounce. She told me she was seventeen and asked how old I was.

"I'm seventeen too," I lied, hoping my voice didn't break as I said it.

We shared soft drinks and danced until the church hall shut its doors at eleven. She was staying in Shiphay, just a mile from where I lived. Not wanting to say goodbye to this gorgeous girl I offered to walk her home and she said she'd like that. Our path took us through the grounds of Torre Abbey and suddenly I found myself making out with Elizabeth standing up against a centuries-old oak tree.

As our session got hot and heavy I readied myself to hear the inevitable *no* which always came right at the good part. But not tonight.

Holy shit, I thought, *No fucking way!*

She hiked her dress up and still in a state of disbelief I unzipped my fly. *Is it really going to happen?*

She kissed me hard as if to dispel any doubt and I went for it.

I knew roughly what I should do, the physics and biology of it. But it's like explaining to someone how to drive a car and then putting them behind the wheel for the first time and saying, "Just go." It's not that easy.

But I just went. Suddenly I was inside Elizabeth but so was the bottom part of my shirt! It had come out of my zipper along with the essential bits and was going along for the ride. Sadly this was 1967 and I'd just come from a church dance so I was dressed up. That meant a long-sleeved nylon

24

shirt with spare buttons attached. And you know where they sew those two extra buttons? That's right, at the very tip of the bottom of the shirt, the part that was now 100% obscured from sight.

Nylon chafes, and buttons, well they are definitely not the softest things. But I was fifteen: I certainly didn't want to stop, this might NEVER happen again! At that moment I was achieving my life's ambition, having sex with a real live girl. The fact that I was also having sex with a Van Heusen shirt was a little troubling but not enough to stop. And I was so naive I didn't know what to say. "Excuse me, but you're humping me and my dress whites" were not the romantic words I'd heard Cary Grant utter in the movies.

And I didn't know if she even realized we were having sex. What if she hadn't noticed? Maybe she had been so caught up in our kissing that she wasn't paying attention and it had accidentally slipped inside. If I pointed it out she might scream, "What? You're having sex with me? I didn't know. Get it out." I might never have the opportunity to meet a willing girl again and would be resigned to living out my life in a monastery; bowing, scraping and regretting my decision to speak out that night in Torquay.

So I did the only thing I could: I kept going. Sure it hurt and I could feel the end of the family jewels losing skin with every push as the buttons scraped against it but I was finally doing it and that was what was important. And maybe it was meant to feel this shitty.

I had anticipated a slightly better result. A year or so before, my father had tried to give me the birds-and-bees lecture.

"Your mum wanted me to have a talk with you but I figure that a young boy like you with all your girlfriends has a good idea about what's going on. But if you want to know anything just ask." He smiled then added, "You know, Rich, I used to think planes were the best thing in the world until I discovered sex."

He gave me a wink and walked away. Sex talk over, I was now a qualified expert.

Except that I wasn't. I had no clue. And right now a good airplane ride seemed a much more enticing proposition than the shirt that was having its way with both of us.

Finally I just stopped. There was no climax. No fireworks exploding or rockets launching. Just a humiliating withdrawal. It was like the British troops being evacuated from the beaches of Dunkirk, it had seemed a good idea at the beginning but ended in humbling defeat.

I kissed her then put everything back where it was meant to go and carefully zipped up. We walked to her house in silence. As I kissed her goodnight she smiled and said words that at first I couldn't quite comprehend.

"I had fun. Do you want to get together again? I only have a few days left before I go back to Sweden."

Once I understood the meaning of what she was saying we made a date to meet the next night. As I walked away I was almost in shock; she wants to see me again? How on earth had she enjoyed it? Maybe she was into men's haberdashery?

Less than twenty-four hours later it was time for me to head back to Shiphay to where Elizabeth was staying and take her out for the evening. Tonight, just in case that same miracle of young love happened, I would be prepared. I was wearing the shortest t-shirt I could find; it barely reached to my belt and it definitely had *no fucking buttons* on it!

Elizabeth and I travelled in style that night; we rode the number-twelve bus to the harbor. Our destination was Torquay's version of Las Vegas, an amusement arcade called The Golden Palms, where we played the penny slots and laughed at the money tumbler where you feed coins into a machine and watch as it stacks them until the very weight of all the money you've donated makes some of it over-balance so that a small fraction cascades out and is returned to you.

You squeal with excitement at the jangling sound of the coins rattling down into the metal holder that catches the winnings and as you count your plunder you begin to realize that it only cost you thirty-five pence of your money to get back sixteen pence. But you won, and if math, logic, reason or common sense aren't your strong suits then you do it all over again and again until you run out of cash.

Having dined on the finest cotton candy and ice cream that the south of England had to offer we grabbed each other's hands and strolled along the seafront. First we went to the beautiful Rock Walk, a towering cliff covered with trees and bushes and lit by massive colored lights so it looked like a scene from fairyland. It was also one of Torquay's most romantic spots and I was hoping that we might find a secluded alcove . . . Unfortunately I wasn't the only bloke with that idea; it was a Saturday night and there was a line for all the secluded alcoves that evening with dozens of other young, frisky couples milling around.

Time was running out and frustration was starting to build.

"Let's keep walking," I suggested.

We wandered along the seafront talking about school and Sweden and holidays but all the time I was looking for that perfect dark spot. There had to be somewhere. We passed Torre Abbey and both of us looked up the little lane to the stand of trees where Elizabeth, Van Heusen, and I had become intimate the night before. I was buggered if I was going back there to repeat last night's disaster and I didn't want to be standing up if I was to try it again. That's not how I had heard it was done. Move along, nothing to see here.

We reached the outdoor bowling greens and the fenced-off mini-golf course. It was nine holes with sand traps and bunkers. I had played on it a couple of times and it was always fun. Then it hit me. It was closed now so if we hopped the fence we'd have it all to ourselves. I knew a spot where the fence dropped from an intimidating six foot to a more manageable four foot.

"Wanna try and get in there?" I asked.

"Sure," said Elizabeth.

We reached the low point and I gave Elizabeth a boost and we were over. We found a spot on the green that was shaded from the walkway and laid down and starting making out. I was shocked because she seemed as excited about it as me. All four of our hands were everywhere and in just minutes it was round two but this time no men's evening wear was interfering.

"So this is why it's better than an airplane!" I remember thinking as we kissed, rolled and squeezed.

Amazingly, though I had heard all the jokes before, it wasn't over in seconds; in fact I really wanted it to last so I forced thoughts of cold cauliflower, Harold Wilson and slimy earthworms to fill my head and calm me down at each critical moment. Finally, maybe fifteen minutes later, I pushed those nasty images from my brain and said hello to the end of my innocence.

We lay on the cool grass of the putting green for a while and she stroked my hair and whispered something in Swedish into my ear. I wanted to reply but all that the fifteen-year-old boy could think of was, "Thank you for taking pity on me." Even after the rush of hormones I had the sense to know that wouldn't be cool but I had to say something. Then the words came to me as we lay there on the golf course and before I tell you what I said, please forgive me in advance; I was a kid, it was my first complete time and I was over the moon with what had happened. All I could see was this beautiful girl, the moon above and the flagstick with the number seven on it waving softly above us. So I whispered to her, "Hole in one."

Whether she understood the joke or not I'm still not sure, but she laughed and kissed me and we ran all the way back to her house. That night I slept like I had been nailed to the mattress.

I saw Elizabeth for half an hour the next day then it was time to say goodbye. The family she was staying with was taking her out for a farewell dinner that night and then first thing Monday morning she left with the rest of her Swedish classmates on a bus bound for London. I never saw Elizabeth again but I have never forgotten her and I smile every time I see hole number seven on Torquay's seafront. As for that stand of trees and Van Heusen shirts? I avoid both like the plague!

A month after losing my virginity to Elizabeth something else almost equally momentous happened for me—and for millions of other kids in the UK.

CHILDREN OF THE REVOLUTION

In the summer of 1967 the pirates finally made the British government walk the plank! Due to the continually growing popularity of the offshore radio stations the BBC capitulated and was forced to introduce full-time pop programming. They caved in and revamped their entire antiquated broadcasting structure and announced to the nation that BBC Radio One was coming.

On Saturday morning September 30, 1967, I set my alarm clock for 6:45am so I could catch every second of the beginning of this new station that promised to rock Great Britain. At 7am I was tuned in to 247 on the AM dial and listening intently as the countdown started and the familiar voice of Tony Blackburn came over my little radio.

We had all wondered if the BBC would "cock it up" and if the old guys in charge would be so out of touch that they would have no real ability to bring us legitimate pop programming but this was a good start; we all knew Tony Blackburn from his days on pirate radio so at least the Beeb had brought on board "the real thing."

Tony said hello, and I waited with millions of others up and down the British Isles to see if they would play a pop song that we could relate to or just go into some dross like Andy Williams. When he introduced that first record, The Move and "Flowers in the Rain," I was ecstatic and knew right there and then that a new era in pop music had been born. Now we kids could listen to the songs and groups we loved twenty-four hours a day.

The revolution that had started five years before with The Beatles and had been fought on the high seas with pirate radio ships firing musical broadsides was over, and for once we had won and brought down the mighty government of the United Kingdom. The airwaves were finally ours. British music—and my life—would never be the same again.

FUN, FUN, FUN

Torquay had plenty of jobs available for kids during the holiday seasons which in the "Queen of the English Riviera" were Christmas, Easter and all summer. I was fourteen when I got my first job, washing dishes at the Conway Court Hotel. As the seasons came and went I worked my way from behind the scenes at the back of the kitchen to hitting the dining-room floor, first as a food waiter and then as a wine waiter.

What I knew about wine could have been written on a cork: it came in a bottle and you drank it. When I was asked for a recommendation—because I'm sure that you always trust a sixteen-year-old boy to be your sommelier—my go-to was Mateus Rose. I chose that because not only does a rose go with everything but it had the coolest bottle that I could take home to Mum and she would turn into a brilliant candlestick holder. I think my two summers as a wine waiter helped keep Portugal's economy afloat during the sixties.

I worked hard and saved my money and at sixteen took the jump, became a mod and bought a scooter. It was a Lambretta LI 150, white with blue side panels and rabbit fur on the back support of the passenger seat. Now I had transportation that looked cool, I didn't have to pedal and—most importantly—the girls loved it.

Many a time I would see an exchange student waiting at a bus stop and if she was cute I'd pull up and offer her a ride home. It became a great dating machine.

My scooter also gave me something to transport my spearfishing gear on. I'd been snorkeling and spearfishing since I was twelve, and at fourteen bought a roll of neoprene and a design from a company in London and with scissors, glue, tape, a thick needle and nylon thread, made my own wetsuit.

The wetsuit was vital; even in summer the water in Torquay was cold, in the low sixties, so without a suit you couldn't stay out for more than fifteen minutes. Now, incased in my custom neoprene shell I could drift with the tide for hours before my extremities began to shake and turn blue.

I found a secret spot off of Torquay, in deep water nearly a half mile offshore where a submerged rock reef sheltered schools of fish. I discovered it accidentally one day as I floated over it. I made a note of its position by triangulating it with three objects on the shore and it became *my* spot. I never saw anyone else there and never told anyone about it.

I only took fish that Mum, Dad and I could eat and never more than two at most. In the mid- to late summer schools of bass would come in with the warmer water to graze on the kelp and seaweed that grew on the rocks. They only arrived on the incoming high tide which meant that to get to them you had to swim out against the current and after the hunt, whether successful or not, your long swim back to the shore was now against the outgoing tide. It was a workout but one that I looked forward to and loved.

These beautiful silver fish ranged between seven and twelve pounds and were not only amazing swimmers but smart. I swear that if they caught you looking at them they would be gone in an instant. My trick was to lie on the surface motionless until I saw them below me then let the tide take me past them, dive silently down and swim back underwater.

If I was lucky I would have time to get one shot off. Miss and you were done. Hit, and the fight of a lifetime would break out. You were twenty feet down, surrounded by rocks and kelp, with a fish that was desperately trying to escape by kicking and whirling. It would whip up the long, barbed fins on its back in defense and several times over the years I felt the five sharpened points rip through my gloved hands and tear deep into the flesh between my thumb and finger as I tried to subdue the fighting fish.

You had to do this, and quickly, because otherwise its frantic spinning would free it from the spear and the bass would swim off somewhere to die and that would be a tragedy because a fish like this deserves much more than being shot just for kicks. To finally bring the bass to the surface and slip it into my mesh game bag was a thrill and it was great to know that that night my family and I would be eating the freshest catch around.

The ocean became my playground. I loved it and treated it with great respect. Despite the fact that Torquay had very little surf due to its sheltered location in the heart of Torbay, I bought a used nine-foot, single-fin surfboard. I could only use it locally in the dead of winter when the water temperatures had dropped into the forties, because it was then that the massive storms rolling in from the Atlantic and eastward up the English Channel would push huge rollers into the bay.

I would get my parents to drop me off in Paignton, the next coastal town over, and there I learned to surf in the thundering white-water swells that would break at Paignton Pier. Mum and Dad would sit in the restaurant on the pier and have dinner while their son paddled frantically into the pounding foam below them as I attempted to get out past the endless line of waves. In my head I could hear Dad saying to Mum, "He's a little fish, Mary. And if there's any trouble I'll be in there in a flash."

When I turned seventeen I passed my driving test (the second time—damn you, parallel parking!) and sold my scooter to buy a car. I borrowed some money from my parents to make up the difference and bought a Morris Minor convertible. Now I could stash the board in the car and speed off to the surf spots in North Devon and Cornwall, a good sixty miles away.

I had finished my O-levels and had moved on to the sixth form at school where at the tender age of sixteen you

Outside #22 with my first car, a Morris Minor

were required to decide what you were going to do with the rest of your life. To tell you the truth I had no clue.

Stephen was beginning a successful career as an actor in London having graduated at the top of his class at RADA, the Royal Academy of Dramatic Arts, and had just shot his first film with perhaps the most famous movie star in the world, Richard Burton, so I felt like the no-good brother condemned to living an aimless life.

I selected the three subjects I was best at; English, art, and history and they became the three A (advanced) levels I would attempt to pass. Get those and maybe I could find myself a place at university.

My parents suggested teaching but that wasn't what I wanted to do.

"Then what do you want to do?" Dad wanted to know.

"Not sure, but not teach."

Finally I found a compromise. I was at the public library going through their books on colleges and university colleges and found one that was affiliated with Oxford University that also offered a teacher training course, Westminster College, Oxford. This would make Mum and Dad happy and I could take an accredited Oxford University degree. But most importantly for me, it had a swimming pool on campus and a competitive swimming team. This way I could study and pursue my favorite sport in one place.

My teachers advised against me applying to a college that was a part of Oxford University. They said it would be much easier to select a college that wasn't associated with an institute that had such a storied background; after all the University of Oxford is the oldest university in the English-speaking world. Established in 1096 it set the standard for Western education. They recommended I try to get into Plymouth or Reading College instead. I understood their concern but that swimming pool was calling my name and Oxford with its multiple colleges seemed to be an amazing student party town.

I put the naysayers' gloomy advice aside and applied to Westminster based on my academic record and the courses I was taking. Two weeks later I received a letter back. I had been accepted pending the results of my A-levels. Pass, and I was going to Oxford, fail and . . . Well, I didn't even want to visit that option.

SCHOOL'S OUT

I had never been to Westminster College until that day in September, 1970 when I pulled into the parking lot at the top of Harcourt Hill. I had applied—and been accepted—sight unseen, based on my courses and academic record.

For me the choice had been swayed by a number of reasons, the most important being the chance to join the college swim team. Other factors included the fact that Oxford was almost 200 miles from Torquay so I would have the chance to get away from home and meet all-new people in a brand-new city and that I could take an Oxford University degree if I stayed on for a fourth year. That sounded particularly attractive as I had no clue what I wanted to do with my life so four years at college and university seemed a good option. What I wasn't prepared for was that it was a religious college.

Somehow while reading through the endless parade of available colleges presented in the careers section of Torquay public library I must have skipped past the part that said, "Westminster is a Methodist college." That oversight was quickly corrected that very first day at the assembly of all the new students where we were addressed by the college chaplin, who explained in no uncertain terms that while we were not *required* to attend the daily services it was *highly recommended*. The subtext was painfully obvious: don't go to chapel and not only will fire and brimstone rain down upon your head for all eternity, but you'll also be viewed unfavorably by the academic staff for the next three years. You'll be going to hell and so will your grades!

I hadn't been to church since I was eleven years old and my voice broke in the middle of "All Things Bright and Beautiful," ending my budding career as a choir boy. It was all I could do not to jump up from that first assembly, run to the parking lot and speed back to Torquay.

One thing that stopped me from doing that was the ratio of girls to boys in that meeting. It was at least two to one in my favor. Because Westminster offered such a strong teaching course it attracted a disproportionate number of young women who had decided, very admirably, that teaching was to be their vocation. And a lot of those girls were very cute. Maybe I should stay for a while. If I didn't like it I could always do what Timothy Leary had suggested just a couple of years before, "Turn On, Tune In, Drop Out."

I was assigned my dorm. Westminster had more than sixty "houses" on campus with nine bedrooms in each. First-year students shared a room, second- and third-years had their own. It was very basic; just a bed, a small wardrobe and a sink. Communal showers, toilets and the kitchen were downstairs. Your roommate was assigned alphabetically; I was Richard Sheppard so I was sentenced to year sharing a room with Robert Shellard. Aside from our last name being just one letter apart we had nothing else in common. Bob was taller than me at six-foot four-inches and maybe fifteen pounds lighter. I was six two and 168 pounds, twelve stone, so Bob was a bean pole. He also had no interest in partying, music or girls. It was going to be a long twelve months.

Each house had a letter designation starting at A; ours was PP. As I got to know the ins and outs of Westminster College I was thankful every day for where I ended up. Most of the guys' houses were populated by clones of Bob, but two houses had developed a reputation, CC and PP. The word was that the boys in those houses should be avoided by "decent" girls at all costs.

Umm, let me think about that for a moment. You take an attractive eighteen-year-old girl, away from home for the first time, put her in college and then say, "Stay away from those boys, they have a scandalous reputation. The other boys are much nicer and safer, just like the ones back home." Who do you think she is going to be most interested in?

Amongst the residents of PP house were the captain of the field-hockey team, Phil Richards, the captain of the rugby team, Keith Martin and the DJ of all the college dances, Norm Holmes. PP was a good place to be.

My first day at PP put me face to face with Phil Richards. He welcomed me to the house.

"What's your name?" asked Phil.

"Richard Sheppard," I replied.

"Richards is my last name. Too confusing to have two Richards in the house. You're Dick."

And just like that Dick Sheppard was born.

PP was just yards from the swimming pool rather than way across campus, so even in the pouring rain or blowing snow I could make it to the pool to train, often twice a day. I'd tuck my long hair into a swim cap and start by doing laps then sprints. Apart from the late afternoons I usually had the pool to myself. Westminster had its chapel; the pool became my church.

Being a part of Oxford University had benefits that I hadn't anticipated. At our student union orientation we were introduced to the literally hundreds of extra-curricular activities available, everything from needlepoint to mountaineering—which puzzled me as the nearest mountain to Oxford was the hill that Westminster College was located on and most of the students already scaled it twice a day as they made their way to and from the pub.

My roommate chose to take Bible studies while I signed up for Shotokan Karate. It was an intensely physical but fun class that met twice a week, once at the gym at Westminster and once at a dojo in town.

I'd been at college just one week when the first dance was held in the cafeteria. The sound gear that the student union rented was delivered and Norm readied his record collection.

Coming from Manchester, Norm was big into Northern Soul which is an English term for fast, uptempo American black music imports which had at its forefront amazing artists such as Gene Chandler, Al Wilson, The Elgins and Dobie Gray. It was huge in the clubs in the north of England but being a "southerner" it was a style of music that I hadn't been exposed to before and I lapped it up. It made me want to dance and I could immediately hear how effective it would be in a club or played loudly over a mobile disco system.

I worked as Norm's roadie that first night and watched in awe as he kept the floor packed. He didn't arrive with any pre-set plan of what to play; instead, he allowed himself to feel the ebb and flow in the room and would deliberately let the energy start to drop then slam into a huge song to bring it back up and take it on to the next level. *He's reading the crowd,* I thought to myself. *That's how a great DJ does it.*

As the evening wore on I noticed another thing starting to happen. Girls were asking Norm for requests and then hanging around the DJ booth waiting to be noticed. In that college cafeteria on two rented turntables, Norm was the star. He didn't sing, he didn't dance, but he ruled that room with his music and the girls loved him. A light went off and on September 26, 1970, I glimpsed my future.

The dance was scheduled to end at midnight and at around eleven o'clock two third-year girls arrived, Sue and Pauline Cook. They weren't sisters, just friends who had met each other two years before when Westminster's alphabetical system assigned them as roommates. The blond, Pauline, hit the dance floor while Sue came up to Norm at the DJ booth to say hi. She caught my eye and smiled.

"And just who are you?" she asked.

"I'm Dick. I'm in the same house as Norm."

Norm looked over and grinned. "Be gentle with him now, Sue."

Sue waited as the dance wound down and the exhausted students piled out. I started to help Norm with the rental gear but he waved me away,

"You've got other things to do," he said.

Sue led me across the quadrangle to the outside of L house.

"Pretend you're saying goodnight to me then go around the back. I'll open the window for you."

I nodded in understanding. Westminster College had stern policies against a man being in a girl's room or vice versa. It was strictly forbidden after 8pm. If you were caught you had to appear before Donald Tranter, the principal of the college. The second time was grounds for expulsion. Despite that harsh ruling, after dark when hormones were raging, the quad came alive with scurrying young lovers dashing back and forth.

I tumbled through Sue's window as gracefully as possible and within seconds we were going at it on her bed. That's when she stopped me.

"What is your hurry?" she said. "Let's take our time."

"Okay," I replied.

"Wait a minute, this is new to you isn't it?" Sue was smiling now.

I was flustered. Was I so inept she thought I was a virgin? "No, I've done it a lot. I've had plenty of girlfriends."

"But not like this, right? Not alone, in a bedroom, with no worry of your parents coming home? I bet you've always had to be fast so you didn't get caught. Right?"

Sue had seen right through me. There had been plenty of girls but I'd never had the luxury of a private bedroom with no fear of that dreaded knock on the door. There had been many stolen, furtive encounters, all passion and young lust cooped up in the backseat of a small car but no long, safe nights of love-making. I nodded in agreement with her assessment.

Sue smiled, "Then this is going to be fun. All you have to do is relax; I'll show you what to do. We've got all night."

And just like that, on the same evening that I began to learn about DJing from a pro, another expert took me under her wing to educate me in something else equally important, the ways of women.

For the next three months I played Benjamin Braddock to Sue's Mrs. Robinson. I'd come to Westminster for an education and I certainly got one, but perhaps not the kind that my parents or Donald Tranter had planned.

Sue and I were not "boyfriend and girlfriend" or even exclusive. We both saw other people but we still found time for me to climb in through her window four nights a week.

The Christmas holidays came and went and when I returned to Westminster I found Pauline Cook waiting for me. Sue had decided it was time for her to move on to greener pastures and her best friend, Pauline, had volunteered to step in and continue my education. I was not complaining.

Pauline was a very pretty blond and always caught your eye when she would shimmy on the dance floor in her miniskirts and thigh-high patent-leather boots. The only problem was that her room was upstairs on the second floor so, not being a skilled cat burglar, I now had to sneak in and out through the front door which was an equally perilous proposition. But the risk/reward ratio was definitely in my favor and I learned to move quickly and silently through the quadrangle unobserved by the watching prefects. And let me just make a statement here, whoever coined the term "Too many cooks spoil the broth" had obviously never met these two Cooks!

I continued to help Norm with the college dances which were booked every other Saturday throughout the term. I became very proficient at setting up the rental gear and troubleshooting any problems that occurred with the speaker leads and valve amplifiers. Norm began letting me DJ with him and start off the first hour of the dances. I had no record collection of my own at Westminster so I had to use Norm's and I treated his seven-inch vinyl singles like gold.

Soon I was getting the early crowd dancing and began to get confident using the microphone. My initial fear of being laughed at when I said something dissipated and I looked forward all week to getting behind the turntables and playing for the other students. I would emulate my DJ heroes from the radio like Emperor Rosko and Paul Burnett. I didn't yet have a style of my own so I took my inspiration from those I considered to be the best.

In February of 1971 there was a vacancy on the social club and I was elected onto it as secretary. It basically meant that I had to keep track of booking out the cafeteria and dealing with the disco rental gear. There were a few other activities that the social club was involved with like planning barbeques and trips to other campuses for sing-alongs, but none of that kumbaya stuff was important to me; I was focused on the college dances. A seed had been sown in my mind: maybe I could become a DJ.

As June rolled around the college year was ending. I bid a sad but grateful goodbye to the two Cooks, and then said farewell to Keith, Phil and finally to Norm.

He shook my hand and smiled, "Don't let me down. You're the DJ now."

And with that endorsement the baton or at least the two rented turntables and a microphone were handed over to me.

Summer rolled by quickly in Torquay. I worked as a full silver-service waiter at the Rainbow House hotel. My job was to present and serve the food from individual silver platters onto the guests' plates. In return they were expected to come for lunch and dinner dressed up. The minimum of a linen suit and tie was required at lunch, and for dinner a dark formal suit or tuxedo and bow-tie. It was very old-school but the diners loved it as it made them feel as if they had been transported back to a golden age in British history and as a result they were very generous with their tips.

I worked hard and saved a lot of money that summer and used it for two things, the first of which was to put together a record collection that I could DJ with. I did this by scouring the record stores and combing through the used jukebox singles for sale at Torquay's flea market.

The second thing I did with my wages and tips was to pay off the loan from my parents for my Morris Minor. I then sold that car and bought a used sports car for two-hundred and twenty pounds, a bright-blue convertible MG Midget with a removal hardtop conversion perfect for Oxford's brutal winters. I loved that car!

Outside #22 with my beloved MG Midget

September 1971 marked the start of my second year in college. Now I could choose which house to stay in so I opted to remain in P.P. I had my own room and my ex-roommate couldn't wait to leave that house of ill-repute and flee across campus to a more respectable location closer to the chapel.

I was elected again to the social club and I immediately presented the committee an ambitious plan that I had come up with during the summer; we should buy our own DJ setup and stop renting it!

My argument was simple; we were paying fifteen pounds each time we rented the gear and had it delivered. With twenty dances a year that came out to the princely sum of 300 pounds. We could buy a mobile disco setup for less than 400 pounds so within fifteen months it would be paid for and we'd start saving money. This made so much sense that the student union approved it right away and said I should be the one to head down to London and order the disco unit.

LONDON CALLING

Gas (petrol) was expensive in England and driving in London was a nightmare. As it was a straight shot down the M40 from Oxford to London and as the motorway ran right past Harcourt Hill I decided to hitchhike and save both the money and the mental anguish. I made my way down to the busy road and stuck my thumb out. Within minutes a beautiful Mini Cooper S pulled up and the driver wound down the window.

"Where to?" he asked.

"London. Going to Tottenham Court Road."

"That's right by where I'm going, Oxford Street. Hop in."

I climbed into the lovely little car and we zoomed off.

We chatted nonstop as we sped down the motorway. We introduced ourselves and laughed that we were both called Richard. He was excited that I was a DJ and told me he owned a record store on Oxford Street. I knew the store and had been there a few months before in April when I was in London visiting my brother. I'd actually bought a couple of records at his shop including *Bridge Over Troubled Water* from Simon and Garfunkel and *Mona Bone Jakon* from Cat Stevens.

"Both great LPs, especially when you're with a girl," he laughed.

I asked what had brought him up to Oxford.

"Been looking for a place to put in a recording studio that also has some rooms. Kind of like a studio and hotel combo, so the artists can stay overnight and can play and record until they get tired and then just crash there. It's too expensive to find anything like that in London. Prices are crazy there now. I was just up here looking at an old manor house and it seems to have everything I need. I might end up trying to buy that and using it for recordings and maybe even starting my own record label."

I told Richard I was heading to London to look for a DJ setup.

"Tottenham Court Road is good. All kinds of shops down there selling gear and electronics. Might also want to try Roger Squires on Junction Road. It's a bit of a ride on the Tube out to Tufnell Park but it might be worth it because that's all he sells, stuff for discos."

He dropped me off at the intersection of Oxford Street and Tottenham Court Road then zipped off to his record shop. I watched as Richard Branson drove away and wondered if the young entrepreneur would follow through and sign the papers to buy The Manor Studio and start Virgin Records.

I hit about eight stores before I eventually settled on a compact DJ unit with mixer and turntables, a 200-watt amp and two speakers with fifteen-inch woofers and horns. The price was 399 pounds and included all the leads, a microphone and delivery! Westminster College was about to have its own disco unit and I was in charge of it.

THE FIRST CUT IS THE DEEPEST

I returned to college with the good news on the purchase and the promise that it would be delivered before our next dance so we could start recouping its costs almost immediately. I was in a great mood as I wandered back to my room at PP house, my mind buzzing with plans for the upcoming college disco night. As I crossed the quad past L house those ideas turned to fond memories of Pauline and Sue as I remembered our late-night clandestine rendezvous and I was totally lost in thought as I walked straight into someone coming out of the door.

"I'm so sorry," I apologized. "I wasn't looking where I was going."

"That's alright," she replied, "It was just a bump."

My God, she was beautiful. She was five foot six with shoulder-length blonde hair, piercing blue eyes, a face like a model and a body that any nineteen-year-old boy could only dream of holding.

"I haven't seen you around here before. Do you go to college here?" I asked.

"Yes, but I just arrived a couple of days ago. I live in Hong Kong and had problems getting my school papers transferred but they were very understanding and it's all done now. What year are you in?"

"I'm a second-year. My name's Dick Sheppard. And you're . . .?"

"Carolyn Wilson."

It was as if I had known that name forever. It just resonated through my soul. Perhaps I was picking up vibrations from the future colliding backwards with the present. Either way right there in that moment I knew this girl would be an important part of my life. Call it kismet, call it fate, but let me call it as it was, love at first sight.

Carolyn and I became inseparable. She was not only beautiful but also one of the coolest people I had ever met. I loved her and loved being with her. She would come to watch me swim and then dance all night when I DJ'd. She became my biggest supporter. When Carolyn was present I stepped up my game. I wanted to be better for her. My swim times became a little faster, my DJing a little more spot on.

Taking Carolyn surfing

I found out her father was rich, I mean silly rich. He was one of the managing directors of the Hong Kong and Shanghai Bank. They had a home on The Peak in Hong Kong and a house on the Isle of Man, an island 140 miles off the coast of England, which allowed them to have a residence in the United Kingdom without falling victim to Britain's punitive taxation system.

Carolyn and I talked about the future and she said that her family wanted her to marry well. Great! A waiter-turned-college-DJ who was probably going to end up being a teacher. That probably didn't fit within their definition of *well*. But Carolyn wanted to follow her heart and not any financial plan that was imposed upon her. She was head over heels in love

Mum and Carolyn outside #22

with me and I with her.

That Christmas Carolyn flew back from Hong Kong early so she could meet my parents in Torquay. Mum was very reticent about "that girl" coming to stay but within minutes of meeting her, Mum was embracing her like the daughter she never had. Dad, of course, fell instantly in love with Carolyn just as I had. Those were joyous days at number 22.

GOING MOBILE

As college resumed I came up with a little business plan. Oxford University was made up of more than thirty different colleges, all of which had campuses filled with students who loved to drink and party when their academic day was over. Virtually all of those colleges booked outside DJs to play at their dances. Why not book a fellow student who just happened to have all the gear necessary to rock the house?

I made up a flyer advertising my mobile disco services with an address to write to and our house payphone number at PP and took them all over Oxford putting them up in the student-union halls of Christ Church, Exeter, Corpus Christi, Trinity, Magdalen, every college I could find. I also hit the notice boards at the entrance to Bodleian Library and all the major student pubs. Within two days I started getting calls.

I had to keep a tight schedule as to when my swim meets were so I didn't miss a competition or a road trip to Birmingham, Coventry, York or London. On the nights that I was free I took bookings all across Oxfordshire for Dick Sheppard's Stereo Disco Show! At fifteen pounds a night I was doing well.

It was a lot of work lugging all the gear, setting it up and then DJing for up to six hours for hundreds of piss-drunk students but it was more than paying the bills and my record collection started to expand rapidly. After I would get back to Westminster I would unload and store the precious mobile disco equipment then head back to PP. Most nights I would find Carolyn in my room waiting for me. It always had to be my room because she was a first-year with a roommate, but that was fine with me. As long as she was there then all was good with the world.

In May of 1972 my father sent me an ad he had seen in a local paper looking for DJs to work in Torquay that summer. I liked the sound of that and wrote a letter to Brian Clifford at Soundwave Mobile Discos. Two phone calls and three weeks later I had secured a job with Brian to play at events all across south Devon. My days as a waiter were over, now my exploits as a DJ were about to begin in earnest.

Brian Clifford had the biggest mobile-disco company in the West Country. He had five DJ units and a built-in clientele that he had acquired over the six years he had been in business. One night you could be DJing a house party, the next playing for a thousand people at a holiday camp.

Brian stressed to me that he wanted DJs with personality.

"Anyone can play records," he explained, "I need someone who can bring the show!"

He said that for most of his customers their party was the biggest event of the year for them so it had to be memorable.

"If you hide behind the console then you are no good to me," said Brian. "They're paying good money to have you there so make them feel it was worth it."

That resonated with me and from that moment on I wanted to look, as well as sound, the part. If they wanted a show I would give them one.

I went out and invested a little money in some "DJ clothes." This included a sequined shirt with an oversized collar, wide flared pants, a silver jacket and two pairs of platform shoes. My mother nearly had a stroke when she first saw me walk in the house with my "platforms" on.

"You look like a monster in those things!" she exclaimed.

"Yes, and I'm surprised he can even walk in them. Mark my words, you'll end up breaking your neck with those on," said Dad.

And in a way they were both right. I'm a little over six feet two inches tall barefoot so with those four-inch heels on I was rapidly approaching six seven! But couple those platforms with my shiny shirts and for sure you wouldn't miss me as I danced wildly to Slade, Sweet and Bowie behind the DJ console.

The crowds seemed to like it, perhaps because my enthusiastic but lousy dancing made them feel better about their own rhythmic impairment, and I started getting repeat bookings and referrals asking for me by name which pleased Brian no end as it meant more business for his company. For me it was fun and I began to really enjoy the excitement and nervous energy of not knowing what to expect when I walked into a new room except that it was my job to win everyone over and show them a great time.

Brian commented on my voice and said I should make a demo tape to try to get on the radio so for the next few evenings I went over to his house, set up one of the DJ consoles in his garage and attempted to put together a short cassette featuring me doing my best impression of a radio DJ.

My dad helped me type out a resume and insisted I include my previous experience in the "restaurant business" as it would show "backbone" and willingness to work. I was mortified. One look at that and I imagined that instead of the BBC hiring me to be their newest on-air DJ, they would have me work at Broadcast House as a waiter delivering scrambled eggs and a steaming pot of tea to the breakfast show.

So with a ten-minute demo cassette, a resume that proudly featured serving wine at the Conway Court Hotel along with playing records for holidaymakers at Pontins, Barton Hall, I mailed off the demo and waited in vain.

With Mum and my friend Dave, working the boats – Summer, 1972

During the day the ocean was calling my name so I took a job working on Babbacombe beach renting out motor boats. First thing in the morning I would slip a trolley under the heavy, wooden boats and race with them down the steeply sloping, pebbled beach to the water using my body and legs as brakes to slow them down, Fred Flintstone fashion. You couldn't wear shoes because the rocks were too slippery so it was brutal on your bare feet. But I was out in the sun and water all day meeting girls and DJing most nights so I had no complaints that summer.

Actually I did have one complaint. After the freedom of having my own room at college, here I was back in my childhood bedroom at Mum and Dad's house with little to no privacy. That meant I had nowhere to take all the girls I was meeting as a "beach boy" and DJ. I was relegated once again to stealthy encounters in parks and back seats. Knowing this was not an ideal situation for me or for the girls, I started making enquiries for the next summer; I knew if I could get my own apartment to rent then Torquay would become a completely different place.

I rationalized to myself that I wasn't really being unfaithful to Carolyn. She was in Hong Kong, 8,000 miles away, and when we got back together at college we would be exclusive, but if she wasn't even in the same global hemisphere as me how could it be cheating? It's amazing the logic a twenty-year-old boy can come up with.

I started my third year at Oxford as a seasoned DJ. I'd taken what both Norm and Brian had taught me and evolved it into my own developing style. Other students noticed how I was dressing at the disco shows and really trying to "work the crowd." I would get a lot of comments like "You

look like a glam rocker" or "You should be in bloody Roxy Music dressed like that," but they were said good-heartedly as I think they appreciated the effort I was making. Now the college dances were becoming more and more popular and even the hard-core Methodists would show up from time to time.

My artwork for a college dance poster

I was made captain of the swim team and between my increased pool training schedule and DJing around Oxford three or four nights a week my studies were relegated to the back burner which I knew would be a huge problem as in eight months I would be facing a series of major exams. Despite that sword of Damocles hanging over me, I was having way too much fun to be hunched over books when I could be spinning music at parties, beating out laps in the pool or spending precious time with Carolyn. Something had to suffer, so I chose academics to be the victim.

Westminster College swim team

UNDER PRESSURE

In October 1972 the college was approached by RAF Brize Norton who was trying to obtain permission to use our pool. The Royal Air Force was embarking on a program to train its aircrews from 10 Squadron and 53 Squadron in sub-aqua (SCUBA) skills to increase their comfort level in the ocean in the case of a "pilot down" or an open-water landing situation. As captain of the swim team they were passed over to me to handle.

Their request was simple. For the next twelve weeks they wanted to use our pool twice a week for two hours at a time to train their pilots and aircrews in sub-aqua skills. They were flexible with both days and times. Could I find some empty slots to fit them in?

I said it would be no problem but asked one favor of them in return. I had always loved Jacques Cousteau and had wanted to dive since being a little boy. And it wasn't just me. Four of us on the swim team also wanted to learn how to use sub-aqua gear. If they could fit us into their classes then I could find them time in our pool. A deal was struck and for the next three months my three teammates and I went through full military SCUBA training.

These guys were not messing around! We had two weeks of classes and theory before we were even allowed to get our toes wet. We learned first from the lectures the physics and biology of SCUBA including nitrogen build-up times as they relate to depth, decompression sickness and how the body responds under pressure. Armed with that slightly scary knowledge we finally were allowed in the pool where we were told what to do. And I do mean *told*.

Our instructor was a no-nonsense sergeant who would bark orders to us.

"Put the bloody regulator in your mouth and don't take it out until I say you can!"

We were all more scared of him than drowning so we did as we were told.

As we became more confident underwater, all kinds of tasks and obstacles were presented to us. He would swim up from behind and rip off our masks and turn off our air without warning. If we surfaced we were done for the day. We would have to sink to the bottom, find the mask, replace and clear it, shrug off our gear, turn the air back on using the valve at the top of the tank then replace all the gear and continue on.

Other times he would obscure our masks with duct tape then throw all the equipment into the deep end and have us dive down, find it, turn the air on and then don everything completely blind without surfacing.

Perhaps the toughest of all the exercises was drownproofing. We would have to tread water in the deep end of the pool while Sarge watched from the side. After fifteen minutes, just as we were starting to get tired he would hand down to each of us a ten-pound cinder block which we had to hold above our heads for another ten minutes while we kicked frantically to try and stay afloat.

As our legs cramped up from charley horses that knotted our calf muscles and stabbing pains shot through our entire bodies he would yell out encouraging words to us like "Don't you dare get that bloody brick wet. I'm going to be using it tomorrow to build me wife a new shed."

Those ten minutes lasted an eternity as the weight of the concrete blocks would inevitably force our heads to sink underwater and we'd kick desperately to get back to the surface for just a moment to take a gulp of life-giving air.

When the time was finally up we would gratefully hand him back the cinder blocks and crawl painfully out of the pool rubbing our burning, swollen legs.

"I'm doing all this so you are prepared," he explained as we lay there on the pool deck, too exhausted to stand. "What are you going to do if you end up in the water with heavy clothes on and they start dragging you down? You're going to fight to stay afloat, to stay alive, that's what you're going to do. It won't always be easy. You do what you have to do to get through it."

His intense training had me convinced that in the event I was diving one day and a fish swam up with a roll of duct tape, covered my mask, hid all my dive gear under a coral reef and handed me a brick then I would know exactly how to respond.

Our first ocean dive was at the end of November in Weymouth. We met on the base at RAF Brize Norton and were loaded into two green military trucks and headed 130 miles to the south. The trucks were not designed for comfort and for three hours we bumped and banged around on the two wooden benches that ran the length of either side of the military transport.

It was drizzling when we reached the coast and we could hear the surf pounding onto the beach as we were ordered out of the trucks. The waves were nearly six feet high and smashed relentlessly on the rocky shoreline. It was, to say the least, intimidating.

"Here's what our plans are for today," the sergeant barked, "get kitted up, put your regulator in your mouth and hold your flippers in hand. Don't bloody let go of them either or the quartermaster will wreak havoc with me and then I'll have to take it out on all of you. We're going to walk straight into the water, get past the waves then slip the fins on our dainty feet and go for a nice little dive."

As we stared at the angry ocean I think he could sense the reticence among not just us four Westminster students but also the combat aircrews that were gathered there.

"Is there a problem? Did I just waste my time teaching you how to breathe bubbles the last two months? Anybody want to tell me they signed up for the wrong course? If you do then I think a saw a pub down the street that has a beer garden perfect for little girls. You could go there and wait for the rest of us divers. Have a bag of crisps and a nice lemonade shandy and sit in a deck chair as you miss out on all of the fun. Who wants to go?"

I did, but as no one else was moving I stayed put.

"Good, let's all get ready then." He turned and watched a massive breaker roll in and explode on the shore sending spray twenty feet into the air, "Bloody lovely day to go diving."

Amazingly despite the pounding surf and hideous visibility underwater we all survived the dive. On the way back to Oxford we compared bruises that our tumbles on the rocks had given us, but we were all still breathing and ready to go on our next adventure.

Westminster College Sub-Aqua Club, 1973

In December we received certification by the RAF and BSAC, the British Sub-Aqua Club, and in late January the Westminster College Sub-Aqua Club was officially started. The first four members being the survivors of the battle of Weymouth beach.

The summer of 1973 was rapidly approaching and with it my first major exams. I had found an apartment of my own to rent in Torquay and would be returning to Soundwave Mobile Discos but before any of those good times were to happen I had to face the dreaded written papers in English, drama and history.

My professors were expecting me to flunk two of the subjects and maybe scrape through with drama and I was tending to agree with them. The principal called me into his office and told me in no uncertain terms that he had been watching "my antics" for the past three years and as far as he was concerned I had wasted my time at Westminster. I had not been to church once and all I did was "swim, play music and run around to all the other colleges in Oxford every night." Didn't I know I was here to study?

This conceited little man continued to lecture me and when he finally stopped his tirade he said, pointedly, "Well, so what are you going to do?"

I looked at him and smiled.

"I think I'm going to stay on another year and take my degree course," I explained matter-of-factly.

"I don't think that's going to happen," he spluttered. "You'll be lucky to leave here next month with a teaching certificate."

"But if I pass my exams you have to—"

"*If* you pass your exams! But we both know the chances of that happening."

I walked out of his study determined to prove him wrong. I got to work and crammed three years' worth of study into one week and hoped for the best.

As the day of the first exam rolled around I entered the room more scared than I had been facing those monster waves six months before in Weymouth. It was history, the toughest of the three subjects. Here we were dealing with facts and dates. Whatever topic that had been chosen had already happened and it was up to me to know exactly when, how and why it had occurred.

The only good news was the exams were not written by the college. They originated from the education board in London and would be sent back and graded there, so there was no personal bias against me.

I opened the exam paper. The main question was on the rise of the House of Tudor and the formation of the Church of England. I knew this inside out—even if Bummer Stokes had mocked me about it.

I wrote of the Wars of the Roses, how Henry the VII seized the throne of England and left it to his surviving male heir, Henry the VIII. I went into detail on Henry's conflict with Spain over his first wife, Catherine of Aragon, and his subsequent battles with the Vatican. I elaborated on the beheading of two of his wives, Anne Boleyn and Catherine Howard and his wars with France and his obsession to conquer territories there that he felt were rightfully his. I put my pen down and sat back. One down, two to go.

Drama was next and a piece of cake. I had to review three of Shakespeare's plays and explain the subplots and the importance of the secondary characters. As we had produced two of his plays at Westminster in the past two years, *Hamlet* and *Macbeth*, this was a gimme as well.

Finally for English literature the question was to trace the evolution of a genre of literature of my choosing such as the romance, adventure or political novel.

I took a chance on this and traced the development of the spy novel in European literature stemming back to Charles Dickens's *A Tale of Two*

Cities through to *The Thirty-Nine Steps*, *The Thin Man* and finally the James Bond series which marked the arrival of the anti-hero. I wasn't sure if this would be too hip for the examiners but I was going for it.

I called my parents and let them know the exams were done and I was fairly confident that I would get a passing grade and asked what was going on in Torquay. Dad told me that he'd had a meeting with one of the planners for SIS, Scandinavian International Summerschools, and they were looking for teachers of conversational English for their Scandinavian students for the summer. They paid well. Was I interested? My answer came in seconds.

IN THE SUMMERTIME

Summer of 1973 was a mind-blowing experience. Every morning from nine until twelve I would teach Swedish and Norwegian students conversational English and every evening I would DJ for Soundwave. Most nights I would take one of the Swedish girls with me and she would dance while I played the music.

Brian Clifford landed the contract to install the sound equipment at a brand-new club in Teignmouth, just six miles from Torquay. He chose me to open the disco and be the resident DJ there. The club, Barbarella's, bought full-page ads in all the local papers and I was thrilled to see my name spread right across the page. Unfortunately they did misspell it and for a brief moment I felt like dropping one of the *p*'s in Sheppard but thankfully common sense kicked in.

My life became one continuous party and how I stayed away from drink I don't know. Drugs were not a temptation; in the summer of 1973 they were virtually unknown in a little town like Torquay but alcohol was another thing all together. Many of my old school friends spent night after night in the pubs swilling back the beers and then staggering all the way home but that had no real attraction for me. My vices were girls and music.

Just a week after the opening of Barbarella's I had a call from the BBC. When I heard who was on the line I nearly had a heart attack, but sadly it wasn't in response to any of the demo tapes I had sent them. Instead they had been doing their research to find which local DJs in each town were most popular and my name had come up when they were looking at Torquay.

Opening for Emperor Rosko – Summer, 1973

They asked me to 'open' for the BBC Radio One Roadshow when it came to Torbay. I would DJ for two hours and then they would go live on air with none other than one of my radio heroes, Emperor Rosko. It might not have been a radio gig but I was excited to do it.

That afternoon playing on the Radio One Roadshow stage on Torre Abbey green to 6,000 people was a thrill. I'd never been in front of such a huge crowd before and knowing that many of "me mates" were out there watching made me make sure that the music was rocking. Fortunately the British weather upheld its side of the bargain and the sun beamed down through my entire set and during the live broadcast.

Watching the massive response and hearing the cheers that erupted from the crowd when Rosko strode out onto the stage made me want to really step up my game as a DJ and push hard for a job on the radio. I could only imagine how it must feel to have the audience scream for you like that.

As the end of the summer approached I was called into the office of SIS at Castle Circus in Torquay. They wouldn't tell me why they wanted to see me. My mind was racing. Had the parents of one of my girlfriends complained or worse, was one of the girls pregnant? I just knew it would be a bad meeting.

Instead the director of operations sat me down and made me a proposal. He'd been going through my college paperwork and had heard from some of the other teachers about my DJing. His idea was that the following summer I teach only three mornings a week, lifeguard for the students on the beach five afternoons a week and DJ their dances three nights a week.

I couldn't believe my ears. SIS took over a section of a beach in Torbay for the summer every year and it would become semi-private, just for the students, and it was well-known that their dances were students only. You had to show an SIS card to get in; otherwise they were off-limits. But here I was being offered unlimited access to all of it along with the incredible nineteen- and twenty-year-old Scandinavian girls who were here for the summer as both their lifeguard and DJ! It was all I could do not to ask if I could have keys to the hen house as well!

THE LOVE I LOST

My final year at Westminster saw me spending only a few hours a week at Harcourt Hill for my academic studies. I had transferred to the degree course and was taking a Bachelor of Education in English at Exeter College, Oxford. The studies were dry and dreary, but fortunately were only three one-hour sessions a week; the rest of the time I was expected to be mature enough to study at my own speed. The big thrill was that my lectures were one-on-one with the professor of English and he made a point to tell me that the study where we had our meetings and the very chair I was sitting in had been used by J. R. R. Tolkien when he had studied there fifty years before me.

Carolyn and I talked about what we would do when college was over. She wasn't going to stay on a fourth year for her degree; instead she wanted to get a teaching diploma and find a great school to start her career as an educator. One night she unexpectedly exploded into tears. I wrapped my arms around her and asked what was wrong.

"You've been so good," she said, "but I haven't. I saw someone this summer in Hong Kong. My parents took me water skiing and introduced me to one of the bank managers and it just happened. I'm so sorry."

What was I going to say to this wonderful, distressed person? Get mad? No, that would have been hypocrisy central. After all I had done how could I blame for one second this amazing girl for being human?

I held Carolyn tight and whispered, "It's okay. I love you."

I could feel her tears soaking through my shirt onto my shoulder and dreaded the moment we would inevitably break up. I knew our lives were destined to be so different that it could never work out, but until that time I would cherish every moment with her that the next eight months would bring.

As with so many things that we adore and treasure, nature played her cruel joke and time sped up causing those months to race by in the blink of an eye and suddenly, before we knew it, it was late May of 1974 when, with all the exams finished, the third- and fourth-year students were bidding their final farewells to both college and to their friends. For me that meant saying goodbye to Carolyn forever.

Carolyn hoped we would stay together, somehow make it work. We talked endlessly about how we were better together, how our love could overcome any obstacle, how we could build a future as a couple. Even though those last nights were filled with tears and promises it was obvious to me that our ultimate fate was already, irrevocably out of our hands.

I knew that once she was away from college her parents wouldn't let her return to me. And my dreams were also pulling me from her. Many times over that final year I had thought seriously about marrying Carolyn, settling down and becoming a teacher. But I just couldn't do it. I knew that pathway would ultimately lead me to unhappiness and I loved Carolyn way too much to have her stuck with a husband who came home each night full of regrets and discontent. Plus I needed to see where DJing would take me, and that was a decidedly uncertain future that the Wilson family would want their daughter to have no part of.

We hugged, we cried and we held hands until her ride to the airport arrived and we were forced to let go of each other. Our fingertips brushed one final time and I watched as she climbed the three stairs onto the shuttle and prayed that she would find happiness. As crazy as I was when we were apart, Carolyn was more than just another girl; when we were together there was no one else in my life.

My last glimpse of my first love was as she pressed her face against the window of the bus and waved sadly, desperately, as the engine of the old service vehicle grumbled into life and with a shudder, took her away from me in a choking cloud of black diesel smoke, beginning her long journey to the other side of the world and a new life that I would have no part in.

As I lugged my bags to my little MG I stopped for a moment to take a final look back at Westminster College. I was leaving a place that had introduced me to the world of DJing, given me the opportunity to train and swim every day, taught me to SCUBA dive and allowed me to discover a great love like Carolyn.

My farewells done, a wave of sorrow swept over me as I drove down Harcourt Hill for the last time. It was as though I had a hole in my soul, that I'd lost a part of myself. I slipped in a cassette of some of my favorite disco records to lift my spirits. The first song that came on was "The Love I Lost," a track that I played at most of my gigs and it always worked as a floor-filler, but today it was as if I were hearing it for the first time.

The velvet voice of Teddy Pendergrass filled my little car, and the melancholy lyrics hit home and hit hard as in that moment every word seemed to have been written just for Carolyn and me. I *had* lost a sweet love, a complete love and I was sure that I would never love that way again.

Tears began to well up and I had to pull my MG to a stop at the bottom of the hill and even as I did, Teddy reminded me of the good times that Carolyn and I used to share and of how sad and lonely I would be without her. It was all too much so I punched the eject button and the tape popped out of the player.

I sat there in silence with my head in my hands and I cried like a baby. Just what was I doing with my life? What was I thinking that I could let someone like Carolyn go in the wild hope that I might one day be a DJ?

Reality sank in as the song's words continued to play through my head of the love I had just lost. I felt stupid, heartbroken and so alone.

GETAWAY

The summer of '74 came to a crashing close on the evening of September 2 when a major gale swept down across the south of England from the North Sea. The dark, foreboding storm front was driven by category-nine winds which uprooted trees and whipped up massive waves that forced vessels to seek shelter from the Thames Estuary to Plymouth Sound. One boat that didn't find safe harbor in time was the forty-four-foot *Morning Cloud*, the racing yacht owned by former prime minister Sir Edward Heath.

I awoke on the morning of September 3 to see Dad's beloved lawn flooded and littered with debris from a shattered apple tree that was the first thing he had proudly planted in that garden a decade before. As wind-driven rain and hail hammered unrelentingly against the windows I turned on the radio to catch Noel Edmonds's *Breakfast Show* and heard the news of the loss of the *Morning Cloud* and two of her crew.

The BBC newsreader explained that waves in excess of thirty-five feet had pounded the vessel and swept away the life raft. The five surviving members were said to be in poor condition, suffering from broken limbs, a punctured lung and hypothermia. He continued that the meteorological office advised that the storm would continue for a number of days and that all persons in the south and east of England were cautioned to stay inside and "make alternative plans." It was that phrase that triggered something inside of me, alternative plans.

The summer had been fantastic, but now it was over. The long sunny days would become a fading memory and the tourists would flee the sleepy seaside resort that Ian Fleming had used as a disparaging comparison in a James Bond novel, saying "Miami is a lot like Torquay, a town where old people go to die." Even those dying old people would stay inside the comparative safety of their warm homes as the English Riviera wound down and buttoned up for the long, harsh winter.

The amusement parks, tourist attractions and boat rides would not be the only things shuttered for the season. The quiet months ahead meant that the clubs would only open at weekends, narrowing the opportunity for my DJ gigs, and social gatherings would be limited to meeting up at the neighborhood pubs and chasing the same rosy-cheeked local girls that we had all already dated. It sounded like a waking nightmare to me.

Plus what would I do for work? My life had been non-stop since leaving Westminster College; teaching English to Scandinavian girls in the mornings—yes, I know there were guys in the class too, but they weren't my focus—working as their lifeguard at Elberry Cove in the afternoons and DJing their dances at night. SIS paid me good money for my services and that job had fringe benefits beyond belief. But now what?

I was fortunate that my mother and father weren't pressuring me. I'd just moved home three days before after my summer-rental arrangement had concluded and they were happy to have me back. Dad gently hinted that he could get me a job as a teacher starting in January. He knew it would be no problem finding a school to give me an entry-level position after my studies in Oxford and my degree from Westminster, but teaching still didn't seem right for me. I wanted to travel, to meet new people and I was really starting to fall in love with music and being a DJ, but how could I make that combination all come together?

I thought radio might be the answer and had been cutting more demo cassettes of radio shows that I would make on the DJ equipment after the club closed. It was a laborious hit-or-miss process. You used three buttons to make a tape, PLAY, RECORD and PAUSE. If you screwed up you had to hit the dreaded fourth button, STOP, and begin all over again. It took many hours to put together an acceptable five-minute demo. However, my opinion of *acceptable* and the professionals' opinions must have been very different because even though I sent out dozens of cassettes and somewhat exaggerated resumes of my DJing history to the BBC, London's

Capital Radio, 208 Radio Luxembourg and even the United Biscuits Network (UBN) I was not even getting one call or response. So what should I do? That's when the letter arrived and my future was decided by a two kroner airmail stamp.

Tove Amundsen was a beautiful eighteen-year-old Norwegian girl that I had been seeing in July. Her family had sent her over to Torquay for a month with SIS to immerse her in the British culture and improve her already-excellent English.

We met on her second day in Devonshire at Elberry Cove, the beach where I worked for SIS as a lifeguard. She looked stunning in a snow-white bikini and already had a golden tan that accentuated her shoulder-length blond hair and aquamarine eyes. We hit it off instantly and the month blazed by with a series of passionate encounters. And now, five weeks later, I was holding a letter from Tove. She wrote that she had told her parents about me and that they would love for me to come over and visit. They had a house just outside of Oslo and I would be welcome to come and stay there anytime.

This was not the first invitation I'd received from the Scandinavian girls I'd dated over the previous summers. Most would ask me to come and visit them but I'd never taken any of them up on it, but now I was out of college, and with winter barreling in and nothing but time on my hands and boredom looming, maybe I just would . . . I raced upstairs to my bedroom and dragged out my box of letters and photos. Maybe, just maybe, I could put something together?

I flipped through the well-worn correspondence. Britt lived in Gothenburg, Sweden. She had been to Torquay two summers in a row and really wanted me to meet her family. There was a daily ferry from Newcastle to Gothenburg, so that would be a great place to start. Then there was Una. She lived in Jonkoping, which was halfway between Gothenburg and Stockholm. I could stop there for a few days and say hi before moving on.

Stockholm was where Inger lived and worked and she had asked me many times to stay with her in Sweden's capital. From there I could head back west and up to Norway where I'd wrap up my visit to Scandinavia by spending a final week with Tove in Oslo before returning home and facing a dreary winter in England.

I immediately started writing letters asking the girls if it was okay with them and their families to come over, and outlining some possible dates.

In my head I had it all worked out. The trip would have me visiting two countries and last about a month. In reality it would turn out to be more than a dozen countries and take over two years.

Replies came back from the girls in less than a week. All of them said, "Yes, please come and stay." I had lucked out with my timing. Scandinavia was also sliding towards winter so the family holidays were done and the parents were back at work. I would be a welcome distraction from the encroaching nights and a chance for the entire family to practice their English with the genuine article.

My parents were a little apprehensive about me taking off to Scandinavia alone, but they knew there would be no stopping me. Instead Dad posed one question only, already knowing the answer. "How are you going to get around when you're there?"

I held up my thumb. Dad nodded. "Okay, just be careful."

The train journey on British Rail up to Newcastle was long and tiring but nothing compared with the forty-eight-hour crossing of the North Sea on the DFDS ferry. The old, diesel-burning vessel plowed slowly through one of the planet's roughest bodies of water as if she were resigned to the battle ahead.

The entire ship shuddered as the huge waves threw themselves against her towering metal bow and you could have sworn that you could hear the rivets holding the rusty hull together coming loose, but after a moment's hesitation the aging workhorse of a boat continued cutting through the swells on her way to our scheduled arrival in Gothenburg.

Britt and her parents were waiting for me in the disembarkation area at the ferry terminal. I only had a backpack with me so within minutes we were on our way to the suburbs of Gothenburg in the family's Volvo. I wondered if it was a requirement of all Swedes to show their patriotism by driving the country's biggest car brand.

For the next five days Britt showed me the sights of Gothenburg—or Goteborg as I called it after getting used to the Swedish pronunciation of that city. We went to Goteborg's equivalent of Disneyland, Liseberg twice. I loved it. It was much bigger than any amusement park in Britain at the time and had some incredible rides.

But it was at night the fun really happened. After the family had gone to bed Britt would sneak into my room and we would try to keep our trysts as silent as possible. I'm not sure how successful we were because every morning over a breakfast of crispbread, muesli and goat's milk I would see knowing winks and smiles between Britt's mother and father. I could only admire the tolerant attitude that prevailed in Scandinavia towards sex. Whereas in England it was something that should not be talked of lest one would be thought to enjoy it, here it was embraced as both a natural and very welcome part of life.

It was time to move on from Goteborg to Jonkoping. It was a straight shot across Sweden and barely one hundred miles. Britt's parents offered to drive me but I didn't want to push their boundaries too much. I wasn't sure how well they would take the fact that I was leaving their daughter to go and stay with another girl. Instead they dropped me on the main highway outside of town; I hugged them and Britt goodbye and claimed a prime position by the on-ramp to the busy road.

I was no stranger to hitch-hiking. Two summers before I'd "hitched" across Europe with my childhood friend Mike Frost, and we'd always had great success. I'd learned a trick that served me well. Virtually all Europeans learn English from a young age in school and many love to practice it whenever possible. So I had sown a large Union Jack onto my backpack to advertise the fact I was from Britain and positioned the bag so that the drivers couldn't miss seeing the flag. I held up a handwritten sign that said "*Jonkoping*" and stuck my thumb out; ten minutes later I was speeding eastbound along Highway 40 giving a free conversational-English lesson to an enthusiastic Swedish motorist.

Una was thrilled to have me at her family's farm on the banks of Lake Vattern. Even though it was late September, that first afternoon still clung desperately to the sun's remaining warmth and we went canoeing on the lake. It was gorgeous; the calm waters sparkled before us and dragonflies buzzed low across the bow of our canoe. Una paddled us to a tree-lined inlet and we rekindled our relationship.

Her parents had been anticipating my visit and had prepared a magnificent feast fit for a family of Vikings that night. As we sat by their open fireplace enjoying that sleepy feeling of fullness Una's father looked at me and asked, "Would you like to make some money while you are here?"

I said sure and asked how.

Una's family farm was big—massive by my small-town standards—and required a lot of maintenance. There was one area in particular that needed help, an orchard grove that had been hit by a blight that had killed all the trees and now they needed to be removed before the contagion spread further. Would I like to work as a . . . He struggled for the English word and could only say it in Swedish. . . . *timmerhuggare?* Una looked at me and laughed.

"Do you mean lumberjack?" I asked.

Apparently that was the plan, and the next day Una's father equipped me with a jacket, gloves and goggles and after a quick lesson on how to use a chain saw, let me loose on 400 dead fruit trees on two acres of land. I earned 600 Swedish krone (about sixty-six dollars) and two calluses!

Stockholm and Inger were fun. I actually saw very little of her during the afternoons and evenings as she worked as a typesetter for a big Swedish newspaper and had to make sure the articles and photos were ready to go to press each night in time for morning delivery.

Instead I explored the nation's capital by myself and was stunned at how the city was built over and around water on multiple islands. In many areas it was more common to take a ferry than to take a bus.

And water is an inescapable part of Stockholm's history; my favorite place to go became the Wasavarvet, a shipyard dedicated to a mighty Swedish warship, *The Vasa*, which, to the complete embarrassment of King Gustav, capsized and sank in the harbor as she was leaving on her maiden voyage in 1628.

The days flew by in Stockholm and soon it was time to say *adjo - goodbye*. I was off to my final destination, Oslo, Norway, for a six-day trip that would change my life forever.

SIGNED, SEALED, DELIVERED

Tove's family lived on Nesodden, a large peninsula in the Oslo fjord that was a short ferry ride from the city. My first two days were quiet and her parents weren't quite as welcoming to me. It turned out that Tove had a serious boyfriend who was away at university in Stavanger. Tove felt that at this point we should be "just friends."

I was surprised because it was she who had instigated my entire trip. She apologized and told me that during her time in Torquay I was her summer fling and she apologized for it, calling me a "holiday boy." It boggled my mind to have it presented that way. I'd thought of myself as the one doing the chasing but here was this gorgeous girl saying that it was she who was actually in control of the relationship and how it had played out the entire time. The shoe was definitely on the other foot and here was a girl proud to own her independence and sexuality.

As for my visit, Tove said she had gotten to really like me and thought it would be fun for me to come and see Norway. On my third day in tiny Nesodden Tove sensed my boredom and suggested that we explore Oslo and maybe go to a club that night before catching the last boat home. Hitting a disco in Norway's capital? I was in for that!

Our first stop was the spectacular Holmenkollen ski jump which had towered over the city like a colossus for more than a century and had been home to many major skiing events including the 1952 Winter Olympics. Then it was on to Sofienberg Park where we walked through the trees then hung out with students and drank coffee and talked about the latest movies like *Blazing Saddles* and *Towering Inferno*. It was already dark when we headed back to the city center and saw the line to get into Key House Disco.

The club had just opened its doors thirty minutes before but already it was three-quarters full. To get inside you had to first pass an intimidating bouncer from Yugoslavia who looked like he had exhausted the supply of people to beat up in his own country so he'd moved to Norway in search of new victims.

After that it was up a steep flight of stairs which led you straight into the main dance floor. But that was not the only room; Key House had three different areas for dancing and drinking. The décor was decidedly psyche-delic with posters of rainbows and kaleidoscopes pinned to the fifties-style velvet patterned wallpaper that was pasted everywhere.

Despite the club's retro appearance the music was bang up to date and I recognized all of the songs that were playing, Johnny Bristol's "Hang On in There, Baby," Eddie Kendricks's "Boogie Down" and Rufus's "Tell Me Something Good," but I was a little disappointed as they were all on a tape from some prerecorded cassette.

I asked Tove if they had a DJ and she smiled, "Oh yes, they are famous for their disc jockeys!"

Even as she spoke a DJ entered the booth and pulled a couple of records from the built-in wooden bins behind him. I watched as he cued up his first songs. He looked good. He had long dark hair, a drooping mustache that a porn star would have envied and a bright shirt that stood out in the dim light of the club.

He turned to the crowd and picked up a microphone. "Good evening everybody and welcome to Key House. I'm Bobbie Junior and if you are ready to dance here's Barry White!"

Boom, "You're My First, My Last, My Everything" blasted out of the PA and the young crowd raced onto the dance floor. I was stunned. I stared at Bobbie Junior trying to understand what I had just heard then turned to Tove to make sure.

"He's English?" I asked.

Tove nodded. "All the DJs in Oslo are from England, and the best ones work here."

She took me into the other dance room and sure enough another Brit, John Warner, was packing the floor in there.

I watched John and Bobbie work the crowd for about an hour before I said hi. I made my way to the DJ booth and waited. Bobbie Junior saw me, stepped over and bent down from the suspended booth.

"Got a request?" he asked.

"No," I replied. "I'm from England. I'm a DJ too. I like your music."

Bobbie smiled. "That's cool, man. You should meet the boss."

Bobbie called one of the bouncers over and asked him to take me to Anders, the owner of the club. He led me to an office in the back, knocked on the door and let me inside.

John Warner

Anders was tall and skinny with cropped hair. He asked me about my DJ experience and explained that Key House was open seven nights a week with three separate rooms and DJs that rotated during the month. He needed at least one more disc jockey on staff to work into the schedule. Would I be interested in trying out? I didn't have to think about it.

"Sure" I said.

Anders nodded and described how my audition would go. He wanted me to come back tomorrow and observe Bobbie and John playing to the crowd

Bobbie Junior

to learn how his club worked, then the following evening he would have a mobile disco unit set up in a restaurant he owned and I would have my audition there. He couldn't risk doing it at the Key House itself. It was the hottest club in Oslo and he couldn't allow a new DJ he wasn't familiar with to just turn up and spin.

I understood and said that was fine with me and asked what time he would like me to be there the next night.

"I want you here at opening tomorrow so you can get familiar with how we turn everything on and set it up for the evening, and stay through closing so you can do the same with the shutdown."

"Seven until midnight, right?"

Anders nodded in reply. I explained that there was a problem. I was staying on Nesodden and the last ferry left at 11pm.

"Then stay in the city," Anders suggested. "I have a place for you at my flat."

I thanked him and said I'd work out something for sure. Then I asked him if I could go up to the booth and watch Bobbie DJ. He thought that was a good idea and I headed back out to the club.

In between records I told Bobbie what was going on and he paused for a moment and looked me up and down. I didn't know why. Then he said that he would help out. He waved one of the cocktail waitresses over and explained the situation. She gave Bobbie a knowing nod and introduced herself.

Hilde was a good-looking blond in her mid-twenties with eyes that hinted of experience well beyond her years. She said I could sleep at her place those two nights, it would be no problem. We'd go there after the club closed tomorrow. With that taken care of I went out onto the dance floor to tell Tove the news.

As the ferry sliced through the black, mirror-smooth waters of Oslo fjord, Tove and I huddled for warmth under the star-filled sky. Normally I would have been trying to name the constellations or spot a meteor burning up as it entered Earth's atmosphere but instead my mind was racing. A gig at one of the hottest clubs in Scandinavia. That would be the answer to so many of my short-term questions; how to get away from the boredom of the English winter, what to do for a job over the next few months, a way to continue DJing . . .

Tove's voice interrupted my thoughts. "Maybe you should go tomorrow if you really have a place to sleep?" I looked down at her. "You can come back, of course, if it doesn't work out. I invited you to stay so you can be at my house for as long as you like, but if this is what you want then you must do it."

My smile provided Tove with her answer. I gave her a little hug and replied, "*Takk sa mye*," Norwegian for "thanks so much."

I was eager to be back in Oslo and was anxiously waiting outside Key House when the first workers arrived to get the club ready for its opening that night. They let me right in assuming I was one of the English DJs.

I needed to get to know the DJ booth and studied it intently. The mixers were standard—four inputs for music, two for turntables and two for cassette decks—all controlled by rotary faders which were common at the time. There were also two microphone inputs which was great as it gave the DJ the option of a second mic in case there was someone else in the club, like a visiting artist, who wanted to say hi to the crowd. But the amplifiers were the most interesting thing in the booth.

In most installations they would have been tucked away in a rack and fan-cooled to keep them from overheating and shutting down. The prevalent brands in the industry were Orange, RSD, Kustom and Peavey. But at Key House they weren't using pro gear for the heart of the system; instead they had installed four high-powered home-stereo amplifier/receivers in each booth to drive the speakers and had proudly mounted them on display in a vertical hanging position. They were in plain sight and a complete mish-mash. One was a Marantz, two were Technics and one was a Sansui. It should not have worked but somehow it did and sounded amazing.

John Warner told me that once a month on a Sunday afternoon the club would open for a listening party where they would switch the system to Quadraphonic and play the latest albums from Pink Floyd, Santana and Eric Clapton all the way through. At a time when mono was the accepted norm for a club system this was nothing short of revolutionary. Apparently the audience really appreciated it because it was incredibly popular and as the monthly four-hour session came to a close the kids would roll out on the street "stoned" from the combination of the high-fidelity music and Jägermeister shots.

That night my training with Bobbie Junior went really well. I watched the ebb and flow on the dance floor and got a feel as to what worked and what didn't. All the very latest American disco and soul were *big* as was English glam rock like Bowie, Queen, Gary Glitter and Roxy Music, and my old stand bys, foot-stomping rockers like Free, "All Right Now" and Slade, "Cum On, Feel the Noize", were guaranteed to pack the floor.

Bobbie let me spin a thirty-minute set while he partied with his fiancé, Brit. They both gave me a thumbs-up from the floor. I was doing good. Tomorrow night, bring it on. Everyone would be talking about the new DJ in town and his name was Dick Sheppard!

Anders seemed very pleased at the attention I was paying to the crowd and the music. The only thing that seemed to bother him was that I was not drinking.

"All my DJs drink," he said. "It loosens them up."

But I'm not a big drinker and I needed to see—and remember—how everything worked. He had shots and beer sent up to me in the booth throughout the night but I turned them all down. This was my chance and I was focused 100%.

Anders asked me several times if I was certain that I didn't want to stay at his flat, and just to be sure he gave me his address and said I could come over anytime if it didn't work out at Hilde's. But I wasn't comfortable staying with "the boss"; that might upset the other employees thinking I had an unfair advantage and ultimately work against me. I wanted to stick with Hilde's offer, plus she could let me know the ins and outs from a staff member's perspective and that is so important.

Hilde lived just over a mile from Key House on Steinspranget in a cute little apartment she had decorated with posters of Monty Python and Frank Zappa.

Her roommate, Eva, was a waitress at a nearby restaurant and she had already made up a bed for me on their fold-out couch. We stayed up late that night swapping endless lines from Monty Python, "No one expects the Spanish Inquisition" and "This is a late parrot. It's a stiff. Bereft of life, it rests in peace. If you hadn't nailed it to the perch, it would be pushing up the daisies."

In my photo album I have a picture of them and a caption that I hand-wrote that says "Two of the kindest girls that I ever met." They gave me a place to stay, food and drink and asked for nothing but friendship in return. They became a big part of my life for the next month.

Saturday rolled around and audition night was here. I wanted to get to the restaurant early to check out the gear. Hilde knew the location and walked with me to make sure I didn't get lost. As twilight fell across the streets of Oslo, Hilde excitedly pointed out a black-and-white flyer taped to a lamppost. It was in Norwegian but I recognized the words printed in block letters:

FRA STORBRITANNIA ENGELSK DJ DICK SHEPPARD

It was a poster that Anders had put out advertising the evening to make sure there would be some people there. I had picked up a little Norwegian and was learning more each day so I was able to make out the key words.

"*Ti krone*" (ten krone to get in), "Rock'n'Roll, Pop, Disco *og Gammal-dans*"—of course I knew the first three but what was *Gammaldans*?

Hilde laughed and explained that it was the music used for Norwegian folk dances, popular with the older crowd. My *Gammaldans* experience was obviously very limited so I was hoping that no old people would show up – if anyone came who was over thirty I would be in trouble!

As we got closer I saw at least a dozen more posters and flyers taped on poles and pasted on walls. I have to admit that it was quite a thrill to see my name plastered up in a foreign city.

The word *restaurant* was an exaggeration; this place struggled to be a cafeteria on its best day and was lit with hideous flickering fluorescent strip bulbs. It had all the ambience of a truck stop. But there at the end of the long white room was a DJ console set on a Formica table with a pair of big black speakers on either side sitting on the floor. I'd seen worse.

The manager took me into his office where two milk crates full of vinyl albums were locked up and waiting for me along with a box of seven-inch singles. He gestured to them and it was obvious that he'd done all he was going to do. As far as he was concerned this young wanna-be DJ was on his own from here on out.

There is nothing heavier on the planet than a milk crate full of vinyl. If you don't believe me just ask any old-time DJ. No wonder most of them have back problems. I lugged the boxes out and plopped them on the floor behind me. I fired up the system and dropped a needle on the record. It didn't sound half bad. I tested the microphone with the time honored "1, 2, 1, 2, 3." I was good to go.

Even as I was basking in that "I can make this work" feeling, the manager ran up and yelled, "No music now. Not until eight when we will have the dancing. Turn it all off."

As he stomped away I realized that no matter where you go in the world there's always one person who will have zero respect for the DJ and go out of their way to treat you like shit.

I busied myself by sorting through the records and getting to know the music I had available. To my horror many of the albums were Music for Pleasure. That was a cut-price series that had started in the sixties and featured all the latest hits on them, kind of a "best of the charts" compilation. But they weren't the original songs!

To save money and licensing fees the MFP people would hire a group of session singers and musicians to come into the studio and re-record the current hits as close to the originals as possible. Unfortunately nine times out of ten it was painfully obvious that it wasn't the real thing; after all, no one can perform a song by Stevie Wonder or Diana Ross and reach those notes and convince anyone it's the genuine Tamla Motown article!

In preparation for disaster hitting and emptying the floor with one of these counterfeit hits I made sure I had a couple of songs to keep "in my back pocket" that would be certain to have the punters pushing past each other in their race to get back out there dancing.

I pulled Suzi Quatro ("Can the Can"), Hamilton Bohannon ("South African Man") and as I was in Scandinavia, ABBA, with the record that had won the Eurovision Song Contest for them just six months previously, "Waterloo." I was making damn sure I wasn't going to go down like Napoleon that night.

They cleared away the tables at eight to open up an area to be used as the dance floor and surprisingly people began streaming in. The posters and flyers had worked! Within thirty minutes the cafeteria was crowded and I had dancers on the open linoleum area that masqueraded as the dance floor.

I cranked the music and was bouncing around like a crazy man behind the console as Anders walked into the restaurant to assess my audition. Great. He'd picked the perfect time; it was still early, the floor was already packed, all I needed to do was bring the show. I figured I would take a chance and switch it up. I grabbed the mic and with a "Are you ready to rock and roll?" slammed into The Doobie Brothers "Long Train Runnin'." Now you needed a shoe horn to find a spot on the floor and two waiters scurried out and moved more tables to make space for the dancers.

As the record started to fade I decided to push the limits; I knew I had to make an impact and stand out. Among the singles was a new track that had only just been released in the shops. I'd had it for two months as a record company promo and it had worked fantastically for me with the Scandinavian students in Torquay this past summer. It should work here.

I yelled into the mic, "Here's something new for all you rockers. We're off to Canada with B.T.O. and 'You Ain't Seen Nothin' Yet.'"

Randy Bachman's driving guitar tore through the speakers as I leapt onto my chair and pumped my fist in the air. The crowd went nuts and by the end of the song they were singing along with the chorus. I caught Anders's eyes with mine and knew I'd gotten the job.

I was sliding the records back into the crates as Anders walked through the now empty club and approached me.

"That was better than I thought it would be," he said. "I think we'll have you start a week from tomorrow, next Sunday. We'll work out the schedule." Anders paused. "You should stay with me until you get your own apartment. That way if John or Bobbie call in sick you can be there to cover those nights. It won't work as well if you stay with Hilde."

He smiled warmly and put his arm around my shoulder. "Now you are part of my staff I want to make sure you feel welcomed. Come by tomorrow at six and we'll have dinner together and talk."

Anders shook my hand and left. I was thrilled. Oslo, man! This would be *my* town.

A few minutes later I headed downstairs clutching Hilde's address to give to the first taxi driver I could find. As I hit the sidewalk I heard a voice behind me.

"Excuse me."

I turned to see a tall, well-dressed Norwegian man. He seemed familiar. I'd seen him in the club.

"My name is Tor Tendon. I saw you playing up there. I'd like you to think about coming to work with us."

Us? I looked around. Tor was alone. Did he have a mouse in his pocket?

"I have a company called Europa Booking. I place DJs in clubs throughout Europe. I'd love you to be one of them."

Wow! Two job offers in one night. I thanked Tor but told him I had just been offered a gig at Key House starting next weekend.

Tor shook his head slowly. "Did he say anything about a work permit?"

That hit me hard. Anders hadn't mentioned that. Just a part-time job, weekends and fill-ins to start.

"He's going to hire you because he likes you. And if you don't like him back the same way he'll call the police and you'll be deported

and he won't pay you. He's done it before and it's a shame. Ask him about your work permit. If what I'm saying sounds right then call me."

Tor handed me his business card and walked away.

Dinner the next night with Anders was uncomfortable. I so wanted this job at his amazing club but I was not going to be anyone's fool. I asked if he needed a copy of my passport for the paperwork, to which he replied it wasn't necessary, he'd pay me cash under the table. It would be much better all around. No tax for me and no extra employee fees for him to pay the government.

I broached the topic again. How long could I stay in Norway without a work permit? He laughed and said that I could stay as long as I wanted. The paperwork wasn't important; it was keeping the club full and him happy that was. That moment over dinner the stars in my eyes were gone.

I think Bobbie sensed it later that night at Key House. He said that everyone was talking about my audition "blowing off the roof" and that I would be great to work with.

I nodded unenthusiastically and asked Bobbie quite pointedly, "Do you have papers to be here? A work permit?"

Bobbie replied it was the first thing he made sure he had and that every time he changed clubs the manager would take care of the paperwork and he would take that with him to the police station to renew his permit.

"I'm sure Anders will get you yours," he said.

I realized that Bobbie didn't know. He was unaware of Anders's plans for me.

Tor's agency in Skoyenasen was a short five-minute walk from Hilde's apartment and he met with me first thing Monday morning. His office was small and neat and featured something that definitely caught my eye, a large map of Europe with a series of colored pins in it.

I learned that each pin represented one of the clubs he booked. I told Tor he was right about the work permit and asked what he would be able to do if I took a job with Europa Booking. Tor explained that there were two major agencies that booked English DJs across Europe and his was one of them.

He specialized in Norway and Denmark, but also had clubs in Austria and Switzerland that took his DJs. Everything above-board with a work permit granted in advance for each club and country. You would play at each disco for one month and the club provides a room for you, takes care of your food and the first two drinks every night. I found out later why many of the clubs had a two-drink limit and that was because a lot of the DJs were prone to drinking non-stop so the managers, to protect both the DJ and their profits, charged them for all their drinks after the first two.

The clubs booked English DJs because it made them "hip"; all the music being played in Europe came from England or America and featured English vocals and so to the audience it was much better if the DJ was talking in the same language as the songs they were playing. If the DJ was to spin The O'Jays or Silver Convention then bust out on the microphone in Danish or German it would be too jarring. It didn't matter whether the crowd understood the DJ or not, it just sounded much smoother and more sophisticated.

And all the clubs required the DJs to talk between the songs. Their only experience of pop music was through Radio Luxembourg and the rapid-fire patter of their on-air jocks. So that's what the owners expected in their clubs, personality DJs who were entertaining on the microphone.

Prior to the start of disco, most of the countries in northern Europe had absolutely no club culture for the kids, it was all afternoon-tea dances for moms and pops and at night rock or swing bands in local church halls. Now with teenagers demanding their own places to go out to and party so they could mingle, spend money and dance, the discotheque phenomenon was exploding across Europe and the only country that had a history of those kinds of nightclubs was Britain. So that's where the continent turned to for experienced DJs.

"The clubs will promote that you are coming. They will make it seem like you are a famous radio DJ visiting from England. That helps bring in the crowds to the bars. You are going to be like a rock star. People are going to want to meet you. We'll need photographs for you to sign," Tor told me. "I will pay for the first couple of hundred then it's up to you."

Wow. Photos to sign. Who would want my autograph? And could I ever get through a couple of hundred? That seemed impossible. But it also sounded like fun.

"Okay, I'm good with that," I said.

"Don't be surprised if they have posters up that say 'direct from BBC Radio One' or things like that. Go along with it. They just want to make you and the club seem as big as possible," he grinned at me, "You'll be the talk of the town."

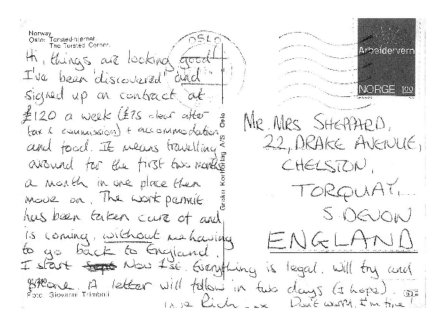

Norway
Oslo: Torsted-hjørnet.
The Torstéd Corner.

Hi, things are looking good. I've been 'discovered' and signed up on contract at £120 a week (£75 clear after tax & commission) + accommodation and food. It means travelling around for the first two months, a month in one place then move on. The work permit has been taken care of and is coming, without me having to go back to England. I start ~~Sept~~ Nov 1st. Everything is legal. Will try and phone. A letter will follow in two days (I hope). Love Richard. xx Don't worry, I'm fine!

Foto: Giovanni Trimboli

Mr. Mrs SHEPPARD,
22, DRAKE AVENUE,
CHELSTON,
   TORQUAY,
      S. DEVON
ENGLAND

I asked Tor how much the pay was and he said I would start at between 100 and 150 pounds a week. That was amazing! My father was the deputy headmaster at his school and made barely 100 pounds a week. Here I was making more than that and being paid to travel Europe and party every night. It was a young man's dream come true!

So when did Tor think he could get me my first gig? Tor picked up his phone and dialed.

He spoke rapidly in Norwegian for a few minutes then hung up.

"You start at the beginning of November in Tonsberg. It's an hour south of here. That's two weeks from Friday. Does that give you enough time to get your records sent over from England?"

NORWEGIAN WOOD

It didn't take me long to work out why Tor had chosen Tonsberg for my first gig. Bonanza was a shit hole. It attracted customers who were uninterested in the music and only wandered in off of the street to find a warm place to hang out, hide their drinking and smoking habits from concerned spouses and shake off the boredom of their repetitive nine-to-five jobs.

The Bonanza crowd were the kind of people you would be more likely to expect to run into at a twelve-step program than as part of a party group out to have fun at a nightclub. And "dress to impress" was hardly a requisite. As long as your fly was partially zipped and you had some kind of shirt on then you were good for a night on the town.

When their alcohol levels rose high enough and they decided to stumble from the bar to attempt dancing it was to Neil Diamond or Tom Jones. "Sweet Caroline" and "Delilah" became my go-to songs. Put on either of those records and the floor would fill with drunken Norwegians who would stand there, link arms and bellow out the chorus at the top of their voices like a soccer crowd in their home stadium.

Tor had said I would be a star in the town. Instead I felt like an interruption not the attraction. I think the busboy received more acclaim than I did as he was called out onto the tiny dance floor again and again throughout the night to mop up the pools of beer spilled by those sloppy drunks. In those first few days I wasn't so much playing records as pulling teeth. It was as if I'd become a dentist not a DJ. But it taught me so much about DJing that stayed with me forever. I learned how to get through a night where I was looked at as simply a human jukebox. I got used to handling drunks with their rude, demanding requests, "Play that song again right now!" or "Play something I can dance to" and I discovered how to win people over who had zero interest in what I was doing.

After the music stopped, the lights came on and the remaining intoxicated patrons staggered out onto the streets I would clean up the booth area of shot glasses and overturned beer mugs and head upstairs to escape in the room the club provided for me. Unfortunately it was no sanctuary; not a place where I could become Zen with the night and evaluate the pluses and minuses experienced during the hours before.

In fact even the word *room* was hardly fitting for where I was staying. *Room* implies space; instead the enclosure the club provided for me was so small that I could stand in the middle of it and touch both of the damp walls with my fingertips and if I jumped I would smack my head against the ceiling. I kept thinking that instead of it being my first DJ gig in Norway I had been sentenced to a month in the Tonsberg jailhouse.

And it was impossible to regulate the temperature in my cell; it was either baking hot or freezing cold thanks to an antique oil-filled radiator that had two heating positions, either fully on or all the way off. And when it was turned on it would *thump, thump, thump* every twenty minutes throughout the night as the boiling oil attempted to flow around the rusted coils.

The metal-framed bed was deliberately narrow and short so it could be squeezed into that tiny space and my feet hung out four inches over the bottom of the thin mattress. The communal toilet and shower were down the hall and shared with six other people who had never been taught about the purpose and use of a flush.

It was trial by fire; maybe Tor figured that if I could survive this I could get through anything. But as the days wore on I resolved not just to survive, but to thrive.

I pulled myself together and pretended that this rundown, wood-paneled bar that could barely hold one hundred people was the best club in Europe. It would become the place to be in Tonsberg—not that the rest of the town gave me much competition!

I took a risk and announced that from now on Fridays would be Countdown Night. I would stay away from the standards they would scream out for, stick to my guns and only play the latest songs from the UK and

US and "count down" from number twenty to number one starting at eleven o'clock until closing at midnight. It was a huge gamble because this was "drunk hour" when the alcohol hit hardest and patience and under-standing were all but forgotten, but it paid off and quickly the crowd grew to love it. By the second week the club was packed early and people stayed until closing.

DJing Countdown Night at Bonanza in Tonsberg

I started a "rock night" on Wednes-days and oldies, "*Gammel* Night," on Thursdays. As word spread new people began coming in and lots of girls started showing up to check out the "En-glish DJ with the cool music" and my single bed became even smaller and it was rare that I had to turn on the heater at all.

Two weeks into the gig Tor drove down from Oslo to see me.

"Here are your promo pictures and your schedule for the next two months."

He passed me the pictures we had taken in Oslo and two contracts. I was at Ands Inn in Bardufoss in De-cember, Sesame Restaurant in Trom-so in January. I was happy. Anything to get bailed out of this prison sen-tence. I couldn't sign the contracts quickly enough as though the very

My first promo picture

act of putting my name in triplicate on those forms would hurry the days away. It was a thrill knowing that I'd passed the test and soon my one month sentence of hard labor in Tonsberg would be commuted and I would be free to move on.

"I got the club in Bardufoss to pay for your flight and for the overweight charge for your records," Tor told me.

Flight? Doubly cool! That really was rock-star territory. "How far away is Bardufoss?" I asked.

"It's a little north of here," replied Tor with a smile.

FLYING NORTH

A little north was an understatement. The NAS 737 flew for more than 1,700 kilometers before skidding to a halt on the icy runway a little after 1pm on December 1, 1974. The two-and-a-half-hour flight was packed full and it was the first time I had seen live chickens carried on a plane.

If you want to travel north in Norway in the winter you have two options: either take an ice-breaker up the coast or fly. It's impossible to drive as the mountain ranges that run up and down the center of the country like a rocky spine for more than 800 miles, are covered with snow and the roads become impassible for several months.

The preferred method of transportation is the flying bus and if you have a chicken or a small goat to take north then you put it in a crate and it goes in the cabin with you. I never knew when I was boarding a plane in Norway in mid-winter if I would end up sitting next to a businessman holding a briefcase or a farmer clutching a turkey.

As I made my way down the stairs to the tarmac it was impossible to tell if it was one in the afternoon or one in the morning. Bardufoss is more than 200 miles north of the Arctic Circle and by December the sun has set for its winter slumber and won't rise again for almost three months when it peeks above the horizon on February 26, giving cause for the drunken celebration known as Sol Fest.

I was met at the airport by the owner of Ands Inn, Knut, a big, jovial guy who helped load my heavy suitcase packed with records into the back of his Mercedes, and off we went to the club. Knut explained that Ands

Inn was in Andselv, a suburb of Bardufoss and had a population of only 900 people!

But the club was always busy because of the NATO base nearby. It was manned by several thousand US troops who were actively preparing counter measures to the Soviet invasion that the Cold War was threatening to bring down upon the free world's head. The GIs needed to blow off steam and they would head off base to Ands Inn to drink and party, and to make sure the soldiers had females to dance with the US Army would helicopter girls in from the nearby towns.

It was a win-win for the military; the night flights were perfect training exercises for the pilots and crew, and it gave the GIs on the ground a chance to escape from the latest issue of Penthouse and flirt with a real girl instead.

Most evenings I would stand outside the back entrance of Ands Inn and gaze into the night sky as I waited to see the blinking lights of the massive helicopters approaching. It sent a chill down my spine every time they swept into view: it looked like news footage I'd seen from Vietnam but instead of Charlie hiding in the brush waiting to shoot them down, the incoming choppers were greeted by the sound of George McCrae and "Rock Your Baby" blaring across the snow.

DJing at Ands Inn was a blast. The American soldiers loved the soul music I had in my collection and I was thrilled to have the opportunity to break out James Brown, Marvin Gaye and Tammi Terrell. I met some great girls at the club but they were, at best, brief encounters as they had to be back onboard the helicopters by 1a.m. to return to their hometowns. So I broke one of my personal rules and dated a couple of the waitresses, though fortunately no unpleasant work situations arose from those romantic interludes.

One thing I really enjoyed was getting to know the soldiers. I've always had great respect for the military and those who serve. My father was in the Royal Artillery during World War II and retired holding the rank of major in 1946, and my time doing sub-aqua training with the RAF while at college filled me with even more appreciation for their selfless devotion to duty.

On my nights off, when the GIs invited me onto their base to watch movies, I was there! I didn't have to be asked twice. They would pick me up at Ands Inn in a half-track, a weird vehicle that looked like the illegitimate love child of a tank and a truck. The front wheels were normal but the back wheels were replaced by an articulated tread. This gave the vehicle the ability to cross virtually any terrain and made for an exhilarating trip.

We would race over the ice and hard-packed snow with the half-track's twin exhausts rumbling like angry thunder behind us. If there had been a recent blizzard or snowfall, which was a common occurrence this far north of the Arctic Circle, the driver would yell out, "Hold on!" and speed towards the biggest drift and plunge the half-track into the mountain of soft powder and blast out of the other side sending geysers of snow exploding high into the sky. It was a thrill ride courtesy of the United States Armed Forces.

Once we reached the base and piled out of the transport, we'd hurry across the frozen ground into the makeshift screening room where a projector would throw the images onto a stretched king-sized sheet. With cold beers in hand from the commissary we would sit on canvas folding chairs, bundle ourselves in camo-green sleeping bags to keep warm and watch two movies in a night.

One that stuck with me and proved to be a major influence on my future was a low-budget western, *They Call Me Trinity*, starring Terence Hill. I had just come inside from a withering snowstorm and sub-zero temperatures as the movie started. It opened with Trinity and his horse crossing a parched desert landscape under a blazing sun and cloudless blue sky. When the caption *"California"* appeared on screen, I made a mental note to myself that I should definitely make a point to go there someday just to escape this numbing chill. I didn't realize then that the seed the film planted within me would grow to end up influencing the rest of my life.

The month sped by and after a raucous New Year's Eve party at Ands Inn it was time to say goodbye and head even further north to Tromso. After a four-hour, hundred-mile bus ride past fjords and waterfalls I arrived at the most northerly city in the world. But it was so different to what I had expected. Instead of igloos and polar bears there were heated sidewalks, endless coffee shops and a bustling shopping area. This town was big!

Tromso is an island just off of the Barents Sea and connects to the mainland by a spectacular bridge which links it to Tromsdalen and the rest of Norway. Tromso alone has a population of more than 75,000 people, plus add to that the crews of the fishing fleets plying the Arctic Ocean and North Sea who would dock to unload their catch and then look for a welcoming bar to spend their hard-earned wages and the population was boosted even higher. As a result, Tromso was able to support three different discos and had a thriving nightlife.

It was there that I met up with two other English DJs who were on the road like me, Peter Brown and Geoff Collins. Peter and I became firm friends and our paths would cross many times as we zigzagged our way across Europe. We also had the same love for the ladies and were amazed to find out just how sexually aggressive the girls were in Tromso. With the city cloaked in perpetual darkness for those winter months there was little for them to do except hang out, go dancing and find a guy for the night. And being the new kids in town and the "star" DJs from overseas headlining their favorite club for a month we became the notches on their belts rather than vice versa.

I'd learned a little about that attitude from Tove two months before, and I was fine with it. It was chauvinism reversed and Peter and I were happy to support this new suffragette movement.

On still nights in Tromso when there was no wind, I would walk the half mile back to my apartment from Sesame Restaurant. Because the temperature would be as low as thirty below zero all the moisture was frozen from the atmosphere and the air became so dry that you didn't feel the cold. However should that change and there be even a breath of wind the frigid air would tear right through your clothes and your bones would lock up from an instant chill. But on those still, clear nights the cold was forgotten as the most-incredible natural spectacle would appear across the firmament.

From horizon to horizon the heavens would erupt in a display the likes of which I had never seen before, the Aurora Borealis, the northern lights. The entire night sky would shimmer, twist and crackle as nature sent her electric pulses through the magnetosphere. Curtains of colors; greens, blues, purples white and even pink, would flex and fold in every direction. A thousand years before, the Norse warriors believed that they were seeing the "Bifrost Bridge" – the gateway to Valhalla. It was easy to understand why they felt that way; the sight was so breathtaking and beautiful. Staring up at that celestial light show became a bucket-list moment for me before I even knew what a bucket list was.

Two weeks into my residency in Tromso I received a call from Tor in Oslo. He asked if I would stay on for a second month up there. The owners loved me and the crowd that I was bringing in packed the house every night and so they wanted to extend my contract. In return they would pay any transportation costs to my next town.

I was fine with the arrangement. Tromso was being very good to me. Tor was happy to hear that and told me that my next gig would be at his number-one club in all of Norway, Hotel Norge, in Bergen, the country's second-biggest city. This was exciting news as Peter and Geoff both said great things about Bergen.

The local paper got wind of the sensation that the trio of English DJs were creating in Tromso and ran an article on us.

I mailed the article along with a translation back home to a couple of newspapers in England and sure enough within a week a big story appeared in the *Herald Express* with the headline:

No Winter of Discontent although in the Frozen North

It began with: *Dick Sheppard's winter currently means perpetual twilight, temperatures of minus-23 degrees and six-foot snow drifts. And he enjoys it!*

My parents saw the article and were thrilled, and they weren't the only ones to read it. I received a telegram and letter from Brian Clifford in Torquay offering me my choice of residencies with Soundwave at clubs for the summer season including The Yacht,

1975

De lever av plateprating

Med flere tusen plater i kofferten har tre engelske discjockeyer invandret Tromsø. De jobber for Europa Booking, et internasjonalt disc-jockey selskap som forsynet blant annet de skandinaviske diskoteker med «platepratere».

Peter Brown (21) er fra Wembley i London. Han prater og spiller plater på Hawk Club og har vært profesjonell i to og et halvt år. I fjor var han blant annet engasjert av klubber i Barbados og Miami.

Dick Sheppard (22) kommer fra Torquay. Han finner man på Senjam hvor han inntok mikrofonen etter å ha pratet plater i Oslo, Tønsberg og Andselv.

Dick har blant annet jobbet i et show i Englands «Radio One».

Engelske «platepratere» til Tromsø med flere tusen plater i kofferten. Fra venstre: Peter Brown, Dick Sheppard og Geoff Collins.

(Foto: Trond Mæland)

Geoff Collins finner vi på Festhus. Han har vært profesjonell i fem år, og kommer fra Essex.

Geoff ble utpekt som Danmarks beste internasjonale discjockey i fjor, mens han i 1973 ble valgt som nummer en hjemme i Essex. Og selv påstår han at han har spilt profesjonell fotball for «Orient» i engelsk 2. divisjon.

Felles for alle tre er at de har et sprudlende humør som de smitter over på publikum.

February 14, 1975

Devon Coast and the peak of them all, The Casino, which boasted three dance floors and a more-than-hour-long wait to get in during the holiday months. It really began to feel that things were happening and moving in the right direction.

As my residency in Tromso wrapped up I boarded another plane and flew south to Norway's west coast and the gorgeous city of Bergen. Tor had been right about Hotel Norge. It was a fantastic club, located in the very heart of the town and packed with beautiful girls who were excited that a new, 'hot' English DJ had come to town. There was nothing I would have changed; the DJ booth was designed by someone who actually knew what a DJ's needs were, with the turntables, records and cassette player all within easy reach, the staff was super friendly and respected the DJ as the entertainer who brought the crowds in and kept them there, and the apartment was beautiful.

Tom's Apartments was the rather unoriginal name of the building I stayed in but that was the only disappointing thing about it. The location could not have been better; it was on the waterfront of Bergen's massive harbor that had been refuge to the raiding fleets of Ragnar Lothbrok and his longships ten centuries before. It featured three rooms and a kitchen and they all had panoramic views over the water and looked towards Floyen, one of the seven snow-capped mountains that ring Bergen.

With spring coming it felt as if I had arrived in paradise. Ten days into my residency it got even better. Tor called and asked if I would remain in Bergen an extra month. The manager had requested it and even though

DJing at Hotel Norge, Bergen, Norway – March 1975

Tor would have to reroute a couple of DJs he wanted to keep his number-one club happy. I was over the moon. This was where I wanted to be!

The next six weeks flew by and with just five days left in April I had no idea where I would be heading next. Tor kept telling me that he had something lined up "for sure" but was waiting on the contract. I arrived early at Hotel Norge that night for dinner and the manager walked over and asked if he could join me. He sat down and after a few minutes of small talk he told me he would be sorry to see me go. I nodded in agreement and said that I was the one sorry to be leaving.

He stared at me for a second and said, "I thought you didn't like it here that much?"

I was stunned. "Are you kidding? Your club is wonderful, the best place I've ever played." I replied.

Now it was his turn to look puzzled. "But we wanted you to stay for the entire summer but your agent said you didn't want to and would only give us one extra month."

You could have knocked me down with a feather. Summer in Bergen would have been a dream—living in my waterfront apartment, DJing at an amazing venue, and dating some of the most beautiful girls I had ever seen.

"Let me call Tor," I said.

There was no answer that night so first thing next morning I called again and got him on the phone. I tried to keep it under control.

"What's the deal with Hotel Norge?" I asked. "They tell me they asked to have me stay on for the summer."

Tor paused. I knew he was thinking of his answer, not because he had problems with his English, he was incredibly fluent, but because he knew I wouldn't like what he was going to say.

"I promised another club that you would go back and play for them," he replied.

"Who? What club?" I wanted to know.

"Bonanza, in Tonsberg. They want you back. They'll pay a lot more."

"No fucking way!" I yelled. "The manager didn't even talk to me once while I was there. They don't want me back."

Tor took a breath. "I don't know what went on there but they like you a lot. You brought a lot of business to the club. So you're going back. It's just one month."

Yeah, right, that's what the firing squad told the condemned man, "It's just one bullet." November in Tonsberg had been the longest, most boring month of my life.

"No. I'm not doing it. I'm staying in Bergen."

"You can't," Tor said. "I have an exclusive two-year contract with the owners of Hotel Norge to provide the DJs there. They won't let their manager break that contract; it would cost them too much money. I have another DJ going in there in four days and you are going back to Tonsberg."

It was my turn to pause. When I spoke I knew what I was saying but it still twisted a hole in my gut.

"Fuck you, Tor. I'm not going back to that hole. I quit. I've got four more days here then I'm gone."

I slammed the phone down and stood there staring at it for at least two minutes without moving, wondering if I'd just hung up on my DJ career.

Five days later I boarded another DFDS ferry. But this one was taking me away from Scandinavia and back to England. I ignored the light rain that fell as I stood on the stern for almost an hour watching the cliffs and fjords of Norway recede into the distance and with them the memories of the excitement of the European clubs and my dreams of becoming a big-time DJ. It was one of the saddest moments of my life.

BLISTER IN THE SUN

Have you ever been away for a job or a vacation that seemed almost life-changing then come home and felt that moment of anti-climax, that feeling of "gone so soon" or even "Did it really happen?" Everything seems a little smaller, a little quieter, the colors muted.

That's how it felt returning to Torquay on May 3, 1975. My childhood friends Mike Frost and John Bennett tried to cheer me up by taking me to our local pub, the Devon Dumpling, and offered kind words like "Well, at least you tried and had a good time while it lasted" but I didn't see it in the past tense. Those clubs were still there, the music was still playing and the girls were still chasing the DJs, it wasn't over, it was just that I wasn't a part of it any more.

So what now? Take a residency at a club in Torquay for the summer and be in the same situation come September? I'd done that before and it didn't seem exciting to me dealing with all the drunken holiday-makers down from Glasgow or Slough for the weekend. Plus, *it wouldn't stop raining*! It was driving me nuts. Sure, it rained in Norway, but not like this. Three days back in England and not a glimpse of blue sky, just a constant downpour. I knew what I had to do.

I hopped onboard the 28A bus and headed into downtown. With my dripping umbrella rolled up beside me I sat facing the travel agent inside Thomas Cook and made a simple request.

"I want to go somewhere sunny," I stated.

"Where do you have in mind?" she asked.

"Anywhere," I said, "as long as it's sunny."

She wrinkled her brow, unaccustomed to clients who didn't have a set destination planned.

"Okay,"—she flipped through a stack of brochures—"and when would you like to go?"

"Tomorrow?" I said.

Now she was really taken aback.

"Are you serious or are you just wasting my time, young man? You don't know where you want to go and you want to leave tomorrow? Well I never . . ."

The sight of the 200 pounds in cash that I slapped down on her desk cut her off in mid-sentence.

"I'm not pulling your leg. I just don't like the rain. I want to go somewhere sunny. If I can't go tomorrow, then I can go the day after. But I'm serious about it."

She looked at the money and back at me. "All right then, let me see what I can do. I'll make some calls. If you'd like to come back in an hour . . . ?"

I killed sixty minutes buying used jukebox singles at Torquay's indoor market then returned to Thomas Cook. This time she was all smiles. "How does Spain sound to you?"

It was not only sunny but hot as I walked across the tarmac towards the Spanish Customs and Immigration at Barcelona airport. I couldn't remember the last time I had been truly warm without being bundled up in fifteen layers of clothing or rubbing my hands together in front of a roaring fire. This was glorious and it was only the tenth of May! I thought about this mini-break; ten days down here before flying back. That should be long enough to get a nice tan before I had to return to the inevitability of England.

The travel agent had booked me on a charter flight out of Luton airport near London. It was part of a package deal that included the round-trip air to Barcelona, ground transportation to Lloret De Mar and ten nights in a hotel with full board. As it was off-season and last minute the whole thing had cost me less than eighty pounds. Squinting up at the blazing sun I knew I would have happily paid double that.

It took the rickety shuttle bus just over an hour to get to Lloret De Mar. As we bumped our way down the cobblestone road into town the Mediterranean lay in front of me like an invitation, glistening in the sun.

Within minutes of checking in I hoofed it through the center of town and dove into that legendary sea's embrace. It felt so good to swim again in the sea that was the cradle of Western civilization and the birthplace of independent thought and democracy. There is something magical about its waters and I could feel five millennia of history flowing though me and washing away my angst.

I wandered back through the town a little slower so I could check out the shops and bars. And there, just steps from my hotel, was a small building with locked double doors painted a bright blue with a logo that read "Moby Dick Discoteca." Discoteca? Right away I knew where I was going that night!

There were a few people lined up in front of me that evening waiting to pay their admission fee to get into the Moby Dick. As I stepped up to the window I slipped my "International Disc Jockey" business card to the cashier and asked if they did a discount for DJs. She looked at it for a moment then called the bouncer over. My business card seemed to disappear in this giant's hand but it served its purpose.

The monster glared down and commanded me to "Wait here" and went inside.

Seconds later he reappeared with another guy.

"I'm Tony, the manager here," said the other guy. "You come for the DJ job?"

I hadn't but if he was offering . . . I gave Tony a quick twenty-second rundown of my DJ experience as he sized me up.

"You're a west-country boy." It was a statement not a question. "I'm from Birmingham but spent a lot of my hols in Devon. Here's the deal. We just reopened for the season and don't have a DJ yet. I was going to play tonight but if you want to do it then I can concentrate on getting the bar up and running. No money, but no charge to come in and your drinks are free all night."

Sounded good to me. I just had a couple of questions.

"Do you have records?" Tony nodded. "And when do you close?"

Tony grinned, "When the punters go home. Could be two, could be five. Never know." This might be a long night but I was up for it.

The Moby Dick was quiet until around ten-thirty, that's when it exploded with people. The club held around 400 but no one at the door could count that high so it wasn't unusual to have 600–700 crammed inside.

That's actually a DJ's dream. The busier it is the easier it is to keep them dancing. Plus if the club is jammed, sometimes even if a song comes on they don't like it's better for the customers to just stay on the dance floor than to have to battle their way off of it. That night I made sure everybody stayed on the floor.

The Philadelphia sound was huge in the disco scene at that time. Elton John was one of the first to notice how popular it was becoming and incorporated it into one of his songs that became a massive hit for him, "Philadelphia Freedom." But the real deal was the music written by the two guys who had created the entire movement, Gamble and Huff.

If you saw their names on a record then you knew you had an almost certain winner going on your decks. I was happy to see that TSOP, The Sound of Philadelphia, was well-represented in the Moby Dick record collection. I would drop in The Three Degrees, "When Will I See You Again," Harold Melvin's "Don't Leave Me This Way" or "TSOP" itself by MFSB and the screams of excitement from the tourists packing the dance floor would drown out the music.

But the ultimate secret weapon for the DJ was the first major disco single to cross over into the mainstream as purely and proudly a disco record not one trying to masquerade as a pop or funk song. Even the title was the dance it was entreating everyone to do - "The Hustle" by Van McCoy. I had two copies of the seven-inch and would mix into them back and forth making a long, extended version and do that five times a night and still be asked to play it "one more time."

Just before 3am the crowd started to dissipate. I was flirting with a tall, blond Dutch girl

With the crew at the Moby Dick, Lloret de Mar – Summer, 1975

who was also just beginning her Spanish vacation and ready for a holiday romance when Tony came into the booth.

He looked at the girl and then at me and grinned. "I see you've discovered one of the perks of the job. You can wrap it up now. Good first night. I'll be here later today around noon to do inventory. Come on by and we'll grab a sandwich and work out what you need to stay for the summer."

With that he turned and was gone. I looked at the girl and was tempted to ask if she too thought that that was a job offer but I didn't want to blow my cool so instead I cued up the last song and said goodnight to the stragglers in the club and "See you tomorrow!"

Being a DJ in Spain during the summer season is like almost nothing else on earth. Everyone there is on vacation, out to have a good time, away from their family and any chance of discovery or ridicule. Put them in a bar that pours cheap, generous drinks and set them loose on a hot, sweaty dance floor that pounds with sexy beats that resonate through your body encouraging any inhibitions to be thrown to the wind and you have a recipe for debauchery that hasn't been seen since the fall of the Roman Empire. Even Caligula would have felt at home inside a Spanish disco in July or August.

It was hard to go home alone when the club closed. Sometimes you just wanted to sleep but there was always at least one girl who would not let you leave by yourself.

"Come on. I'm only here for a couple more days. Why not?" It was a common refrain and it wasn't just me as the DJ who would hear it, but the bartenders and the bouncers as well.

With the dependable weather guaranteeing endless days of scorching summer sunshine and the night's promise of excitement, my schedule became almost set in stone.

I would arrive at the club at nine at night and spin until five in the morning. I'd go back to my apartment with a happy tourist and then sleep until ten in the morning. I'd get up, head off to the beach, stopping on the way to grab a sandwich to take with me. I'd usually meet up with some of the crew who would save me a place on the sand and we'd swim, nap and snorkel until late afternoon. Then it was back to my apartment to recuperate with two hours of sleep before a quick dinner and do it all again with someone new. Party, sleep, party, repeat.

September came far too quickly. It had been an unforgettable four months. Mum and Dad had come down to visit in July and I found them an oceanfront apartment for two weeks that was owned by the local family of one of the bartenders. They were hesitant at first to stay in such a busy holiday hotspot, but apart from an intense sunburn that savaged my poor father and blistered his skin on his second day and restricted him to the darkness of their rental unit for forty-eight hours, they loved it!

After Dad recovered and we put on the sunblock, he and I would swim together in the warm water for hours, and on the two evenings that I had off while they were visiting we went to flamenco clubs and danced the night away, drinking sangria and feasting on paella. On their last morning in Lloret De Mar Mum and Dad hugged me tight and said how sorry they were to have to go.

Now, two months later, with the season winding down and the town empty of tourists, I was the one who was sorry, as I sat on the bus to Barcelona to catch a flight back to England to once again ponder my options.

HOME AGAIN

It was strange to be at home in my childhood bed at number 22 in Torquay. It was almost exactly twelve months to the day that my European adventures had started but there I was, a year later, and back in the same situation.

Dad reminded me that I only had until the following May to validate my degree for teaching. If I didn't get a job in a school by then my degree would count for very little and I would have to go back to college for a year and take a separate teacher's diploma if I wanted to teach.

"It would be good to have something to fall back on," Dad cautioned me.

But I didn't want to teach and I certainly didn't want to fall back. My theory was if I had something to "fall back on" then if the going got tough I would eventually give up and use that safety net. I wanted to push forward, to give myself no alternative but to succeed and if there were the inevitable bumps in the road, then so be it.

I loved music, I loved discovering new songs and I loved playing live to an audience. I needed to talk to someone who could relate to what I was feeling so I called my friend Peter Brown at his house outside of London, on the off-chance he was there. He wasn't, but I talked to his mum, who told me he was DJing in Switzerland and she'd let him know I was back in England and that I'd called. I didn't want to just sit around and do nothing so I got busy trying to do anything to advance my stalled career.

Back from Spain in my home studio with my record case

I was already on a few promotional mailing lists so I used the time to write letters to the other major record companies in London telling them I was a DJ and listing all the clubs I had played at and the thousands of potential record buyers who were exposed to my music every week. I asked to be placed on their mailing lists so I could get the records free and ahead of their release date and that way promote them to my audience. I think I forgot to include that I was actually unemployed at the time.

I set up a makeshift recording studio in Mum and Dad's front room using my DJ gear and ubiquitous Phillips cassette recorder and started making new demo tapes for the radio stations that were beginning to pop up around the UK as the British government was forced to release their iron grip on the airwaves. In addition to the usual suspects—the BBC, Capital Radio, 208 and UBN—I also sent tapes to Radio Clyde, Swansea Sound and a half dozen others.

To keep my hand in the music scene I volunteered at Torquay's Hospital Radio and for two hours a day I would play requests for the patients languishing in the recovery wards and the intensive care units. After my shift I stuck around to work on redesigning the antiquated studios to make them more DJ-friendly and brought the wiring up to code so that the station wouldn't go off the air every thirty minutes or so due to a short in the circuits.

On September 20, I got a phone call.

My parents didn't actually have their own phone in the house. Instead they had an arrangement with our next-door neighbors, a lovely couple named Tommy and Margaret Northcott. Tommy was the former captain of the Torquay United football team whose crowning achievement of his playing career was leading Torquay to a three–three tie against the then-unstoppable Tottenham Hotspur, "*Spurs*," in a thrilling 1965 FA Cup matchup. But those days were behind him and Tommy now worked as a plumber and was a fantastic family man.

He and Mrs. Northcott were more than happy to have calls come in for us and would yell over the fence that "so and so" is on the phone. On that day I heard her shouting for me.

"Richard. It's the phone for you, my love. Better come quickly, it's long-distance." She dropped her voice to almost a whisper as if the authorities might be eavesdropping. "I think it's from somewhere in Europe!"

I hopped over the privet hedge and ran into Mrs. Northcott's hallway where the large black handset lay waiting for me next to the receiver.

I grabbed it and uttered a quick "Hello?"

I didn't recognize the voice but I instantly knew the caller's name.

"Richard, this is Alan Lawrie from IDEA. Can we talk?"

Alan Lawrie was the founder and owner of IDEA, International Disc Jockey and Entertainment Agency, the largest booking agency for DJs in Europe. Europa Booking had started to compete with IDEA but Alan's company was still, by far, the biggest, having more than 160 clubs throughout the continent.

Alan continued on the phone. "Peter Brown called me. Says you just returned from Spain. Bet that was fun. If you want to come back out to Europe I would love to book you. Interested?"

He'd obviously been hoping I'd say yes because within five minutes Alan had laid out a touring itinerary for me. I would start in just eleven days on the first of October in Helsingor just north of Copenhagen, then head over to Jutland, central Denmark, for two months, then down to Switzerland in the new year where I could meet up with Peter Brown again, then stay on in Switzerland for another month but move to Basel and from there I would go to Vienna, Austria. Did it sound good?

To me at that moment it could not have sounded any better. Alan advised bringing a car if I had one as it would make getting around a lot easier, and unlike Norway with its mountainous ridge running right through the center of the country, mainland Europe has the best roads in the world. I had ten days to get it all together; car, insurance, ferry tickets . . .

I realized that my much-loved MG would be too small to hold me, my record collection, my clothes and everything I'd need for a year on the

ON the first night of his two-week package holiday to the Spanish resort of Lloret de Mar, Torquay disc-jockey Dick Sheppard was asked if he wouldn't mind spinning the records at the hotel's discotheque as they were without a dee-jay. Needless to say he ended up working the turntables all summer and has just returned to his home at 22, Drake-avenue, Chelston.

But not for long. This week Dick is off to Denmark and Sweden for six months disc-jockeying and the bulk of his luggage is made up of 1,000 singles records and 200 L.P.s. During the three weeks he has been at home Dick has helped with the setting up of the radio station at Torbay Hospital.

"I shall begin working at a club just outside Copenhagen. As they are behind with the new releases I'll be taking all the latest sounds with

Herald Express, September 1975

road in Europe. With Dad's help I traded it in for a more sensible vehicle, a red Vauxhall Viva with all the trunk space I could need. It wasn't my little blue sports car but hopefully it would be perfect for my upcoming exploits.

The local press gave me a very nice send-off. Dad called the newspaper that had run an article on me in February and filled them in on the adventure ahead of me. The editor sent over a reporter and photographer and the story ran in two papers blanketing the south of England, *The Herald Express* and *The Western Morning News*. That's when I knew for sure that my Dad, despite his entreaties for me to teach, was secretly proud of my travels and was living vicariously through my exploits. And boy, was I happy to share them with him.

GOLDEN YEARS

The ferry crossing to Copenhagen was anything but smooth. An early seasonal storm rolled south from the Artic and whipped the North Sea into a frenzy. The normal twenty-foot waves reached the towering heights of fifty to sixty feet causing the decks to be secured, meaning we were locked beneath and couldn't go outside for fresh air for fear of being swept away to our certain death. Below deck the vessel stank of diesel and vomit and even though I don't normally get seasick, on this crossing I threw up with the best of them.

I was curled in a fetal position in one of the three deserted restaurants on board when an old salt came up to me and handed me a tomato.

"Eat it," he commanded.

"I can't," I replied. "I've been throwing up for hours."

"That's why you need to eat it," he continued. "Something slimy like this in your belly will come right back up and bring all the bile with it. It'll clean you out and you'll feel better."

I took the tomato and staggered across the pitching deck to the cramped bathroom. I only managed one bite before I regurgitated the red-skinned fruit along with the remainder of my stomach lining. He had been right about it triggering your vomit reflex, but he was wrong about something else—I didn't feel one bit better.

I arrived in Copenhagen on September 28 with two days to spare. I planned that deliberately so I would have time to meet Alan and get to know him a little. He promised that he would find me a place to stay while I was there so I could have a couple of days to play around in the big city before heading forty miles up the coast to Helsingor.

Alan and his glamorous wife, Julie, made a lovely couple and Alan was true to his word. He had a stack of contracts for me to sign and set up a photo shoot to take some updated publicity shots. He introduced me to Zed and Baba Bailey, a husband-and-wife DJ team that lived in Copenhagen and said I'd be staying with them.

Zed and Baba lived on Landskronagade, a street that stayed busy all year long because situated at the end of their road was the liquid equivalent to a pot o' gold, the main Carlsberg brewing company factory which conducted daily tours of their facility and were very generous at handing out samples of their product. It was common to see a large group of tourists walk in and then roll out about an hour later.

Their apartment was a gathering place for British DJs. Zed and Baba were the friendliest, most welcoming people in the world and would go out of their way to help you. As a result it was more common than not for them to have a DJ or two crashing on their floor. You didn't even have to give them any notice, just show up and they'd find a place for you to sleep. For two nights I helped them uphold that "open door" reputation as we sat around swapping war stories from the road.

They told me I'd like Helsingor and they weren't wrong, it was beyond amazing. The town was set on Oresund, a body of water that connects the Baltic Sea to the Atlantic Ocean. Barely three miles across Oresund is Sweden, so close that at night you could watch people turning on the lights in their houses.

And Helsingor held a major attraction for me. One of the Shakespearean plays I had studied and acted in at Westminster College was *Hamlet, Prince of Denmark* and here I was walking the grounds of the very castle that inspired the Bard to write his masterpiece. All he did was change the name of Helsingor's castle from Kronborg to Elsinore, inspired by the name of the town itself. I felt as if I were stepping back into the past.

But history was not the inspiration for the club, Svingelport; it was anything but old. It was everything I loved about Scandinavian discos and more. The sound system cranked, the lights were cool and the girls were red-hot. But it did have a very unusual time schedule. The doors opened at eight and the bartenders would put on a cassette that the DJ had left for them. At ten I would go on live and crank the music until a little after midnight. Then it would be a mellow mix for about forty-five minutes as you awaited the arrival of the Swedes. Then, by 1 a.m., you were rocking out again and stayed, full throttle, until five in the morning when the club closed.

This unique format was put together because in Sweden (like Norway) the clubs closed at midnight. So at that time all the young Swedes would empty out of the bars and clubs, stampede to the ferry terminal and cross the Oresund from Helsingborg (Sweden) to Helsingor (Denmark) where the licensing laws were a lot more liberal. Plus as the ship sailed between two different countries the tax laws were relaxed and on board during the short ten-minute ferry crossing the cigarettes and booze were all duty-free and therefore less than half the price they would cost in the regular shops.

So every night, like clockwork, at 12:40am the club would suddenly double in capacity as it filled to the brim with drunken Swedes reeking of nicotine and Bacardi. But they staggered in ready to party and I was the guy to make sure that these tipsy Norsemen and women had a good time. When closing time rolled around I would attempt to mellow out the rowdy dancers and send them home with a huge ballad like "Feelings" by Morris Albert or "I'm Not in Love" by 10cc.

After the crowd dissipated I would leave the club and head back to my apartment which was a short walk through the old town. Those early mornings were magical. Most people were still asleep and the timed security lights that burned all night mixed with the first rays of the sun as it rose over the Oresund. Often a fine mist would drift in from the waterway and make the cobblestone pathway slippery. I would hold on tightly to the girl that I was with to make sure that she didn't take an unexpected tumble on those smooth, damp pebbles.

Without exception my route home would lead me to Falhlmans Konditori, a wonderful little bakery whose store window promised an unending assortment of delights. Though the shop would be closed for another hour, ten feet below street level the bakers were hard at work mixing flour, water, butter and sugar into pastries until they were ready for the wood-fired oven. The smell of their delicious baking filled the air, teasing your taste buds and luring you to Falhlmans.

Several of the bakers were regulars at Svingelport so when I bent down and knocked on the old wooden hatch in the alleyway behind the store they would be anticipating my appearance which had become as regu-

DJ DICK SHEPPARD

Promo picture, October 1975

lar as the dawn and would pop open the ancient trapdoor and hand me a freshly baked loaf straight out of the oven at no charge. I would heed their warning, *"Forsiktig det er varmt!"* with a smile.

Good, I'd think to myself, *I love it hot.*

We would tear the loaf apart right there and then and chew on big chunks of that incredibly delicious fresh bread, its crust crunchy, the insides still steaming and soft, almost melting in your mouth. Whether it was the time or the place, or both, that contributed to the experience, it remains one of the best things I've ever eaten. My companion and I would laugh, hug and finish off that freshest of breads before we even reached the door of my waiting apartment.

It was an unforgettable time to be young and in Europe, working as a DJ, and a brand-new song from David Bowie that I had just been sent and had started playing summed it all up for me, these were "Golden Years."

I received my new promo pictures from Alan and suddenly my white suit and I were all over that Danish coastal town.

My other regular routine was going to the club a little early and putting together demo tapes for the radio. As great as DJing in the clubs across Europe was, I remained determined that one day I'd get on air with my own show. After an hour or so of working on that I would take a break from recording and get on the empty dance floor to stretch and practice my karate.

I'd been studying Shotokan since my early days at Westminster College but because of my traveling had not been able to take a class or visit a dojo for almost sixteen months. So I would work through the moves on the empty dance floors in the clubs I was playing as it gave me the space and height that even the biggest of the DJ rooms couldn't provide.

When I went back to Europe this time around I was in a car and I had room for a few extra things so I brought my nunchucks with me. These Japanese fighting sticks were a homemade pair I'd put together using two fifteen-inch pieces of one-inch birch linked with six inches of thick nylon twine. They were perfectly fine for my use which was practice and fitness. At quite a few of the discos, the barbacks, who were the only other people in the club with me at the time, would ask to try them out, occasionally resulting in hilarious outcomes and more than a few bruises.

I really didn't think anything about them apart from that they were a sporting hobby item like my speargun back home. I didn't have any idea how grateful I would be just two months later that those nunchucks were with me in Denmark and not at home in Torquay in my top drawer.

November had flown by and my memories of my month-long gig in Horsens, Denmark were already thankfully fading. It was a small town with a club that didn't go out of its way to impress the clients. And they in turn didn't seem picky. As long as the beers were cold and the music was loud, they were happy. The hours were shorter there than in Helsingor as I was now on the mainland of Denmark—Jutland—rather than on the island of Sjaelland which is home to both Helsingor and the country's capital, Copenhagen, so there were few tourists. But it was during my stint in Horsens that I came across a record that became a springboard to disco's worldwide explosion and an artist who was destined to be its figurehead.

I had been reading about this song in several of the music publications and it intrigued me to no end that the BBC had banned it before it was even released. The record was described as "sex on vinyl" and the more I heard about it the more I wanted to play it. I had my father order me a copy from London and send it over. He called to tell me it was on its way but cautioned, "I tried listening to it at home but your mother had me turn it off. She said it was far too rude." That was just what I was hoping for and I couldn't wait for it to arrive in the mail.

When it finally came I was shocked to see it was over sixteen minutes long. My first thought was that it would be perfect to play if I needed a bathroom break. Then I slipped it on the turntable. Wow, it was as if the future had just exploded in my room, I had heard nothing like it before; the vocal was repetitive and hypnotic, the background beat came from a synthesizer not a drum set, and the message was perfectly clear, "Let's have sex!" Perfect for a Dick Sheppard disco set.

I played it that night at the club but I deliberately held it back and waited until the evening was drawing to a close, the alcohol had kicked in and the beer goggles were on. I introduced it with a simple "Here's a song for anyone who is looking for a little love tonight," and started the twelve-inch.

At first everyone gave me the sideways glance that every DJ is used to getting when they play a new track that the audience doesn't recognize—I'm always tempted to get back on the microphone and yell, "This *will* be your new favorite song in about a week so just go with it"—and no one got up and danced. After two minutes the floor was still empty but I noticed that the people at the bar and sitting at the tables were starting to move in their seats and look around with a kind of "Should we be the first?" vibe. Then three girls got up and starting dancing, almost swaying together on the floor and then singing along with the chorus as it repeated over and over.

It was as if they had opened the floodgates and made it safe to dance. The whole club seemed to move onto the floor as one and quickly couples matched up and began to grind on each other. My gut was right, it was the perfect late-night "let's hook up, go home and get wild" song.

"Love to Love You, Baby" played for sixteen minutes, packed the floor and changed so many people's minds about what disco could be. I knew that night at that small club in Horsens that I was witnessing an evolution in music and the birth of a superstar, Donna Summer. After the song finished I was mobbed by people wanting to know what they had just danced to. I was happy to tell them, knowing that from then on out it would be one of my top requests.

After the club closed I read the label carefully and saw that the track was written and produced by someone called Giorgio Moroder. I remember thinking that I hoped this wouldn't be just a one-off record for him. I wasn't the only one impressed by his music; unknown to me in places as far apart as Liverpool, Basildon and Paris, kids would also hear his music and decide that they too would want to play a synthesizer like that and the only way to do it would be to start a band.

Winter was coming on strong as I wrapped up my month in Horsens, and my short, fifty-mile drive to Herning was treacherous due to black ice on the roads. I was already dreading my next road trip, all the way to Kreuzlingen in Switzerland, 1,200 kilometers away. And I'd have to do it in one day to make it to my gig the next night. That upcoming trek stayed in the back of my mind all month.

The club in Herning was a mess when I arrived on Monday afternoon, December 1. Less than forty-eight hours before, during a raging Saturday night party, a big fight had erupted on the dance floor. There was only one bouncer in the club so all the bartenders leapt over the counter to help break it up, but the turning point was when the DJ, a tough-as-nails ex-seaman from Grimsby, got involved and waded in throwing haymakers.

He seriously hurt two of the people who had started the fight, one so badly that he had to be transported to hospital. Two tables were broken and three of the speakers surrounding the dance floor had their fronts kicked in and had to be replaced. As a result there was no dancing the first two days because the sound system was down. Instead the club just opened for drinks and bar food.

Wednesday, December 3, was almost a re-opening party. It was also my first night playing and one that gave me a permanent reminder of what went down.

I arrived early to test the new replacement speakers. I don't know what the previous ones had sounded like but these had some great bottom end and I knew they would be perfect for songs like B.T. Express' "Do It 'til You're Satisfied" and The Bee Gees' "Jive Talking." I did a quick workout on the floor for thirty minutes, then cleaned up in the manager's office and got ready for work.

The night was uneventful and a little slow, but it was midweek and people were still nervous about the violence that had happened there that past Saturday. We closed early, at midnight, and with just a few people remaining in the club I didn't wait for it to clear out. Instead I said goodnight to the bartenders, trying to remember as many of their names as possible, grabbed my bag with my workout clothes and cassette player in it so I could have music in my room, my practice nunchucks; and walked outside to my car.

The flame-red Vauxhall Viva was parked close to the club in the spot saved for the DJ and I opened the passenger door and put the bag on the seat. I was just about to toss in the nunchucks when I heard "*Fanden!*" behind me. I knew that word. It is almost the same in Swedish and Norwegian and was one of the first curse words I had learned. It means "Devil" and is directed at someone you don't like.

The person yelling "*Fanden!*" definitely didn't have me on their Christmas card list. He had been hiding behind the car next to mine. He was around my height and build but he was holding a broken beer bottle.

He thrust the jagged glass hard at my face. I reacted spontaneously. I raised my right arm and swept it across my body, right to left to protect myself. Whether I was too fast or too slow I still haven't decided but I stopped the bottle with my arm. It didn't hit my face but instead ripped through my jacket's sleeve and sliced open a four-inch gash on my wrist just an inch from my main artery. But at that moment with the surprise, the fear and the adrenalin pumping I didn't even feel the cut.

Instead the impact from my arm sent the bottle flying from his hand and he stepped back momentarily. That was his big mistake. He gave me a three-foot space in which to move. In my left hand I still had my nunchucks.

Just as I had practiced a hundred times while doing my katas on the empty dance floors I raised the fighting sticks up high and in the same continuous move flipped them hard downwards. That was it, the fight was over. I opened a huge cut through his right eyebrow and crushed the bridge of his nose.

He was still down when the police and ambulance arrived to ironically take both of us, victim and assailant, to hospital. I had fourteen stitches in my wrist to close up the wound and till this day still have a four-inch scar running down the inside of my right forearm. He was not quite as lucky as I was told his forehead and nose would carry a very visible scar for many years to come.

Sadly, the ambush and fight should never have happened. It was my attacker's brother who had been transported to hospital the previous Saturday and he had come looking for revenge against the DJ who had put him there. What he didn't know was that IDEA DJs changed on the first of every month and the person he thought was responsible was long gone to another town and another club. He just knew I was the DJ and mistakenly thought that I was the one he was looking for. For my remaining three weeks in Herning the doormen walked me to my car every night and I must say I was glad of the escort.

AUTOBAHN

The Longest Day, January 1, 1976. "*Godt Nytar*" was still ringing in my ears as the manager and doormen went with me to my car at 4am on New Year's Day. It had been a wild New Year's Eve at the club in Herning and perhaps their busiest Wednesday night ever. The manager stood with me at the car and wanted to talk for a while. He told me that the club was really fun in the summer and I should definitely come back. I didn't want to be rude but I had to get going.

Waiting for me was a trek like none I had ever done before; I had to drive the length of Jutland, right through Germany and get to Kreuzlingen in Switzerland in time to go on stage by 8pm That gave me just less than sixteen hours to cover three countries and nearly 1,200 kilometers. Couple that with the fact that this was the dead of winter and snow and ice were everywhere and it made for a daunting journey.

Fortunately the night was clear; no rain, sleet or snow was falling. But I had to get going. One handshake later and I was on my way. I had been planning this trip for a month. I had water, sandwiches and—most importantly—a stack of TDK C90 cassettes that I had put together to keep me company. With the opening notes of Golden Earring's "Radar Love" blaring from my speakers I shifted the car into gear and sped south. Within two hours I was passing Handewitt, Germany and Denmark disappeared in my rear-view mirror. Soon speed limit signs were gone and I was on the autobahn.

Europe was forever shaped by World War II and nowhere is there more evidence of this than on the German autobahns. Arguably the greatest highways in the world, they were designed for a secret, sinister purpose: to move divisions of armored tank columns across Germany to invade the neighboring countries. Initially started in 1929 as a jobs project, to create employment for the German people who were suffering terribly from the Great Depression, their peaceful purpose changed in 1933 when Hitler rose to power.

As undisputed leader of the Third Reich he saw another use for them, one that would aide him in his goals of conquest and destruction.

For the next eleven years until the Allies landed on the beaches of Normandy on June 6, 1944, Der Fuhrer ordered a construction plan for the autobahns that is almost unmatched in the history of our planet. At first they were built by Germans desperately needing to work but as the economy recovered and Hitler's iron grip on his country tightened he realized that it would be more cost-effective to build this network of high-speed roads using slave labor.

As part of his "ultimate solution" hundreds of thousands of imprisoned Jews, Gypsies and homosexuals were loaded onto trains and brought to these work sites and forced to toil night and day to build this massive transportation infrastructure. Most died during the project due to the inhumane conditions and many of those were entombed where they fell in an unmarked grave of concrete and tarmac. These highways, constructed by a river of human blood, crisscross Germany to this day.

And now I hurtled down the autobahn, tracing the path of the retreating Panzer tank convoys fleeing south to protect their homeland as the war neared its bloody climax. I sped past Hamburg, then Hanover. The next major city was Frankfurt, four hours away. I was now more than five hours into my drive, and apart for a stop for gas and the bathroom, I hadn't taken a break. But I could feel the weight of my tiredness catching up with me.

I'd been going for two days straight, including that crazy New Year's Eve party but if I could just keep my eyes open everything would be good. Frankie Valli's heavenly falsetto floated from my car speakers as "Who Loves You (Pretty Baby)" was next up on my cassette. *Good. This one always gets me going.* I cranked the volume, wishing it went up to eleven, and sang along with The Four Seasons. I was flying now.

Dad had helped me pick out a great little car. Whatever measurement you used; miles or kilometers, this German autobahn was being gobbled up by four Michelin tires and a motor made in Cheshire, England. I relaxed into the rhythm of the road, letting the music power me on. Track after track played as my odometer racked up the distance traveled.

I remember being puzzled, I wasn't sure what song it was but it had a strange tempo; a fast *cuh, cuh, cuh, cuh* followed by a loud *toot, toot*. I didn't recognize it but it repeated again. *Cuh, cuh, cuh, cuh—toot, toot. Did I put this on the cassette? Could you dance to it?* I woke up as the *toot, toot* became a continuous blast on an air horn.

The deafening klaxon jolted me out of my sleep and I found myself in a waking nightmare, speeding out of control at more than 100 miles per hour with my tires thumping out an unholy beat as they pounded over the raised cats' eyes that marked the lane dividers. I was drifting into the path of an eighteen-wheeler that was thundering towards me, desperately blasting its air horn to get my attention before the massive big-rig smashed into me and reduced the car to scrap metal and its fatigued driver to road kill.

Even as I wrenched the steering wheel hard to the right to avoid the catastrophic collision my car violently rocked sideways as the wind from the hurtling juggernaut hit and shook me like a cat shakes a mouse. My little Vauxhall Viva bounced wildly towards the hard shoulder and I could feel the rear wheels sliding as I braked hard while struggling to straighten out the careening vehicle. I finally got the car under control and my heart raced at the realization of what my exhaustion could have caused.

My car filled with the acrid stench of burning rubber so I rolled my window down and the freezing January air roared in shocking me awake. How long had I been asleep; a second, a minute? It had almost been a lifetime.

I wrapped a sweater around my chest to keep warm but left the window down so that the icy chill blowing across my face and head would keep me from dozing off again. Only another two hours to Frankfurt. Then it would be on to Heidelberg, Stuttgart and finally Kreuzlingen. Switzerland here I come.

Kreuzlingen is set on one of Europe's most picturesque lakes, the Bodensee. It is a border town, walk down the narrow main street and you pass a small hut with an armed, uniformed guard in it. You've just entered Konstanz, Germany!

Suddenly I was in exactly the opposite situation of the one I'd encountered in Helsingor. The stringent Swiss drinking laws meant that my club, The Green Apple, closed at midnight. So as the clock struck twelve the club would empty and the intoxicated dancers would stagger their way from the bosom of Swiss hospitality to the anxiously waiting arms of the German club owners.

Every evening it resembled a scene from *Night of the Living Dead* as the border's floodlights illuminated hundreds of drunken Swiss kids as they weaved and lurched like zombies stumbling their way down the short road that led from one country to another.

Lena was from Konstanz. She was one of the bartenders at the club and was drop-dead gorgeous. But no one ever went near her. She seemed to have walls around her that were higher and stronger than the ones that divided her country's capital 400 miles away. One quiet night she opened up to me, we started talking and hit it off. The next morning we woke up together in my room above the club and I asked if she wanted to grab breakfast. She said that might not be a good idea. She had a boyfriend and didn't think that people should see us together.

Rocking the crowd in Switzerland

I asked where he was; I'd been at the club for nearly three weeks and had never seen anyone with her. She explained that he was away, training in the Bavarian mountains.

"Training? For what?" I asked.

"The altitude is good for him. He's got a big fight coming up. He's a middleweight boxer."

Lena was lovely, but now I knew why no one ever even attempted to flirt with her. I just hoped that her boyfriend's training would last at least another ten days because after that I was out of there. I dreaded him coming back early because I would have made a lousy sparring partner for a seventy-two-kilo German pro boxer.

IDEA had clubs across Europe and Alan Lawrie was a great booking agent but not so hot on routing a tour. My next gig sent me backwards over a hundred miles to Basel. This was a much bigger city but also unique as it sits on the crossroads of three countries and tourists can visit "the border triangle" and literally step from one country to the next. France, Germany and Switzerland all meet up here so it's a great way to impress your friends by telling them that you visited all three countries in one day—or truthfully, in three steps!

Happy Night was the name of the disco in Basel and they loved their English DJs so much that the booth was a hollowed-out London taxi—one of the famous "black cabs."

The management were not content with only the DJ entertaining the crowd; twice a night I would have to stop the music for a show. One performance would be a stripper and the second, a magician. The magic acts rotated in and out; sometimes card tricks and mind reading with the audience, sometimes fire breathing and other weeks a knife thrower with his scantily clad assistant strapped to the "Wheel o' Death." And if you've ever seen knife throwing up close, you know it's terrifying. There's nothing fake about it and twice during my month at Happy Night I watched as a knife flew close enough to the scantily clad assistant's body to draw blood. No wonder the audience gasps!

My room in Basel was just that, a room. It was cramped and had a bed that had seen plenty of use. As the incoming DJ you learned to shake out the sheets before you lay down just in case they hadn't been washed well enough to get rid of any creepy crawlies that the previous DJ might have left behind. The room was directly above the club and had probably been a former office. My clues to that origin were two empty file cabinets that were jammed in the corner because it was probably easier to just leave them there than to lug them down the stairs. Those metal cabinets were the only decoration in the entire room. No pictures of the town square or the river or cats playing cards, just four blank walls to comfort you during your stay.

Several of the DJs, evidently rife with boredom, had written on the walls in ballpoint pen. Some of the words were warnings, "Stay away from Susie, she has the clap" or "Buy your beer in Germany. It's cheaper." But one caught my eye. It said, "Radio. You can sing along with it, but you can never be on it."

I would find myself going back to that sad graffiti day after day. I could feel the despair of the person who had written it flowing through those words. Like most of the club DJs I wanted to get on the radio but again and again had found it to be a "closed shop." But I was not giving up—ever! Whoever had scribbled this on the wall had obviously resigned themselves to failure. The more I stared at this hopeless phrase the more I could feel the determination building within me. There had to be a way to break in, there had to be.

On my last day at Happy Night I knew I could not leave without re-plying to that haunting negativity. I would not let it win. Nine words to answer it kept ringing through my head and on that final morning I scrawled them out on the wall right below the phrase. The next DJ follow-ing me would now read:

Radio. You can sing along with it, but you can never be on it. Then one day you can sing-along with me.

I stopped and added two more words—*Dick Sheppard.*

That was the moment I signed a contract with myself.

As my time in Basel drew to a close I readied myself for another journey. As I mentioned, Alan was fantastic at getting the gigs but not at planning how to get from club A to club B. He'd sent me backwards to Basel, now I had to drive due east 850 kilometers to Vienna, Austria, passing Kreu-zlingen on the way. Nine more non-stop hours in the car. I was definitely becoming Dick Sheppard, road dog.

———\◇\———

VIENNA CALLING

Winter had not yet surrendered to spring, and snow still clung to the ground as I pulled my car up to Magic Discotheque in Vienna with just minutes to spare. I would unpack later; right now I had to get to work.

The club was situated in Volksgarten, on the grounds of Hofburg Pal-ace. It was in the center of Austria's capital and the most important club in the city. I'd been told it was big but the description didn't prepare me for just how huge it was. Inside the main building there were several dance floors that held more than 2,000 people. The side walls had massive powered sliders that in the warm summer months pushed them open to a vast exterior area that could accommodate another 4,000 party-goers.

The sound system was tri-amped with Earthquake bass bins and the lighting was state of the art with sweeping overhead Par cans and neon wall displays. I had a dry-ice fog machine at my disposal and a confetti cannon. Magic was a forerunner of the mega clubs that were starting to appear in Ibiza and Mallorca and would then spread across the world to London, New York and Las Vegas.

As I entered the club there were already people inside enjoying the cheap drink deals that were part of the Austrian version of "happy hour." The DJ booth was located right next to the main bar and after assessing the gear I unloaded my records and plugged in my microphone. I changed into my white suit which I always liked to wear on the first night in a new club to make an impression, came back out, put on a mid-tempo song to start the evening and looked around to absorb the ambience.

121

Taxi at the bar at Magic, Vienna, March 1976

The theme running throughout Magic was pink velvet. Everything was covered in that fabric and even the roof had thousands of pink stalactites hanging down. It was funky but somehow it worked and with all the plush material acting as acoustic baffles by absorbing any stray echoes from the loud speakers the club sounded amazing. I knew right away that this would be the perfect setup to showcase some of my favorite bass-heavy tracks like Brass Construction's "Movin'" and Earth, Wind & Fire's "Shining Star" and that as the night wore on and the drinks kicked I could get this club going off big-time. But there was one other thing that caught my eye.

Sitting at the bar, surrounded by her friends, was a vision in white. She almost looked too pretty to be real. An overhead spotlight hit her from be-hind and lit up her platinum-blond, shoulder-length hair like a halo. *Holy shit*, I thought, *she was so worth that drive*. I caught her eye and smiled. I turned away to cue up the next song, thinking that I was going to go right over to her and say hello but as I turned back around she was standing there on the stairs to the DJ booth.

"I'm Taxi," she said simply.

So many lines rushed through my head but they were all cheesy or rude, so instead I replied, "Great name. I'm Dick."

It was Taxi's turn to smile. She took one step back and looked me up and down. "That's not right. *Du bist nicht dick.*"

My knowledge of the German language was limited to just a few words and phrases but from what Taxi said I picked out a couple that I recognized. *Du* is *you*, *bist* means *is*, *nicht* is *not* and dick is my name. She was saying I wasn't who I said I was.

I leant forward. "Really, I am Dick. Look, this is me." I pointed to the poster advertising my month at Magic that was pinned on the wall of the DJ booth. The picture on the poster looked just like me; hell, I was even wearing the same suit.

She laughed. "Yes, that is you. But *du bist nicht dick.*" She stepped forward and put her hands on my waist. *Dick* in German means *fat*. You are not fat."

Oh great. I was hoping to learn a little German but to find out in my first impromptu lesson that

DICK SHEPPARD
DISC-JOCKEY
APPEARING AT

my name has a specific meaning in that language was certainly not what I was hoping for. Kids across Vienna would see the flyers that read "Dick Sheppard" and would want to come and party with the chubby DJ. Just wonderful.

Taxi's hands lingered on my waist for a few more seconds, perhaps a little longer than they should have. The message was clear. I looked into her eyes, "How long are you going to be here tonight?" I asked.

She held my gaze and said without hesitation, "Until you finish." I knew the game was on.

As they locked the doors of the club behind us, Taxi and I climbed into my car and she directed me to the address of my apartment on Mariahilfer Strasse. It was easy to find as Mariahilfer Strasse is one of the busiest streets in the city. It's the Viennese equivalent of Oxford Street in London or 5th Avenue in New York.

We climbed the stairs of this classic seventeenth-century building lugging my bags and unlocked the massive door. I was hoping the room wouldn't embarrass me and turn out to be yet another converted janitor's closet. I didn't have to worry. It was a full one-bedroom apartment with separate sitting area, bathroom, kitchen and bedroom. The floors were hardwood and the ceilings were high with ornate crown molding. It was awesome.

Taxi was impressed, "Very nice. Apartments like this are very hard to find in the city." How hard I'll never know because I reached forward, pulled her to me and kissed her.

The next morning we had breakfast at a little *kaffeehaus* just below my centrally located apartment. Taxi told me her story. She had just turned twenty and was a working model in Vienna. Her real name was Romy but everyone called her Taxi because she was born in the back of a speeding cab as her mother was being rushed to hospital. Her modeling name was

Publicity shots with Taxi – March 1976, Vienna

Tarquin. She laughed that she had three names and asked what I wanted to call her.

I grinned and said *Leibling* which means *cutie*. She giggled and said "You do speak German!" To which I replied, "Just the important words," which earned me a good-hearted slap. From that moment on there was no doubt that we would be together for my entire time in Austria.

We explored the world-class museums and art galleries of Vienna and drove to the banks of the legendary Blue Danube River where we picnicked and skimmed pebbles over the surface of the water. We shared each other's dreams and hopes and time slipped through our fingers like water spilling over a dam.

Taxi's photographer offered to shoot new promo pictures for me and we headed into his studio. We shot most of the day and I had Taxi appear in several of the shots. They became very popular handouts to the club regulars who would come up to the DJ booth asking for autographs.

With just a week to go in Vienna the manager of Magic approached me and asked if I would continue on at the club. He'd already spoken to Alan Lawrie and told him he'd like me to stay through May. Alan, fearing that I might turn on him as I had on Tor when he insisted on my returning to Tonsberg, said he could make it happen but it was my decision. I told the manager I was so up for the extra two months and asked if I could use his phone to call my girlfriend.

In just less than a month I had made a mark in Vienna. The club was sold out five nights a week, the record companies whose main offices were just down the street from my apartment on Mariahilfer Strasse would come to Magic to present me with all the latest new releases to premiere plus I was dating the hottest girl in the city. How could it get any better? By saying yes to a simple offer.

Wednesdays got a good, early crowd of regulars who were eager to get a jump-start on their partying and shake off the mid-week blues. I was in the DJ booth when a man in his late thirties approached me. He asked if I had ever thought about doing any radio. I said yes, of course I had. He continued that he was with an Austrian radio station and was wondering if I would like to try doing a rock show on the radio. It would be one hour, once a week in English and I would play all the hottest rock bands around like Queen, Roxy Music, Slade and Rod Stewart. It would be on Friday nights from six until seven and then I could head over to Magic for my regular DJ show. I'm sure my immediate handshake answered his question.

That Friday night doing my first show on one of Austria's national radio stations was terrifying. I felt like everyone in the country was tuned in and listening and I was scared stiff that I would screw up. Plus I had zero control over actually playing the records and I'm a very tactile person. I like to cue the vinyl up, adjust the volume and do the cross fades and starts when I DJ, not let someone else do it for me.

Instead they sat me alone in a voice-over booth with a large glass window facing the engineer and the show's producer. I had just two buttons to worry about; an *on* button for my microphone and a "talk-back" button so the engineer could hear me through the soundproof glass for cues and suggestions. I could hear him and the outgoing mix of the broadcast in my headphones. I put together a list of music and we were on the air.

It was the fastest sixty minutes of my life. My nerves were playing up and I kept thinking I had to go to the bathroom but I didn't want to leave the booth and risk missing the end of a song. And I was continuously second-guessing myself; there was that little voice in the back of my mind

On my trusty Vauxhall Viva   *Outside of Magic disco*

that repeated over and over in a continuous loop "Maybe there's a reason you're not on the radio. You're just not good enough." But somehow I got through it and after the show was congratulated by both the programmer and engineer and invited to do it again the next week.

Back at Magic an hour later I was amazed that person after person lined up at the DJ booth to say hello and tell me that they had listened to my rock show on the radio. More people had heard me DJ in just sixty minutes than in the previous four years of spinning in England and Europe. I knew there and then, on that Friday night in Vienna, that my dream of radio was not just a far-fetched goal; it was something I had to make reality at all costs.

Taxi took me out for lunch on my birthday. I had a week left in Vienna before my three months were over and I was set to return to Denmark for the summer. We had talked about my leaving but she didn't think I was actually going to go. After all, I would not only be leaving her but also Magic and the radio.

I explained that I had come to a realization. Here I was just a novelty doing a one-hour show on a German language radio station, that "foreigner with a cute accent." It wasn't mean, it was just a fact. To make it on the radio, to really make it, I had to be in a country where English, my native language, was also the native language of the listener. I wrote out a list on a napkin.

"These are the places I can go. I have to choose one," I said as I slipped her the napkin. It read:

America
Canada
Australia & New Zealand
South Africa

"What about England?" Taxi asked.

"No. I'm not going back there."

"But it's your home?" she said.

"It was. But I can't go back. There doesn't seem to be any drive or excitement there; not in the country or in the people. "It's . . ." I struggled for the word, "grey, dreary. I think in German you say *trostlos*. Everyone gets beaten down by the weather and they don't seem to even want to try. Have you seen *The Wizard of Oz?*"

Taxi nodded.

"It's like that. You know how the beginning of the movie is black and white and then turns to color? That's how I feel leaving England. England is black and white then you leave and the world explodes into Technicolor. And that's what I want. I don't think that's so wrong, is it?"

"No, it's not," she agreed. "So where will you go? Which country?"

I laughed. "I know this is going to sound nuts but I was freezing my buns off one day in Norway and I saw this movie that was shot in California and it was hot and sunny and it made me want to go there. So I think maybe America."

"Because of a film?" she asked.

I smiled and nodded. There was a long pause, then she asked that question I had prayed wasn't coming. It was just three words but I knew the answer would be something she didn't want to hear.

"Can I come?"

The reply to that should have been simple and honest—*No*—but I couldn't be that brutal. I struggled to find the words.

"It would be great but . . . but I don't know how it'll work out. We'll stay in touch and see if we can make it happen."

Taxi slumped a little in her chair. She had cut through my babble and deciphered the real meaning; she had heard *no* and realized I was saying goodbye!

Our remaining week together was great. We laughed, explored the city together and made love as if our conversation had never happened. On Monday May 31, 1976 Taxi was there to help me empty my apartment and load up my car. She even brought me pastries for the twenty-hour drive back across Europe and into Denmark.

We hugged, kissed and said our tearful goodbyes. Taxi stood there waving as I pulled away and left her and Vienna behind as I began my drive out of the city to start the long journey north.

NEVER CAN SAY GOODBYE

It was another long haul, almost 1,000 miles, heading west along the banks of the Danube through Switzerland and Germany before entering Scandinavia. I could have shaved more than 200 miles off the trip had I been able to go north but unfortunately that direction would have taken me through Czechoslovakia which was part of the USSR and a shortcut through Soviet territory in the spring of 1976 would have ended with me heading for a Siberian gulag, so instead I stayed on the roads that ran through NATO countries and remained free to rock.

Darkness was falling and the street lights were on as I arrived in Copenhagen. I drove through the busy streets packed with tired commuters anxiously heading home and made my way to Zed and Baba's.

I spent the night at their apartment, playing cards and listening to another Brit, Roger Keisha, strumming guitar as he contemplated quitting the world of DJing to become a professional musician. Roger was staying in the room I normally slept in so Baba made a bed for me on their couch, but I wasn't complaining because they'd put me up several times without any notice and asked for nothing but friendship in return.

That morning, after a very welcome homemade English breakfast, I headed out and a little over an hour later I was in Helsingor. It felt good to be back. It was the beginning of June, the sun was out and people celebrated its warmth by flocking to the beaches. This small, coastal town might not have been as exciting as Vienna but its familiar welcome gave me time to relax and plan my trip to America. I was surprised at myself that now I had no doubt as to my destination. It was to be the US of A for sure. Now I just had to work out how to get there and when to go. But my plans were about to be interrupted by the most unexpected event.

I'd been in Helsingor for just three days and had slipped easily into my old ways as I embraced my regular haunts. I'd met up with a couple of girls I'd dated the last time I had been in town, Bitten, who was a pretty, fun-loving regular at Svingelport and Gerd, a tall, gorgeous redhead who was the most easy-going person you could ever meet. I'm glad that it was Gerd that I was with that afternoon.

We were walking together through the town's central square to see if my friend, Ian Johnson, a.k.a. Dr. Disc, was at home in his apartment, when I noticed something across the fifteenth-century town square.

Denmark, like its sister Scandinavia countries, Sweden, Norway and Finland, is a nation of blonds. Flowing golden hair is the norm, not the exception. But this was not normal blond hair that I had just glimpsed. This was a flash of white, of platinum-blond hair glistening in the sun. I had only seen hair like that once before.

Concerned, I turned to Gerd and said, "I've gotta go." I sprinted across the crowded square towards that hair, towards Taxi.

She saw me coming and a huge smile lit up her face. "I found you," she said.

My head was spinning. "What are you doing here? Why did you come?"

Taxi reached for my hand. "To be with you, so we can be together again."

Fuck, she looked beautiful but I was having none of it.

"Come with me," I said as I half dragged her to the phone booth at the edge of the square.

I pulled out several Danish krone coins and dropped them in the phone and dialed.

"Are you angry?" Taxi asked. I raised my hand to quiet her as Baba answered the phone.

"Hello?"

"Hey, sorry to bother you. It's Dick," I said into the handset. "Look can I ask you for a big favor? I'm going to put someone on the train to Copenhagen. Could you meet her at the station and get her on a train to Vienna?" I turned to Taxi. "Do you have money?" She nodded.

I continued on the phone to Baba. "I'll call you back in a few minutes with her train number and what time it arrives. Should be within the next two hours. The girl's name is Taxi. She has short, white-blond hair. You can't miss her. Just help her find a connecting train to Vienna if you could. Thanks."

Taxi tried to make small talk as I led her to Helsingor's tiny regional train station. I don't think I said anything back to her. I was a sea of emotions: shock, anger, surprise, sadness.

After today there would be no chance that we would ever get back together which was a shame because she was such a special girl. But this was bat-shit crazy. She'd come halfway across Europe to a country she'd never been to and full of people who didn't speak her language to look for me in a town she'd never even heard of until a few days before. And somehow she had pulled it off! My mind was reeling.

I bought the eleven-krone ticket for Taxi and put her on the train. I waited until it left the station and watched as it built up speed and rumbled down the tracks to make sure that she didn't jump from it like I had seen in many a western. With her safely on her way I called Baba back to let her know the train number and arrival time. Still stunned, I decided to walk to Kronborg castle to sit on its battlements, to collect my thoughts, and go back to the time of Hamlet and clear my head.

My month in Helsingor sped by way too fast and soon it was time to get back on the road again but this time it was just a short journey. I was heading south to one of Copenhagen's major suburbs, Borgergade, to play at Circle Club. My parents were scheduled to come out and stay with me in the middle of July and I was excited to see them; it had been nearly ten months and I wanted to show them Denmark.

Circle Club was a small disco but had a good urban crowd that liked the funkier tracks I was playing such as The Commodores' "Brick House,"

The Isley Brothers "Live It Up" and Candi Staton's "Young Hearts Run Free." The hours were long, and it wasn't unusual for me not to get back to my apartment until 6am. As a result I would sleep until noon then get up and hit one of Copenhagen's many beaches like Amager or Bellevue. I was in Copenhagen almost a week before I had the opportunity to visit Zed and Baba and thank them for bailing me out with the "Taxi thing."

Baba looked surprised when she opened the door and saw me. She ushered me into her front room and said she'd put the kettle on. She came back from the kitchen and sat and talked with me as we waited for the kettle's whistle.

"I can't thank you enough," I told Baba. "I really didn't know what else to do."

"It was no problem," Baba replied. "You know the train station is no distance from here. And she's so nice."

I nodded. "She is. But loony, right? I mean coming all that way. Nuts."

Baba wrinkled her nose. I could see she wasn't on the same page as me.

"Haven't you done something like that? Been so in love—"

I interrupted her. "That I would travel a thousand miles to barge in on someone who wasn't expecting me? No, I can honestly say I haven't."

The door opened slightly and Taxi popped her head in.

"Did you want biscuits with the tea?"

I think I froze. Maybe not completely because I do remember looking from Taxi to Baba and back again. For the second time in two months I was gobsmacked.

Baba smiled at Taxi, "Biscuits would be lovely."

Taxi turned and went back to the kitchen. I could only stare at Baba in disbelief. What the hell was going on?

Baba spoke first. "There were no trains the day she got in. I couldn't have her wait at the station all night by herself. So I brought her home. And she's so sweet, no trouble at all. What else could I have done?"

I rubbed my face with my hands. "You could have put her on the train the next day, or the day after, or yesterday! She knew I was coming to Copenhagen after Helsingor, we'd talked about my schedule, she's just using you."

"To get to you?" Baba was getting defensive. "No, not true. Zed and I like having Taxi here. We asked her to stay if you must know. It's got nothing to do with you."

My brain felt like it was about to explode. Nothing? Then why the hell was she even in Denmark and not home in Austria if it had nothing to do with me? And now I had burdened this great couple, my dear friends, with a potentially psycho ex-girlfriend. I could see the headlines of tomorrow's *Dagbladet* reading "*Mand og kone myrdet*" (Husband and wife murdered).

At that moment Taxi walked in but instead of wielding a carving knife she carried a tray loaded with tea and biscuits. Baba and I sat in uncomfortable silence as she set the tray on the table.

Taxi turned to Baba and smiled, "Let me know if you need anything else," and left the room.

Baba looked at me and nodded knowingly, "She's great."

Baba could have added "and beautiful and sexy and fun and intelligent" and she would have been right on all counts but it was over; I was not going back there, I'd obviously screwed her up enough already. As soon as I'd finished my cuppa I left without saying one word to Taxi. I figured that was the best way as I didn't want to find myself losing it and getting into an argument and souring my friendship with Zed and Baba.

Mum and Dad arrived in Denmark the following week. Dad brought a stack of vinyl that the record companies had sent me. Apparently my request to be put on the promo lists had worked and Dad said I was getting at least fifty new albums and twelve-inches every week. And God bless my father, he would open the packages, listen to all the new releases and sort out what he considered the good from the bad. He was my personal music director.

He handed me a package and said "These are all pretty good. The two best are on the top."

Wouldn't you know it, this fifty-nine-year-old math teacher was right, he'd picked The Bee Gees' "You Should Be Dancing," the song that would convince Robert Stigwood that these three brothers should be given the opportunity to write the songs for a little disco film he was working on with John Travolta, and the other was from Abba.

Dad grinned, "The letter with it says it comes out next month. They sent you an advance copy. I thought you might like it as they are from Scandinavia."

I looked at the twelve-inch from Polar Records and read the title, "Dancing Queen."

I said, "Hopefully it lives up to its name!"

I played it that night at Circle Disco while Mum and Dad danced the bump on the floor. It was an immediate hit with the crowd and that night—and for the next five months—I must have played it every hour.

The next day Zed came over to my apartment to meet Mum and Dad. While he was there he handed me a small box with a dozen cassettes inside. "Could you make copies of the new Abba song on these? All the DJs want to play it but it's not in the shops yet."

It was a treat having Mum and Dad in Copenhagen. I was able to discover the city all over again as I saw it anew through their eyes. We explored Tivoli Gardens, which is like taking Central Park and adding roller coasters, we rode the ferry across the Oresund to Malmo in Sweden and took photographs together at the statue of The Little Mermaid in Copenhagen harbor. And every night they would come to Circle Club to dance into the early morning hours.

On their final day we went for a late breakfast and I told my parents my decision that I was going to America.

"When?" they wanted to know.

"I'm not sure, but this year."

"Where in America?"

"Maybe California?" I said.

They asked if I knew anyone there. I shook my head.

"What will you do?"

I knew the answer to that one, "DJ."

I took out an envelope and gave it to Dad. "I hope you don't mind taking this with you. It's £500, I changed it at the bank. When I work out when I'm going to America I'd like you to buy my ticket for me because I'll be flying from London."

"So you'll come home first?" asked Mum.

I grinned at my lovely mother, "Of course I will."

It was Dad's turn to smile, "Well that makes me feel better."

I got in my car and had them follow me about sixty miles to Odense. They were heading down to France and still had two weeks of vacation ahead of them.

We exchanged tearful hugs goodbye at the side of the road and I watched their Fiat 124 motor west towards Jutland. I thought then and still think to this day how blessed I was to have those two as my parents. They taught me to love people and to love music, and six years later, my father would give me one more, final gift that would forever influence the way I lived my life. But that was in a distant future and I still had a hectic present to cope with.

For my final two weeks in Copenhagen it seemed that every time I went to the beach Taxi would show up and each time she made damn sure she looked hotter and hotter. But I did a gut check and forced myself not to be weak.

As the month came to a close I hit the beach one last time and sure enough Taxi was there along with Zed and Baba, but this time she looked different. She'd dyed her hair graphite-black to match the tight bikini that clung to every curve of her incredible body. The hair color didn't look great on her, but I wasn't going to tell her that, I'd already done enough damage. Baba positioned the towels to make sure that Taxi was lying next to me on the sand.

Taxi looked at me and said softly, "You're leaving tomorrow."

I nodded, "Yup."

She grabbed my hand and whispered, "I'm sorry if I hurt you coming here."

I was shocked at her unnecessary apology. It took me a moment to process it and reply. "You didn't hurt me, it's okay."

I realized I had a tear in my eye. This beautiful girl was something else; rather than hate me which would have been the easy thing to do after all that had happened, she was blaming herself for everything that had gone down. Her only fault was trying to give our love affair a second chance.

For a split second I thought about my choices in life and that maybe . . . No. I stood up and said I had to leave to get my things packed. I bid farewell to Zed and Baba and then finally to Taxi.

"You're a very special person, Taxi. Don't ever let anyone tell you anything else. I truly hope you have a wonderful life."

As I walked away across the warm sand of Amager beach I knew it would be the last time I would see her.

I write this with a smile as I know how things turned out for this love-sick girl. Less than two weeks after I left she returned to Austria and her modeling career. Several years later she fell in love again, got married and had children. She continues to have a life filled with love. How did I get this information? Courtesy of Mark Zuckerberg who wasn't even born when Taxi followed me across the length of Europe. Almost forty years to the day that I left Taxi on that beach in Copenhagen a message appeared on my Facebook page. It was from Romy.

It read: "Hi, I just watched a video of you on YouTube. You are still a very attractive boy, enthusiastic and energetic like ever. Are you deeply satisfied with your life? I want to congratulate you, you have achieved all your dreams and goals you had when you were 24. You will always be in my mind as my first great love, God bless you Richard!"

I clicked on Taxi's name and Romy's page appeared showing her in the arms of her family. I was thrilled for her and smiled from ear to ear as I saw the black hair was long gone and she had gone back to being that beautiful platinum blond.

NOTHING TO FEAR
(BUT FEAR ITSELF)

I had three months left in Denmark and I made it my mission to learn as much as I could about America.

Playboy Club, Varde, Denmark – September 1976

At night I was spinning at The Playboy Club in Varde, during the day I was at the local library getting details on Miami, New York, San Francisco and Los Angeles. I kept coming back to LA.

New York was too cold, and at that time, way too violent as made known worldwide in movies such as Charles Bronson's *Death Wish*. Miami seemed too undeveloped and San Francisco damp and foggy. LA appeared to have it all, sunshine, blue skies and surf. It also had more than fifty radio stations and Hollywood. I guess I knew what city was calling my name.

My contracts with IDEA were up for renewal at the end of October so that forced my timeframe. I got in touch with Alan and told him I was going to America to try and make it there. He wished me well and made me promise I'd call him first if I returned to Europe. He told me to watch the mail—he was going to send me something.

Sure enough, three days later an envelope arrived at the club with a cassette inside. It was a tape Alan had in his archives from a random radio station in New Mexico that someone had recorded for him. Every night for the next six weeks as I drove back and forth to my gigs I would listen to this cassette over and over. *This is what American radio sounds like!* I thought as I tried to copy the DJ's inflections as he read a live commercial for Heinz ketchup between songs. I practiced and practiced until I was sure I could sell condiments as well as the guy on the air.

I knew I was done with Denmark at the end of October but I had to decide exactly when to go to the US. I sat down with a calendar and circled a date. This was the day I'd leave London for California. I wrote to my father and asked him to buy me a ticket for Tuesday, November 16, 1976. As I dropped the letter in the post box on the main street of Varde I knew I had put the wheels in motion and I was committed to trying to find a future in America.

This time back at number 22, Torquay felt different. I had returned with a purpose rather than finding myself there between gigs. Things had to be gotten ready for my trip to the USA and I was busy putting it together.

My ticket arrived in the mail from TWA and with it came the booklet "TWA's Guide To Los Angeles." I have never forgotten the opening words of that comprehensive little pamphlet; "In Los Angeles you need a car like you need your liver"! It went on to describe how spread out LA is and with a noticeable lack of good public transport available the only way to get around was a rental car. It was back to the travel agent for me!

In 1976 the only way to confirm something overseas was either by writing a letter and sending a money order, hoping it got to the right person at the correct destination or by having a travel agent take care of the details and book it for you. For something as essential as my liver I decided that using the latter would be the smart choice. The clock was ticking rapidly to my leaving home when fate decided to test my resolve not once, but two times.

With just one week to go before I was scheduled to depart a letter arrived for me from Sussex. It was from UBN, United Biscuit Network. As silly as that name seems, UBN was well respected and looked upon as a gateway to radio opportunities in Great Britain.

Headquartered in Osterley, just outside of London, UBN broadcast on a landline from professional studios to five factories up and down the country entertaining their workers to take their mind off the drudgery of laboring away packaging biscuits. I had tried to get on to UBN for three years and now, just when I was getting ready to leave, I found myself clutching a letter asking me to come up to Hounslow to meet with their program controllers to discuss a presenter position.

Finally someone liked one of my audition tapes but why now of all times? There had to have been something special about that particular demo tape because three days later I received a second inquiry letter from Swansea Sound, a "real" radio station in South Wales, who also wanted to meet with me. They had only been granted their license and started broadcasting two years before and were now looking to boost their on-air lineup.

This was what I had wanted for so long and finally I was holding in my hand two chances to break into the seemingly closed shop that was British radio. Three months previously I would have given my left arm to have had a shot like this but now, strangely, I found myself drawn to the unknown horizons of America rather than taking a radio gig in the UK. After all, in England we all knew winter was coming while LA held the promise of an endless summer and hadn't I always wanted to live somewhere sunny, ever since making that list as a ten-year-old boy?

I showed the letters to Mike and John over a pint at the Devon Dumpling and they both thought I was crazy to pass on the potential offers.

"Do it, Dick," said Mike. "Why risk going to America? They're crazy with their guns over there and you don't know anyone and you'll probably spend all your money and it won't work out. If you stay here you'll have a job for sure and be closer to home."

Ironically Mike's words simply reinforced my desire to take my chances in the California sunshine. It seemed to be a place that was full of opportunities and potential, plus, in addition to the promise I had made to myself nearly two years before on that American military base in Bardufoss, I had grown up with the myth of Southern California from watching *The Monkees* on TV and playing songs by The Beach Boys who sang of distant far-off places like Malibu, Redondo and Doheny. But if everyone was telling me no . . .?

I think Dad sensed my uncertainty and he made an excuse to Mum to drive me into town. We parked along the seafront and the two of us walked for a while along the promenade to the spot where he had taught me to swim all those years ago.

"Just before you were born I was offered two jobs abroad," Dad said. "One was in Canada and one in Australia. Both countries really needed teachers at the time, and I was asked if I would take over the position of headmaster at schools either in Sydney and Vancouver. I would have my choice. They were going to pay for everything; sending the family there, a house for the first year and a big cash incentive up-front to help with the relocation."

He looked out over Torbay but his mind was thousands of miles away; he wasn't seeing the still waters in front of him, he was gazing at a different shoreline.

"Your Mum would have none of it. She wouldn't leave Bristol. I wanted to go so badly. But I loved her and Stephen so much and you, you were growing in her tummy, so I couldn't leave."

He took a deep breath and looked me square in the eyes as he continued to confide in me, "That's my one regret, not insisting that we all go. I should have put my foot down and had us all move there as a family. That's what I did a few years later and that's how we ended up here in Torquay."

I'd never seen Dad this open, this vulnerable. He'd always been such a giant to me—quiet, strong, steadfast.

"This country is going to hell right now. Inflation is what, seventeen percent? When my pupils leave school they are struggling to find jobs that don't exist and end up on the dole, and with the riots that are happening up and down England it's pulling everything and everyone down."

He put his hand on my shoulder.

"You're a lot like me, my son. But you have the chance to do what I couldn't. This has to be your choice, not someone else's. Just remember, as you get older, it's not what you attempted that you regret it's what you didn't attempt. You've got nothing to fear from trying something new. If I could do it again I know what my choice would be."

He smiled to change the mood. "Come on. Let's walk a little."

With those words spoken that afternoon, any remaining doubts were dispelled from my mind.

I wrote two identical letters to the program controllers at both Swansea Sound and UBN thanking them for their interest but letting them know I was leaving the country to DJ (again I think I may have forgotten to include that I didn't actually have a job yet!) and that I would be in contact with them if I were to return to the British Isles.

Two days later everyone at number 22 was awake before the first rays of dawn to be certain that I'd make my flight to Los Angeles. Mum whipped up a plate of scrambled eggs to tide me over for my journey, and then held me tight as she said her tearful goodbyes. She stayed behind as my father drove me to Newton Abbott railway station in time to catch the London-bound train.

We stood together on the platform as the train appeared through the early morning fog and pulled to a stop in a billowing cloud of steam and coal dust. Dad gave me a final hug.

"Your mother was too upset to come. I know you did it in Europe and in Spain, but America might be different, my son. It's a big country. They don't mess around there. I think it's great that you are going, and what you are trying to do, but if you need to come back, there will be no shame in it, we're here."

I looked into his bright blue eyes and saw nothing but love and encouragement. "Thanks, Dad. You're always there for me, aren't you? The next time we see each other you'll be visiting me in Los Angeles."

I grabbed my suitcase and climbed the two stairs onto the train. I lowered the window of my second-class carriage and leaned out as the green and grey Pullman began its eastbound journey to Paddington station, 200 miles away. Dad watched me and gave me a thumbs-up and a grin. It was a genuine smile and in that moment I could feel the excitement he had for me. It meant so much as I knew right then that I wasn't going alone, I had him with me.

With my father's blessing I left England with one suitcase, $450 and a round-trip air ticket that I was determined to only use one half of.

YOUNG AMERICANS

I was unprepared for what I was seeing. The dazzling glow below me stretched forever. The 747 had been descending for some time but the sea of red, orange and white lights showed no signs of letting up, if anything, they were getting brighter. I tried to do the calculation in my head, if our airspeed was averaging 200 miles an hour and we'd been on the descent path for more than fifteen minutes that meant we'd already flown over fifty miles of buildings and freeways and lights. Was that even possible? Just how big was Los Angeles anyway?

We touched down at 7:20pm on November 16, 1976. As I walked towards customs and immigration a huge poster of Mayor Tom Bradley welcomed me to "Los Angeles, The City of Angels." I was actually here; I was in America for the first time. Like millions of hopefuls before me I had come to seek my fortune and build a new life. I carried with me a backpack, a suitcase, a return ticket on TWA departing December 15 and a headful of dreams. I had less than thirty days and $450 to build a base here or to return to Torquay with my tail between my legs.

I arrived at my hotel in Hollywood considerably poorer. Lesson one learned, taxis aren't cheap and LA is so spread out. Hollywood looked close to LAX on the map but I quickly grasped the fact that in Southern California distances aren't measured in miles, they're measured in time. Ask any local a question like, "How far is downtown LA from Disneyland?" and they won't say "twenty-seven miles." Instead they'll come back with, "Well, if you leave now it's about an hour, if you wait much longer it'll be more like ninety minutes or so." According to Einstein, time and space are constants, but then again Einstein was never forced to commute on the freeways of Los Angeles.

My nut was reduced to $427 as I got out of the yellow cab to check into my hotel, the Hollywood Studio Apartments. It had sounded so perfect back home when I had read those words in the TWA booklet. However it failed to explain that *studio* in America meant a small room; I had thought that the building had been given its prestigious title after being construct-ed for the sole purpose of serving the Hollywood Studios.

I imagined getting up in the morning and over breakfast running into Robert Redford, Clint Eastwood or Stanley Kubrick. We would share small talk about the difference between shooting in 35mm or 70mm and debate as to why no one had ever made a great filmed version of *Othello*. Instead, the Hollywood Studio Apartments on North Whitley, just a half block from Hollywood Boulevard itself, was a run-down, roach-infested dive whose main clients were ladies of the night who picked up most of their business from disillusioned tourists who were saddened by the total lack of glitz and glamour that awaited them on that boulevard of broken dreams.

It was almost midnight when I was given the key to my tiny room on the sixth floor. It seemed clean enough and it had a shower so in many ways it was better than a lot of places I'd stayed in Europe. What I wasn't prepared for were the screams and yells coming from the street below all night long and the persistent wailing of police sirens. What the fuck had I gotten myself into? I collapsed onto the bed and courtesy of jet-lag fell asleep on top of the covers with all my clothes on.

A little after 2am I was woken abruptly by someone hammering on my door and yelling, "Mary, Mary, Mary!" over and over. The handle shook up and down but the door remained locked. I flipped the light on and lay there not making a sound. I heard footsteps retreating down the corridor so I got up and maneuvered the old, heavy dresser across the room to block the door just in case Mary's despondent suitor returned.

The next morning was a lot better. I was greeted by a typical mid-No-vember LA day; cloudless blue sky, sunshine and temperatures around seventy degrees going up to a high in the mid-eighties. All those jokes about weathermen in Southern California are true. They have just two lines to memorize and then they are set for life.

I walked down to Hollywood Boulevard and was shocked to see it looked even worse during the day. At least at night it had a few lights to brighten it up, now, in the unforgiving glare of the harsh morning sun, it highlighted the fact that the famous "walk of stars" was actually littered with bottles, cans, flyers offering nude massages and homeless unfortunates lining the sidewalk. And where were all the celebrities? I walked at least half a mile and didn't recognize one person. What was the deal with that? I had been led to believe that all the world's major actors came from Hollywood and here I was in the epicenter of it all and there was no one around who looked like they even owned a television let alone been on one!

I found Avis, located right next to the Grauman's Chinese Theater and proudly presented my international driver's license and picked up the rental car that my travel agent had pre-paid for me before I left England and headed out in that rust-red Chevy Chevette. I cruised west-bound on Hollywood Boulevard only to find that it ended abruptly less than a half mile further and merged into Sunset. But that was cool because Sunset Boulevard was not only home to TV shows like *77 Sunset Strip* but it also led to the beach and after reading *Surfer* magazine for so many years back home I couldn't wait to see Malibu for myself.

With my rental Chevy Chevette, Hollywood, November 17, 1976

Ummm . . . The Pacific wasn't quite as blue as I thought it would be. In fact it looked a lot like the water back in Torquay with perhaps, if anything, even more of a brownish tint, but maybe that was unusual. Either way I knew it would be warm. I pulled on my Speedos (Hey, I'm from England and new in America; I didn't know!) and sprinted into the water by Malibu pier. I was running so fast that I couldn't stop even as my feet desperately tried to send me warning signals that perhaps the temperature wasn't what I was expecting. I plunged headfirst into that sixty-one degree water and got out just as quickly. It was freezing. Now I realized why the American guys wore baggy shorts rather than tight, competition swimsuits—because it was so cold!

The sun soon warmed me up and very quickly I grasped the attraction of the Southern California lifestyle. The white sand, the laid-back vibe and the girls in bikinis looked like they had been assembled by a set director ready to shoot a sequel to *Beach Blanket Bingo*. All it needed was for Gidget to show up and they could roll camera.

I rented a board from a van parked by the pier and paddled out into the small three-foot waves. As long as I didn't wipe out too badly in those polar waters then it was almost idyllic. As the swells broke into perfect little curls that you could ride for more than 200 yards, I understood why Malibu's point break had become so celebrated and was looked upon by many as the birthplace of surfing on the mainland.

That night I went out and hit my first club. Everything was rock and roll on Sunset apart from one disco right in the center of the strip at 9000 Sunset. It was called Disco 9000 and I could almost envision the conversation the owners had had while coming up with that name, "So what are you going to call your disco at 9000 Sunset?" I planned to go there a little later but as it was a Wednesday I thought I would give it a little time to get busy first so I went to the club right across from it, The Roxy.

Before coming to America I'd promised myself I'd visit The Roxy as so many artists that I loved had played there including Bob Marley, Genesis and the jazz/funk group The Crusaders whose music I would play during the early part of the evening at my gigs in Europe. I stepped inside and looked around, imagining what it must be like to stand on that legendary stage.

I jostled my way through the early crowd and ordered a beer at the bar. As I was thanking the bartender a girl next to me asked, "Where are you from?" Within minutes I was sitting at her table with her friends and realizing that being a young Englishman in Los Angeles definitely had its benefits.

The girls advised me against going to Disco 9000 and instead invited me to their place at Mount Olympus. I nearly choked on my beer; the only Mount Olympus I knew was in Greece and home to Zeus and Hercules. They thought that was adorable and we all left together. Only in America can an accent cover up your stupidity and make you "adorable."

California girls really are everything that Mike Love sang about on the Beach Boys' classic, but along with my romancing I had to remember my true agenda. I had come to LA to try and make it in America and I only had twenty-nine days to do it and the clock was ticking.

I'd brought with me more than two dozen demo cassettes and resumes to deliver to radio stations and hopefully land myself a job. I had recorded one especially for American radio based on the cassette that Alan Lawrie had given me that I had devotedly listened to over and over again in my travels across Europe but right before I left England I felt it sounded too fake. It came across as me attempting to do an American accent and a slick top-forty presentation. It just didn't ring true. It got to the point that I couldn't even bear to listen to it. So instead I dubbed multiple copies of the "magic" demo that had sparked the interest of Swansea Sound and UBN before I left England. Both of those outlets were run by professionals and maybe if it was good enough for them then it might work here.

I went to every station in the Hollywood area I could find, KHJ, KRLA, KMET, KLOS, KWST, KBIG, KIQQ, KIIS, etc . . . If it began with a *K* I was there.

In most cases my polite, low-key approach and DJ business card got me inside the station but that was as far as the interest went. The assistant program director was usually the one who was burdened with having to deal with me and after a quick tour of their studios would take my demo and send me on my way. As I left the station I knew that my cassette would never be listened to and would probably end up being dubbed over or slipped into someone's answering machine.

At KPOL AM 1540 it was the program director himself that met with me and laughed when I told him I was looking for a job at his station.

"Everybody wants to work here," he said. "But without experience you've got no chance at getting a job."

"But I do have experience," I explained. "I've been DJing for five years."

"Five years? I've got DJs whose headphones are older than that," he cracked. "Go get yourself a job in a smaller market then come back when you have done something. That's when we'll talk. I'll have one of our interns give you a tour so you can see what a real radio station looks like."

He walked me to a bank of phones and introduced me to Steve Smith, a tall, lanky kid in his early twenties. After he walked away, Steve rolled his eyes.

"Don't mind him. He thinks his shit doesn't stink. I'm Steve."

I introduced myself and we talked as Steve showed me around the smug a-hole's station. Steve was a student at Saddleback College in Mission Viejo, which Steve explained, using Southern California's unique measurement of distance as "about an hour and ten minutes away." He was studying television and radio broadcasting and as part of the program he was getting credits for interning at a radio station.

As he learned about my story he had an idea. Why didn't I come down to his college and do a TV interview with him about my career in Europe that he would edit and put together as a project for part of his course? I was up for anything and the following Tuesday I found myself crossing into unknown territory, Orange County, California.

The shoot was fun and interesting. I'd never done anything like it before and I was surrounded by eager students who all had their own roles to play so they too could get college credits for being part of this feature. There was a makeup artist, a lighting director, a sound engineer, two cameramen, a director and Steve Smith, the star interviewer. They all took it extremely seriously and it felt very real for a taped piece that would only be seen by the class and their professor.

TV interview at Saddleback College, November 1976

Steve took me for a late lunch at a burger place to say thanks and as we talked he brought up an idea he'd been kicking around.

"You really want to stay here, right?"

"Yeah, I do."

"If you can't get a job right away on the radio do you have any other plans?"

I thought for a moment. "I wouldn't mind working in a club but there's no discos around, at least not like there are in Europe."

"They are just starting here. There's one in Irvine and I just heard yesterday about one that's going to be opening in El Toro. And I know they're looking for staff, because they've been putting up flyers on the campus. They might need a DJ. Do you want to go there with me and talk to them?"

I had no problem with that, plus as it was after four in the afternoon, Southern California's space/time continuum had shifted again and if I was to leave now the horrendous traffic would have made that seventy-minute drive more like two and a half hours!

The disco was set in a mini-mall about ten minutes north of Saddleback College and six minutes inland from the El Toro Y, the intersection of the 5 and 405 freeways. It had been a neighborhood bar in a former life, the kind of place brow-beaten husbands go to drink and escape their wives.

It was small with a maximum capacity of barely a hundred people. On one side of it was a liquor store and on the other, a pet shop. There was some painting going on inside but not much in the way of construction or major remodeling.

Steve introduced me to the two owners who were onsite overseeing the work. They showed me a basic wooden framework where the DJ booth was going to be which was positioned on the far side of the room away from the dance floor. That's never a good idea as it limits the contact between the dancers and the DJ and it makes it hard to read the mood on the floor. I explained that point and they said that maybe they could move it later. They weren't clear about whether they meant the dance floor or the booth.

They did get excited about the fact I was English and seemed to know what I was talking about and asked if I could be there on Friday for the grand opening. I didn't see anything that looked "grand" but they assured me the club would be ready, the turntables would be in and they would even have records for the booth. It would be fifty dollars a night, four nights a week Thursday through Sunday. Did I want the job?

Memories of Tonsberg came flooding back but I had nothing else going for me and I had to start somewhere. I was in.

The bar would open at 11am, happy hour was four until six and I would start at 7p and play until 1:30am. I told them I'd be there early, by five, on Friday to get familiar with the gear and Steve and I left the dingy bar.

We stood in the parking lot and Steve shook my hand, "Looks like you're here to stay," he said with a big smile.

I can't say I wasn't excited about having a job. I like to work and this was my start, but I knew the club wasn't going to be a long-term thing for me. I couldn't even understand why they were bothering to change it from a local bar to a disco, it didn't seem like it would attract that nightclub crowd, but I was the rookie there and they obviously knew the area much better than I did.

Friday rolled around and I went for an early lunch to give myself plenty of time for my drive down to El Toro. Around one o'clock my head started pounding and a searing pain shot from my forehead down through to my left eye. Multiple star fields swam in front of my vision and it was hard to hold my head upright. I was having a migraine attack.

I staggered towards the door, left my room and was blasted by the blazing sun that threatened to incinerate my throbbing eyeballs as I searched Hollywood Boulevard for a store that sold anything that could help me. But sadly this was 1976 and there was no effective migraine medicine available over-the-counter. I returned clutching a bottle of Beyer aspirin which proved to be as useful against migraine as a witch doctor's chant and a bath of nettles picked under the light of a new moon.

I drew the blinds and huddled under the sheets in my hotel room. The darkness felt good. No way could I get up. No way could I drive. I slipped in and out of consciousness throughout the afternoon. I kept meaning to go downstairs to the reception and call Steve but I couldn't find the strength to move from the bed. And I didn't have the number for either of the two owners of the club. So I just lay there as my skull split asunder and the clock scorned me as it approached and then swept past 7pm.

Morning came and I was surprised to find I was human again. I could stand and walk and maybe even talk. And boy, was I hungry.

I ploughed my way through eggs, bacon, pancakes and hash browns washed down with an orange juice and decided it was time to see if an apology might work. I sat in the reception of the hotel which was obviously a burial ground for old, red naugahyde couches and put a quarter in the lobby's payphone and dialed Steve's house. He answered on the second ring.

"I'm so sorry about last night," I said.

"So you heard?" replied Steve.

"No. I haven't heard from them. I don't think they know how to reach me. I was so sick—" I hadn't even gotten to the apology as Steve cut me off.

"The club. You haven't heard about the club?"

"No. Did it go well?"

"It burned down."

"What?" I was stunned. "When? How did it . . ."

"Right after they closed. It was on the local news this morning. They think it was an electrical fire. Burned the entire club down and half of the mini-mall."

I couldn't believe what I was hearing. I thought that everything in that dump was half-assed, but a fire? I'd never even got close to experiencing anything like that.

"I was there last night for about an hour then left when I realized you weren't coming. It was pretty dead," continued Steve.

"Who DJ'd?" I asked.

"Not sure. I think it was a busboy or a bartender. They just put on the records. Like I said it was dead."

I told Steve I was going to drive down and see him and I would be there within two hours. I hung up and sat there in the lobby trying to take in what I had just heard.

Steve was waiting for me by his parents' pool when I arrived. He'd driven to the mini-mall and talked to the fire crew who were on hand to make sure there were no flare ups. Steve had interviewed them for his communications class and the firefighters had told him that it looked like the fire had started by the DJ booth—they'd found a flashpoint in that area with the charred equipment.

The first theory they were working with was that maybe the DJ hadn't shut the gear down correctly and after everyone had left some faulty wiring ignited the blaze. But the firefighter stressed that these were still "early days" and they were still looking to confirm the real cause of the fire. The saddest thing was it also burned through most of the pet shop next door. I think that upset me as much as losing my gig. As bad as that was, Steve waved the thought away.

"It's a good thing you weren't there last night," Steve said.

"No." I shook my head. "If I'd been there I would have made sure it was all turned off correctly. There would have been no fire. The club would still be there, the animals would be alive."

"Listen, man, they are blaming the busboy or whoever it was in the DJ booth last night." Steve dropped his voice. "If it had been you then they would have arrested you and then deported you for working illegally. Don't you think that's a little too easy?"

I didn't follow him. "Too easy for what?"

"Maybe they wanted it to burn down. And maybe they wanted someone to blame it on. That's all I'm saying."

Oh my God. If he was right then I would have been in such trouble that it would have followed me for the rest of my life, wherever I went. What Steve was saying made sense. That's why they weren't spending any money or effort changing the place from a bar to a disco. And that's why they offered me the job simply based on me having a business card. They were going to set me up! It wasn't important to them that I could DJ, what was important was that I would have been an illegal immigrant breaking the law and the responsibility for the fire would have fallen squarely on my head. Case closed.

As night started to fall Steve and I drove over to the burned-out mini-mall to see the extent of the damage. It was far worse than I had imagined. It looked like an old bombsite in England left over from the blitz. More than half of the mini-mall had been gutted and the exterior walls had been reduced to rubble when the roof had collapsed in the raging inferno.

Three days later Steve's suspicions were proved correct when the local papers reported that the cause of the fire had officially changed from an electrical fault to probable arson and that police were questioning the staff and the owners. Had I been working that night there is no doubt that I would have been provided with a one-way ticket back to England with "Do Not Return" stamped on my passport. For the first and only time in my life I was grateful for a migraine.

The burned-out disco and mini-mall in El Toro, December 1976

I went back to pounding the pavement and knocking on radio stations' doors. One that I hadn't tried before was KMPC 710 AM. They were very kind to me and I was introduced to several of their DJs who were part of their "Station of the Stars" lineup that included Gary Owens, Wink Martindale and Robert W. Morgan. One who was exceptionally cool was Sonny Melendrez who let me sit in on his nighttime show on multiple occasions.

But time was running out. It was now Wednesday, December 8 and I only had one week left before I was due to return to England. I was in the KMPC on-air studio answering phones when Sonny, who was flipping through a radio industry trade magazine, spotted something. He passed the magazine to me.

"Look at that. They're advertising for disco DJs. Isn't that what you do?" Sonny asked.

Sure enough, the ad said, "Disco DJs wanted for clubs across America. Experience a must." It had a phone number to call.

"Can I keep this?"

"Sure," said Sonny. "Hey, I know it's not radio but you'd still be playing records, right?"

The next morning I called the number. It was for Far West Services, a massive restaurant chain that included brands like Coco's, Snack Shop, Moonraker, Reuben's, Rueben E. Lee, Baxter Street and The Plankhouse. They were expanding rapidly and putting discos in a number of their restaurants across the country. The girl on the phone asked where I was calling from and when I said *Hollywood* she paused as she looked down her list.

"There's a Plankhouse on Western in San Pedro. Is that close to you?"

I wasn't sure but I took down the address and number. I hung up then dialed. Auditions were tomorrow, Friday, and I could choose 11am or

153

1pm. I took the morning slot just so I could avoid the traffic and beat the LA space/time continuum.

I got there early and surprise, surprise, this place was for real. The booth had instant-start, direct-drive radio-style turntables and a Shure SM58 microphone which to me, is the industry standard. It had two built-in bins for albums and a basic set of on/off switches to control the mirror ball, pin spots, strobe and sound-activated chase lights. It had the potential to be a good little club.

The audition was in front of the regional entertainment director and the restaurant's manager, Maria. They explained that they didn't want any mixing; they wanted the DJ to spin "radio-style" and entertain the dancers as I had done in Europe. For the audition I should get on the microphone, introduce a record, wait until it finished, talk into the next one and keep going like that until they said stop. For me that was a piece of cake. I'd spent so much time after hours in empty clubs working on demo tapes for radio positions that I could do the "DJ thing" without an audience at the drop of a hat. I just had to take the energy up a couple of notches to simulate the live crowd they were hoping for, and make sure the songs I selected were fun dance cuts. I flipped through the albums and pulled the first few records I'd be using.

I locked eyes with my two judges. "Ready?" I asked.

They nodded and it was time for me to bring the show.

"Welcome to The Plankhouse, I'm your DJ, Dick Sheppard, and for the next few hours you and I are going to be sharing a little dance party together. And if you're shy about getting on the floor don't worry, I promise my moves will make you look good, and after all this is 'The Best Disco in Town.'" And with that I slammed into The Ritchie Family hit of the same name.

I wanted to keep a dance beat but show that I knew how to work in different styles so I cued up Ohio Players' "Love Rollercoaster." As soon as it was ready I faded out The Ritchie Family even though it had only been playing for maybe forty seconds. I was going to keep this sucker moving.

"Love The Ritchie Family, and don't forget if you love our food here at The Plankhouse make a reservation tonight to guarantee your table for this weekend, then afterwards come in here and dance off your dinner." I hit *start* and the heavy beat of the Ohio Players filled the room.

I knew this was the suburbs and just like in Europe where people's tastes vary from the big cities to the smaller towns I thought it was important to demonstrate that I understood that not everybody is super hip, so my next song was from one of the biggest pop albums of the year but it still had a cool, soulful edge. Down came the Ohio Players and on went my mic.

"Getting funky with the Ohio Players and now I've got a request for David and Cheryl who are here at The Plankhouse celebrating their wedding anniversary. They are right there in the corner," I gestured to an empty table and was thrilled to see my two judges turn to look where I was pointing. That showed me they were into it!

"And they promised they would come on up and dance if I played their favorite song on the radio these days. It's Boz Scaggs with that dirty "Lowdown.""

As that huge hit from *Silk Degrees* came on the two judges raised their hands and walked over towards me. I stopped the music. The entertainment coordinator spoke first.

"That was very good. That's exactly the kind of thing we're looking for." He hesitated for a moment. "You are the first person we're seeing today. We have four more to hear. Would you mind sticking around until they are all done? The last one is scheduled for 1pm."

Maria jumped in. "If you're willing to stay, the kitchen will be open in just a few minutes at 11:30. We'd love to buy you lunch while you wait."

I didn't want to get too excited but I was getting such a positive feeling from the two of them. They just wanted to do things correctly. They were representing a huge corporation and needed to honor their obligations. They'd scheduled other potential DJs and didn't want to simply blow them out; I respected that.

By 2:30 the deal was done. I would start at The Plankhouse on a trial basis the next two nights, Saturday and Sunday. On Monday I would drive up to the Federal Building in downtown Los Angeles and file papers to start the process of getting a work permit and a social security number. The moment those papers were filed I could then get on the payroll on a conditional basis until the official approval came through. My salary would be $300 a week for five nights DJing and free food every night I was working. They assured me I should have no problem with the filing as many of the chefs at their restaurants came from out of the country and went through exactly the same procedures.

"Also on Monday, if you come back here after the papers are filed we can give you a $120 signing bonus to say thank you," said Maria.

I knew instantly what she meant. That would be the money for my trial period of Saturday and Sunday night. They wouldn't pay me until they knew I had paperwork accepted by the immigration department and could legally work. These people were 100% on the up-and-up.

Those first two nights at The Plankhouse went brilliantly and even though it wasn't the biggest club I'd ever played at I had a great time, and so, hopefully, did the crowd. I left late Sunday night with a package of papers that Maria had prepared for me. They were for me to take to the INS in Los Angeles the following day. I was ready for my next step.

I had never seen so many people crammed into one place as there were in the application room of the Federal Building at 300 N. Los Angeles Street. There were literally 500 hopefuls like me waiting to be seen by a clerk at one of the fourteen booths. I took a number. It was in the high 400s and the red display showed they were only serving number sixty-eight. It would be a while before they got to me. I killed time by exploring Olvera Street which, even though I'd never been there, made me feel like I was in Mexico. An hour later I returned to the Federal Building and was shocked to see they hadn't even reached the 200s yet. I had a long time to wait.

Finally, around 3pm it was my time to go up to the window. The clerk shuffled through my papers which showed the multiple advertisements that my employer had run trying to find DJs, the locations owned by Far West Services across America, the number of employees they had on payroll and finally their job offer to me. The Immigration clerk looked up and forced a smile; it had been a long day for her as well.

"Okay, it looks like it's all there, everything I need from your employer. I can get you in the system but before it can go further we're going to need a few things from you. Photographs, social security number, address where you can be reached, a phone number outside of work and fingerprints."

I asked how I went about getting her my fingerprints.

"You can either find a notary to do them for you or I can set up an appointment to have it done here. That way you know it's done correctly and there's no charge. I can get you in . . .," she looked at her schedule, "one week from today. Get here early, pull a number, and then go upstairs to the second floor. They'll fingerprint you and you come straight back down and submit all your completed paper work. How's that sound?"

My smile told her yes and Monday, December 20 was set in stone.

I dropped off the papers with Maria at The Plankhouse that night. She was happy to get them and paid me my "bonus." She asked where I was staying and when I told her about the Hollywood Studio Apartments she shook her head.

"Look, why don't you stay with me? My husband and I have a big house just down the road in Lomita and we'd love to have you stay there for a while. Hope you don't mind kids, I've got two young boys who'll want to talk to you nonstop about music."

I wasn't sad packing up my things and leaving Hollywood. It had been a long, crazy month. It would be nice to be in a family household again. The only thing weighing on my mind was the plane ticket. Today was my scheduled travel day, December 15 and this was a non-refundable fare. I had to use it or lose it. But ironically by using it I would be losing the dream that had brought me to America. I stared at that ticket for a long while and then tore it in two and tossed it in the trash bin as I said good-bye to the Hollywood Studio Apartments. Come hell or high water there was no going back now.

I felt good on Monday, December 20. I had been at The Plankhouse for a little more than a week and the club was getting busier and busier. My room at Maria's house was wonderful and she and her family were spoiling me with home-cooked meals. I'd even bought a small car to replace the rental that was eating up my dollars. It was a little Datsun B210 that Erin, one of the servers whom I'd become great friends with, sold to me for $500. It was beat up and would need new tires soon but it ran and it was mine. I left Lomita around six in the morning to get an early jump on pulling a number at the Federal Building.

The doors opened at seven to allow access to the number allocation machine and my number was barely over one hundred; that was a good start. My appointment for fingerprinting was at 9am so I was there promptly on time to have my right hand recorded for the FBI to run through their files. With that done and signed off I was ready to submit my completed papers.

I took my seat on one of the metal chairs and waited in the packed room for almost an hour before my number finally appeared on the red-lighted display. I was excited as I stepped up to the counter and slid my papers under the Perspex to the waiting clerk. Without even looking up at me she opened the thick envelope, flipped quickly through the paperwork and then stuffed them back inside.

"I can't file these. Sorry."

I didn't understand. "But everything is filled out correctly? What did I miss?"

"Just filling out the forms means nothing. There has to be a reason to grant you a visa to live and work in the United States. I don't see one here. Sorry." She passed the envelope back to me under the Perspex window.

"But I was here last week and told to get my fingerprints, social security—"

She cut me off in mid-sentence, "Yes, because your application was incomplete without them. I can see all that here. But just because your paperwork was on hold with us doesn't automatically mean I can issue you a work visa."

"So what do I need to do?" I pleaded.

"There's nothing you can do. If there are no adequate grounds for a work visa to be issued it means that your application is rejected and can go no further with the INS. You are welcome to stay in the United States until your tourist visa expires, but if you do any form of work or employment or if you stay on after your tourist visa expires, you'll find yourself in big trouble with the authorities and will be deported." Her words were final and as far as she was concerned, I was dismissed. She hit a button and the lighted number on the back wall changed. "Next."

I walked back through the crowded waiting area in a daze. I thought I'd done everything right. I had an employer who wanted me. I had years of experience. I had a degree from college. I had gotten a social security number as I had been told to do so Far West Services could withhold the necessary taxes. I had entered the US legally, not overstayed my three-month tourist visa and had gone directly to the INS to submit the required paperwork before even taking one dollar but now I was told it was all in vain. One word, *next*, had destroyed my future and thrown me into despair. What could I do now? I had no return ticket to England anymore and not enough money to buy one. I was sick to my stomach.

I felt stunned as I left the room that had held all my hopes and dreams and shuffled into the massive lobby of the Federal Building. I slowly pushed my way through the crowds of people waiting patiently for the bathrooms in long lines that almost blocked the exits to the street. I looked at their faces; black, white, brown, people just like me, and wondered how many of those poor souls would also have their lives and futures upended today and be told that their applications were refused and that there was no place for them.

Then it hit me. That clerk might have decided to take away my chance for a new life but I could not let that stand, I had come too far not to try again and in doing so create another chance for myself.

I turned and hurried back into the overflowing holding area. I scanned the huge room and its fourteen booths. They were all busy but it wasn't just any open one I was looking for, I was trying to find the female clerk who'd helped me the week before. And there she was, talking with a Korean couple and their lawyer. I worked my way past the mob of people and waited behind the trio at that window. As soon as they were done, I stepped up.

"I'm so sorry, I think I missed my number being called. The line for the bathroom was so long." I looked at the clerk and caught her eye and smiled. "Oh hey, you helped me last week and set up my appointment today for fingerprinting. Thank you so much. I got it done."

I grinned and pulled out the freshly inked form from the envelope. "Here it is. I really appreciate your advice on that; they were really nice about it upstairs. Got everything else done that you asked me to do as well. Should all be in there." I slipped the paperwork to her.

She nodded in recognition. "Yeah, I remember you. You're the DJ. Let me look at your papers."

She went through them quickly but thoroughly then looked up and smiled. "It's all there. I keep the paperwork here to file and distribute and you get this." She pushed a single sheet of paper under the Perspex. "Go back upstairs and give it to the people in the office right next to where you were fingerprinted. They'll take it and issue you a number. Whatever you do, don't lose it, that's your file reference. It means you are in our system and can stay here in the country until we contact you for a final interview."

"And when will that be?" I asked.

"Look around. There are a lot of people being processed. It could be six months or more. But until then you are good to stay and work here. Couple of things; try not to change your employer because then you'll have to resubmit all your paperwork and do not use any social services. That's a big no-no because we want to know you are not going to be a drain on the economy. And stay out of trouble. Any felonies and your number will be revoked immediately. Got it?"

I nodded vigorously. "Thank you so much. I really appreciate this."

"Glad to help. Now go play that funky music, Mr. DJ."

I think I floated upstairs to get my official number from the INS and as I left the building it shook me as I realized how much impact one person can make on your life. Perhaps the first clerk had argued with her husband that morning, or maybe her kids had been misbehaving and she had taken out her anger on me. Whatever reason she had for shooting down my application I considered myself fortunate that I'd run afoul of that line at the bathroom and that it had given me the inspiration to go back into that government building a second time. Now I was legal and welcome in this country and I wasn't going to blow this amazing opportunity.

I'M YOUR BOOGIE MAN

Christmas sped by and soon it was the New Year and hello to 1977. Things were going well at The Plankhouse but I didn't want to wear out my welcome with Maria and her family, so I grabbed at the chance to rent a room in Ken's condo which overlooked the ocean in Redondo Beach. Ken was one of the three full-time bartenders at The Plankhouse and had been looking for a roomie to offset his rent so he was more than happy to have me move in. As for me, I was thrilled to be so close to the beach as it gave me a chance to surf more and it was only a fifteen minute drive to work.

The location of the condo was a plus with the ladies as they were impressed by the view of Santa Monica Bay and Palos Verdes. However my actual room was not quite as spectacular as the only furniture was a folding chair and my "bed" was a six-foot-six by five-foot piece of foam that I bought for twenty two dollars at an industrial store in North Hollywood. But I was young and it was all I needed.

I received notification from the INS that my interview was set for Wednesday, July 13 at ten in the morning. I arrived at the Federal Building early and changed into a shirt and tie. I wanted to make a good impression but there was no way I was going to drive all the way from Redondo Beach to downtown LA on a scorching summer day all dressed up. After all, it was July and my little Datsun lacked air conditioning.

A secretary showed me into my interviewer's office and had me sit and wait for him. As he walked in he saw me there and said, "Stand up!"

I jumped to my feet, thinking I had done something wrong and didn't move as he looked me up and down.

"How tall are you?" he asked. He didn't have a threatening tone; he just seemed puzzled.

"I'm six two," I replied.

He took a breath before responding, "That's very tall for a jockey."

I couldn't help smiling. "I'm actually a disc jockey."

He looked at the paperwork he was holding and burst out laughing,

"My mistake. I didn't read it right. Never had a disc jockey in here before, " he said. "And how old are you?"

"I just turned twenty-five in May."

"Really? That's funny; you're the same age and same height as my son. Sit down, I'll be right back."

He put the paperwork on his desk and I watched him unclip my two small headshot photos from the stack of forms and take them out to his secretary. In seconds he was back.

"Okay. Let's get into it."

He asked me about coming to America and finding my job, and then said he had to go through a list of required questions that he read verbatim from an official document on the top of the pile. They included if I had been on unemployment, committed a felony or was planning to overthrow the lawfully elected government of the United States. He seemed happy that I answered no on all counts. Within ten minutes the interview was over and he left the room again for a moment. He returned carrying a small newly laminated ID, barely bigger than a business card. I could see that my photograph was on it. He handed it to me.

"Here's your Green Card, son. Welcome to the United States."

Wow, I had been accepted. This was not something to be taken lightly. I had a new country. As someone who loves history I appreciated all who had come before me to build America, to pave the way, to make this possible; I hadn't done it alone, I understood that I was standing on the shoulders of giants. I actually felt different inside, the best way I can explain it is by saying that my English blood still flowed through my body but now it was pumped by an American heart. That day I found my home.

Now I could really make plans. I could buy furniture and just like every good American consumer, go into debt. I had been told again and again that you need credit to get anywhere in the States but getting credit without having credit first was almost impossible. My answer to this Catch-22 was Montgomery Ward.

I bought a seventeen-inch TV there for $299. I put $190 down and financed the remaining $109. I could have bought it outright but that wasn't the plan. In America you had to owe money to prove that you were creditworthy. Try explaining that to a visitor from outer space. But for me it worked!

Within four months I was inundated with "you are pre-approved" credit card applications from Master Charge and Visa. Soon I would be able to owe everybody money and that was the surefire sign of success!

In September I rented my own place in Redondo Beach. It was at 107b Paseo De La Playa, just three buildings from the Esplanade and the sand. The two bedroom, one bath plus fireplace, enclosed garage and private courtyard unit was $275 a month.

Over the next weeks I slowly furnished the place by using my credit cards to buy an inexpensive couch and table set that I would have rather paid cash for, but I was getting established and trying to do everything "the right way."

I put together a home studio using an AKAI reel-to-reel tape recorder, a cassette deck, two Garrard turntables and a Shure microphone and mic mixer from Radio Shack. I was determined to use any free time I had to break into the closed shop that was the LA radio market.

In my first year at The Plankhouse there were many memorable female encounters including one with a Playboy model who came to the club wearing tight white jeans with unique embroidery on the back pockets. On one pocket it said "USDA" and on the other it read "CHOICE." For once there was definite truth in advertising. We had an unforgettable night together but when I asked if she wanted to meet up again she said no. It turned out she was using me for "revenge sex" against her cheating husband and was just looking for one wild night to pay him back for what he'd put her through.

It was during this time that I met a great girl, Katy Manor. She was pretty, sexy and made me laugh. We started dating on and off, then quickly became exclusive. A couple of months later she moved in with me.

I received a letter from Mum and Dad letting me know that Mum had finally given in to my father's pleas and was willing to make the eleven-hour flight from the UK to California. They would be coming over to stay with me in mid-January for two weeks to escape the British winter. I was ecstatic that I would get to see them again and soon!

Just days before Christmas a tall, good-looking gentleman approached me in the DJ booth at The Plankhouse.

"Would you like a request?" I asked.

"No, you've been playing everything I like," he said. He passed me his business card. "Call me. I might have a job for you."

As he left the club I glanced at the card. It read, "Ron Newman, President, The Red Onion."

Due to a complicated legal settlement there were two chains of restaurants in California both called The Red Onion, Ron Newman was the owner of one of those chains with three existing locations and two more about to open. When I met with him at his offices in Carson, California on December 22, 1977 he told me of his intended expansion and introduced me to his entertainment coordinator, Gary Gunn.

The bar business for The Red Onion was already huge and growing exponentially, and now with *Saturday Night Fever* having just opened in the theaters they were jammed to capacity every night with long lines of new customers waiting to get in as everyone wanted to go out to a club and experience what "disco nights" were really like first-hand. Walk into any of The Red Onions and you would see a dozen wanna-be Tony Maneros begging the DJ to play "Stayin' Alive."

Gary oversaw all the entertainment at The Red Onion including booking the live bands that now alternated with the DJs he'd brought in to keep the music going non-stop and the dance floor packed. With the upcoming expansion it was going to be too much work for just one person to coordinate so when Ron saw me DJing he figured I was the one to step in and help.

The offer was for me to work directly beneath Gary. I would be program director of The Red Onion in charge of the recorded music and DJs. I would oversee the schedules and music for all five locations, Redondo Beach, Canoga Park, Mid-Wilshire, Beverly Hills and West Covina.

Gary wanted the clubs run like a radio station; we would supply all the records and give the DJs promos to read twice an hour—food specials, drink deals, shots, upcoming bands, etc. I would DJ four nights a week on the days and at the locations of my choice and make sure the rest of the nights were covered. The salary was huge, $500 a week plus an additional $600 in vouchers that I could use to comp food and drinks for regulars and for any visiting celebs that might come to the clubs.

This was a deal I couldn't turn down, so I gave my notice to The Plankhouse and after a final New Year's Eve party I bade farewell to my friends and the employer who had helped me come to America, and started 1978 with a new job and new responsibilities.

Thanks to John Travolta and The Bee Gees, disco was now breaking all over the world and I continued to ride that wave. Ron Newman wanted his largest club, The Red Onion in Canoga Park, to be a showcase so he and I flew out to New York to check out the mecca of disco, Studio 54. It had taken a number of cross-country calls but the owners finally placed us on their VIP list for the time we were in the Big Apple and each night the velvet rope was opened for us and we were escorted past the throngs of would-be dancers outside, desperately clamoring to get in and become a part of the legend on 254 West 54th Street.

Everything you have heard about Studio 54 is true. It set the standard for sound and lighting in clubs that is still hard to beat. Nudity and cocaine were everywhere in the club. Topless girls danced with ripped black guys wearing only thongs and a horse would suddenly appear from nowhere and be led across the floor. It was an acid trip come to life. Nothing made any sense but somehow it all worked. While the lights flashed and Donna Summer's disco beat pulsed, everyone there became a star even if in reality they had to suffer through the routine drudgery of a nine-to-five workday.

We returned to Los Angeles energized and Ron Newman and I conjured up a lighting design for the club that would be unique. Ron had his crew, including technical engineer Bill Motley, make our fantasy become reality and within two months they had taken our pencil sketches and put together a special-effects rig which included a neon lightning storm that crackled around the dance floor and four motorized towers filled with strobes and beacons that descended from the ceiling to illuminate the dance floor from all angles.

If you were in southern California in 1978 and wanted to go out to a disco then The Red Onion became number one on your list. All of the locations were packed seven nights a week with people looking to drink, dance and hook up. Guys with hairy chests and shirts open to their waists busted out their best disco moves with girls in halter tops and tight, shiny Spandex pants that left nothing to the imagination. The staff would joke how only carnivores came to The Red Onion because we were a total meat market, and the very lyrics of the songs encouraged the sexual atmosphere. When I put on Donna Summer's "Bad Girls" or pumped The Andrea True Connection's "More, More, More" through the speakers I could spot from the DJ booth just who would be going home with whom. And often these eager couples wouldn't even make it back to their apartments; every night you'd walk through the parking lot and see people going at it in their cars. The security were told to turn a blind eye to it; after all, this was the disco era and sex had never been freer or more available.

Word of the huge success The Red Onion discos were having spread, even outside of America, and I received a call from Jerry Gilbert in the UK. Jerry was the Editorial Director of Europe's, and the world's, best-selling disco publication, *Disco International*. This full-color monthly magazine was the bible of the disco industry and Jerry wanted to know if I would like to be the American editor and writer for it. The answer to that was a no-brainer and thereby began a long relationship with Jerry, writing for that London-based magazine.

As the American editor it fell upon me to cover the stories from this side of the Atlantic along with all the major interviews with artists breaking out of the US and Canada. Within just a few months one of my interviews hit the cover of the magazine when I sat down with the queen of dis-

Disco International exclusive with Donna Summer

co herself, Donna Summer. For me personally it was a landmark moment; it was not only my first big celebrity interview but it was with the artist who had never been off my turntables since that chilly night in Horsens, Denmark three years before.

I started to get requests from some of our regulars to DJ private parties at their houses. As I was in charge of booking my own nights I tentatively agreed to do a couple of these events and cleared my club schedule to make myself available.

Gary Gunn let me borrow some of the old sound gear from The Red Onion including a power amp, two speakers and a Meteor Clubman mixer which he pulled from their trash and gave me to keep.

"It's too small for our clubs, so you might as well have it," said Gary.

That little unwanted mixer became the heart of my mobile DJ system for the next two years!

I had to rent a van to lug all the heavy gear to the parties but despite the back-breaking load in and load out and a three hour set up time, the gigs went fantastically.

As the second party wrapped up, the caterer asked me for a card and said she had a client whose son was having a Bar Mitzvah and was looking for a DJ. I said great and handed her my Red Onion business card and scribbled my home number on the back. What I didn't tell her was that I had no idea what a Bar Mitzvah was. I came from a community that had a very small Jewish population so I wasn't exposed to that ancient culture growing up. For all I knew a Bar Mitzvah could have been something that happens at a NASCAR race. But whatever it was, I was ready to learn about it and do my best to make sure that everyone there had a great time. The word *bar* was in the name so how hard could it be; I'd worked at plenty of bars all over the world in the last eight years.

I met with the caterer in Malibu and we caravanned to her client's house, just inland on a private road above Paradise Cove. The property was a gated compound of three homes that she had acquired over a period of time to protect her privacy. All three houses had spectacular views of the Pacific. She was waiting to greet us as we parked our cars. The caterer spoke first.

"Dick, I'd like you to meet Miss Streisand."

"Please!" The music and film star offered me her hand. "Just call me Barbra."

At the time I was not a huge fan. Of course I was aware of who she was. I would have had to have come from Siberia instead of Torquay not to have heard of Barbra Streisand, but her music was not what I related to. To me she was just another popular singer and actress. It was only later that I realized the magnitude of her success and what an icon she was. So instead of standing there, speechless, I took her hand, shook it, and said, casually, "Hey, Barbra."

She turned out to be so down to earth. Those stories I heard later about what a bitch she could be held no truth with me. She was simply a loving mother who was planning a party for her son, Jason, and wanted to make sure he had the best night possible. And making sure you had a good time was my specialty so I was all confidence and no nerves. Sometimes being ignorant of your surroundings can actually be a benefit.

Her plans included bringing in a real three-ring circus tent to enclose the paddock that lay between two of her houses. The dance floor would be in the middle of the tent and around each of the three massive supporting poles would be food stations; one Mexican, one Chinese and one French cuisine. She would have the sound system provided for me to plug my turntables into. I just had to let the coordinator know how many speakers and where they should be placed and it would all be taken care of. I only had a couple of questions, how many guests—500—and when would it start—6pm until whenever.

Barbra told me that she wanted mostly disco, to please not play any of her songs and that of course, at one point, they would do the Hora.

She turned to the caterer, "And make sure that we have a chair for Jason when Dick plays the Hora."

As Barbra Streisand was saying that, Dick was making a mental note to self: "Remember to find out what a Hora is and why Jason is going to be sitting down when it's playing!"

As I walked back to the car with the caterer she asked me, "How much do you need to DJ the party?" I thought for a moment; Malibu, Barbra Streisand, 500 guests . . . I figured shoot for the moon, a dollar per guest. "Would $500 work?"

The caterer nodded. "I think we can handle that."

The party went perfectly. Dancing started almost immediately and there was no stopping for dinner as all three stations featured continuous buffet service. I had read up and asked two of my friends at The Red Onion who were Jewish about Bar Mitzvahs and Horas, and armed with "Hava Nagila" and the *Fiddler on the Roof* soundtrack—when I brought Barbra out to dance with her son to "Sunrise, Sunset" I had nearly everyone in tears—you would have thought that the Rabbi himself had instructed me in how to put together this classic rite of passage.

Around eight o'clock Barbra approached me in the DJ area.

"Have you eaten yet?" she asked.

"No. I don't like to leave the DJ console in case a record skips or something."

"Let me get you some food. What would you like?"

"Chinese sounds good, but really you don't have to bother . . ."

"It's no bother," Barbra replied. "I'll be right back."

Less than five minutes later my famous singing waitress returned with a plate of Chinese noodles.

"Just let me know if you need anything else." Barbra Streisand handed me the haute cuisine Chinese food and returned to her Bar Mitzvah boy. And I had just been served dinner by perhaps the most acclaimed singer in American music history. Bitch? No way; I would defend her reputation until my dying day.

Our hostess was not the only famous person at Jason's Bar Mitzvah. The guest list read like a who's who of Hollywood. Along with her ex and Jason's father, Elliott Gould, Donna Summer was there, Neil Bogart of Casablanca Records, Larry Hagman, Neil Diamond who had just recorded "You Don't Bring Me Flowers" with Barbra, Donald Sutherland and

Ryan O'Neil. For this kid from a little town in the south of England it was an extraordinary night.

And suddenly my home phone was going crazy. All of Jason's classmates who were planning their Bar and Bat (*What's a Bat Mitzvah?* I thought.) Mitzvahs and their parents wanted the DJ who had played for Barbra Streisand's son. I had booking after booking coming in. And Lorimar Television called. Larry Hagman was throwing a wrap party at his beach house for the first season of his new TV show that had debuted on CBS to massive ratings and wanted to celebrate. Did I know who J. R. Ewing was?

I needed a mobile DJ setup fast but there were no stores in Los Angeles at the time selling DJ gear and most of the clubs were using big, cumbersome mixers that had been designed for bands and not disco DJing. But I had that little Meteor mixer from England that Gary Gunn had given me; I could use that!

I sketched out a DJ console similar to the ones I had used at mobiles for Soundwave in Devon but decided I would build in switches to control any lights I wanted to use. That would make it look clean and elegant for my higher-end gigs. I pulled the two Garrard SP 25 turntables from my home studio and removed them from their bases. I took their measurements and had the design ready to go.

It was off to the hardware store to buy a jigsaw, drill, screws, particle board, wiring, switches, plugs and corner brackets and then to a fabric shop for faux leather and glue to stick it down and cover the console.

The beach was forgotten. Every afternoon I shut myself in the garage of my apartment measuring, sawing and building my console. The tenants in the neighboring units must have wondered what was going on; I would emerge after a couple of hours covered in dirt and sawdust and behind me, on the floor of the garage, lay a partially assembled custom "coffin." (Yes, that's what the hard shell for a DJ console is called!) But I was on a schedule. Just four days to build and test it before my first gig!

I needed speakers for my mobile disco setup and Cerwin Vega were the state of the art at the time. I reached deep into my pockets, drove to Pacific Stereo and bought four of those monsters that had horns, fifteen-inch woofers and weighed more than eighty pounds each. They sounded great but needed an amp to drive them so I picked up a Crown DC 300 and, just for backup, a Marantz 125-watt home receiver.

I spent the best part of a day soldering and checking all the cables until I was certain that everything was in place and working, and now Dick Sheppard's Mobile Disco was ready to hit the road. I had spent every cent I had on this gear. If the gigs didn't work out I'd have to ask Ron Newman for a loan just to get through the month.

But the gigs did work out and soon I found myself booked every Friday and Saturday night, and with the prices I charged for a disco show, starting at $300 and going up to $600, I was making amazing money.

Most of the party planners in Los Angeles and Beverly Hills were recommending me and even my weekday schedule was filling up; disco fashion shows at Robinson's and Nordstrom stores,

My hand-built mobile disco system

movie premiere events and album release parties, including for Dan Aykroyd and John Belushi with their debut Blues Brothers' album, *Briefcase full of Blues*.

I did the arithmetic and realized that with all this business coming in and the gigs I was having to turn away, it was actually costing me money to work at The Red Onion, so I gave Gary Gunn and Ron Newman my notice and took the chance and struck out on my own.

After so many successful parties I began getting referral after referral. It reached the point that I was getting enquiries from people wanting to throw a disco party on nights when I was already booked. I hated to lose that potential client and their business but I couldn't clone myself so I did the next best thing; I taught my girlfriend how to DJ and had her pick up the excess gigs.

Katy was a natural. She had been to most of my shows so she knew how to read the crowd and structure the flow of the music through the night.

After just a couple of solo gigs she became a great DJ and very comfortable on the microphone and within just a few weeks clients were asking for her by name.

With Katy getting not just my overflow but also her own gigs, it meant I had to build a second DJ console from scratch, so I had my father send over a Citronic mixer from England along with two four-channel "chase" units and sixty feet of rope lights. When it all came together it was the best looking and sounding mobile disco I had ever seen.

With two complete units and two DJs I couldn't just call it Dick Sheppard's Mobile Disco anymore so I borrowed the name of the company I'd worked for back in the UK and Soundwave Mobile Discos was reborn in California.

The celebrity parties continued and I spun for "the Penguin"— Dodger baseman Ron Cey, Jim Nabors, Gene Simmons and Diana Ross, Regis Philbin, Mac Davis and Zsa Zsa Gabor.

Zsa Zsa Gabor held the party in her two-level home in Beverly Hills. While her guests dined upstairs I set up my mobile disco downstairs in the game room. I was the only one there until a young black guy came in and joined me. He asked if it was okay if he looked through my records and I told him no problem. He pulled out a couple of singles and wanted to know if I would play them for him. They were two of my biggest tracks, Earth, Wind and Fire's "Boogie Wonderland" and Marvin Gaye's "Got to Give It Up." As the songs played he started to dance to them.

Watching Michael Jackson out there, alone, on the dance floor, putting together moves, stopping, correcting himself and then doing them again until he was satisfied is burned indelibly into my mind. As Marvin Gaye finished I told Michael that I had The Jacksons' brand-new *Destiny* album to which he got excited and asked for "Shake Your Body (Down to the Ground)." He had no hesitation dancing to this; he had already perfected the moves for his own song and he floated over the dance floor as he sang and spun to the beat.

Michael walked over to me at my booth setup as the last notes of The Jacksons' hit faded out.

"Do you have a cassette player?" Michael asked.

I said yes and pointed to the Panasonic beneath my console.

"Okay," said Michael. "I'll be right back!" He raced away up the stairs.

Within two minutes he lived up to his word and reappeared clutching a cassette. He handed it to me.

"Could you play this? It's a track I was working on today."

I slipped in the cassette and pressed play. I wish I could tell you the name of the song, but it was the first time I'd heard it and I was just too busy taking it all in to remember, but it was either "Rock with You," "Off the Wall" or "Don't Stop 'til You Get Enough." I was mesmerized seeing Michael out there, singing a little, dancing a few beats then raising his hand to me.

"Can you stop it and play it over?" he asked.

Sure. It was just me and him and as far as I was concerned I would happily play it all night. I rewound the tape and restarted it. At exactly the same spot Michael had me stop the tape again.

"Sounds great, Michael," I said.

"No," he shook his head, "it doesn't. The strings fade up. They need to come in with a strong attack and be much louder right after the break. Can you play it again and when I point to you can you turn the volume all the way up please?"

I did as instructed and Michael clapped his hands.

"So much better," he cried out happily. "I'll get that fixed."

I stayed quiet. What was I going to say—good? It already sounded incredible to me.

For the next twenty minutes we talked about the music scene, disco and funk. Michael told me how much he liked English people and how great the audiences had been when The Jackson 5 toured the UK. "More people came to see us than saw The Beatles," he said proudly. "And I met the Queen. Do you know her?"

Sadly I had to tell him that we were not acquainted.

All too soon we were interrupted by the guests coming downstairs for Zsa Zsa's disco party, amongst them my all-time favorite actor, Sean Connery. It was a night for my personal record books.

I thought my time with Michael was done. After all, I was just a hired hand and most celebs never stay in touch, but three days later I received a call from Epic Records saying that Michael had requested I DJ the platinum album presentation party that the label was throwing for The Jacksons to certify their latest record selling more than one million copies.

The record executive then said mysteriously, "You'll have to get FBI clearance for the party."

The event was being staged inside the vault of City National Bank in Beverly Hills. Michael, Randy, Marlon, Tito, Jackie and I were to wait inside the vault with all my DJ gear set up, along with rope lights, fog machine and a single-beam red LASER. When the door of the vault opened I'd hit the music and The Jacksons would dance out through the fog and LASER to "Blame It on the Boogie." And because we were not bank employees and were being left alone in a vault for an unspecified length of time, we had to be screened to make sure we – The Jackson gang - were not potential bank robbers.

After their appearance and the platinum album presentation, everyone would move to the lobby where I would have another full sound system and lighting rig set up and then DJ a disco party for The Jacksons and all the invited guests and press. It was a lot of responsibility that would entail using top-of-the-line gear and I knew I would need help.

A couple of months before I had been approached by Tim Mahoney and Mark Rowlands, two English transplants to LA, to join forces with their rapidly growing disco company, Towards 2000. They had invested in great equipment and already had a lot of gigs on their books but as good as they were, they didn't feel that being the front person, the DJ, was for them. They were more into growing the business which they were both exceptional at.

Their idea was to join their business skills with my DJ reputation to create an unstoppable force in mobile DJing. I put off deciding on this as Katy and I were doing so well by ourselves, but in this situation, partnering with Tim and Mark made perfect sense.

We met up at their small showroom in North Hollywood and struck a deal. Soundwave Mobile Discos merged with Towards 2000 and now there would be no event too big for us to handle.

The Jacksons' party went flawlessly and TV footage from it was shown around the world. The *Los Angeles Times* ran a front-page story about the party on July 31, 1979.

The headline was "Rent-a-disco: Dance Party Comes Home" and the article featured a big picture of me DJing in front of the lighted Jacksons logo with the caption:

*At The Jacksons' disco party in City National Bank in Beverly Hills, To-
wards 2000 disc jockey, Dick Sheppard, starts a record on part of the $25,000
worth of traveling equipment the company uses.* We were making waves.

George Lucas booked me to DJ his Christmas party for Skywalker
Sound in San Francisco and Mark, Tim and I drove up there with all the
gear doing terrible Darth Vader impressions the entire length of the 5
freeway.

Clubs began contracting with Towards 2000 to supply equipment for
their discos and I designed a number of sound systems including one for a
bar in Torrance and another for the first disco that opened in Anchorage.
Mark and I flew up to Alaska in the dead of winter to oversee the installa-
tion and to train their DJ.

When we returned there was a message waiting for us from the Playboy
Mansion—Hugh Hefner wanted us to do a sound and lighting installa-
tion at his famed home in Holmby Hills.

Driving into the mansion through the security gates and up the long
curved driveway was nothing short of mind-blowing. It felt like stepping
back in time to visit a stately chateau in France; that is, if the chateau was
populated by nearly naked Playboy bunnies! Inside we were shown the
organ room—literally that, a massive church pipe organ—and the inner
sanctum of Hugh's bedroom.

He wanted his church organ augmented by hidden amplifiers and
speakers and a light system designed to shine down inside the organ pipes
and "dance" with the music. Upstairs he wanted to replace his existing
speakers with a new sound system that hooked up with his three tele-
visions in the bedroom. We
took measurements and
notes and returned a week
later to do the two-day in-
stallation.

Another huge name came
into the picture when Elton
John booked me to play
his thirty-third (actually
billed as thirty-three and a

With Olivia Newton-John

175

Torbay disco-king wows them over in LA

third—the speed of a vinyl LP) birthday party at Le Dome in Beverly Hills, and as the word continued to spread Towards 2000 also became the recommended DJ company for LA's restaurant to the stars, Spago.

Many other celebrity parties followed including one for Olivia Newton-John who was red-hot after her massive success with *Grease*.

I was making money, business was booming and I wasn't happy.

It wasn't Katy or Mark or Tim who were making me unhappy; it was me. I had come to America to get on the radio and for the past year I'd done nothing to make that happen. Sure, I could stay with Towards 2000 and continue DJing live and probably make more money doing that than if I landed a radio job but it wasn't just about the money. It was the promise I had made to myself. I was no longer pursuing my dream; I was letting myself down.

I have few fears, but one that terrifies me is the fear of regret. If you don't at least attempt to chase your dreams then how will you face yourself when you are older? Too many people live a would-have, could-have, should-have life—I saw that all the time growing up in England where fear of failure stifles you from even trying. Was I letting my runaway success in one area distract me from my true goal? There was only one thing I could do and that's get out there and try all over again.

With this re-energized drive I locked myself in my home studio and worked on a new radio demo tape. A week later I was ready to walk the streets of Hollywood, cap in hand, and ask the radio programmers to please listen to my tape.

But no one would. There was no interest. My knuckles became bloodied from knocking on all the doors. One radio station after another would politely tell me to go away. No, I couldn't try out on an overnight spot for no pay just to show them what I could do. It was very nice that I DJ'd all those big parties but that means nothing to us.

I was at my lowest when I went back to KMET, the Mighty Met, at Metromedia Square. Through some confusion at the front desk, I was shown into the program director's office at that powerhouse rock station.

The PD was something of a rarity at the time in radio; she was female. She was a good-looking redhead who had carved out a major niche in the FM rock market as the talented program director of that legendary station. I hoped that just as she had come up through the ranks, paid her dues and then shattered the glass ceiling that had prevented women from running radio stations, she would have some sympathy for my story and ongoing struggle.

I spoke to her about my years as a DJ in Europe and America and slid her my resume, card, press cuttings and tape. Without even looking at them she put her hand on the envelope and pushed them all back to me. I'll never forget her words as they cut through my soul and dashed everything I'd worked for.

"I don't need any of this," she said. "Because you'll never be a DJ in this town with that accent." She almost seemed to enjoy watching my obvious disappointment as she waved me away and went back to her work.

Minutes later, I stood on the dirty sidewalk at the corner of Sunset and Van Ness burning with anger as I looked up at the Metromedia sign. "Fuck you," I thought. "One day you can sing along with me on the radio." I didn't know how, but I was more determined than ever to make that happen. I hadn't come this far to give up now.

It was a few days after my birthday in 1980 that I heard the promo on KWST. "We're looking for the best unknown DJ in Southern California. Win cash and a one hour slot on LA's finest rock station, K-West. Call for more information."

Within minutes I had found out what the contest rules were and what they were looking for. They needed a cassette, no longer than ten minutes, showing off your voice and DJ delivery. Simple. I could do that. But I wanted to send in something that stood out from the thousands of tapes that they were certain to receive.

I hunkered down and produced two unique KWST jingles and opened my tape with one of them. I then went into a voice break that teased "a K-West exclusive! A remix coming up of Pink Floyd's 'Another Brick in the Wall.'" This was a *huge* risk that could be looked upon as being almost sacrilegious, messing with a major track from such a legendary band, but maybe it just might be enough to keep them listening through my entire tape.

I got to work on the remix, extending vocal bridges "We don't need no education, cation, cation," working in sound effects of pigs grunting during "If you don't eat your meat, you can't have any pudding," and phasing the beat so it would drop in and out. It took me a long time on the analog equipment I was working with but after much sweat and second guessing, it was done.

I sent in the audition cassette along with a high-speed reel-to-reel in case they wanted to play the remix itself on the air, and I waited. The day finally arrived when they announced that they would reveal the winners that evening at 8pm. Winners? Katy and I looked at each other. Wasn't there just meant to be one winner?

At eight o'clock J. J. Jackson hit the airwaves and told his listeners that they had *two* winners for the best unknown DJ in Southern California. Both would get cash *and* a one-hour shift on KWST. He'd have their names right after this break. Yikes. It was the longest five minutes ever. J. J. came back on the air and gave the name of the first winner. It wasn't me. Okay, the odds had just lengthened.

". . . and our second winner is . . . Dick Sheppard."

I think he carried on talking but Katy and I didn't hear another word he said. We were holding each other, screaming and jumping up and down. Finally I was going to get an hour on a major station in Los Angeles. It was what I had been chasing for so long, it was the reason I had left my parents, my country and my career in Europe. I would have sixty minutes to prove that it hadn't all been in vain.

A week later, on July 28 I was at KWST ready to go on the air with J. J. Jackson. He was a big, friendly bear of a man who greeted you with a huge smile and words of encouragement. And he knew his music. I remember thinking how fortunate I was to have him set up the board for my on-air DJ session.

I had studied KWST's format at length and had been told I could pick whatever songs I wanted from their playlist for my show. I'd done the math in my head. An average of twelve minutes of commercials in the hour meant I had forty-eight minutes for music and talk. I picked a couple of mainstream rock hits from Boston and 38 Special, 'Suffragette City' from David Bowie because it came from the *Ziggy Stardust* album which featured David on the cover standing outside a recording studio which was also called K-West, and the title track from a just released album by AC/DC, *Back In Black*. No one was going to be sleeping during my hour.

The show flew by and despite my nerves I had no major problems. I knew Katy was recording the show back home in the apartment, but I was so happy when J. J. Jackson handed me two cassettes.

"One is scoped," he explained. "Just you talking, most of the music is cut out; and the other is the complete show. Hope that's good for you."

I was on cloud nine when I left the studio.

The next day I made a dozen dubs of the scoped cassette of my hour on the air in Los Angeles at KWST and sent copies along with my resume, to radio stations in Santa Barbara, Palm Springs, San Francisco, San Diego, Bakersfield and Fresno.

On the morning of July 31, 1980 my phone rang. A cheerful voice came on the line.

"This is Dave Lawrence. I'm the program director at Magic 98 in Bakersfield. Would you like to talk?"

FOR THOSE ABOUT TO ROCK

It took me ninety minutes to drive to Bakersfield. I was pleased that it wasn't too far from Los Angeles because I knew I would be coming back. That had always been my goal and it wasn't changing now.

The offices for Magic 98 were located in downtown Bakersfield. I cruised through the town and saw nothing but faded store fronts and low-rise buildings, two and three stories at the most, none of the gleaming high rises that were popping up all over Los Angeles and Century City. The center of Bakersfield felt old, as if time had stopped for it in the fifties and the town was resigned to being stuck there.

As I pulled up at a stoplight I saw that all the vehicles around me were pickups, their windows rolled down and Buck Owens's hillbilly twang blaring out proudly for all to hear. Several of the trucks carried migrant workers squatting in the flatbeds. I had arrived in cowboy country, California, but the horses had left and had been replaced by Dodges and Chevys.

Dave Lawrence was happy to see me. Dave was the PD and morning drive DJ on Magic 98, and as our meeting got under way at 1pm he made sure to let me know he had just finished his show an hour before.

"We work six hour shifts at Magic," Dave explained. "I've been looking for a nighttime guy for a while now. You'll be working six until midnight. Would that be OK?"

"Yeah, sure," I said. It sounded like he was offering me the job. This was going well so far!

"We're owned by a company that's actually two brothers, Anthony and Rogers Brandon. That's Rogers with an *s*, not Roger. Took me a while to get used to that," Dave laughed. "But both are very nice people and leave us alone as long as we do our jobs and get their names right. The lack of interference from the owners is pretty rare these days. Do you know our format?"

I'd looked up Magic when I'd put together the list of stations to send my demos to. I answered Dave with the one word that kept popping up to describe KMGN Magic 98.

"Rock?"

Dave nodded, "Yes, it's rock; in fact that's our slogan, 'The Rock of the Valley,' but we're not a regular rock station like KMET or the one that your tape was from, K-West. We play hard rock exclusively, the harder the better. We day-part a little, being a bit softer in the morning and then going all out at night. Your job as the music director will be to listen to the new stuff that comes in and decide what time of day those tracks go on the air."

My head started to spin. "Music director?"

"Bakersfield is a small market. We all wear more than one hat here. I'm the morning guy, the program director and do some sales on the side to supplement my income. You'll be the nighttime jock and the music director, and maybe you'll find something else you'll want to do after you've been here a while."

This was sounding like it was a done deal. But picking the music for a hard-rock station was not something that was in my wheelhouse. I was Disco Dick. I could put together sets with Anita Ward, Chic and Sylvester all day long, but hard rock?

"What's your criteria for adding songs?" I asked.

"Good question. Come with me."

I followed Dave through the bustling radio station into his office. He sat at his desk and gestured for me to sit down across from him. He flipped through a stack of records and pulled out Ted Nugent's *Double Live Gonzo*. He slipped one of the discs on his turntable, switched it on and dropped the needle into the middle of "Wang Dang Sweet Poontang." Instantly the room quaked as a blistering guitar solo roared out of the speakers, rattling the walls and threatening to dislodge the posters and pictures hanging there. Dave looked up at me and yelled over the screaming licks.

"That's as mellow as we get."

I forced a smile and screamed back at him over the uproar, "I can do that." Inside I knew I had some serious learning to do!

I had already decided that if I got the job I would only spend one year in Bakersfield to get the experience I needed before leaving and going back to try again in Los Angeles. I could put up with "the Nuge" and his ilk for twelve months if that's what was required.

Dave's offer was simple. Start as soon as possible, do my music duties from noon until five, then go on the air at six and rock the San Joaquin Valley through until midnight. He took a long breath and his tone dropped a little. The tough part was coming.

"It's not a lot of money. It's Bakersfield, so it's a lot cheaper to live out here, but we can still only pay you $800."

The numbers ran through my head. That was about what I was making now every week with my mobile DJ bookings and this would be a lot more hours, but the idea of hard work didn't scare me. I was willing to work twenty-four hours a day if necessary to break into radio.

"That's okay. I can live with that."

"You understand that's per month?" Dave added.

So much for my math. I would be going from living at the beach, making nearly $40,000 a year to a dustbowl in the desert for less than two hundred bucks a week. But if you really believe in your dreams you have to be willing to make the necessary sacrifices. I didn't hesitate.

"I'll do it," I said and reached out my hand.

Dave took it and beamed. "I'm so glad," he said. "You'll start next Monday, a week from today. It'll be great to have you here."

With those words and that handshake I was to begin my professional career in radio.

The next few days rank among the busiest of my life. I had to tell Mark and Tim at Towards 2000 that I was leaving, let Katy know that we were moving out of LA, and do multiple journeys back and forth speeding over the California Grapevine to find an apartment in Bakersfield and move all our stuff.

Mark and Tim were cool when I broke the news to them. It really wasn't a surprise as they knew how driven I was to get into radio and after winning that slot on KWST they could feel it coming.

I sold them my mobile DJ gear and we met with an up-and-coming club promoter, John Dunn, to help find a couple of local club DJs who could cover my gigs for me. Mark pointed out that a few of the existing clients had insisted that I be their DJ and there would be no getting out of those engagements, so I promised I'd drive back and spin at those parties for Towards 2000, and to be quite honest I was actually glad to do that as I knew the money would come in handy based on the pittance Magic 98 would be paying me.

Katy was thrilled for me and I gave her the choice of whether she wanted to come to Bakersfield or not. As wonderful as she was, we were both young and were already having our occasional ups and downs, plus her family lived in San Pedro and she would be leaving them behind. But Katy didn't hesitate; if I was moving then she was coming with me and I was happy she was.

We rented an apartment right off of the 99 freeway and started to get it ready to settle into. It was mid-way through our move that I found out that Magic 98's on-air studio was not in the building where I had met with Dave Lawrence. The programming and sales offices of Magic were housed inside that building which was actually the base for another Rogers Brandon station, KERN. The studio for Magic was out of town, *way* out of town, in the middle of nowhere—Shafter, California, population 7,010.

It was a plain concrete-block building barely eighteen by eighteen feet, which contained the transmitter, a studio, a tiny bathroom and a cluster of black widow spiders. It was topped by a 220-foot-high broadcast tower. To get there I had to head up the 99 then drive through endless tracts of barren fields that made it look as though the farmers were spending their days attempting to grow sand. All in all, it was nearly thirty miles from our apartment. But I had moved to Bakersfield to learn and pay my dues and that's just what I was going to do.

Every day I would head to the KERN building and work with their production director learning how to edit, loop and splice. In the afternoons I would go out on sales calls to find out the inner workings of selling a radio station. I would listen to the music that came in from the record companies as soon as it arrived in the mail and on Tuesdays I'd take calls from their promo people then report our "adds" to Magic's playlist to both Billboard and Cashbox. And Sunday through Friday as the sun started to set into the endless desert I'd race out to Shafter to be on the air from 6pm until midnight, rocking the valley with Ozzy, Priest, Motorhead, Leppard, KISS, Scorpions and Zep.

Katy and I quickly felt the financial pinch from the meager wage I was bringing home each week. After taxes, social security, etc. I was barely clearing $135. We had the rent, utilities, gas and a car payment to make with that. Soon I was using my credit cards to support us and quickly running up a growing monthly balance that the banks were more than happy to carry at a 21% interest rate.

There was a Wendy's right down the street from our apartment and that became our regular place for dinner. We'd get a single to-go container from the salad bar and cram it full of chicken strips, beets, tomatoes, garbanzo beans, carrots, eggs and croutons and bring it home along with a dozen packets of dressing. We'd buy a head of lettuce at the supermarket because it was cheap and saved us space in that precious to-go container for the other more expensive items, and make a salad that would last us two days. We stole teabags and sachets of coffee from the KERN offices along with toilet paper and kitchen supplies—anything to make sure that we could pay that month's rent.

In the Magic 98 studios, Shafter, California

In December, Dave received another job offer and left Magic 98. That's when I realized there were only two kinds of radio DJs in Bakersfield, and that's those on their way up or those on their way down. The old joke there was you could always spot a radio DJ's car. It was the one with a U-Haul trailer permanently attached to it. I related to that 100%. Eight more months and I would be gone too.

With Dave across the country, the owners of the station approached me with a proposal. They wanted me to take over as program director and morning drive DJ. And with the increased responsibility I would get a 25% pay raise. Now I was up at four-thirty, on the air until noon and then in the offices of KERN until at least seven at night. I did a quick calculation; factoring in all the extra time that had been placed on my schedule my salary increase came out to a princely sixty-two cents an hour, but I didn't complain because Katy and I were grateful to have that extra fifty dollars a week.

My first job was to find someone to fill my vacated nighttime shift. I moved the midday guy to nights and filled his position by having Katy take it. She quickly got a handle on the rock format and proved to be a natural on the air and an amazingly good radio personality.

One of the few good things about Bakersfield is its proximity to Los Angeles. It means that if a band is on tour and they want to pick up an extra show, then Bakersfield is always available and has a built-in audience of people starved of excitement.

With heavy metal having a huge following in the desert it made good sense for the record companies to have their acts play Bakersfield, and naturally, they would approach us at Magic 98 as "the rock of the Valley" to sponsor and promote the shows.

This gave us huge visibility for the station and for me it marked my first experiences of walking out on stage in front of thousands of people to introduce their favorite group. Amongst the ones that I was privileged to work with when they came to town were Motorhead, The Babies and Ted Nugent. When I was asked to introduce the Nuge, Ted took me aside to explain his opening and make sure we were on the same page.

"Make sure you finish with my name, *Ted Nugent*, because that will be my cue, then you run to stage left as quickly as you can," he told me. "That way you definitely won't get hurt."

Ted's concern was that I didn't get burned, and I certainly appreciated that. His opening was spectacular. As I wrapped up my introduction by screaming his name, he swung down from the rafters like Tarzan, dressed only in a loin cloth. He dropped from the rope, grabbed a bow and arrow that was waiting on stage, set fire to the arrow and shot it across stage to a target that had been soaked in kerosene. As the arrow hit, the target exploded in a massive fireball.

It was a phenomenal start to a show and the whole audience jumped to their feet as one, gasping at what they had seen. It was also a very expensive stunt, because in addition to the props needed, a fire marshal, three firefighters and a paramedic had to be present at the side of the stage in case anything went wrong. Fortunately, that night at the Bakersfield Sports Arena, Ted Nugent's aim was perfect and set the tone for a "balls to the wall" rock show.

Interviews with the bands were as important to us at the station as they were for the groups themselves. Their presence on our airwaves gave us credibility and we gave them a chance to promote their latest album or tour to a big audience.

In February of 1981 we had been hyping for weeks that one of the gods of heavy metal, Judas Priest, were coming in to the station to be live on my morning show. They were releasing the follow up to an album that had been gigantic for them and for us, *British Steel*. The new LP, *Point of Entry*, was coming out the following week on February 26 and they were trekking across the country making sure their fans knew about it.

They were due to arrive at the studio at 7am which is normally the time a touring metal band would be going to bed. Seven came and went, and no Judas Priest.

At seven-twenty, my counterpart, the morning guy from KERN, called me on the hotline.

"Do you know anything about five guys in leather doing an interview with you this morning?" he asked.

"Absolutely. That would be Judas Priest. I'm waiting for them to get here and go on the air."

"Well, right now they are standing outside the KERN building."

"Oh my God, how long have they been there?" I asked.

"Their car dropped them off about fifteen minutes ago and left and they've been banging on the door but I didn't know who the hell they were. I thought they were a biker gang or something, so I wasn't going to let them in. After all, it's just me here until eight. What do you want to do?"

The record company's limo driver had made the same mistake as I had and thought that Magic's broadcast studios were in the same building as KERN instead of all the way out in Shafter. So Judas Priest had been dropped off in error and now had no way of contacting the driver to have him return for them. All I could think off was that this multi-million album selling band had come all the way from Birmingham, England, woke up with the dawn to make a scheduled interview with a little radio station in a one-horse town and now was pounding on the windows, pleading to get out of the cold and to be let inside the building.

"Let me call Katy," I said. "Tell them someone will be there in minutes to get them and bring them to Magic."

I hung up, called Katy and stressed, "Get there as quick as you can!"

I kept the outside door of Magic's little concrete bunker propped open so I could greet them as soon as Katy pulled up. Sure enough, forty-five minutes later her tiny Toyota Tercel squealed to a halt right outside our breeze-block building. I had to stop myself from laughing as I saw Katy and five big guys dressed head-to-toe in studded black leather, chains and boots try and extract themselves from that little Japanese import. It was a clown car full of five of the world's most popular heavy metal rockers.

Rob Halford and the rest of Priest stayed on the radio with me for more

than an hour promoting their upcoming tour, album and then taking questions and talking with listeners live on the air. They could not have been nicer and despite their escapade in the desert they went on to see their new album be certified "gold" within a week of its release.

As program director and on-air talent, plus doing promotions

With Rob Halford of Judas Priest outside Magic 98 with DJ Katy's little car!

188

and appearances, my schedule had become non-stop. It was rare I had a minute to myself as I was all about learning every aspect of the station and of radio. Katy was working hard as well; she was on the air right after me and at nights would often have to go straight to the production studios at KERN to do voice-overs for local commercials.

All of this created a huge problem for us on a personal level; now I would only see Katy for a few minutes when I was handing over my shift to her at noon and then again when I stumbled in to our apartment at night, too exhausted to do anything but fall into bed and sleep.

Time became our enemy and those moments we had shared in the past—road trips to surf spots in Mexico, hikes along the coastline, movie nights and lazy dinners—were long gone. Now we were like strangers who pass each other at the same time each day as they travel to and from their work.

The station took off in the ratings book, but as Magic climbed, Katy and I began our long, inevitable fall as we started arguing more and drawing further apart.

It was the middle of June when some insignificant spark ignited into a raging blaze between us and we laid into each other with a verbal assault that would have been wrong to launch at your enemy, never mind your lover. But anger is an evil beast and we both gave each other as good as we got.

Two days later, our emotions still flayed raw, I knew it was time to have that inevitable talk with Katy about the future.

"We can't go on like this," I said. "Either you move out or I move out. I really don't care which. Let me know by the end of the month. I'm good with whatever you decide."

Katy was a smart, clever girl and said nothing in reply. She didn't want to unwittingly start World War III all over again. And for the next two weeks we attempted to continue on as if nothing had happened. But some things you can't forget or ignore, and silence can be as powerful as a scream.

On Wednesday, July 1, 1981, I told Rogers Brandon that I was giving the company one month's notice and leaving Magic 98. He was upset and wanted me to stay.

"We thought you liked it here," Brandon said.

"I like you; you've been great to work for. But I was upfront with everyone when I was hired that this would only be for one year, and the end of the month will make it a year. And I can't stay here in Bakersfield."

"So what are you going to do?"

"What I said I would do," I continued. "Go back to LA and try and get a job there. That's always been my goal."

"So you're staying in radio?"

"Definitely."

Brandon thought for a moment. "We have a station in San Luis Obispo. It's a rock station but much more mainstream than Magic. We just heard from Arbitron that they have finally approved the San Luis Obispo market for its first ever ratings book. There's never been a ranking of radio stations taken on the Central Coast before. This is crucially important to us. Would you go there and do mornings and be the program director? You will, of course, get a raise."

I shook my head. "It's not about money. I made a promise to myself and I have to keep it."

"And I respect that," said Brandon. "But these ratings are a huge priority, both for the company and for me personally." He took a moment then continued, "Have you ever been to San Luis Obispo?"

I shook my head.

"Then we'll fly you there. We'll go tomorrow. I'll get someone from KERN to cover your shift on Magic and you and I will fly to the coast and I'll show you the Z93 studios in person. It might change your mind."

I was blown away. I had no idea how they would take my leaving, but flying me in a private plane to try and keep me working for the company? This was something that took me completely by surprise. I'd never been in a private plane so why not? I was certain it wouldn't change anything, I'd still be going back to LA, but this would be a fun little adventure.

"Okay," I said. "Just let me know where and when."

I drove back to my apartment and waited for Katy to come home from her air shift. I broke the news to her that as she hadn't come to a decision about what was to happen between us I had been forced to make that choice. I told her that I had given my notice directly to Rogers Brandon and would be leaving come August 1 and she could have the apartment and everything in it. I assured her that I was positive that Magic 98 would want her to remain on the air because she was such a talented DJ.

Tears flowed that night but we kept it civil and restrained and on that Wednesday evening our love affair ended.

CALIFORNIA GIRLS

After a year of driving back and forth across the arid deserts and oil-fields of Bakersfield, it was a thrill to be up in the sky and soaring over the California Coastal Range of mountains that separate the San Joaquin Valley from the Pacific. The barren sand quickly gave way to rolling hills and vineyards loaded with grapes ripening for the harvest. The view was spectacular. Rogers Brandon had the pilot fly slightly north and over a dramatic chain of peaks called the Nine Sisters and then out above the Pacific at Morro Bay. He pointed out the famous landmark rock that gives the bay its name and then turned south to hug the coastline.

There was a light haze hanging low over the ocean that only served to accentuate the beauty of Avila Beach and approaching those sands, like vast columns of marching soldiers, were endless lines of incoming swells readying to break and release their pent-up energy on the shore after their 2,000-mile journey across the ocean. The pilot dipped the plane to the left and throttled back as the small four-seater turbo prop began its final approach into San Luis Obispo Regional Airport

A car was waiting for us and we headed to the studios of KZOZ on Higuera Street. Z93 occupied a free-standing, one-story brick building and I was happy to see everything was right there; the sales offices, the management offices and the studio. No more driving back and forth, a definite plus. I was introduced to the staff and the station's consultant who the company had brought in, Mark Driscoll, a legendary DJ out of New York.

We went over what was being offered to me, morning drive from 6am to 10am, overseeing the running of the station as program director and a salary increase to $1,800 a month. It all sounded good but I wasn't swayed. I wanted to get back to LA.

One of the DJs, Harlon "the Wingnut," whose long hair and tie-dyed t-shirt marked him as a holdover from "flower power" and the sixties, spoke up.

"You should walk around slow town and check it out. It's a great little place," he suggested.

Mark agreed and said we should go for lunch. As the two of us walked along the main street to the restaurant that Mark had chosen we talked about a number of things including San Luis Obispo's nickname.

"They call it SLO town," laughed Mark. "And sometimes it is. I spent a lot of time doing radio in New York and believe me, I'd see more going on there in a day than you could see happening here in a year. The biggest tourist attractions close by are a wacky motel called the Madonna Inn that has a "cave room" and Bubblegum Alley, which is just that, a little alley where the kids have stuck their gum on the walls over the years. It's kind of gross, but kind of quaint too."

Mark was right. This place had a quirky small-town vibe. But as we reached the restaurant I'd noticed something else and I had to bring it up to him over lunch.

"Was I just seeing things after being locked up in Bakersfield for a year, or are there an inordinate number of beautiful girls in San Luis Obispo?" I asked Mark.

"Your eyes do not deceive you, my friend. You're not only in a beach town, but this place is also home to Cal Poly. Just wait, when the college is in session and all the students are back, it's like a parade of supermodels every day."

What was said during the rest of lunch was a blur. My mind was racing. A California beach town full of hot college girls and I would be the newly single morning DJ on the only rock station on the entire central coast? That was a recipe for disaster and I was all in.

As Mark picked up the check I heard a voice saying, "I think I can do this. I'll stay through the ratings book and then leave." That's when I realized that voice was mine.

Rogers Brandon was so happy that his "show and tell" had worked and wanted me to leave Bakersfield and take over in San Luis Obispo immediately. He had the afternoon DJ from KERN assume my duties at Magic 98 and by the end of the week I had said goodbye to both Bakersfield and, sadly, to Katy.

The Arbitron ratings period was scheduled to run from mid-September until mid-December. The numbers (results) would be released during the second week of January. I would stay until then and get the station through "the book." I had only eight weeks to prepare Z93 for the upcoming ratings battle.

The monster that loomed over us was KSLY, a long-established country station with a huge following. If we could be a strong second to them that was all that was hoped for. But to achieve that we had to get our name out there. Mark and I pleaded with our owners to free up some money and soon we were able to order t-shirts, jackets and stickers that we could use as promo items. We wanted every bumper on the central coast to display "Z93—The Music FM." But how do we convince everyone to stick one on?

The answer was simple: prizes. We see your sticker, read out your license plate number and you have thirty minutes to call in and claim your prize: an album, t-shirt or maybe even a pair of concert tickets. But it bothered me. That wasn't big enough to guarantee that mom and dad would let you place a sticker on the rear end of their beloved Ford, let alone change the dial from KSLY to Z93.

Then it came to me: What if we saved *all* of the winners' names throughout the twelve-week ratings period and on the last day of Arbitron's survey threw a free outdoor party for our listeners and drew one name from our entire existing winners' list and that person would get a grand prize from Z93? But what would be big enough and catchy enough so that our name was always in your head, Z93?

The answer was obvious and it tied in so perfectly with a car bumper sticker campaign,

"Win a Z from Z93"

The sales manager, plus Mark and I, approached the biggest Datsun dealership on the central coast and persuaded them, along with the promise of on-air mentions and a number of sales incentives, to give us a used, but perfect-condition, loaded, two-year-old 280Z for our contest. Now we were ready.

Mark and I cut a series of promo spots to run around the clock on Z93. Working with Mark Driscoll was a true learning experience; not only did he have one of the greatest voices in radio but he was also a whiz at production and putting together spots, promos and commercials. Those times in the studio with Mark became invaluable to me because learning from the best really makes you want to step up your own game.

It was the middle of August and we were just four weeks away from the start of the ratings book. I was having a meeting with the jocks and going over the new music I'd added to the playlist. Punk and New Wave were happening, and along with Journey's *Escape* and Stevie Nicks's *Bella Donna*, I'd put into rotation The Go-Gos, Wall of Voodoo and The Pretenders plus several big records from England that Dad had sent me, "Tainted Love" from Soft Cell, "Fade To Grey" from Visage and a track that had so much energy I felt it would hold its place against any of the rockers we were playing during the evening show, Spandau Ballet and "To Cut a Long Story Short."

I was going over the music details with my crew when one of the most stunning girls I had ever seen strolled past the window of the station. For a moment my eyes couldn't quite take in this moving fantasy. I stopped talking mid-sentence and my gaze followed her down the street. I knew I couldn't miss this chance and just let her disappear. As incredibly unprofessional as it was, I leapt to my feet, said to the group, "Hang on a minute," grabbed a t-shirt and sprinted outside.

I caught up with this walking loveliness in seconds and tapped her on the shoulder. She turned around and greeted me with a dazzling smile.

"Hi," she said.

"Can I ask you what radio station you listen to?"

"Z93 of course," she beamed.

"Great. That's who I DJ for and I can't think of a better way to advertise our station than to have a beautiful girl wear our t-shirt."

Okay, so it was corny, but sometimes corny works.

Darcy lived just twenty minutes north in Atascadero. Her parents had a small ranch there and she was getting ready to start her second year at Cal

Poly. I was hosting a station party that evening at a local Mexican restaurant and invited her. The attraction was instant and we hit it off.

As Darcy and I started to doze off that night, I saw the two of us reflected in the mirrored wardrobe doors in my room. She was laying there, already breathing deeply, her body looking flawless as she drifted away—Sleeping Beauty in person. Then I caught a glimpse of myself in that unforgiving mirror and a realization came over me. I was getting fat.

My year in Bakersfield had been nothing but endless hours of work punctuated by short breaks where I only had time to grab junk food, eat then sleep, and I had continued that habit in San Luis Obispo. Now all those empty calories were starting to show. I was probably twenty pounds heavier than I had ever been. I turned off the dim bedside light and hoped I was the only one of us who had noticed.

The next evening there was a slight chill in the air and a light rain was falling but that didn't deter me. I pulled on tennis shoes, shorts and a hoodie and left my rented room on Laguna Lane and hopped the fence onto the grounds of Laguna Middle School right next door. Their sports field and track were empty and waiting for me. I accepted their invitation and knew those first laps would be hard; after all, I'd done nothing physical for fourteen months—no surfing, karate, swimming—just work. But now I had to do something for myself. That August night in 1981 I started to run and I have never stopped.

I had been looking for a model for an ad we were putting together for our Z93 t-shirts and jackets and knew that we could do no better than Darcy. Close your eyes right now and imagine the ultimate California beach girl. Congratulations, that's Darcy. Her blond hair tumbled down to the small of her back and her toned legs went on forever.

I shot three rolls of black and white film getting the picture for the ad but in all truth any of the photos would have worked. When we looked back at the pictures the caption wrote itself.

The Z93 Jacket—Wear It or Wear Nothing at All

The weeks sped by and fall arrived. Our bumper sticker contest was working even better than we could have hoped. Every time we read out a license plate number between 6am and midnight the winner would call in within five minutes; it was exciting that there always seemed to be some-

Darcy modeling the
Z93 jacket
– November 1981

one listening, tuned in, and waiting to win. Our main fear became that we would run out of prizes and giveaways before the end of the bumper sticker contest.

Finally December rolled around and with it the last day of the Arbitron ratings period. All our planning and preparations had led to this, the culmination of the twelve-week promotion and the massive final party at the Datsun dealership. More than a thousand people showed up and the 280Z sat in pride of place, polished and gleaming in the front of the showroom. We drew the winner's name and he was there in the crowd. As we handed the screaming winner the keys the press took pictures and we cranked the station over the loudspeakers we'd brought in. It was the perfect end to an incredible campaign.

Later that evening Mark Driscoll and I drove back to the station to wrap up everything. Mark was a veteran of Arbitron ratings wars and was a lot less concerned about it than I was. He sensed my anxiety and he looked over at me and said reassuringly, "Relax, we've done all we can do. We're at the mercy of the ratings now."

With almost a month to go before Arbitron released the all-important numbers, I went up to Atascadero and spent Christmas with Darcy and her family. Darcy and I hiked in the fields behind their ranch and talked about my plans.

"I don't think you should go to LA," she said. "You're so popular here on the coast. Everyone knows you. It'll never be like that for you down there; it's too big."

I knew she was right, but it was something I had to do. Darcy knew that too, and as the year drew to its close so did our fling.

It was mid-January 1982, ratings day. We all knew that word of the numbers would come in first to the Bakersfield office. A little after ten the business line lit up. I grabbed it on the first ring; this was the all-important call. Rogers Brandon was on the other end of the phone. His voice was subdued.

"We just got the numbers," he said softly.

It was my turn to speak. This was not sounding good. How badly had we done after all?

"Did we come second to KSLY?" That was our hope, our goal, our prayer.

"No, we didn't." His voice was emotionless and somber as if he were contemplating all the money his company had wasted on this first, all important survey, helmed by this young, talentless British DJ.

"So how did the numbers come out?" I had to know the worst.

"Okay," he said. "Well, KSLY got a solid nine share."

"And us? How did we do?"

Brandon's voice exploded over the phone, "We got a *twenty*-eight share! No one can believe it. You didn't just beat them, you crushed them! Get on the air now and I want you to say 'Z93—the Central Coast's number-one music station!'"

If you're not in radio that doesn't seem such a big deal, but if you are then you know it's like winning the World Series, the Stanley Cup and the Super Bowl all at once and then someone tosses in the Masters, the Daytona 500 and a few Olympic medals just for good measure.

Brandon's voice continued: "We're number one! It doesn't get any bigger. You are the program director of the biggest station on the Central Coast. Are you going to stay now?"

"I'm thrilled with the numbers, but I can't."

I was honestly sorry—these were genuinely good people but my dreams were elsewhere. San Luis Obispo had been a fantastic town for me but

The day after the ratings – in the Z93 studio

the cliché of "big fish, small pond" resonated through my brain. I had no alternative.

"I'll be here through a week on Friday, and then I have to go just like we arranged. I've got to get back to LA."

"Then you are going to miss out on an amazing year for the station. With this under our belt everything around here will change, and for the better. I wish you would stay and be a part of it. We'll be sending you something tomorrow." He hung up.

The next day, halfway through my morning show a card, flowers and champagne arrived. The card read, "We'll be here for you." Like I said, genuinely good people.

My return to Los Angeles was now a little over one week away. I called Mark and Tim at Towards 2000 to let them know I was heading back and Tim offered to let me room with him at his little place in Sherman Oaks. Now that I knew I had a place to stay it was time to lay the groundwork for the future and land that elusive radio job in LA.

UP ALL NIGHT

At the same time as our ratings book had come out for the Central Coast, Arbitron had released the ratings for all its other markets across America, and that included Southern California. I managed to get a copy of the Los Angeles ratings numbers and marked which stations had gone up and which ones were struggling. It was those weaker radio stations I targeted, figuring that they might be planning changes to strengthen their on-air position and therefore be the most receptive.

I put together a package with Z93's amazing results along with Magic 98's increased ratings from the previous year and prepared to send them out. I called a dozen stations in LA who had big drops in their audience figures and asked if I could send their program directors my resume, tape and Arbitron package. That's when I found out how self-absorbed and myopic most of these PDs really are; little green men from Mars could come down and take over all the radio stations in Texas and they wouldn't care; their only concern was their particular station and their market. To them, nothing else existed. No wonder they were such losers!

The exception was the program director at KNAC FM 105.5 in Long Beach. Jimmy Christopher actually seemed interested in the huge numbers that Z93 had pulled and set up an appointment to meet with me as soon as I was back in LA. That gave me hope and as I left SLO town and cruised south on California Coast Highway 1, I was filled with excitement at the unknown prospects ahead and finally returning to Los Angeles and the promised land.

KNAC was located just three blocks from the ocean on the tenth floor of the F&M bank building at 320 Pine Avenue. The on-air studio was huge and the offices spacious, if a little run down, from too many years of partying and abuse. I met with Jimmy Christopher a little after ten on Monday morning. Jimmy was a sports guy at heart but loved music and was passionate about it. He also was the afternoon drive DJ as Jimmy "the Saint" Christopher. We immediately clicked and talked for just a few minutes before he offered me the job. Then it was déjà vu all over again.

"It'll be a six-hour shift," Jimmy said, "Midnight until six, and then you hand over to Norm McBride. It's won't be a lot of money because, as you probably know, our ratings aren't that great because of our limited signal."

Jimmy wasn't kidding about that. The FCC regulates every radio station in the USA and KNAC's transmitter power was so low that it could only be heard up and down LA's coastline. Drive a few miles inland and they were gone in a crackle of static. As a result, their advertising income was drastically restricted and so was their budget.

"I can only pay you a thousand a month for five overnights a week. That would be Monday through Friday. Will that work?"

It was a radio gig in Los Angeles. This was the reason I had come to America. I wasn't going to turn it down no matter how small the salary.

"When do I start?" I said.

"How about tonight?" replied Jimmy. "The guy we've been using will be more than happy to go back to his wife and kids. He's been bugging me for months to return to weekends."

"I can do tonight, boss," I smiled. "Can I check out the studios?"

"Sure," said Jimmy. "I'll take you in there and introduce you to Sylvia Amerito. She's on the air now."

Technically it was Tuesday morning, February 2, 1982 that I made my debut on LA radio doing the overnights on KNAC "Rock and Rhythm." The format was rock, punk and new wave. I had a lot of freedom on the air—even more after 2am when I knew that the bosses were asleep—and anyway Jimmy wanted his station to be unique in the market; that's why he'd instituted the format of having the newest music available played right next to "hip" rock standards.

It wouldn't be unusual to tune into KNAC and hear The B-52s "Planet Claire" followed by The Beatles "Back in the USSR" into Elvis Costello

"Pump It Up", Romeo Void "Never Say Never" and Van Halen "You Really Got Me".

Our main radio competitor was KROQ in Pasadena who also played new wave and punk. KROQ was famous in the industry as being totally disorganized and constantly on the verge of going bankrupt. The urban myth—which proved to be true—was that they were so behind on their rent that they had actually moved their studios across town in the middle of the night to avoid being evicted and having their equipment seized.

Stories of bounced checks, FCC lawsuits and days when the station just turned off its transmitter because they couldn't pay their electrical bill were known to everyone. But somehow despite all of that they were starting to make an impact with the younger audience in Southern California. The kids didn't care about the business side of radio; they just wanted to hear cool music that no one else was playing.

Jimmy wanted to stay ahead of KROQ musically and encouraged me to bring in new music from England to play first. He was talking to the right person as my Dad continued to send me new songs on a regular basis.

On my overnight show I debuted a number of great records and twelve-inches including Depeche Mode's "See You," Fun Boy Three's "It Ain't What You Do" and Haircut 100's "Love Plus One." I started combing the record stores and found some gems from closer to home including a local group called Berlin who had a song called "Tell Me Why." I liked it but thought the B side was even better so I flipped it over and started playing that track every night. Jimmy heard it on my show and had it added to KNAC's playlist so suddenly it was all over the station. Tune in to KNAC in the spring of 1982 and very soon you would hear "The Metro" booming out of your radio speakers.

The biggest problem about doing overnights at KNAC was my commute from Long Beach back to Tim's apartment in Sherman Oaks. I would hit the 710 then the 405 starting at around six twenty in the morning and anyone who has ever faced the morning rush hour on the freeways in LA can feel my pain. It would take a minimum of an hour and a half to make it the thirty-nine miles to the valley.

It was all I could do to keep my eyes open on that stop-and-go crawl of a drive and the only thing that kept me going was tuning into the energy and humor of the morning team on our competitor, KROQ.

Ramondo and Evans were fresh, funny and unlike anyone else on radio. I couldn't believe the stuff they got away with. They made my long, tedious drive bearable. But by the time I arrived at Tim's apartment and crashed on my ever-present foam mattress on the floor of my room I was ready to sleep the rest of the morning away.

Tim and Mark's company was going gangbusters. They were happy to have me working with them again and before February was over I was back DJing four nights a week at private parties and discos. They introduced me to another DJ they used, Egil Alvik, "the Swedish Eagle," and we became instant friends. Amazingly we had both arrived in America on the same day—November 16, 1976, within an hour of each other. It was fun to practice my limited Swedish with Egil and he made sure that I had an instant refresher course of all the bad words.

I also got to know John Dunn, the club promoter, really well and spun for him every Monday in Encino at Le Hot Club. I had no idea that John and his one-club gig would be the ticket to everything I'd been looking for. My set would be from eight until eleven and then I'd race to my car and shoot down the freeway to Long Beach to make it in time for my overnight radio show. As the weeks sped by the hours began to take their toll.

One night in late March I was already more than halfway through my overnight shift and it was a little after four with still no hint of any morning light to chase away the darkness.

I cued up a record from one of my favorite rock bands of the late sixties, The Doors. It was the opening track of side two of an album that I consider a "must have" for anyone's record collection, The Doors' *Greatest Hits*. The cut I put on was "Break on Through." It had always been a song I loved, from the beginning bossa nova beat through to the Vox organ and Jim Morrison's haunting vocals that build and build to become almost a primal scream. I introduced it on the air, cranked the studio speakers and leaned forward with my elbow on the console and put my head in my hand to enjoy that archetypical California sound.

The listeners got much more of the California sound than I did. When I opened my eyes "LA Woman" was playing, the final cut on the LP. I had fallen asleep during "Break on Through" and stayed asleep, sitting up, as the entire album side had tracked through. The most amazing thing to me was that "Break on Through" is less than two and a half minutes long; I had gone right out as if I'd been decked!

I jumped on the microphone as "LA Woman" faded away. "Great to hear an entire album side from one of LA's most important bands. Kind of a mini nighttime concert from The Doors here on Rock and Rhythm, KNAC. I'm Dick Sheppard, and now, let's cross the Atlantic and come up to date with The Human League."

For the next couple of days I waited to get called out on what had happened but nothing came. No one had heard my screw up. No listeners had phoned in to make fun of me, no staff had been tuned in. Was I talking to myself? Is it radio if there is no one listening? I knew it would soon be time to move on again if, in the words of Jim Morrison, I ever really wanted to "break on through."

WORLD IN MY EYES

ON YOUR RADIO

It was John Dunn's idea, but I was for it 100%. Le Hot Club was packed with the hip kids on the disco nights he promoted and John, ever the entrepreneur, saw a fresh opportunity with the rise of New Wave music and decided to expand to two nights a week with the second being a "New Wave dance party."

He needed to get the word out quickly, so he bought time on KROQ. I'd asked him to advertise on KNAC but John said no because its low signal didn't reach that far inland, while KROQ and its transmitter blanketed Encino in the San Fernando Valley where Le Hot Club was located.

John's brainwave was that I voice the commercials for him. I didn't care that the real reason he wanted me to do the commercials was that he would be saving around $400 a week by not having to pay one of the KROQ jocks to use their name to endorse the club; instead I was thrilled to have the opportunity to get my voice heard on a station with a decent signal that could be picked up all over Southern California rather than staying stuck on one that was limited by the FCC to just a few towns up and down the coast.

John set up a time for me to go to the KROQ building and record his commercial so on an unusually warm day in late March of 1982 I headed out to Pasadena. Like many American cities at that time, Pasadena was run-down and had sections filled with homeless people and drug addicts sleeping on sidewalks and in doorways; its main thoroughfare, Colorado

Boulevard, had been taken over to the point that it had become a no-go area and was unsafe to visit at night.

As part of a major, concerted effort to turn things around, the city council was instigating a number of far-reaching changes to Pasadena including introducing a very confusing one-way system that had just been implemented so try as I might using my trusty but now outdated Thomas Guide map book and John's hand-written directions I couldn't find my way through the maze to Los Robles Avenue.

After circumnavigating the streets of the city three times I was so frustrated that I almost gave up and turned around. Instead I took a series of deep breaths, pulled into a gas station, found a pay phone and called KROQ's office number.

Within moments I received directions that were completely different from John's. I had actually passed KROQ twice and it was less than a half mile away. In minutes I was there and safely in the parking lot behind the building.

To say KROQ was underwhelming is an overstatement. Located above a hospital clothing supplier, "Look for Uniform Circus, then you've found us," the receptionist told me, KROQ was reached through an unassuming ground-floor door with a hand-painted wooden KROQ sign above it, the only clue that a radio station existed within.

The stairway was covered with a worn and dirty avocado-green carpet and the walls were painted a deep plum purple. There had obviously been a contest to find the two most clashing colors in the world and this peculiar combo had won out.

The friendly receptionist, Angela, whom I'd spoken to on the phone just minutes before, greeted me with a smile from behind her aging wooden desk. "You found us?"

It was as much a question as a statement. Yeah, I was as amazed as her at how tricky it was getting around the Pasadena streets. She directed me to the production room barely ten feet behind the reception area.

As I walked down the corridor I realized I could see all the way from the front to the back of the building. It was less than fifty feet long and thirty feet wide! Where was the rest of the station?

I knocked on the production room door and John Logic waved me in. John was a tall, lanky surfer type who hadn't been told I was coming but that didn't perturb him; he seemed pleased to have the interruption. His acid-washed shorts and t-shirt fit in with the décor of the studio which was casual and young; posters of The Ramones and Gen X jostled for wall space with pinups and calendars of bikini babes. The room was small and basic—like the rest of KROQ—but everything you needed was right there.

John showed me how it all worked and then stunned me by saying, "You got it? I'm going for lunch."

As he left me alone in the studio I was almost in shock. What? You're leaving me with all this gear? What if I was to sneak out with a TEAC reel-to-reel recorder under my arm? But petty theft was not on the agenda today so I set to work on the two commercials. One was for "This Tuesday"; the other, for a "Tonight!" version.

I voiced the spots, laid down the tracks over some music borrowed from John's production library albums and dubbed the finished ads onto two blank "carts." I copied the typed format of the labels from the other commercial carts in the studio and awaited John's return.

When he got back he was visibly impressed that I'd done all his work for him. I said I thought it was all in place except for the colored dots on the carts which I hadn't been able to make sense of.

John explained, "That's so we know the order of which commercials run first or last on the air. Red means they have music or are a beer or movie spot and those are exciting so they go first in a stop set; blue is a produced spot but nothing to jump up and down about, you know a car commercial or a sale at a store; and green is hideous like an insurance commercial or loan company! Those are cold reads, no music, just audience killers. Those go last."

He pulled out two red dots and stuck them on my carts. I would be running first in a commercial block; the audience would have a chance to hear me before they tuned out to avoid the hard sell.

For the next month I went back every week to update the commercials. John Dunn didn't pay me one cent to do them but that was okay. I got to know my way around KROQ and the staff became used to having me in their building. I would walk straight in from the street and get a happy wave from Angela without being questioned or even stopped.

During that time I found out just how disorganized KROQ really was. I'd thought John Logic was the production director, the guy who supervises the recording of the commercials, jingles, and "bits" that go on the air, but he wasn't. KROQ didn't have one. Instead, the DJs were responsible for recording their own commercials and at certain times of the day would have to battle to have access to that one little production room. And it wasn't uncommon at KROQ to even have the salespeople push their way in there and dub spots for their clients.

I'd never seen anything like it before—not in Bakersfield, San Luis Obispo and certainly not at KNAC. But here we were in one of the world's biggest radio markets at a station that had no rules. It was the wild west of radio and the sheriff had left town!

I got to know several of the jocks plus the station's music director, the brilliant Larry Groves. One of the DJs from the morning show, Mike Evans of "Ramondo & Evans" came into the production room while I was there and asked if I was the guy with the English accent. When I replied yes—my voice giving me away—he wanted to know if I would cut "drops" for a couple of the morning show features that he and Ramondo, Raymond Bannister, did.

I was excited to do this for him. I had become a huge fan of Mike Evans on my morning commutes and I did my best to act as professionally as I could around him while all the time inside the little boy in me was screaming "Get his autograph!" But I restrained myself and casually asked exactly what he needed.

One recording he wanted was for a hilarious character Mike had created called Yolanda and the other was me saying his nickname in a very British accent, "Well, hello and good morning! You are listening to the Hose." Liking what he heard he also had me track several variations of "Go to bed with April Whitney; wake up with Ramondo & Evans" that would act as promos and run on-air throughout the day on KROQ. Suddenly my voice was all over KROQ on virtually everyone's shift.

Jimmy Christopher, the PD of KNAC, called me at home to chat and brought up that he was hearing me on KROQ. I explained about Le Hot Club and how it had all happened and instead of chewing me out, Jimmy was very supportive and wished me well. He made no threats against my job and if anything I felt encouraged.

Now I was in a situation where I would get off the air at KNAC at 6am and as I made my ninety-minute morning slog back to my apartment in Sherman Oaks I would listen to Ramondo & Evans and hear myself on the air at least twice an hour.

It was a month later, just a couple of days after my birthday, that Larry Groves came into the production room while I worked on a new promo for the morning show. "When you finish up in here Rick wants to see you in his office." Larry was very matter of fact and didn't wait for a reply before he left.

"Rick?" I thought. That could only mean Rick Carroll, the program director of KROQ. After all these weeks I still hadn't met him so this was a big moment, unless he was going to kick me out of the station which was very possible.

Rick's office was tiny and cramped and filled with gold and platinum albums. Unfortunately because of the lack of wall space they were just piled on the floor in a towering heap that looked as if they could fall over and come smashing down at any time. Two big speakers hung from the wall and on his desk a turntable fought for space with an unruly stack of papers that screamed out for organization.

Rick looked up and gazed questioningly at me through his long, curly hair, "You're the English guy I've been hearing on the air?"

I nodded as Rick continued, "In the middle of June all the jocks are going away on a station trip to Hawaii for two weeks. I've got some local names to cover most of the daytime shifts like Elvira and the lead singer from Oingo Boingo, Danny Elfman. But I'm short one person, and that's someone to do Denise Westwood's program from nine until noon. Do you want to do it?"

"Fuck yes I do!" Those were the words that instantly leapt into my brain but I managed to contain the extent of my excitement and answered in a semi-controlled manner, "Yeah, I could do that."

Rick continued, "Good. Couple of things. We can't pay you, so for the two weeks on the air you'll be working for free. How do you feel about that?"

"Fine," I said.

"And the other thing is that I can't have you on the air at another ra-dio station if you are doing a show here at KROQ so you'll have to quit KNAC."

This was a hammer blow. As limited as KNAC was it still gave me a job on a station in America's number two radio market. This was a huge setback. No money and no job.

I thought for a second and then asked, "Are you going to Hawaii?"

Rick shook his head, "No, I'm staying here."

Then this was my chance, maybe if I did this I could achieve everything I had dreamed of since those early days at Oxford a decade before. But it meant leaving behind all I had accomplished so far. Did I dare? Yes, I hadn't come to America to play it safe and wonder "what if." I was going to roll the dice again and this time it would be all or nothing.

"If you're going to stay I'll do it because you'll get to hear me on the air."

Rick instantly picked up on what I meant and spoke slowly as he tried not to pop my bubble. "I know what you're thinking but it's not going to happen. There are no jobs available here at KROQ. It took me two years to put together this team. No one is leaving. They're going to Hawaii and then they are coming back to their shifts. Unless their plane goes down and kills them all I won't have anything for you."

To this day I don't know where I got the balls to say this but I looked Rick dead in the eyes and said quietly and deliberately, "I'll quit KNAC because you will find something for me here."

And just like that I made it my game to win or lose.

WHAT'S MY NAME

I was sad giving my notice to Jimmy at KNAC. Everyone there had been so friendly and had encouraged me in my quest to move up through radio's ranks. As my final day approached, their talented morning guy, Norm McBride, took me out for lunch to wish me well.

I carried with me a lot of appreciation for that good-hearted staff on that underpowered little station as I walked into the KROQ building on that fateful day, Monday, June 14, 1982, to do my first shift there.

I arrived early and ran through some bits I wanted to do on air. If there was the chance to do a contest then I planned on some music trivia; I had a great question ready: "What is the name of the club on the east coast where The Ramones and Blondie first played?" I also wanted to work in a character that I had unabashedly stolen from Noel Edmond's breakfast show on BBC Radio One, that of a blustery, rude old tea lady barging into the studio on her daily rounds. I figured that would be perfect in the eleven o'clock hour just as everyone's thoughts began gravitating towards lunch and if it went well I could make her a regular.

One thing I couldn't decide was what name to use on the air. It was time to put Dick Sheppard to rest for a number of reasons. First, in my naiveté, I didn't want to steal any listeners from the struggling KNAC—they were friends and already had enough problems getting an audience with their low-wattage signal—and secondly, ever since Taxi put her arms on my waist and teased me about "Dick" I had decided I should eventually revert back to Richard.

But Richard what? Richard Sheppard was way too mundane on a station whose jock lineup included Freddy Snakeskin, Jed the Fish, Dusty Street and Sam Freeze. I needed something catchy and a little out of the ordinary. I had been going over this again and again ever since Rick offered me the slot but was no closer to coming up with anything original.

At exactly nine I walked into the on-air studio of KROQ and took over. I'd been in there before the previous week for two nights and run the board as I trained with Dusty Street so I'd be technically competent for my fill-in shifts, but much of the training was Dusty sending me out to Trader Joe's down the street to buy her a liter and a half of Gallo Chardonnay which amazingly didn't detract from her on-air performance but definitely did affect her in other ways because as the alcohol kicked in she would lock her eyes on mine from across the console and say in that unforgettable gruff voice of hers, "You and me, boyfriend, it's just a matter of time!" But now Dusty was in Aloha Land and I was alone in the studio.

There were two turntables on my left, a third on my right, a sixteen-channel mixer in front of me, six cart machines in two stacks of three and a Sennheiser microphone on a flexible stand. Behind me was a five-foot-high carousel holding the commercial and promo carts, a plastic file box with the live copy typed on cards and the rear wall was all shelves filled with albums and music carts filed in a fashion that almost made sense.

There was a window into the studio but strung up across it to conceal the goings on inside was an old, ugly green and red curtain that my mother would have refused to have in her house. The studio was anything but glamorous but it had everything I needed to succeed or fail. But what name was I going to use?

The top of the hour song was fading and I cued up and started the next one, A Flock of Seagulls' "Telecommunication." Two minutes and fifty seconds to decide. On the other side of the soundboard, lying on one of the chairs where the in-studio guests would sit, was a *Los Angeles Times* Calendar section from the day before. I grabbed it in an attempt to find inspiration.

The Calendar's Sunday edition was thick and comprehensive; on the front page was an article by critic Robert Hilburn. *Richard Hilburn?* I thought. No, that was as bland as Richard Sheppard. Forty seconds to go before I had to turn on the microphone and be committed for ever after.

On page three there was a full-page ad for a movie opening in two weeks directed by Ridley Scott. Richard Scott? That made no sense; I was English not Scottish and I had already gone through a list of "origin" names—Richard England, Richard London and in a salute to the Royal family, Richard Windsor—but none seemed right to me. But this movie's name was cool, *Blade Runner*. I made up my mind there and then; it would be Richard Runner. Catchy, short, had alliteration and I could put together a fun logo using the two *R*s mimicking the famous Rolls Royce insignia.

Fifteen seconds to the song's fade. My nerves kicked in. I have never had a panic attack but this was as close as I ever want to get. I felt as if all of Southern California was tuned in, hunched around their radios, listening intently with pen and paper ready to make notes of all my screw ups and mock me endlessly for them.

I tossed the paper onto the floor, rolled my chair into position at the console, pulled my headphones down and hit the red *on* button for the mic. "Flock of Seagulls' 'Telecommunication' or Telecom as it's known affectionately back in my native England. Denise Westwood is on vacation in Hawaii so you're stuck with me on K-Rock. I'm . . ." *What's my name?*

The planet's biggest brain fart hit. I flashed a glance down at the newspaper to jog my memory but the paper had folded when it landed and half of the page was obscured. I could no longer see the full ad; all I could pick out was "Opening June 25, Blade R—" What was the other word? Too late, no time! You've got to say something, the world is listening!

I heard the words come out of my mouth, "I'm Richard Blade and if you are in the mood for Elvis Costello or Madness then they are both on their way in minutes, but before that a new group from Sheffield, England, whose just released album is a killer, never off my turntable at home; this is ABC and 'Poison Arrow.'"

I started the song and closed the mic. I slipped off my headphones and collapsed back in the chair and ran the name through my head. Richard Blade. I'd heard worse. It would have to do.

Hard to believe it was almost noon already. My first three hours on the air at KROQ had flown by. I'd made it without a major screw up. Sure, I'd fallen over a couple of words and almost miscued a song but caught it before I'd put it on the air so that was good and no one knew about that potential disaster apart from me. I hadn't left the studio once, not for a pee break or to make a cup of tea in the closet that masqueraded as a kitchen, but now as I was playing my last song I realized just how tired I was. That last 180 minutes had been non-stop pure adrenalin for me; it had been my prime-time LA debut. Maybe I hadn't scored a touchdown but I hadn't fumbled or thrown an interception so I felt good.

I hit the pre-recorded top-of-the-hour ID, "K-R-O-Q Los Angeles, Pasadena, 106.7 FM," and slammed into the Talking Heads' "Life During Wartime." That was it. I was done. Just one thing missing. Danny Elfman wasn't there yet to take over. I couldn't leave the studio unmanned.

I cued up the next song from Larry Grove's hand-written music key that more resembled a child's pie chart than a radio station's playlist and waited for the lead singer of Oingo Boingo to take over. Danny had planned to come on the air under the pseudonym of *Moscow Eddie* but he was nearly five minutes late already. Was he sitting, listening in his car somewhere, pounding the steering wheel, caught in LA's notorious traffic?

My unspoken question was answered as the hotline blinked red. "KROQ," I answered.

"Yo! Can I speak to the DJ?"

"That's me," I replied.

"OK. It's Danny Elfman here."

"Hey, Danny," I said, "Are you running late?"

"No, I'm not going to make it. I'm stuck in the studio with Steve and Johnny rehearsing a new song for our live show and I can't get free," explained Danny. "I'll be there tomorrow for sure but I can't get out of this rehearsal today. Can someone take care of things there for me?"

I didn't hesitate; sometimes you have to step up. It's like when you're playing a gig and you're dog tired and just want to go home and crawl into bed but the client and their friends are having such a great time that they want "one more hour!" You put on your brave face and do your job.

"Not a problem, Danny. I'll cover your shift. Looking forward to meeting you tomorrow," I said.

"Good. See you then!"

The line went silent and Danny was gone, back to his Oingo Boingo session where he was prepping for a concert tour to promote their new album *Nothing to Fear* that was due out in just days. And just like that I was doing my second show on KROQ, except it was consecutive to my first, six hours straight and now with zero prep.

This time I would be filling in for Jed the Fish. Jed was an incredibly talented and unpredictable on-air personality whose laugh had its own unique sound, unmatched or unequalled by any other jock in the United States. It was often imitated by listeners but none of their impressions ever came close to the real thing.

He also liked to suddenly break into nonsensical, made-up words and phrases. His music taste was esoteric and he was well-known as an early champion of Devo and Oingo Boingo which is how the station had been able to persuade Danny Elfman to come on board as Jed's fill-in DJ. His were tough shoes to fill.

I decided that rather than attempt to be Jed I would lean towards my own personal favorites, new British bands like Spandau Ballet, Duran Duran and the emerging Depeche Mode. If people didn't like the jock choices that I was allowed to insert twice an hour then so be it. Better to upset a few listeners than pretend to be a carbon copy of someone I could never be.

Right at the beginning of the shift I went for it and put listener calls on the air and they seemed positive. It wasn't easy airing the phone calls as I had to first record them on a reel-to-reel tape and shorten them for brevity and content if necessary.

That editing process was awkward and time consuming; the tape had to be listened to, the editing points marked with a white wax pencil, the tape lifted onto a splicing block where you cut it with a razor blade at a forty-five-degree angle to make a clean audio transition and then joined the two ends together using a thin, sticky splicing tape. After all that was done you would listen back to it to make sure the call flowed naturally before playing it on the air. If you were good and didn't run into any complications like tape drop outs or marking the wrong section then you could have it done within ten minutes.

Around twelve-forty the red "hotline" blinked into life. Very few people had the number for this internal line and you had to answer it ASAP as it meant someone important was calling. I picked it up and was instantly greeted by radio's most identifiable laugh!

"It's Jeddum Fishum here. Where's Danny?"

I explained that he wasn't coming in and I was covering for Danny covering for him which Jed thought was the single funniest thing he had heard that year. He'd planned the call with Danny so we went ahead with it anyway and I put him on the air and for the next three minutes we chatted live about the adventures the KROQ listeners were having with the jocks in Oahu.

We wrapped up the call with Jed introducing the new Oingo Boingo single, or "Ingy Bingy" as Jed liked to call them, "Private Life." Having Jed endorse me doing his show on the air meant a lot and filled me with new confidence.

I'd brought with me a half-dozen records that Dad had sent from England and I decided I'd start trying out some of those as my twice an hour jock's choice rather than continue to play it safe by slipping in already approved cuts that were available in the studio.

I punched the *on* button and leant forward to the mic, "It's Richard Blade in for Jed the Fish who right now is swimming around in the waters off of Waikiki, and I wanted to play you something new. I just received this from the record company back in the UK. It's a white-label twelve-inch that doesn't have any information on it except for two words that are hand-written so all I know about it is that it sounds totally awesome. Whether those two words are the name of the band or the name of the song, I'm not sure, but either way I'd love you to check it out so here goes; this is "Talk Talk" on K-Rock!"

As the needle tracked across the vinyl all four of the request lines lit up with excited listeners. Thirty minutes later as my next jock's choice rolled around I debuted another new song, this one was "Pale Shelter" from a group hailing from Bath, England, just seven miles from my birthplace, Bristol, Tears For Fears.

I flew through the next two hours fueled by pure energy that the music pumped through my body. The endless stream of calls on the request line encouraged me to keep going and play tracks that weren't ever heard on the radio, album cuts like "Europa and the Pirate Twins" by Thomas Dolby, B sides such as "Late Bar" from Duran Duran and fun dance tracks like The Thompson Twins' "In the Name of Love."

I also snuck in that seven-inch single that I'd fallen in love with after finding it in a used record store in Long Beach. I'd been playing it during the dead of night on KNAC and thought it sounded amazing on the air. It was on a small record label based in Southern California but the band had a European name and sang about London and Paris. I figured it would be perfect for KROQ so I introduced that band on my very first day on the air with, "Let's all take a little trip to Berlin, and if you're not sure how to get there, don't worry, we're riding 'The Metro.'"

That second three-hour show was, in a word, fun. I learned to relax and be myself, and whatever was to happen with Rick Carroll, I knew I'd done as well as I could. Even if it wasn't what Rick was looking for it had been the best I could do; I'd brought the show, put it all out there on the air and left nothing on the table. I was spent, exhausted but thrilled. It was that same feeling a runner gets when crossing the finish line after a 10K. You might not have the fastest time but you pushed yourself to a personal best and no one can take that away from you. With those endorphins flowing through me I inserted the top-of-the-hour ID cart and waited for the arrival of Elvira.

And waited. The required FCC ID played and I started the first song of the 3pm hour. No Mistress of the Dark. I stared at the studio door and willed it to open but the Force was weak in me that day and it remained closed. Now it was on to the second song of the hour and that meant a talk break was rapidly approaching. Now what? Freddy Snakeskin was in Hawaii and Elvira was nowhere to be found. I had to do something.

Maybe she was outside waiting in the reception area? I hated to leave the studio empty but I jumped out of my chair and hurried into the narrow corridor to look for her. No sign of the exotic, and AWOL, Elvira. Larry's and Rick's offices were empty too; I would learn later that it was rare for either of them to show up on a Monday as they would both be in their respective apartments face-down at the start of the work week, recovering from their wild weekends.

The only person in authority I could find was Pat Welsh, the station's general manager. His door was open, but despite the emergency, I acknowledged my lowly place in the scheme of things by knocking softly before going in. He was a tough-looking ginger with a ruddy complexion, a pockmarked face that hadn't seen a razor in years and a no-nonsense glare.

"Yes?" he boomed as he hit me with his intimidating stare.

"I'm Dick—Richard Blade, the guy on the air. The next DJ, Elvira, isn't here yet. Should I keep going?"

Pat looked puzzled. "You didn't get the message?"

My blank gaze obviously answered his question.

"She can't make it today. Her channel-nine TV taping got changed; she's shooting all afternoon. You okay to cover for her?"

I had two choices, say yes or tell him I was walking away and leaving the station to close down. I didn't think that would impress him.

"I can stay," I told him confidently.

"Good. Do you need a coffee or anything?"

"No. I'll grab some water. Better go before the song finishes." I sprinted down the hallway to the studio to start my third shift in a row and hour number seven on the air.

I completely understand that most people reading this book work much longer than seven hours a day on a regular basis and have little sympathy for my plight and in all honesty I don't expect any. My shift at KNAC, midnight to 6am, was six hours but it's very different doing an overnight program than being on during the busy daytime slots.

There's a reason most radio DJs only have three or four-hour shows and that's because the programs are so intense. No, you're not saving lives, chasing down bad guys or putting out fires and in the grand scheme of things being a DJ ranks right up there with unicorn handlers in terms of importance, but if you are doing it to the best of your ability, it is exhausting.

Some DJs just cruise; it's time, temperature and station ID—that's it. They don't care about the music and certainly have no interest in the listeners. They are just there because they lucked into the job and it's better (a lot better) than digging ditches. They are the ones you almost tune out on the air and you have no clue or even interest as to what their names are or the things they do when they are not on the radio, because they are not relating to you on a personal level.

The ones you remember, the ones who become your personal favorites, are the ones who come on the radio to work, to entertain you, to be that other person in the car next to you as you drive home, to be your friend when no one else gets you. They are the ones I continue to aspire to be as a DJ, so as I entered my seventh hour I forced any tiredness aside and tried to be that personality I would want to tune in to and hear on the radio.

For my jock's choices I worked in two more songs my father had sent me from England; one was a great track with boundless energy from Echo & the Bunnymen called "Back of Love" and the other was from a group that I was really starting to love, New Order with "Temptation."

My other jock choices were requests for records I had played earlier in the day from Berlin and Talk Talk and it made me feel great that the listeners were already so involved with the show that they remembered the names of the songs they had only just heard for the first time a few hours before. Not only that but they remembered my name too and were excited to talk with me!

But the biggest moment of the entire nine-hour marathon came at 5:25pm when a swear word changed the course of my life forever.

DJing the three shifts back-to-back was baptism by fire and so far I hadn't been burned. As I entered the five o'clock hour, my final sixty minutes on the air, I wanted to end strong.

At five twenty I broke for a stop set and ran the produced commercials first. I was into the final spot which was a live read for The Parrot Place in Van Nuys. I held the yellow four-by-six-inch card in my hand and read the live copy that extolled the virtues of the exotic birds in stock.

I had just reached the line "And through this weekend, macaws are on sale—" when the studio door opened and an older white-haired man wearing a suit leaned in.

"Where's Snakeskin?" he demanded.

I hit the microphone off for a second; said, "Hawaii"; turned it back on and continued, "so now through Sunday macaws are—"

"What's he doing in Hawaii?" the older man blustered.

I hit the mic off again and pleaded, "Please! I'm on the air right now."

I went back to the live read, "for only forty-nine, ninety-nine. Also available—"

"I need to speak to him," the interrupter announced loudly.

I am not a tough guy, and most people will tell you that I'm not a rude person either, but at that moment I was thrown for a loop and completely done. I punched the mic off and leapt to my feet. "Get the fuck out of the studio or I'll come over there and fucking throw you out."

Silence. The two eyes framed by that shock of white hair burned through me but he stepped back and pulled the studio door shut before things got totally out of hand. I sat down and attempted to pull myself together as I finally finished the live read.

I was back together and composed as I handed the studio over to Spacin' Scott Mason at 6pm. I stepped outside and ran into the GM, Pat Welsh, in the hallway.

"Good show," said Pat. "You were on for six hours?"

"No, nine," I replied. "I was in for Denise Westwood; started at nine."

Pat nodded respectfully. "That's a long time. Hopefully Elvira shows up tomorrow."

And Danny, I thought to myself.

Pat continued, "I've got someone who wants to meet you. Come with me."

I followed Pat down the short corridor to his office. He waved me in and sitting behind Pat's desk was the well-dressed white-haired man.

"I want you to meet Ken Roberts. He owns KROQ," said Pat as he pronounced my death sentence.

It had been more than eleven hours since I had eaten but the urge to throw up swept over me. Before I could do that, Ken Roberts spoke.

He addressed his question to Pat, ignoring me entirely, and said, "Ask him why he told me to fuck off."

Pat turned to me, and just in case I was stone deaf, repeated, "Why did you tell Mr. Roberts to fuck off?"

I took a breath and then stepped forward one pace so that I was right in front of Pat's desk and facing Ken.

"From what I understand the only way a radio station makes money is by selling commercials. I was on the air when some guy I didn't know barged into the studio and interrupted me three different times while I was reading a live commercial for the station. At that point I had two choices; one was to tell that person to shut the fuck up and get out of the studio and the other was to put the commercial down and have a nice little chat with him while I should have been working, and that would have meant that K-Rock wouldn't have gotten paid for that spot. And that's not going happen when I'm on the air. No one is going to take money away from a station I'm working for."

I finished and stood there, waiting for the death blow. The silence in the room was palpable. After a moment Ken Roberts leant forward, put his elbows on the desk and rested his chin in his hands. His gaze continued to be fixed on Pat Welsh, as if I weren't in the room. He finally spoke and when he did it was six words that would change everything for me from then on out.

"I like the kid. Hire him."

ROCK THIS TOWN

My parents could hear the joy in my voice when I called them Tuesday morning, June 15, 1982. I had so wanted to get on the phone and share the news with them the night before as soon as I walked out of Pat Welsh's office, to let them know that I'd gotten a job at KROQ, but even as excited as I was I kept in mind the eight-hour time difference between LA and the UK and I didn't want to wake them in the early hours of the morning.

Mum, always the reserved one, gave me a "That's nice, my love."

Dad was a lot more forthcoming. "Well done, lad," he said. "Let's see where this takes you."

Those were exactly my thoughts. Just where would this gig at KROQ get me? After all, as soon as the full-time DJs got back I would be relegated to weekends so I definitely had to make the most of doing a daily show during my remaining two weeks on the air. I had to give the audience my very best every second I was on the radio; to try and make an impact and "bring the show" just as I tried to do when working in a club.

Midway through my program I took a call from an excited young listener. She seemed "safe" so I took the chance and put her on live and unedited. I punched the phone line onto the air and hit the mic on. "It's KROQ. You're on the radio. What do you want to hear today?"

She giggled as she answered me, "Oh my God, Richard Blade, I love your accent. You sound so cute. What do you look like?"

"Two arms, two legs and all the good bits in between," I answered.

"Can you send me a picture?"

"Sure. Just let me have your request first."

"I don't want to hear anything special. I love all the music you guys play. But I do want your picture," she continued.

I was getting a little embarrassed. I wanted to be "the music guy," not have some listener rattling on without giving me a song cue. "Send me a letter at the station with a stamped addressed envelope inside and I'll send you a picture."

"You promise?"

"Yeah, I promise. Now let's play Missing Persons on K-R-O-Q!"

What I didn't realize was my casual promise created a monster. For the remaining ninety minutes of my show virtually every call was from listeners asking if I would send them a photograph as well so they could check out the new English DJ on their favorite radio station. I gave them all the same pat answer about mailing me a stamped addressed envelope.

Two days later when I arrived at the station the receptionist handed

My first KROQ publicity picture, June 17, 1982

me a large box with more than 200 letters in it. They were all requests for pictures!

That afternoon I had Scott Mason take a photo of me in my ever-present flight suit against the brick wall at the entrance to KROQ's little parking lot. Then it was off to Photomat to have 250 small three-by-five prints made. It was just a quick "snap" but it would have to do as a publicity photo because it was all I had and could afford and I was sure that 250 photos would more than take care of it.

At least, that's what I thought. The next day there were 200 more letters and by Saturday I had to print another 500 photos to sign and send out. At eleven cents a picture

I was already into it to the tune of approximately one hundred dollars. If the requests kept up at this speed I'd be broke before I even moved to part-time.

I became aware of some of the many idiosyncrasies of KROQ. The entire building had no electrical ground circuit. The engineer—and part-time DJ—Scott Mason had done a great job in dampening any hum in the studio and over the air that would be caused by the lack of a common ground, but because the building was ungrounded it meant that if there was a spike in the power in one area it could have an effect everywhere.

This was particularly noticeable with the copy machine. The entire top of the big Xerox would slide back and forth as it took the original being copied across the lighted tray below. Unfortunately, as it clicked its way back and forth, those loud clunks could be heard over the air and all across Southern California! This was really obvious during the slower songs we played like Duran Duran's "Save a Prayer" and Freur's "Doot-Doot."

What I had to do before I put on one of these quieter tracks was run out of the studio and plead with the sales staff to stop making copies of their billing or proposals for the next few minutes. If it was urgent and they couldn't hold off on their work, I would race back into the studio and stick on something loud and pumping like The Nails' "88 Lines about 44 Women" or Romeo Void's "Never Say Never." That way, the driving beat covered up the *click, click, click* of the copy machine, and if the listeners did hear those noises they would hopefully think they were extra beats coming from an exclusive KROQ remix.

Another huge problem that KROQ had was getting the signal from the control room of the KROQ building in Pasadena up to the transmitter in the Verdugo mountains that ring the San Gabriel valley.

Most stations used a microwave signal to send the transmission but KROQ was stuck with an old-fashioned underground landline system. Unfortunately the line was prone to problems including flooding during heavy rains or after any earth movement; this meant the signal could be lost and suddenly, without any warning, KROQ would go off the air.

I was in my second week filling in at KROQ when a sudden transmitter failure happened to me. All four request lines blazed with listeners saying they couldn't get KROQ. The music sounded fine in the control room but that's where it stopped.

Scott Mason made some calls and found out that our line had been severed during a road excavation. He zipped off to assess the damage and I sat in the studio with nothing to do.

Thirty minutes later Scott called and said it was pretty serious and it could be hours before it was fixed. I told him to let the next DJ, Danny Elfman, know about it and not to come in and I would stay on at the station until it—hopefully—came back on the air.

Three hours passed and Pat Welsh walked into the studio. He was a salesman at heart and our lost signal had made him very upset. And that was understandable; we had missed playing almost forty minutes of scheduled commercials already. That meant a lot of refunds going back to the advertisers.

"This is terrible," he said. I could see the frustration written across his face as he paced back and forth in the tiny control room.

I had an idea. "Can you let me have one hundred and six dollars and seven cents to give away?" I asked.

"KROQ *never* gives away money," he stated. "And anyway, how would that help?"

"When we do get the transmitter line fixed I'll play all of the commercials non-stop, back-to-back until they have all aired. Then you don't have to do any refunds to our advertisers."

"Okay. But why the money?" Pat asked.

"Because we'll make it a contest. 'Count the commercials.' We've already missed so many. No one would sit through all of them without an incentive and your clients know that. But if we do a contest and give away the money to the first caller who has correctly counted the number of spots then we can keep everyone listening."

It only took the businessman in Pat a moment to see the logic in my idea: spend one hundred and six dollars and seven cents to save thousands.

"I like it," he said. "I can clear the money. Just get me the winner's name and number. And tell me when we get the signal back." With that Pat left the control room.

Twenty minutes later Scott called and said the problem was fixed and the transmitter was on the air.

I punched up my microphone, "And we are back. Hope you enjoyed that little quiet interlude for reflection and meditation, but now we return to punishment as usual with The Ramones, and right after that I'll let you know how you can win money, real money—one hundred and six dollars and seven cents from 106.7, K-Rock."

As the song played I readied the stack of commercials. Because we had been off the air for over four hours several of the commercials would play more than once so I had to keep track and make sure the listeners counted them each time they played.

I teased the contest again and spun two more songs to allow the listeners to return and then went over the rules of the contest. Each time a commercial played regardless of whether it was sixty seconds long, thirty seconds or a live read it counted as one. Keep track of them all, add them up and be the first caller with the correct total and you win the money!

I started on the longest commercial stop set in American radio history. We had been off for close to four and a half hours and on average had a commercial load of fourteen minutes an hour. That meant our poor listeners had to endure almost sixty-three minutes of ads back-to-back, a total of one hundred and eleven commercials!

Amazingly, all the request lines were blazing throughout and after I finished with the final sales pitch I started picking up the phone and by the fourth call we had a winner who screamed so loudly down the line that I thought she would blow out the transmitter a second time.

We had zero complaints from the sponsors or the listeners. Instead I received a thank you from Pat and from our sales manager, John McLaughlin. It made me feel good and I knew I was slowly building a legitimate place for myself at the station.

Quay Hays was the promotion director at KROQ. His job was to keep the radio station's name out on the streets and make sure that our image came across as hip to the kids. Quay was perfect for the job. He oozed cool. He was tall, blonde, wore blue-tinted glasses and Italian leather shoes. He looked as if he had walked in from hanging out at an all-night movie premiere party in the Hollywood Hills. In truth he had just walked in from the airport.

Quay had come back from Hawaii more than a week early because he was needed to coordinate all of the activities that KROQ was involved in and to make sure they went off as planned. He strolled into the studio and waited until I was on a break.

"Next Tuesday afternoon at one you'll be off the air, right?"

"I should be," I replied. "What do you need?"

"We're doing a free lunchtime concert at the Country Club in Reseda. I need someone to introduce the band. Can you do that?"

"Sure, I'd be happy to. Who's the group?"

"It's Joan Jett. Do you know her?"

Joan Jett! I'd loved her music since the days of The Runaways.

"No, I've never met her but I know her music of course."

"Okay. So I can count on you being there?" Quay asked.

"Sure. It'll be fun."

"Great. I'll get you the details by Monday. Feel free to talk about the show on the air." Quay turned and left the studio.

It was already stinking hot by noon the day of the show. This was the kind of LA weather that alerts you to the fact that Southern California is in for a long, blistering summer. The Country Club was packed to the rafters for the free show and its already inadequate air conditioning system was struggling to even circulate the air, never mind cool it. With a capacity crowd jammed inside and the sun burning down outside, it was way too hot to change into jeans and a t-shirt so I hit the stage for my very first KROQ concert in a striped tank top and Dolphin shorts.

Even though I'd introduced much bigger shows in Bakersfield I was nervous; I wanted to make a good impression. Plus Joan Jett was famous as a "punk"; I didn't know how she would be in person. But everything went incredibly well. I threw t-shirts out from the stage, got the crowd screaming and when Joan walked out she gave me a big smile and said into the microphone, "Let's hear it for Richard Blade."

That was a big deal for me; it was the first time an artist had acknowledged me onstage. She didn't have to do that but she did, and I was elated by her kindness.

As I started my second week on the air at KROQ I received a letter from Dad, one that touched me

Introducing Joan Jett at the Country Club, Reseda – June 1982

deeply. I had always hoped he was excited for me and not mad that I had walked away from my education, and as I read his hand-written words I realized that his love exceeded even my wildest dreams. His letter was dated Monday, 21 June and read:

Hi—Congratulations on your appointment at such an important LA Radio Station as KROC. By the time this reaches you work may have commenced. We wish you all the best and sincerely hope you will be happy with your colleagues and programming etc. Thanks for phoning to tell us . . . we were really thrilled and talked of it for quite a while after we put the phone down! It is good too that your journey finally has been rewarded. Do tell us more when you have settled in . . . I expect that your present colleagues will miss you very much. We are so happy for you at the progress you are making, and determination, skill and professionalism like yours will surely get you to the top.

Those words meant so much to me. So often in life we don't express what we feel, particularly coming from England where we are raised to keep our emotions to ourselves, but here was my father telling me to go for it. I couldn't imagine having better parents and couldn't wait to see Mum and Dad again and hold them and tell them everything that was happening.

I folded the letter carefully and knew that I would keep it forever.

They say all good things must come to an end, and sure enough, my two weeks filling in sped by and the full-time air staff returned from Oahu, tanned and exhausted. They had partied so hard for fourteen days straight that they could barely function for their first couple of shifts.

Rick Carroll held a rare jock meeting to introduce me as the new production director and weekend guy then brought in Quay to go over the station's largest promotion ever. It was a concert, but one that was bigger than anything held in Southern California before.

Quay stood up in that tiny room and addressed the jocks. "It's called the US Festival. A big computer guy is putting it on. It's three days during Labor Day weekend. We have the first day exclusively, New Wave Day, Friday, the third of September. Every band on the lineup is one of ours."

"I hope they booked some good ones," said Dusty Street sarcastically. "I'm not going if it's Killer Pussy and The Buggles."

"Oh yeah, they're good. Gang of Four, The Police, Oingo Boingo, The English Beat, B-52s, The Ramones and Talking Heads. They are saying that they should have 200,000 people there."

"Wow. Woodstock 1982," exclaimed Jed the Fish.

"Exactly," smiled Rick. "But this time it's our Woodstock and our music."

It was my job to get the promos for the concert cut and I tried to make them as exciting as possible. This was in addition to recording the commercials as soon as the sales people brought them to me and cutting drops for the jocks. I spent most days at the station with barely a break.

I'd only been full-time at KROQ for a little over a week when Quay approached me directly.

"We have a commercial buy coming in from The Roxy on Sunset," he said. "They want to do a regular KROQ night once a week and the booker there likes the sound of you on the air and thinks you would be right for it with your accent and everything. Have you ever worked in a club before?"

"KROQ Night at The Roxy with Richard Blade" got underway on July 13, 1982. It was every Tuesday from eight until two, but I would only have to DJ from 10pm until 1a.m.; their house DJ would cover the rest. Right away the night was a hit and attracted not just the local Hollywood crowd but also kids from as far away as the Valley and the South Bay. And for me to have my own night at a legendary venue like The Roxy was almost beyond belief. I would get misty-eyed seeing my name on that marquee.

It was my third week at The Roxy, on July 27, when I received a visitor in the DJ booth. He was the lead singer of the band who had performed earlier that night at The Greek Theatre. Simon LeBon had wanted to go out and party after his show and had heard that The Roxy was the place to be. He showed up without an entourage but clutching a white-label twelve-inch record.

"It's the dance mix of our next single. Would you play it?" Simon asked.

I grabbed the microphone and announced to the crowd that the lead singer of Duran Duran was there and this was their new single. I put on "Rio" and almost immediately lost half of the dance floor.

"Shit," exclaimed Simon. "That's not good."

"It's new,'" I reassured him. "They'll love it when they get to know it. Watch."

I segued into "Girls on Film" and in seconds the kids were pushing and elbowing their way back onto the dance floor.

"That's more like it," said Simon. "One of the things John and I always try to do is make music you can dance to." And with that he was gone, off to the bar for a drink and to flirt with his growing number of female fans.

With Simon LeBon at The Roxy, July 1982

KROQ was a unique radio station to work for. You felt as if you were a part of something special. Everywhere you went, you would pick up on the buzz on the street. KROQ was the barometer for hipness in Southern California. If you weren't listening to it constantly you felt that you were falling behind.

This applied to the jocks as well. In Bakersfield, San Luis Obispo and at KNAC, when you got off the air the last thing you wanted to hear was the station you were working for. You'd put on anything else. The reason? All the other stations were predictable. You knew what was going to happen next, what song would play, what promo would run, even what the DJ on the air would say. But at KROQ it was different.

We were allowed so much freedom that no one ever knew what would come blaring out of their radio next. The genius of Rick Carroll was that he encouraged you to be better than the music. If you had something exciting, funny or great to say then say it. If you had a new song that was better than the one scheduled to play then pull off the one from the rotation and play yours. If someone walked in the studio who was interesting, put them on the air. It was radio like it should be, radio designed to entertain the listener, not just to sell them commercials. Rick made a point to stress this.

"There are no bad shifts on KROQ," Rick told us. "The same listeners that tune into Ramondo and Evans in the morning will be back at lunch time, then in the afternoon and last thing at night before they go to sleep. They are always there. And if they are being that loyal to us then we have to be loyal to them. We need to constantly be reinventing the station and ourselves, making sure there's nowhere else for them to go for our kind of DJs or music. Remember, we don't play new wave or punk or rock; we play KROQ music."

Sadly, for all his brilliance and innovation, Rick was a deeply troubled soul and struggled constantly with drugs. Sometimes he would disappear for weeks at a time only to reappear with a phone call from a motel room in Orange County or Santa Barbara. When Rick was gone Freddy Snakeskin would step in as acting program director and make sure that things got (mostly) done. It was during one of Rick's benders that I got a huge opportunity.

It was the end of the first week of August that Denise Westwood gave her notice. She was leaving and heading across town to KMET for double her current salary. This meant the nine-to-noon shift was open. No one had heard from Rick Carroll for over two weeks and Pat had put Freddy back in charge of running the station. Faced with Denise's sudden departure, Freddy called us all in for a meeting that Friday afternoon.

"So Westwood is leaving. That's fine with me," he said. "Now we can put someone in who's got a grain of talent and get some ratings there at last. I've asked Rachel Donahue to join the station and take the slot. I've already put together a new ad showing the change."

Freddy showed us the ad, then continued with some rather unsavory comments about Denise and her personal habits.

What Freddy—or any of us—didn't know was that Denise Westwood was dating Mike Evans and they were getting serious. As Freddy laid into Denise's reputation, Mike started to boil. He was going to do one of two things: knock Freddy out in that meeting or embarrass him on the air. Fortunately for me, Mike chose the latter.

As soon as the meeting was over Mike secretly called KMET and asked them for a job, any job. That night he met with the bosses at the Mighty

MET and they offered him a position as sports reporter on their morning show and he took it. With that in place, Mike made his plans to exact revenge on Freddy.

The next morning, at around 9:30, Mike drove to the station in Pasadena and walked into the studio while Ian Whitcomb, one of KROQ's weekend jocks was on the air doing his Saturday shift.

"I was in the area and thought I'd come by," said Mike with a big smile.

Ian was flattered. It was not often that one of the full-time DJs, especially one half of the fabled morning team, would drop in on his show.

"Do you want to say hi to the listeners?" asked Ian innocently.

"Sure," replied Mike and he walked around to Ian's side of the console.

Ian hit the microphone on as the record faded, "It's K-R-O-Q and look who is in the studio with me. Mike Evans! What brings you here this morning, Mike?"

Mike leant forward and held his finger down on the *on* button for the microphone. Now he couldn't be silenced. "Well, Ian, I know what you and all the listeners are thinking and that's 'What's the Hose doing at KROQ on a Saturday morning?' The answer is that I came here especially to tell you I'm leaving this shithole and going to KMET starting Monday with Jeff Gonzer on their morning show, so you can join me and Denise Westwood on 94.7 or stay here listening to that fat idiot Snakeskin. And by the way, his real name is Scott Campbell but he answers to 'asshole.' Talk to you on the Mighty Met Monday morning—whoo yah!"

Mike strode out of the studio and the station leaving Ian sitting there, stunned. Behind him the hotline lit up and furiously blinked red as Freddy Snakeskin desperately called in to silence the broadcast.

Two days later I received a phone call at home from Freddy. "Mr. Snake here. How do you feel about getting up early tomorrow? If you can be at the station by six I'd like you to do the morning show with Ramondo." And that one simple call created the morning team of Ramondo and The Blade.

For me, having the opportunity to do mornings with Raymond was a match made in heaven. His timing was superb, his wit dry and funny, and his hands-on technical ability with the equipment was precise and kept

RAMONDO AND THE BLADE
KROQ 106.7 FM

Photo courtesy of Joel Gelfand

our show driving non-stop through the morning. Every day I couldn't wait to get on the air with him and I bounded up the back stairs of the KROQ building eager to learn new tricks and techniques from Raymond.

And the enthusiasm wasn't just on my side. The listeners responded in droves and within days of our becoming a team we had girls at the back door bearing donuts and coffee as gifts, waiting for us to arrive. We were inundated with offers to appear at store openings and to MC fashion shows and school dances. Even Pat Welsh noticed and actually spent some money on hiring a photographer to take official publicity shots of his new morning show team. We knew we were at the beginning of a wild and crazy ride together.

Rick returned to KROQ and took back his position as program director. With me now on the morning show it meant that I was only working one Saturday shift every other week so the station was short of weekend air personalities. Rick asked if I knew anyone who was good and could fit in with the KROQ format. I didn't hesitate. I recommended Katy Manor, telling Rick that she was as good as it gets. I knew that Katy had left Magic 98 in Bakersfield and was now working at KBOS in Fresno but was desperate to get out of there.

In minutes I had Katy on the phone with Rick and he arranged for her to do an on-air tryout that coming weekend. As soon as he said that I knew Katy would get the job. I was so happy to be able to help her a little. Even though there was no longer any romance between us, I still considered her to be a dear friend and a great asset to any radio station lucky enough to have her on staff.

Considered the ultimate KROQ '80s on-air lineup, August 1982

With Rachel Donahue doing mid-days and Katy rocking the weekends, the station sounded as Rick had always wanted it to, with no bad shifts, no wasted day parts. Tune into KROQ anytime and you would hear someone who was giving you their all. Just like that, one of LA's most formidable on-air lineups was in place.

At the end of August I began getting some ribbing from the other jocks because that's when a book was published that featured me in it. It was called *Lady's Choice: A Guide To The Eligible Bachelors of Los Angeles*.

I'd been approached to be in it about five months before when I was DJing at Le Hot Club. They arranged for me to go to a studio to shoot some photos and took down my bio and then I heard nothing more from them. That was until my first day on the air at KROQ. I received a call from the editor who said he recognized my voice and asked if Richard Blade and Dick Sheppard were the same. When I asked why he said I had made the book and they were going to rush and try to have my name corrected before it went to press. And now I was holding the book.

The shock was that I not only made the top one hundred bachelors, I was voted the number-one most eligible bachelor in Los Angeles! I didn't talk about it on the air but the other DJs did and a lot of listeners saw the book and the mail I was receiving more than doubled. The person who was most excited was my mum. I sent her a copy of the book and she called me with a word or two of advice.

"Better be careful now, my love," she cautioned. "A lot of women will see this and get the wrong idea about you, that you're out there just to meet girls and you wouldn't want that now would you?"

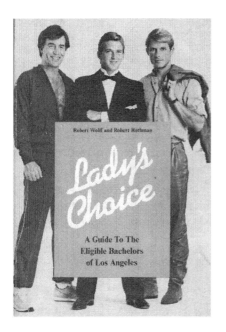

HERE COME THE BACHELORS—beginning with the top vote getter, Richard Blade. Following Richard are 114 of the finest bachelors Los Angeles has to offer, in alphabetical order.

RICHARD BLADE

Height: 6' 2"	**Hair:** brown
Weight: 160	**Eyes:** blue
Birth Date: 5-23-52	**Place of Birth:** Bristol, England

Occupation: Production Director and Disc Jockey for KROQ

Here he is, ladies—our highest-rated bachelor. Richard says that "a person's reach should exceed their grasp—so reach for the stars!" This Oxford-educated bachelor left England to embark on a radio career, and when he was firmly established as the top-rated disc jockey on the central coast (Z93 in San Luis Obispo), he flexed his muscles and reached out again—this time to Los Angeles, where he currently is the production director at KROQ, co-hosts the morning show, and also uses his English background to host the nationally syndicated "BBC Rock Hour."

Richard's friends describe him as being "honest, reliable, and a lot of fun." Witness the following story: "When I was program director of Z93 I was having a meeting with the disc jockeys. Suddenly, one of the jocks said, 'Did you see that?', obviously referring (from the tune of his voice) to a passing lady. Something struck me— and for some reason I grabbed a record and dashed out of the station after this girl whom I had not yet seen. I tapped her on the shoulder and she turned round—and boy, was she gorgeous. However, I kept my cool and said with a straight face, 'Excuse me, what radio station do you listen to?' She replied, 'Z93.' I then told her that was the correct answer and she had won two prizes. I gave her the album. She thanked me and asked what the other prize was. I told her it was a date with a disc jockey. She paused for a second, then with a big smile she said, 'You, right?' That night we had dinner at a lovely beachside restaurant. It was a very exciting start to what turned out to be a great relationship."

Seafood, backgammon, and dancing constitute an ideal date for Richard—provided it's with a woman who has a keen sense of humor, alertness, "and a sparkle in her eyes." He's turned off by cold, aloof, unreliable women.

"If I like a woman, I will certainly go out of my way to pursue her, but the more I pursue, the more I'm aware of the pursuit—and if it doesn't work out, I'll back off. I don't believe in forcing myself upon another person."

Comparing American to English women, Richard says, "American women are much more open in their attitudes, emotions and sexual behavior. Their ambitions go beyond the kitchen sink. Equality is the goal in American relationships; in England, one person or the other is dominant."

Richard loves the fact that miniskirts are coming back. "I also love

3

Errr . . . actually I would but I couldn't say that to my mother so I agreed with her antiquated views and sent my love to her and Dad down the transatlantic phone line.

With everything that was happening at KROQ, time began to speed by and even gather momentum, like a race car accelerating from the starting line. Before we knew it September 3 had arrived and Raymond and I were shuttled out to Glen Helen Regional Park to appear onstage at the US Festival. We were awestruck at what we saw waiting for us.

The stage was massive, almost as big as a football field, and the scaffolding around it towered a hundred feet into the air with giant video screens stretched out on either side. But that stage paled in comparison to the crowd; they reached as far as the eye could see. The entire level area in front of the stage going back over 400 yards was jammed with people standing shoulder to shoulder and that mass of new wave fans continued all the way up the hills that framed the natural arena.

HERALD EXPRESS, SATURDAY, OCTOBER 2, 1982 **7**

THE BEST OF THE BACHELOR BUNCH

WHO do you think is the most eligible bachelor in Los Angeles? Burt Reynolds? Ryan O'Neal? Wrong — the man a panel of wide-eyed women voted the best of the bunch is Torquay man Richard Sheppard, now one of California's leading disc jockeys.

Richard has been working in the States for the past six years and came home last week for his father's funeral. His mother lives in Chelston.

Known as Richard Blade on

KROQ, the station on which he has a morning show, this former BBC radio announcer is becoming hot property.

"I did a TV special hosting the Playgirl magazine search for a centrefold, and I have one of the lead roles in the movie," he said.

However, he does not feel he is eligible for centre spread poses! "I want to get into television and I do not want to ruin my career that way," he laughed.

The two of us stood side by side in the wings waiting to go on. We had nothing prepared and now we had to fill for ten minutes before bringing on The B-52s. Raymond's look spoke volumes, and those words were "Holy shit!"

The sound tech signaled that he was ready to the stage manager who said to us, "Go out there. Be funny," and physically pushed us onto that cavernous stage. We hit the center mics and Raymond went first.

"I'm Ramondo," he yelled into the microphone.

"And I'm the Blade," I said.

The crowd roared when they heard our names. They were all KROQ listeners and pumped to be at such a revolutionary show. The screams continued for what seemed like forever and we had to pause because there was no way to be heard over that wall of sound. Finally we had to speak. I went first.

"Are all you guys in line for the bathroom?" I joked.

"Damn, I knew I should have gone before we got here," responded Raymond picking up on my wisecrack.

"Which one of you brought the toilet paper?" I asked.

The audience loved it and the next few minutes flew by. I think I was almost in a trance up there until I heard Raymond and myself saying together, ". . . The B-52s!" We ran offstage and promised each other we would never forget the thrill of that moment.

Onstage at the US Festival, Sept 3, 1982

Forty minutes later when The B-52s finished their set, their lead singer Fred Schneider came up to us backstage and said, "I am officially changing the name of this from the US Festival to the Dust Festival!"

When that incredible party band from Athens, Georgia, had hit the stage with "Private Idaho" the whole crowd started pogoing and those 200,000 people turned the US Festival into the world's largest mosh pit, stirring up the dry, baked soil and creating a dust cloud that obscured them from the stage. The dust and the heat remained merciless as the anvil of the sun beat down upon the concert-goers for the entire weekend with daytime highs being recorded at around 111 degrees. But I loved every red-hot second of it.

Four days after the US Festival wrapped up I received a call from Anne Beats. She was a five-time Emmy-nominated writer on *Saturday Night Live* and was now filming her own show that she'd created for CBS. She wanted to know if I would like to be one of the recurring characters in it.

The show was *Square Pegs* and starred a young girl called Sarah Jessica Parker. It was about trying to fit in at high school and Anne had thought it would be funny if I played the manager of all the bands that stopped by the school to perform. The joke would be that my accent was so thick that the only per-

With Stewart Copeland of The Police, Backstage at the US Festival – Sept. 1982

son who could understand me was one of the students who was a hip punk kid and he had to translate my words to everyone else.

The bands she had lined up for her TV show came straight from the KROQ playlist—The Waitresses, Jimmy and the Mustangs and Devo. Of course I said yes and just two days later I was on the set at an abandoned school in Long Beach shooting the first episode.

Anne Beats wasn't the only one in the industry to hear about what was happening over at 106.7; KABC TV picked up on the buzz and on Tuesday, the fourteenth of September, sent over a crew to shoot us for *Eye on LA* as host Paul Moyer described us as "LA's fastest-rising morning show."

It seemed that every phone call Raymond and I got brought nothing but good news, with more and more offers coming our way. We were unstoppable. But nature has a way of keeping you grounded. For every high there is a low, and for me the worst low of my life arrived in the form of a call I received on Thursday afternoon, September 16, 1982.

On the set of Square Pegs with The Waitresses – September 1982

MAD WORLD

It was a little before five in the afternoon and I was still at KROQ, locked in the production room working on features for tomorrow's morning show with Raymond. There was a soft knock on the door and Katy leaned hesitantly inside.

"Dick—Richard," she said, her voice subdued as it is so often when someone is the bearer of bad news. "Pat Welsh wants to see you in his office."

I stood up and somehow knew immediately what I was about to hear. I looked Katy in eyes and said, "I'm either being fired or my dad's dead."

There was not a trace of humor in my voice. I knew for a fact that it had to be one of those two things.

Tears welled up in Katy's eyes and I knew it was the worst possible scenario. I pushed past her and ran to Pat's office as if my speed would change the news that I knew I was about to hear.

Pat stood there, waiting for me, behind his desk. His phone was off the hook. He looked down at it and said simply, "It's your mother. I'll leave you alone." Pat left his office, shutting the door behind him.

I stared at the phone. I hated it. Picking it up was the last thing I wanted to do. If I smashed it or hurled it out of the window maybe that would silence the horrific message it held for me. But I could do neither; my mum was waiting to talk to me and now, more than ever before in her life, she needed to hear my voice even if I was dreading her words.

I picked up the phone, "Mum?"

"It's your Dad," the little voice said over the phone. "He's gone. We've lost him."

Somehow words formed in my mouth, "How?"

"He was in bed. One minute he was there with me and the next he was gone. I'm waiting for the doctor but the ambulance man said it was a heart attack." She paused, not believing her own words, "He just died. My big, strong husband died. Reg is gone."

The world became a tiny place at that moment. There was only my mother and I who existed, no one else, the two of us united by my father's death, both of us also dying inside.

I forced myself to keep control, "How about Stephen? Have you told him?"

"He's in the south of France with Winky. I can't reach him."

"Mum, I'm going to the airport right now to fly over and see you. I'll be there tomorrow, I promise."

"Thank you, my love. Travel safely, please."

I hung up and left Pat's office. He was waiting for me outside his door. He spoke first.

"Take as much time as you need. We'll all be thinking of you."

I raced home to Sherman Oaks, grabbed my passport, money and some clothes including my dark suit and hurried to LAX. I caught a flight leaving at 9:30 that got me into Heathrow the next afternoon.

It was pouring rain as I picked up a rental car and sped the 200 miles south to Torquay. The motorway had a speed limit of seventy but despite the weather I pushed "a ton"—one hundred miles an hour—most of the way. I tuned into BBC Radio One and *Rosko's Round Table* was on. It was a weekly show that had celebrity guests reviewing new music. Rosko introduced a song that was about to be released the following week.

"Check this one out; it's a band from Bath with their third single. Their first two didn't do anything in the charts but they are hoping this one breaks that losing streak. They're called Tears for Fears and this is "Mad World.""

The song came on and everything about it grabbed me, from the title, to the vocals, to the beat that matched the sweep of the wiper blades across the windshield as they battled the torrential rain.

To me I was living in a mad world. How could there be any sanity when this man who had done nothing but help people all his life, spent years serving in the military and worked on early radar to combat the German blitz and then raised his two boys in a house full of love and laughter was struck down and taken from us so young?

Curt Smith's hauntingly beautiful voice tore through my heart as he sang about having no tomorrow. I felt the same way—how could there possibly be a tomorrow when my father, the person who had been responsible for my life, was no longer here to share it with me?

On the plane over from LA, I had been unable to sleep for any length of time and during those restless moments images of my Dad had filled my mind; in them he was still alive, still so vibrant and strong, so I totally related to Curt and Roland's words as their song continued to speak just to me that the dreams in which they were dying were the best that they had ever had. Now it would only be in my dreams that I could find happiness and see my father again. Would those be my best moments?

My body shook as tears poured from my eyes and I became two people; one who was in an instinctive mode driving that speeding car as it cut through the downpour, and the other, a lost little boy running home to get out of the rain and find comfort and safety with his heartbroken mother.

Mrs. Northcott, ever the kind neighbor, was sitting with Mum when I arrived a little after six that evening. She gave me a hug, went into the kitchen to put the kettle on for tea and left Mum and me alone.

My mother told me the story of what had happened. Some of it I knew from Dad's letters.

Stephen and his girlfriend/mother of his child, William, who was barely one year old, were away on an extended vacation in Monaco, France. Stephen had left his newborn son at number 22 for over two months and Dad and Mum had been given the responsibility of looking after the baby boy and auditioning nannies to take care of him. With everything my father had taken upon his shoulders, he was stressed and not sleeping.

The night of the sixteenth a new girl had just started in the hopes of becoming William's nanny and was staying in the guest room.

Mum and Dad went to bed late, around midnight, and Mum tearfully went over those final terrible minutes. "He said he felt fine. He was talking about coming back to see you in America again. He couldn't wait. He told me how much he was looking forward to that holiday and finally getting some rest. We got into bed and he kissed me goodnight. I reached over to him to give him a kiss and he was stiff."

She caught her breath as she realized the accidental double entendre. "Not like that! I mean he was stiff, dead—just suddenly. I tried to roll him out of bed and beat on his chest but nothing worked. The poor girl came in, saw Reg lying there and screamed and ran out the door. She just left in the middle of the night. I don't know where she went. I called the ambulance but by the time they got here they couldn't do anything."

The enormity of everything she had been through hit her. "What are we going to do?"

My mother cried in anguish and despair, and I held her tightly in my arms as she wept and wept for her husband.

Her pain was deep on so many levels. Both she and Dad were children of World War I, born into a time of great uncertainty and terror. My mother was only a few weeks old when her father passed away and as the youngest of eight children she watched as her mother struggled to make ends meet.

Twice her mother, my Nanny McCann, fought off bailiffs and police who arrived at her door to drag her off to Eastville Workhouse at 100 Fishponds Road, the dreaded paupers' prison that no one ever left alive. More than 3,500 bodies are buried in unmarked graves on that site and Nana was determined not to become another fatality.

"Who will look after my little ones if I'm gone?" the tiny Irish lady screamed as she beat the police away. "And don't you be coming back neither!"

Nanny and her children all worked hard to get by and just as my mother reached her teens, instead of finding the fun and freedom that kids of that age long for, she watched the planet plunge into the Great Depression. If times were bad before, now they were much, much worse.

Things changed when she met my father. Mum was working as a bus conductor and Dad fell instantly in love with this uniformed, auburn-haired beauty. He changed his schedule going to and from the school where he had just started as a math teacher and made sure he only rode on the routes she was working even though it meant an extra half-mile walk each way.

They married in 1938 and less than a year later my father was approached by the Ministry of Defense to use his math skills on a radar program called

Chain Home. The clouds of war were gathering and Britain needed to be prepared for the onslaught that was coming.

Dad was taken from Bristol and from Mum and relocated to the east coast of England where he remained for four years. The program he was working on was so secret that he was forbidden to even reveal its name and what he had done with them until twenty-years after the war's end because of the Official Secrets Act.

When he came home on leave he was unable to tell his wife what part of the country his unit was located in and what they were developing, but he did find time to take her away from Bristol and the massive bombing raids there to the West Country. It was during one of his leaves that they discovered Torquay.

Mum and Dad strolling the Torquay seafront, 1943

He became highly respected amongst his fellow soldiers and the civilian scientists who oversaw the project and in his free time was quite an athlete, playing football and becoming captain of the cricket "eleven" that played other units around the country and gave everyone's minds a much needed respite from the horrors of the war around them.

My father, Reg Sheppard, with his regiment's "eleven"; he has the bat

He left the army in 1946 with the rank of major in the Royal Artillery. They asked him to stay and become a career officer but Mum was having none of that. She didn't like to travel and certainly didn't want to raise her son Stephen, who was turning one year old, as an "army brat." Reluctantly Dad left the military, his friends and his already esteemed career and returned to teaching.

Dad took care of all the finances for Mum. She ran the house, and ran it well, but Dad made sure the bills were paid and that we had enough to make it through each month even on a meager teacher's salary. When times got tough he would take a second job, evenings and during the summer, using his math skills to oversee the cashiers at Newton Abbott Race Track. It was a long, thankless job and it meant he had to arrive before the first race and stay long after the track was closed to make sure the books were balanced, but our family needed the money so he worked hard providing it for us.

With him gone Mum was understandably devastated. Not only had she lost the man she loved but she didn't know how to drive and had never written a check in her life or used a credit card. That was Dad's world and now she was flung headfirst into it. I spent hours with her explaining how to fill out a check correctly, how to use a ledger and keep a rolling balance. She was frustrated at first but quickly stepped up and grasped the information.

It took two days to locate my brother, Stephen. By the time he arrived in Torquay I had taken care of the death certificate and, with Mum's help, the funeral arrangements. Dad was to be buried near his parents at a cemetery in Bristol. I asked Mum if it would be all right to see Dad before he was moved there. He was being kept at a mortuary nearby.

I had never been in a mortuary before. I stood outside the room where the mortician had my father's body prepared and waiting for me.

"He's inside," he said.

I stepped into the freezing room and saw my hero lying there on a table. My knees buckled and I fell to the floor. But I didn't want to leave. My father deserved more. I had to say goodbye to him.

I picked myself up and lay my head on his chest. His body no longer had any semblance to anything living. It was hard and he felt like a cold plastic doll.

Tears poured from my eyes and I cried like I hadn't since I was a young child. They fell from my face onto his. If this had been a movie my teardrops would have caused some essence of life that remained within him to stir; his fingers would twitch, his eyelids would flutter and he would come back to me, come back to us.

But there was no musical crescendo, no Hollywood happy ending. He lay there unmoving. My tears pooled on his face and then streamed down his cheeks as if he were crying for me as I was crying for him.

I wiped my eyes and gently dabbed his face dry and spoke softly to my father, telling him how grateful I was for his love and his caring and oh, how I would miss him. As I stepped back something amazing happened.

I'm not a religious person but I do believe that somehow we are all connected, and I don't mean just humans, I mean *all*, everything that lives somehow shares the same bond of life. And at that moment I felt the spirit of life fill the room as my father gave me his final gift.

Suddenly it was me lying there on that slab, dead. And I was standing looking at my own body. I turned to my left and my father was right there next to me.

He looked me in the eyes and spoke to me so clearly: "That will be you one day, my son. Remember that. Don't waste a minute, because one day it will all end." He smiled, that warm, beautiful smile he had, and he was back on the slab and I was alone, standing there in that cold room.

I know this may come across as dark and depressing, but for me, in that instant, I was given an amazing awareness of life itself. Too often we go through our lives thinking that everything will last forever and we forget to *live* to our fullest potential, believing we have all the time in the world.

My father showed me how wrong that viewpoint is. When you know that something is finite you enjoy it so much more while you have it; you cherish it; you want to make the most of it, to take every opportunity you can.

From that day on the way I looked at life altered. I was freed of so many doubts. We can plan for tomorrow but we have to live today, in the moment, because time is so fleeting that we may never have that chance again. The worst thing that ever happened to me, my father's death, allowed me to glimpse the inevitable future and in doing so breathed new life into my soul.

Time itself changed in that room. The awareness that swept over me, that swept away any fears I had, became my new starting point for life. It was no longer September 20, 1982, it was Day Four A.D.—After Dad. I vowed that from that second onwards I would keep my father's spirit with me and share my life with him. During every high, and even during the lows, I would take a second to stop and say "This is for you, Dad."

I left Torquay a week later. Before I headed out I made Mum promise to keep to the plans that she had made with Dad to come to Los Angeles in just a few months and stay with me.

As I drove back to Heathrow I had two things with me that I didn't have on the drive down: I wore my father's wedding ring on my right hand to carry his love with me everywhere I went, and in my bag was a copy of "Mad World" which had arrived at the house two weeks before in a promotional mailing. It was the very last record package that my Dad had opened and listened to for me. He had rejected most of the rest but on that Tears for Fears' twelve-inch he wrote "I think you'll like this one." He was right as always.

"Mad World" would be the first song I played on my show when I returned to the air waves on KROQ days later. It was his final musical pick, not just for me but for all the KROQ kids.

Part Two: A.D.

NEW LIFE

It was a relief when I was welcomed back to KROQ by both the jocks and the management. In the back of my mind I was concerned that they were going to say they had found someone else while I was gone but instead it was just the opposite.

With those final moments I had spent with my father still flooding my mind and body with inspiration I threw myself into my work and found that with everything that was happening I had virtually no free time which in many ways was a good thing as it stopped me from dwelling on my loss.

After our morning show Raymond and I would head straight to the production room to work together on produced bits to air on our show the next day. Then I would put together a two-minute segment that I'd started when I was part-time called *ROQ Notes* which ran every morning and afternoon on KROQ. When that was finished I would voice commercials for the station, then race down to Long Beach to shoot my cameos for the TV show *Square Pegs*. Virtually every evening you would find me behind the turntables in a club: The Roxy on Sunset, Marilyn's Back Street in Pasadena, Florentine Gardens in Hollywood, Dillon's in Westwood, The Odyssey on Beverly Boulevard, Seven Seas in Hollywood. It was a crazy non-stop schedule.

My buddy Egil Aalvik came to meet with me at the station. He was putting together a promotional evening and was looking to book me into a club in Santa Monica called Moody's. They wanted to do a Richard Blade New Wave Monday night.

I was all for it, particularly if it meant DJing with a friend like Egil. Then I had an idea. Why didn't he work with me at KROQ assisting with production and using his unique voice, complete with his Swedish accent, on some of the commercials? Maybe that way I could introduce him to the station much as I been able to work my way into KROQ just a few months before. Egil was thrilled with the idea and within just a few weeks "Swedish Eagle" became an integral part of the station lineup.

Monday nights at Moody's at 321 Santa Monica Boulevard were an instant hit, and with two levels and a 600 person capacity, overnight the club became *the* place in Southern California for young people to show up in their hippest clothes to mingle, dance and find a new romantic partner. For me it was reminiscent of my time at Magic in Vienna as record company reps would make a point to hit Moody's every Monday to meet me in the DJ booth with stacks of albums and twelve-inches for me to promo and give away.

Within less than a month, Lloyd Moody, the owner, announced that he was using this new-found success to revamp the club by putting some money into the décor and sound system and changing the name to The 321. That name lasted about one minute because even though the club was officially eighteen and over, the doormen were notoriously lenient and never enforced that age limit, so when you asked a hip kid, a rude boy or a new romantic chick where they were going on a Monday night the answer was inevitably "*the 3-2- young.*"

With all this new-found success I had no shortage of female admirers and there was always that dreaded moment when I would take them back to the little apartment that I shared with Tim Mahoney in Sherman Oaks and they would see my tiny room with the paint peeling from the walls and the foam mattress stuffed into the corner and wonder just what the deal was with this apparently successful DJ.

Egil had the same thought when he came to pick me up one afternoon and drive me to a gig.

"Dude, what are you thinking?" he asked after seeing the squalor I was living in. "You are the 'golden boy' right now and it's going to be that way for at least another year. You've got to get yourself a better apartment!"

I knew he was right but I'd been so crazy busy with both my gigs and the loss of my dad that I was just thankful to have a place to lay my head. But in the back of my mind I knew it was just a few months until my mum would be flying over to visit and she definitely wouldn't enjoy sleeping on a piece of foam on the floor. A new apartment was a must.

We had barely driven three buildings down the street when Egil hit his brakes. He pointed to a brand-new condo complex at the corner of Mammoth and Ventura. There was a "For Lease" sign swinging gently in the breeze.

He grinned at me. "We have time, my friend. Let's check it out."

We went inside and it was perfect. Everything was new with a sunken living room, dining room, kitchen and two bedrooms on an upper level. It had a separate two-car garage and a Jacuzzi.

The potential landlord showed us around, then asked, "So what do you think?"

"He'll take it," said Egil.

For a second I was going to shoot him down because the rent was so much higher than anything I'd paid before but then I realized that life is short. I found myself rubbing Dad's ring on my finger and feeling good about the place. So I nodded in agreement. And just like that I was committed to $1,200 a month in rent and a mass of furniture to buy.

I've often found that when you take a risk in life good things happen. I don't mean by being foolish but by doing something that your gut tells you might be a stretch but that it'll work out. It's almost like putting vibes out into the universe saying "I'm willing to take a chance" and nature replying "Then I'm willing to help you."

I think nature approved of my choice because over the next ten days two amazing things happened: I received a phone call that would make my KROQ fame pale in insignificance and I met the second great love of my life.

T.V.O.D.

The phone call was totally unexpected but the words I heard coming down the line were something I had dreamed of and hoped for since being a young boy. I think as we're growing up many of us secretly wish to be on television. It had certainly been in my thoughts as a kid, so much so that I put it on my list when I was just ten years old.

I knew I would never be a great actor; my years studying drama at Oxford had convinced me of that. I could hit my mark and remember my lines but I could never get lost in the role and become the character. When I was on stage a part of my mind was always saying to me "What would he do next?" rather than letting myself be in the moment and playing the part as it happened.

Working with the talented cast of *Square Pegs*—Sarah Jessica Parker, Jami Gertz and Merritt Butrick—as young as they were, reinforced my thoughts. Those young actors were so fluid and natural that they were already at a level I had to struggle to keep up with. So my problem became: If I couldn't be someone else on TV who could I be? The answer was simple: myself.

In January 1981 while I was in Bakersfield at Magic 98 I read in a trade publication of a small cable channel planning to launch on the east coast that summer that would play nothing but music videos. I knew immediately that could be huge.

I contacted the local TV station that worked with my radio station and they helped me film a five-minute on-camera demo which I dutifully mailed off to Les Garland and Robert Pittman at that start-up channel in New York. The months went by and I heard nothing back and watched sadly as MTV debuted on August 1 of that year.

Now, sitting in the production room of KROQ on that Thursday morning in October 1982, I picked up the phone expecting a sales call and instead received the chance of a lifetime.

"This Richard Blade?" said the voice on the phone.

"That's me. How can I help you?"

"My name's Steve Poole. I'm putting together a music video show for television. We're looking for someone to do a daily rock report on it. Think you could do that?"

"Yeah, absolutely," I said.

"Do you have all your hair and teeth?"

I laughed, "Yes, last time I looked."

"Our studio is in Burbank. Can you be there this afternoon with a sixty-second piece on a band prepared? That way we can test you on camera."

As I wrote and voiced *ROQ Notes* every day for KROQ that would be no problem for me. I would just use that day's segment.

"Sure, give me the address and time and I'll be there."

Two hours later I was heading west on the 134 freeway, running the script out loud to myself in the car. As I sped downhill towards Glendale I clearly remember thinking that if I pulled it off and landed this gig that everything would change for me once again.

Steve Poole's studio in Burbank was a converted warehouse. I parked next to his chocolate-brown corvette, got out, took a deep breath, kissed my Dad's ring for luck and walked inside the building. What I saw there was impressive.

There was a large dance floor, a full overhead studio lighting rig, a thirty-foot raised stage at one side and on the other wall, framing the dancefloor, a huge painted television towing twenty feet high with the screen painted a bright blue.

Three people were waiting for me, Steve Poole, John Farley and Monty Gast, all producers and executives on the show.

Steve stood out from the trio in his leather jacket, late sixties style shaggy hair and orange face that screamed "fake tan." He spoke first.

"Well, you've certainly got your own hair," he quipped.

"And most of my teeth," I answered. "I'm Richard Blade."

I held out my hand and we made our introductions.

Steve went over how it was going to work. He wanted me to stand in front of the giant blue-screen TV where he would frame me in one of the cameras, call *action* and I would go into a run-through of the MV3 World Rock Report.

"MV3?" I asked.

"That's the name of the show."

"Great name. And this is a pilot for television?"

Steve looked at John and Monty and grinned. "No. The pilot was sold months ago. We go on the air in January in more than thirty cities."

"Wow." Now the stakes were even higher I realized. "Even here in LA?"

"Especially here in LA," said Steve. "We're on KHJ channel 9 five days a week at 4pm. Perfect for when the kids come home from school." He took a moment and continued, "So anytime you're ready . . . ?"

"I'm ready," I said and turned and walked to my mark trying not to show my nervousness.

Steve went behind the camera and focused in. Happy with what he was seeing he called out, "Don't worry if you screw up; we can do as many takes as you need. Okay, in 3, 2, 1, action!"

I locked my eyes on the huge square lens of that massive broadcast camera and remembered Brian Clifford's words to me in Torquay all those years ago when I was starting with Soundwave and he told me to "bring the show." Now, like never before, I had to bring it.

"I'm Richard Blade and this is *MV3*'s World Rock Report. Today we are going to cross the Atlantic to introduce you to the band Yazoo, except for one thing," I paused, smiled and raised my finger to the camera, "and that one thing is that over here in North America they are known simply as Yaz due to a copyright problem with their name. But legal complications and the lack of two *o*'s aside, their music speaks for itself and that's no surprise because one of the two members of this talented duo is Vince Clarke, the guy who founded Depeche Mode just two years ago. Now Vince has left that group and started a new band with an incredible vocalist called Alison Moyet and together they've released their debut album *Upstairs at Eric's* named after their engineer, Eric Radcliffe."

"This LP features eleven amazing tracks including a salute to disco on 'Goodbye Seventies'; a dance floor stomper called 'Situation'; a beautiful ballad for any love birds watching, 'Only You' and an up-tempo track about unhealthy obsession called 'Don't Go.'"

"And that's the video we're going to leave you with right now as Dracula, Frankenstein, skeletons and bats pursue Yaz through a haunted house of horrors. Don't get too scared and I'll see you tomorrow right here on *MV3*."

I finished and there was silence. You could hear a penny drop in that huge sound stage. Steve emerged from behind the camera and walked quickly over to Monty and John and the three of them huddled and talked for a few seconds. John hurried away from the stage and disappeared upstairs. Steve turned to me.

"If it's okay with you we're going to have you do that again."

Fuck. I blew it.

"Okay. What would you like different about it? The song—"

Steve cut me off, "Do it exactly the same. John's going up to the control room to fire up the lights and we are going to roll tape on this one." He grinned, "That is if you want the job?"

And just like that my audition became slated to become the first World Rock Report on episode one of *MV3*.

Over the next month things began to fall into place for the launch of *MV3*. The first thing was my salary. Two days after my taped screen test Steve Poole had a contract drawn up and waiting for me.

"Look it over, Daddy. I think you'll find it's all standard," he said.

Steve had a vocal tick of calling everyone Daddy even if he was older than them. I figured it was a sixties hangover like his hairdo. As long as he didn't call me "fired" I was okay with it.

I skimmed the contract but couldn't see the amount I would be getting.

"Does it have my salary in here?" I asked.

"Yeah. You're down for fifteen hundred. Should work, right?"

I was used to this. Fifteen hundred a month was a little more than KROQ was paying me for being one half of the morning show. Just over $350 a week. Not great but with my gig money on the side it would work, plus it was a TV gig and who knew what that could lead to.

Steve continued, "And when we get picked up for a second season there's a built-in increase from fifteen hundred a week to two thousand. After that we can renegotiate for a third through fifth year."

Wait a minute. Was I hearing correctly? He was offering me $1,500 *a week*? As a starting salary? Apart from one change, and that was including a line allowing me to continue appearing on *Square Pegs*, I couldn't sign the contract fast enough.

I met the music coordinator of *MV3*, a fellow Englishman, who hailed from Yorkshire, Peter Facer, and the two hosts, comedian David Maples and a beautiful, nineteen-year-old actress, Karen Scott.

The show was to be shot on Steve's soundstage with teenage dancers in front of the giant TV which would be playing videos on its blue screen using a process known as an Ultimatte. The dancers wouldn't be able to see the videos but to the viewers at home it would look amazingly cool. I was introduced to the girl who was booking the dancers and suggested that she come to my club gigs and pick some of the trendy kids there. Everyone loved that idea.

Two days a week we would have live bands on the show and before their performances we'd do an interview with the groups. Then the bands would play two of their hits while the dancers swarmed around the stage.

I looked over the list of groups already booked to appear and it was very hip with acts like Oingo Boingo, X, Thomas Dolby, Wall of Voodoo and Falco. I suggested Berlin, and also my good friend Jeffrey Spry and his group, Felony. Both made the cut and our lineup for the first few weeks was in place.

Our debut air date was Monday, January 10, 1983, and we started shooting pieces for the daily hour-long show in early December. Halfway through our first day of shooting Steve called me upstairs to his dual-purpose studio and control room. I noticed several lines of white powder on his smooth desktop. Steve saw me looking at it.

"Want a line, Daddy?"

"No, I'm good, Steve. You wanted to see me?"

"Yeah. I've been watching everyone's segments and we've been talking up here. John and I think that you are wasted just doing one report a day. We want you to be one of the hosts. It was going to be just David and Karen but we want you to be there on camera as well throughout the show. Would that work for you?"

"Sure!" I was thrilled at the idea.

"Good. You'll do most of the band and music stuff, we'll have David do the comedy and Karen will be on the floor with the dancers. Sound good, Daddy?"

"Yeah, I love it."

"And it makes sense. The name of the show is MV3 and now the audience will think that means that you, David and Karen are the three.'"

"So what does MV3 mean, Steve?" I asked.

"Do a line with me, Daddy, and I'll tell you."

"Can't, Steve. I have to shoot some more stuff today. I gotta go."

I turned and hurried out of his office. As happy as I was to get higher billing I was taken aback by the cocaine. I'd never done drugs and didn't want to start. But if it was that common . . . ? I made my way downstairs where the first shots of "the MV3" were taken of us together on the set.

MV3

I didn't spend much time with David or Karen off camera as my radio and club schedule was keeping me super busy, but when we were shooting we got on really well; there was never any arguing or friction between us. The really fun days were when we had both the dancers and the bands on the set. Each group would do their performance twice so we would have extra footage to edit from, making it look like we were using six cameras to shoot them rather than three, upping the show's production value.

I was excited when I watched tape of some of the daily footage that we'd shot and couldn't wait to see it on the air. I invited the other KROQ DJs down to the set, but apart from Raymond, Egil and Katy no one else came. I began to feel a little jealousy from them.

The New Year rolled around and TV Guide came out for the week of January 8–14 with John Madden on the cover and there it was, proudly on page A-59, the ad for *MV3*. That's when I knew it was real. The show was actually going to air.

TV Guide ad for January 10th, 1983

I was shocked to see I had top billing on the ad. I sent a copy to my mum and prayed that somewhere my father knew that his little boy was still chasing both their dreams.

That Monday afternoon in January about forty of us from the *MV3* crew crowded into Steve Poole's hillside house in the valley to watch the premiere of *MV3* live on channel 9. The show looked amazing. Unlike MTV which was just a series of video clips and the occasional interview, here we were with real dancers dressed in the latest street fashions, cutting-edge bands putting on the performances of their lives and a massive video screen which the camera would fly into or out of, "the million-dollar move" as Steve called it.

As the show finished we all applauded. Karen, David and I were hugged and kissed by the producers and crew. We had a hit on our hands. The euphoria was everywhere. But I had noticed something very troubling.

Steve and John had told me that *MV3* was syndicated across the country in cities like Chicago, San Jose, Detroit, Charlotte, Atlanta etc. on what is called a barter basis. That means that the TV channel gets the show for free and in return gives back to the producers approximately six minutes of commercial time within the program to sell. Now this is great if you can get national sponsors to step in and buy the open spots; the money from companies like Coca Cola, Ford or McDonalds can not only underwrite the show but yield massive profits to the production company. However I saw none of those on *MV3*.

Maybe I was more aware of this having worked in radio and producing commercial spots to air on a daily basis, but to my eye the direct-response "1-800" ads selling cleaning products, hand-held sewing machines and the perfect egg poachers would hardly generate enough money to feed the group of people at the screening party, never mind fund the TV show. And if the money wasn't coming in then just how long could *MV3* stay on the air?

On the MV3 set with David Maples and Karen Scott

That night after the show's premiere it was off to the 321 for my regular Monday night gig. I parked around the back of the club as usual and as I walked along Third Street and turned towards the club's entrance on Santa Monica I noticed a group of kids pointing at me.

They were young, too young even for the "Three-Two-Young," but they seemed to know who I was. They all ran across the road as one, disregarding the traffic, and surrounded me.

"You're Richard. You're that English guy from the TV show!" one of the girls cried. "Can you sign something for me?" She searched her purse and pockets for something, anything, to have signed.

As she fumbled for a pen a couple more kids came up and had the same reaction. It had barely been five hours since the first episode of *MV3* had aired and already this was happening.

One of the bouncers from the 321 saw the kids around me and moved quickly towards us.

"Everything okay here?" he asked.

"Yeah," I replied, "they just want an autograph."

I looked at their faces and saw myself in them, that fanboy who is desperate for a memento. And now they wanted one from me. But I was no different. I hadn't changed from yesterday. It was only that I'd been on TV, in their house, in their room that afternoon and now they wanted proof to show their friends that they'd met "that guy from the TV show."

I signed the autographs happily and would have stayed out there on the street talking with them all night if it wasn't for the fact that the club was calling me. As I walked inside the 321 I realized that even if *MV3* might already be in trouble because of the lack of well-heeled sponsors the fans didn't know that and my ride into the TV spotlight was just beginning.

MV3 had only been on the air for two weeks when Glen Brunman from Epic records, whose music I played on KROQ, approached Peter Facer with a music video he was trying to get on the show. Peter called me in to the meeting to watch the clip.

"Before we play it," said Glen, "I have to tell you it's a black artist."

That didn't bother us one bit; we were playing Prince ("I Wanna Be Your Lover" and "Controversy"), George Clinton ("Atomic Dog"), The Gap Band ("You Dropped a Bomb on Me") and Musical Youth ("Pass the Dutchie") and the kids loved them all.

Glen continued, "To be upfront with you we've taken this video to MTV several times and they refuse to play it because it's 'too black.' The president of the record label, Walter Yetnikoff, is furious and has made this a priority for us. It would mean a lot to me personally if you could get this one on."

Glen switched his gaze and looked straight at me. "I know you've worked with this guy before and like his music and I promise you it's going to be a big track. It just needs exposure."

Peter smiled, "No problem. If it's good we'll play it. I don't care what color he is as long as the video's great. Do you want to show it to us?"

Glen nodded and hit play on the three-quarter-inch tape machine.

Peter and I sat back and watched in awe as Michael Jackson danced down the street, illuminating paving stones with his feet while singing about Billie Jean.

When it finished Peter took a breath and asked Glen, "Can we see it again?"

Glen looked disappointed, "So you're not sure?"

"No way," said Peter. "The video's brilliant. I just want to see it again for myself!"

Glen rewound the tape and as Michael's masterpiece played a second time Steve Poole walked in and saw the images on the TV screen. He stopped and watched, like Peter and I, transfixed.

As it faded out I explained to Steve, "It's new. Michael Jackson. MTV won't play it because he's black."

Steve wrinkled his brow, "That's why they are fucking losers." He turned to Glen, "How soon can we play it?"

Glen pointed to the tape machine, "The video's yours. Whenever you want."

Steve thought out loud for a moment, "The crew's gone home. But I can run camera myself and we can put together an intro on the fly." He spoke directly to Peter, "You and me, we'll edit it into tomorrow's show, okay?"

Peter nodded.

Steve had one final question for Glen, "Has anyone else played it?"

"No, it's been turned down everywhere. ET ran their credits over twenty seconds of it but that's all. It's your exclusive if you want it."

"Damn right we do. Tell your boss that we're going to world premiere 'Billie Jean' tomorrow on *MV3* and fuck MTV."

Steve Poole might have had drug issues but there wasn't a racist bone in his body.

MV3's premiere of "Billie Jean" had huge implications for the music world. As the song took off and exploded on the charts, MTV realized the magnitude of the mistake they had made.

They went back to Walter Yentikoff, the president of CBS records, and pleaded with him to have the next Michael Jackson video before *MV3* or anyone else. In return they would create a new category, the MTV World Premiere Video, which sounded suspiciously similar to how we had introduced "Billie Jean" as the MV3 World Premiere Video.

CBS agreed and on March 31, 1983, MTV debuted their very first World Premiere Video. And what video was it? Michael Jackson's "Beat It," because now, faced with scorn and ridicule, MTV had decided that Michael wasn't "too black" after all.

Six months later a package arrived at my door. Inside was a framed and mounted *Thriller* album signed by Michael. It also included a note that said, "Richard, thanks for everything you did." I hung it on my wall that day and it has been with me ever since, a reminder of one of the most talented artists in the history of recorded music.

MV3 was a sensation in every market it was airing in. The press jumped on the bandwagon in February with articles headlined "*MV3* Rocks TV," "A Syndicated New Wave Dance Party Takes Hold" and "*MV3* Dance Bandstand Rocks to New Wave Beat," but even with massive ratings in

thirty-one cities and critical acclaim the "1-800" ads remained and the big corporate sponsors stayed away.

During the first week of February when the salary checks for our fourth week of shows were due, Steve called Karen, David and me into his office.

"We've got a slight problem with the bank. I'm sure you all know about thirty-day billing cycles?" He looked at us as if we should have a complete grasp of advertising sales and spread sheets, "Well, we are right in the middle of that cycle so in about twelve days we'll be flush with money from our sponsors but until then if you could give me a little time before issuing your paychecks . . . ?" His voice trailed off.

As the MV3 left Steve's office all three of us now knew that something bad was going down in Burbank.

By the beginning of March we started to notice things were going missing from the set, big things like the camera crane. No longer could the show do sweeping moves in and out of the blue screen and over the dancers' heads. Now we just had three cameras on stationary tripods, or "sticks" as the operators called them. Though no one talked about it we all knew what had happened to the crane; it had been repossessed.

Despite our problems the show remained a huge promotional vehicle for not only the record companies but also the movie studios. In the second week of March, Warner Brothers Pictures contacted us to arrange an interview to promote a new movie they had coming out called *The Outsiders*. Steve Poole joked that it was the perfect fit for us because that's what we often felt like, so he confirmed that the stars of the film could come in.

Two days later I found myself on the set interviewing C. Thomas Howell, Matt Dillon, Ralph Macchio, Patrick Swayze, Rob Lowe, Emilio Estevez and Tom Cruise about their film and we laughed together about movies and music.

I had a shocking wakeup call at the end of that month when The Psychedelic Furs were our live guests on the show. They had rehearsed and sound checked and were ready to go. The lead singer, Richard Butler, was dressed in a long, heavy coat which gave him a dark, mysterious air and looked great on camera. The problem was no one was rolling tape and Richard was starting to sweat.

It got hot quickly on the *MV3* set. With more than a hundred excited dancers pressed up against the stage, the band in full gear and the incandescent Klieg lights blazing down like artificial suns on everyone assembled there, the air conditioning just couldn't cope. And the clock kept ticking.

After more than an hour the band was understandably at their breaking point. Something had to be done. The floor manager chose me as the one to do it.

"Go up to Steve's booth. Break the door down if you have to. Tell him we have to roll tape or we lose the band and today's shoot."

Steve did not like to be disturbed in his office on a tape day but the lot had fallen on me so I shouldered it and went upstairs to confront our director and executive producer.

I knocked gingerly on the door. No answer. I knocked again and again.

"Come on, Steve, I know you're in there. It's Richard. Let me in, please."

"It's open. Come on in," said a voice from inside.

I opened the door and stepped into the control room.

"Shut the door," demanded Steve.

I closed it quickly behind me. I had expected to find Steve at the switching board looking through the large glass window which gave him an unrestricted view of the set and stage; instead he was at the other side of the room hunched behind his desk, and there on the desk top was a mound of white powder with a revolver lying next to it.

"What do you need, Daddy?" he asked.

"We need you to roll tape. The band's going to leave if you don't."

"No, they'll wait. They want to be on television. Everyone wants to be on television. Just like you do, right?" he said.

"Steve, seriously, we have to roll tape."

"Look, Daddy, let's make a deal," he said. "I'll roll tape if you do a line with me. Then I'm done here and we can get going."

"Steve, I can't. I've got to introduce the band when they start."

"You can do that in your sleep," he seemed to be getting angry. "Just do one line. It'll make you better on camera," he held up a rolled up twenty to me, "Just do it."

"If I do a line you'll roll tape?"

"Are you deaf? That's what I said," he thrust the twenty at me again. "Come on, do it!"

We needed to get this performance taped with The Psychedelic Furs and I was not about to get into a shouting match with someone who was obviously stoned out of his head and had a loaded gun just inches from his grasp.

"Okay," I said. I stepped forward and watched as Steve sliced out a line for me.

"It's good stuff," he said proudly.

I bent down and snorted the powder into my nose. It felt sharp and slightly acidic. I had a slight rush, my eyes felt bigger for a moment and I had the urge to grind my back teeth, but that was it. I'd never done drugs before and I was expecting to feel like I was floating or see rainbows and hear a chorus of "Lucy in the Sky with Diamonds," but instead I had less of a rush than I got when catching a wave or finishing a competitive swim.

"That's better, Daddy. Here let's do another."

I stepped back from the desk.

"Steve, come on, you promised," I was frustrated and I certainly wasn't going to do another line.

"You are no fun are you, Daddy?" Steve shook his head at me. "Tell them to roll tape without me. Peter can fix any shots we don't get in post."

Steve raised his head from the desk and glared at me, "And if you don't have the balls to do another line then get out and shut the door behind you."

As I hurried back down to the stage to give them the "roll tape" order I knew that *MV3* would soon be crashing down around our heads.

Just a few days later Steve called a meeting with the hosts and told us that the "overwhelming research" he was getting indicated that the viewing audience didn't like the dancers, that they were getting in the way of the videos. So there would be no more dancers on the set as of that day.

This was the exact opposite of the real-life feedback that I heard every night in the clubs. People *loved* the dancers. They looked forward to checking out their hairstyles and hip street clothes, and when the ska boys and girls would hit the *MV3* dance floor and skank to videos from The Specials or Madness it was like a party happening on your TV.

But if the dancers were gone, the catering and craft table bill would be cut as would several jobs including the dance coordinator. It made sad sense to us. Now Karen, David and I would be the only ones on the set adlibbing our intros to the clips on the show. The videos would play on even as *MV3* began to sink.

As April rolled around we were down to just one camera on the set. It was an older broadcast camera that Steve owned and had dug out of storage; the rest had been grabbed by angry rental companies and returned to their stock. The stage was now a lonely place with Steve running the camera and David, Karen and me moving from corner to corner desperately trying to make each shot look different.

It became Peter's job to take the tapes and edit our "stand ups" with the latest videos and then mix in older clips from the show of the early live performances and even ones with the dancers filmed during our first few weeks on the air. It saved Steve a fortune in shooting new footage but it meant that *MV3* became a chaotic mish-mash of old and new, but somehow, despite itself, the show still continued to pull huge ratings.

As we entered May, the MV3—David, Karen and myself—had still not been paid since the end of January. We were working long hours, under crazy conditions with drugs and guns in plain sight and doing it all for free. It wasn't so bad for me because my club gigs were so lucrative and the TV exposure was certainly helping the morning show ratings on the radio, but for Karen and David times were getting very tough. Steve's promise was that at the end of the month things would change for the better.

The second US Festival was happening May 28–May 30 and Steve had scraped up enough money to secure a camera crew to go with us to the mega-concert in San Bernardino to shoot the performances and backstage interviews. He was convinced that with that footage he could finally get major sponsors to come onboard and pay off all of the bills—and our salaries in full. We had nothing to lose so we stuck with his plan; after all, it was the only one we had.

I reached out to Steve Wozniak and obtained all the clearances we needed and we were ready to reclaim *MV3* and make it a financial success.

My all-area working pass, US Festival, 1983

Our shoot at the US Festival went without a hitch and we interviewed virtually all the major artists on the bill for *MV3* including The Clash, Van Halen, Men at Work, Berlin, Missing Persons, Stray Cats and INXS. It looked and sounded sensational on camera and on the show. But sadly it was all in vain.

With David Lee Roth backstage at the US Festival

Despite the superstar footage Steve was unable to land any national sponsors. At that point David Maples was understandably done and just walked off the set when he heard the news. Steve responded that he was in talks with CBS to do a prime-time video show, a network version of *MV3*, and if Karen and I would just stick with him we would be the hosts.

Our Burbank sound stage that just months before had been seething with life and energy and had been the focal point for everything hip and cool with the youth of America was now desolate and all but abandoned.

Steve Poole would shoot our intros directly onto a bulky old one-inch tape machine that he owned. Peter would then race with the tape to an edit bay in Hollywood and cut together the next show with whatever available video clips he could find. We had no help, we had no hope, we only had each other. I suppose what happened next was inevitable.

It had been a depressing day shooting our thrown-together intros without David and then being constantly interrupted by Steve disappearing to his office "for a few minutes." When we finally wrapped Karen asked if I could give her a ride back to her apartment which was only a couple of miles from mine. I said it was no problem and the two of us took off in my car.

We talked for a few minutes about how sad the situation with our show had become and then we forced ourselves to change the subject and I asked how Karen's acting career was going outside of *MV3*.

As I drove and listened to the stories of her auditions I felt this formerly aloof co-host who had now become my comrade in arms, open up to me and I started to pick up on that unspoken chemistry that often passes through two people prior to their first sexual encounter together.

A few minutes later I exited the 101 at the Woodman off-ramp that Karen and I both used. North would take us to Karen's place, south and we would be at my condo. I deliberately took the middle of the three lanes, and pulled up to the stop sign.

I looked over at Karen and said, very simply, "Left or right?"

They were three little words but there was no room for doubt in their meaning. Karen glanced in the direction of her apartment for a moment and then put her hand on my leg.

"Left," she replied.

I said nothing, just smiled and swung the wheel toward my apartment.

That night we began our illicit affair. Karen was fun and beautiful and we both needed each other to get through the shit-storm that *MV3* had become.

I continued to do everything I could to keep *MV3* going. Every intro I did on camera I tried to make fun and interesting. If I heard a new song I'd ask Peter to see if he could get the video for it so we could play it on the show. I set up wardrobe trades with several clothing stores in LA for Karen and myself, including at The Factory on Ventura Blvd.

So in that spirit when KROQ returned to Hawaii in June of 1983 I arranged to have Karen and Peter fly over to the islands with me to shoot a week of intros for *MV3*. Steve Poole said he would have a camera crew waiting for us in Oahu but at the last minute broke the bad news that he had been unable to book one—something we knew really meant that he had no money to hire them. Instead I picked up a home VHS camera that Peter could operate and hopefully the quality would be good enough to use on the show. I loaded up my carry-on with the camera and a bunch of blank and pre-recorded VHS tapes and we boarded one of two DC10 aircraft that KROQ was using to fly our listeners to Hawaii.

The first plane was entirely filled with KROQ fans, almost 350 of them. Karen, Peter and I were on the second DC10 which carried another 150 loyal listeners, making 500 in all. The rest of that private charter, the other 200 seats, had been sold to another group heading to the island paradise.

I was exhausted having been up since four that morning to host my morning show and was dozing in my seat when a stewardess came up to me and woke me gently. "I'm sorry to disturb you," she said, "but some of the passengers asked if we could show a tape of your TV show on the monitors instead of the movie."

I nodded through my sleepy haze. "Yeah, there's a bunch of tapes in my bag in the bin overhead. Just grab one that isn't sealed. It'll either be a show or a video album." I was way too tired to get up and shuffle through them myself. Within seconds I was back asleep.

I'm not quite sure how long my slumber lasted. I estimate based on the tape that it was about twenty minutes but however long it was this time I was not woken up gently. Instead the stewardess along with two male stewards were leaning over me and shaking my seat violently. I was immediately awake.

"What's going on?" They looked so serious that I was concerned that we were going to crash.

"How dare you bring pornography onto our plane!" exclaimed the stewardess.

"What? I don't have any porn with me."

"I beg to differ." Her eyes went to the screen.

There, in glorious color, was a freeze frame of a nipple with an ice cube being rubbed against it. I recognized it instantly; it was the uncensored video for the twelve-inch version of "Girls on Film." The stewardess had grabbed a Duran Duran compilation tape that I had received from their record label and had put that on. Everything was fine during "Planet Earth," "Hungry like the Wolf" and "Rio," but when the raunchy extended "Girls on Film" started and the sexy models clad only in tiny thongs started their oil wrestling, the passengers on the plane went nuts—but in a good way. The big problem was that it wasn't all KROQ listeners on board; the other 200 travelers were Catholic choral groups bound for a competition in Hawaii.

To make things worse the Catholic schoolgirls LOVED the video as they all had crushes on the guys in Duran Duran and they booed as their Mother Superior stormed down the aisle to have the video turned off. In the confusion the crew had hit *pause* instead of *stop* and now that chilly nipple was being immortalized on the multiple screens throughout the aircraft.

The three crew members who were boxing me in seemed so furious that for a moment I really thought they were going to march me to an exit door and jettison me over the Pacific.

The crew insisted I go back to apologize to the choral groups, which I did, but even as I said sorry I was met by cheers from the frisky schoolgirls who wanted nothing more than to keep watching Duran Duran do their thing. But instead of Simon, John, Roger, Nick and Andy rocking out, we were all relegated to an awful movie that was the regularly scheduled entertainment.

Everything else about the trip to Oahu went flawlessly. We shot intros at the beach, at Diamond Head, at the KROQ nighttime parties and from the top of the hotels that towered over the white sands of Waikiki. Peter and I had hoped that some of the takes might work but we were amazed that when we returned to the mainland it all actually ended up on the air as "*MV3* Invades Hawaii Week." Steve was so desperate for material at the time that even the low quality of home video would do.

In August Peter pulled off a real coup and arranged for Robert Smith of The Cure to come to the Burbank studio for an interview. This would have been huge for our audience as The Cure was already an incredibly popular new wave band in 1983.

Peter met Robert and a representative from his record company outside of the studio but couldn't get in. Steve Poole had forgotten about the interview and had locked everything up. Peter stood on the sidewalk trying to explain to the lead singer of The Cure what had happened and watched helplessly as they drove away.

Peter was broken-hearted that even with all his efforts and everything he'd personally done to try and keep the show on the air it was still in a downward death spiral. He realized that after that day's debacle he'd reached his limit and phoned me that night to tell me he was done.

Three days later Karen quit the show. Steve called me up and had me come over to his house. He was frantic when I arrived.

"Daddy, I have made *the* deal of deals. CBS has signed to do a season of music video shows with me. Here's the contract."

He waved several pages of closely typed legalese with a CBS logo imprinted on it.

"*MV3* was just the beginning. This is the big time. *MV Network* is born. Tell me that you are in, Daddy."

Hell, why not? Even though I'd only made $4,500 for nine months of work on *MV3* it had given me gigantic exposure at home in Southern California and in many states across America.

"Okay, I'll do it. But it better be real, Steve."

Steve waved the contract at me again. "It's real. We are going network, Daddy."

Apparently CBS wanted to make a big splash with the show. Because so many of the most popular videos were coming out of England that's where the network decided they wanted the series' premiere to be shot. But as I would quickly find out, there seemed to be little money upfront for the show to hire staff. As a result it fell on me to be both the on-camera talent and the booking agent.

I spent close to a week on the phone calling bands and artists that I knew in England and convincing them to be on the pilot for the show.

The first to say yes was my dear friend George Michael, who said he would be there 100%. With Wham! and George onboard, I was able to book Spandau Ballet who were coming off one of the year's biggest hits, "True."

Three other favorites were also quick to sign on with me, Tears for Fears, Blancmange and Kim Wilde. To balance things out we needed an American act and who better than Brian Setzer of The Stray Cats?

CBS seemed thrilled with the lineup I had put together and with that in place we shot the first interview for *MV Network* with Brian in Los Angeles and then it was off to London.

With Brian Setzer of Stray Cats

With Blancmange

With Spandau Ballet

With Kim Wilde

With Tears for Fears

With George Michael and Andrew Ridgley – Wham!

Shooting in London was crazy. The British film crew couldn't get used to Steve running around everywhere wearing his California shorts even as the UK plunged into winter. And they didn't take kindly to be called Daddy either and started responding with "Okay, Yank." But somehow we got the footage we needed, all in the space of four non-stop, jam-packed days.

At night Steve would take off by himself and I would spend the time with my mum, who had come up by train from Torquay to be with me. Even though it was just for a few days it was wonderful to see her and she got quite a kick watching her little boy being followed around by a camera crew to iconic locations all over London like Marble Arch, Hyde Park, Buckingham Palace and Big Ben.

With our shooting in England wrapped Steve and I flew back to Los Angeles. He talked the whole flight about how big *MV Network* was going to be, how in the second season we would shoot in Australia and that we would stage an *MV Network* live concert on both coasts.

After we landed at LAX we went our separate ways with plans to get together the following week to lay down voice-overs and any necessary on-camera pickups. Then nothing. No phone calls from Steve, no studio appointments, no edit sessions.

I drove to his house and couldn't get anyone to answer the door. After beating on it for thirty minutes I scrawled out an angry handwritten note and left it in the mailbox but knew it was in vain.

I got together with Peter and Karen and we hired a lawyer. We worked out that Steve Poole owed Peter at least $50,000 in unpaid salary; Karen $65,000 and me, with the *MV Network* "deal," a minimum of $75,000.

The lawyer, being a lawyer, rounded up the amount we were asking for to an even $100,000 each. He hired a detective and a process server but Poole had disappeared and try as they might, even the professionals couldn't find him, and very quickly we discovered that we weren't the only ones looking for him. There was a long list of people and rental companies interested in his whereabouts.

Even without Steve present or even being served, the three of us and our attorney, Arthur Pollack, went to court. That's when I learned the term *in absentia*.

The lawyer presented a mountain of evidence: our contracts of employment, dated video clips from the actual show, press cuttings, our records of deposit from our bank accounts and finally the reports from the process server and detective. The judge decided in our favor and passed a binding ruling that should the defendant be found or come forward now or in the future he would be liable at that time for all monies and court costs due Peter, Karen and me.

We left the court winners. To this day we have not collected a penny of the award or been able to locate Steve Poole.

NO MORE WORDS

They say you can never plan for love and you don't see it coming. I certainly had no idea that Cupid would be waiting for me, her bow drawn, her arrow ready to fire, while I was on the radio that morning.

KROQ was unique in the fact it required the full-time jocks to work a weekend shift every other week. It wasn't a programming decision; it was because the station operated on a shoestring budget. I hosted a Saturday show from 10am to 2pm as it gave me a chance to plug my gigs and plenty of time to get off the air, get changed and head out to my live shows. But I didn't let any of that interfere with the content of my radio program; I was all about what went out over the airwaves and making sure that the listeners got nothing but the best "KROQ music."

It was during my Saturday shift in early October 1982 as I was cuing up the next record that I imagined all the kids who were tuned in as they headed for the beach on that warm fall morning or off to the mall to pick up some new threads and figured it would be a good time to share a story with them.

"This next song is kind of special to me," I said. "I was working at another radio station a few months ago doing overnights when I found this single. I used to put it on during the dead of the night, maybe at three in the morning when the city had fallen silent and it felt like I was the only person still awake. As the record played I'd stare at the girl on the cover of the single and wonder if she was the singer of the band or just some model they had found to help sell the record. Either way, she's one of the most beautiful women I've ever seen. If you buy a copy of it you can check it out. So here it is, Berlin and 'The Metro.'"

The record played and I reached for another song.

About fifteen minutes later as I was going through the request lines I answered a call that would rock my world.

"Hi K-Rock, it's Richard."

"Yes," said a quiet female voice on the line, "you were asking about the girl on the cover of 'The Metro'?"

"Yeah, I was. She's beautiful. Do you know who she is?"

I could clearly hear the smile in her voice as she replied, "It's me."

"Really? How do I know that?" I reached back for the single, slipped it out of its sleeve and looked over the label. "So who wrote the song?"

"John Crawford," she replied without hesitation.

"And who produced it?"

"Daniel Van Patten. And depending on which copy of the single you have it's either from MAO Music or Enigma records, but I think the picture you're talking about is on the Enigma release."

Holy shit, I thought. *This may just be her.*

"Did I tell you you're hot?" I asked.

She laughed, "I heard you say something like that on the radio and I wanted to say thanks."

"So are you single or married or what?" I blathered.

"Single."

"Cool. Hey, do you want to meet up?" I asked

"Sure. Where?"

"Where do you live?"

"Santa Monica," she answered.

"I have a gig in Santa Monica on Monday, The 321 Club. Do you want to meet there?"

"Yeah, that's just a few blocks from me. What time?"

"I'll be there from ten until midnight. I'll leave your name at the door."

"That works. So I'll see you then."

"Great," I went to say goodbye, then realized, "Wait, wait, wait! What is your name?"

"Terri Nunn," she said. "I'll see you Monday."

I'd met girls on the request lines before, sometimes with scary results, but never the lead singer of a band and never one whose photograph looked that hot. Monday couldn't come fast enough for me.

The energy at the 321 was pumping that night. I arrived early, about thirty minutes before my scheduled 10pm start time, to make sure Terri's name was on the guest list. The last thing I wanted was for her to get there and to be turned away at the door.

I took over in the booth right away and was cranking some of my favorite go-to new wave club songs such as B-Movie's "Nowhere Girl" and Pete Shelley's "Homosapien." The floor was packed and I needed a track to keep it that way. I bent over and was hunting through the milk crate full of records for the twelve-inch of The Thompson Twins' "Lies" when I heard Terri's first words to me.

"Nice ass!"

I stood up and turned around quickly. "Thanks, you mu . . . ," my words trailed off as I drank in her beauty. I was stunned for a moment. She literally took my breath away. The picture on the record sleeve didn't do her justice. I doubted that there was a lens crafted on this planet that could.

Terri was short, blond, slim and incredibly gorgeous. But that wasn't it. She radiated an attraction that can't be put into words, an aura that reached into your body and grabbed your soul. She locked her eyes on mine, smiled and said hello and with that simple word I was done.

I managed to form enough words to ask her to hang on, then grabbed the microphone and paged the club DJ to come back to the booth and take over for me. For the first time in my entire DJ career I walked away from the crowd and the booth and neglected the job I was being paid to do.

Terri and I sat at the bar and talked. Our conversation went in every direction under the sun—music, travel, movies, food, politics—there was nothing we couldn't get into. Together we closed the place down.

I walked her to her car and asked if I could see her again, maybe dinner? She smiled and said she was free all week.

The next night she drove to the valley and met me at Rive Gauche in Sherman Oaks, a restaurant known for its great food. They could have served cow slop that evening for all I cared; I just wanted more time with this dazzling person. At the end of the night I asked if she wanted to come back to my apartment which was just blocks away.

She shook her head, "Thanks, but no. I never have sex on the first date."

I nodded and was about to explain that I completely understood when she grabbed my hand and said with a smile, "But I'm free tomorrow if you want to come over to my place."

From that moment on we were inseparable.

Amat ROQS

If you attended this year's Thanksgiving Dance, you were well aware of the events which took place. Richard Blade of KROQ was the primary reason for the great success of the dance. Accompanied by the "Poorman" and Terri Dunn, lead singer from the group Berlin, the Blade ignited great enthusiasm and energy throughout the night. They handed out issues of "The Rag", KROQ's official newspaper, distributed "KROQ ROQS AMAT" bumper stickers, and judged a dance contest among students.

The gym was packed like a can

of sardines, alive with the sounds of KROQ. The energy ran high, Richard Blade directed the masses in thunderous chants and cheers, recording the wild exotic sounds of the Amat students. The following morning the recording was heard on KROQ 106.7.

The dance was probably the best in Amat history, the Blade drawing a mob of females asking for an assortment of things, ranging from autographs to kisses. For all those who attended, the ROQ will live on in the hearts of Amat.

(Top Right) Rocking the night away, students show the excitement of the evening.

(Above) Rocking Amat, Richard Blade and Terri Dunn take a moment out of the hectic evening. Over 800 students attended the memorable event.

(Left) An enthusiastic crowd seeks an autograph or "anything else" from Richard Blade.

Terri came to a lot of my gigs when she wasn't rehearsing with Berlin. My club and personal appearance schedule had me DJing mostly on weeknights. The clubs would book me then because those were the days that needed the most help—weekends could take care of themselves—so they had Richard Blade from KROQ come in on those slower evenings to spin and pack the place. As a result my weekends were mostly free. I made it a point to spend them with Terri, and we would be together every second from Friday afternoon until Monday morning when I would be up with the first rays of the sun to kiss her goodbye and drive to the station in Pasadena.

Terri loved to act things out and enjoyed role playing. She asked me to surprise her on dates, to be different, unexpected.

I just wanted to make this incredible girl happy, so after she told me that I figured that I would play along and the next night showed up in my flight suit pretending to be in the military. She loved it so I continued with the fun and turned up for our next date which we had planned as a casual dinner in a full tuxedo and black tie. Terri in turn played along and I never knew just who would be waiting for me at the door.

However after just a few dates all the planning and dressing up started to get exhausting for me; maybe my imagination was lacking or I just didn't have the time and energy, but I had to sit down with Terri and have a talk.

"Look," I said, "there is nothing more in this world that I want than to be with you but I can't keep doing all this dress up. I'm running out of things to put on and people to be. I'm a man, I'm not a pirate or a secret agent or a submarine captain; I'm a man and that's it. You're so good at being all these different characters and I do love it, but I'm a man and I don't know what else to be."

Terri took my face in her hands and kissed me. "You being a man is enough for me. You be my man and I'll be your babe."

I had no idea that night that our conversation would be set to music and turned into one of the hottest dance songs of the early eighties.

To make up for my lack of spontaneity we did all the usual things that young couples do: we went to Disneyland and Knott's Berry Farm, visited Griffith Park Observatory and rode the roller coasters at Magic Mountain. I also started planning long weekends away with Terri and we would escape together to San Diego, Newport Beach and one of our favorites, my old stomping grounds of San Luis Obispo and the eclectic Caveman Room at the Madonna Inn. Those times away together were so much fun as we would laugh and explore together as if there were no one else in the world.

Terri became all I could think of, and with Berlin starting to blow up in popularity in Southern California I invited her into the radio studio on my Saturday show, rather than with Raymond and me in the morning, as I wanted her first interview on KROQ to really concentrate on her music and the band. There was no one else in the small KROQ building that morning, just the two of us.

The interview was going great and Terri was taking calls from the listeners who were telling her how much they loved her voice and how "The Metro" was their favorite song when Terri turned to me on the air.

"You've been interviewing me all morning, so can I ask you something?" Terri said.

"Sure, go right ahead."

"You've been a DJ on the radio for a while now, right?"

"Yes," I replied, "Coming up on three years."

Her eyes sparkled mischeviously. "Have you ever had sex while you've been on the air doing your show?"

I took a deep breath. "Errr . . . no, actually I haven't."

Terri smiled, "Then why don't you find a long song to put on and we'll change that."

What to do? That's what instantly flashed through my brain. What would Rick Carroll think if I went along with Terri's plan? And what would the listeners think of me if I didn't? Only one thing I could do.

I reached back and pulled out the remix of Soft Cell's "Tainted Love/ Where Did Our Love Go" that ran almost nine minutes and just in case the seven minute vinyl of Depeche Mode's "Just Can't Get Enough."

I punched the microphone on. "By special request, for the lovely Terri Nunn of Berlin, here's a couple of extended versions back-to-back on K-R-O-Q." Then I thought, *What the hell, just go for it*, or as the Bishop said to the actress, "How would you like a twelve-inch on a Saturday morning?"

As the opening drum beats of "Tainted Love" pulsed through the studio speakers Terri was already on her feet and coming around to my side of the console.

In late November of 1982 I took a few days off from KROQ and Terri and I flew to Oahu. It was the first time for either of us to visit Hawaii. We stayed in a little hotel just off of Waikiki's main tourist strip and after a day of exploring the legendary beach and playing in the clear waters there we rented a car and headed up to the unspoiled North Shore.

As we cruised Highway 72 past Makapuu Lighthouse an intense panorama appeared before us of an endless sapphire-blue ocean flecked with breaking whitecaps echoing the line of small cumulus clouds on the horizon.

Terri gasped and urged, "Pull over, pull over!"

We stopped a mile down the road at the appropriately named Lookout Point and jumped out of the car. Terri threw her arms in the air and danced and twirled in the sunshine to a song that only she could hear, perhaps played to her by the warm trade winds that blew in from the east.

She turned and flung her arms around my neck saying, "There is a paradise on this Earth!"

She kissed me and held me tight, laying her head against my chest. She was right: there was a paradise, but it wasn't the view of the mighty Pacific or anything on the islands of Hawaii that was showing me Heaven; it was this diminutive beauty who showered me with her love.

It was in Hawaii that I asked Terri if she would marry me. It just seemed right. Everywhere around us the stores and hotels were getting ready for the holiday season; Christmas ornaments were going up and signs saying "*Mele Kalikimaka,*" Hawaiian for Merry Christmas, were being hung. The season of joy was coming and nothing I could think of would give me more joy than being with this amazing girl forever.

I dropped to one knee and proposed the old fashioned way. Terri had tears in her eyes when I asked her. She knelt down, put her hands out and cradled my face.

"I will, but not yet. I'm not ready right now. But I will be one day I promise."

And with that we kissed and hugged and knew our destiny was determined.

Berlin at the record company showcase at S.I.R. Studios

Terri and her band, Berlin, were now an inescapable part of the KROQ playlist and were generating a huge buzz all over LA and Orange County. Tune into 106.7 and within an hour Berlin would be roaring out of your speakers.

The band's manager, Perry Watts-Russell, felt the vibe they were generating and knew they were ready to take it to the next level. He booked time to put on an industry showcase performance at S.I.R. Studios in Hollywood where I introduced them on stage to an invited audience of record company scouts who were so blown away by what they saw and heard that night that a bidding war erupted for the rights to sign them.

After multiple offers they decided to go with Geffen Records. As part of that deal, Geffen acquired the rights to the first album, *Pleasure Victim*, from their original smaller label, Enigma.

Geffen was one of the biggest players in the business and their roster of artists read like a who's who of the recording industry with John Lennon, Donna Summer and The Eagles as part of their lineup. This mega-corporation loved what Berlin had achieved with their debut record and decided to re-release it without changing a thing about it, not the production, mix or even the artwork. And the bigwigs at Geffen were right; the album quickly was certified gold and I was thrilled when several of the executives showed up at the radio station to present me with an RIAA Gold Disc to commemorate the milestone and my little contribution to the group's success.

I did everything I could to help get the word out about Berlin. Everyone who heard them or saw them live was won over by their raw talent and recognized almost immediately what a wonderful front person Terri is. But there are definitely other ways I could help as well.

I was shooting the TV show *MV3* and arranged to have Berlin perform live on the show. Terri consulted with me before the shoot and was concerned that people might take our relationship the wrong way.

"Look," she said, "I know you have to do the interview with us before we go on but we can't give it away that we're together. Is that okay with you?"

I agreed 100%. The last thing I wanted to do was hurt Terri or the band's chances of being judged fairly. The big fear was that other radio stations would not play Berlin if they found out the lead singer was dating Richard Blade of KROQ, and without airplay the group's momentum could stall.

The day of the TV taping arrived and the band rehearsed, sound checked and blocked for the cameras. I stayed as far from them as possible.

When I got the word to report to the set and introduce the Berlin segment of the show I trotted over right away and avoided even looking at Terri until the cameras were rolling. After the interview one of the producers came up and asked me, "I thought you liked the singer from Berlin? I guess I was wrong." Apparently the act that Terri and I put on was too good! But whether Terri and I came across as distant or not, Berlin staged a rocking show on what was their very first national television performance.

The other opportunity to give Terri a little push was when I received a call from "the Woz," Steve Wozniak. We had hit it off a few months before at the first US Festival and he wanted to come on my show at KROQ and ask the listeners who they would like to see on the bill for the second US Festival that he was planning for Memorial Day.

I arranged for him to join me on my Saturday morning program and in early February the Woz showed up and started taking calls on the air from the excited KROQ audience. However before the show started I got together with my phone op and interns at the station to have them call in themselves and ask for Berlin to be in the lineup. With that in place I was ready to go.

I talked with Steve on the air and went to the phone lines. I had no monitor or display to tell me who was on what line or what they were calling about; I just had to hope for the best. Almost immediately the calls were for Berlin. I saw the Woz write down the name and then the next call was for Berlin and the next. That's when I realized that it wasn't just my interns calling; the request lines were exploding with KROQ listeners who really wanted Terri on the bill!

By the end of the show the tentative lineup for New Wave Day was in place and included The Clash, David Bowie, U2, Stray Cats, Men at

Work, INXS, Oingo Boingo, English Beat and, of course, Berlin. I was thrilled that my girlfriend would be a part of such an event and I also knew that she would steal the show.

To ensure that the band's exposure continued Geffen sent them out on the road on tour. This meant Terri was gone for more than a month and our magical weekends away were over. But instead of simply saying good-bye for a month we came up with a brainwave; we just pretended that she had gone ahead to our weekend away and I would fly out to join her at whatever location she was performing at.

For the next five weeks I'd hop on a plane to see her in concert across North America and after the show we would retreat to our private sanctuary. Among the cities I flew into were Chicago; Detroit; and Athens, Georgia. It was in that home of The B-52s and R.E.M. that something mind-blowing happened.

Berlin was onstage and rocking into their second song as I watched from the audience. You can't appreciate a show from backstage; the sound is never as good and you are seeing the artist from behind and can't experience their moves and facial expressions as they work to give the audience their best. I leave backstage to the poseurs who don't really care about the music. I want to be where it's loud and sweaty, on the floor in the auditorium; that's where the real action is. That night was different.

As the song progressed I noticed the buzz in the audience was changing. The crowd was no longer looking at the stage; they were looking at me! A circle formed around me and one brave girl broke ranks and stepped forward. "Are you Richard Blade from *MV3*?" she asked. That's when I realized that my TV show was on in Georgia and obviously had a huge following with exactly the same crowd that would of course love a band like Berlin.

Within moments things were getting out of hand and security had to rush me through the barriers to backstage. Terri saw the whole thing from onstage and that night, tucked up together in her hotel room, we laughed about what had happened. Over the next two weekends Terri had me come up onstage to introduce Berlin and the audience loved it. For me it was incredible to have the privilege to bring my girlfriend out onto the stage, then watch her raw talent win over the crowd.

During the week when I was back in Southern California and away from Terri, I returned to DJing in the clubs. It was there that I fell victim to temptation, and sadly not just once.

I found myself straying almost every night. It started when I was judging a bikini contest in Newport Beach. My co-judge was a former Miss California. Later that evening I found out just how qualified she was for that title.

It seemed that at every gig there was always a fun-loving, club-going girl who wanted to get together and have a good time so I went for it. And the sad thing is I knew I was so wrong to do what I was doing and that I had no excuse or reason to cheat. I was an asshole for doing it. But the flesh is weak and mine was weaker than most. I realized if I kept this up that there would not be a happy ending to it but I couldn't stop.

Terri returned from her tour and with her back in town I ended any extra dalliances and devoted myself to her once more. We drove together to the US Festival and I brought her onstage and watched as she pulled off an unbelievable performance for more than 180,000 people at the Glen Helen Regional Park on May 30, 1983. I could not have been any prouder as that tiny girl with a miracle of a voice captivated such a massive crowd.

Backstage at the US Festival – May 30, 1983

Terri & Berlin rocking the US Festival, 1983

As much as we tried to keep our love affair secret it became impossible, and at the US Festival there were so many journalists backstage that it was inevitable that someone would see us together. Within just days there were a number of articles about the two of us being a couple.

Terri, John Crawford and David Diamond, the trio that made up the writing core of Berlin, hunkered down in the studio to prep their next album. I stayed out of their hair for those sessions but Terri and I still made time to see each other as much as we could. As our relationship grew even stronger we became close with each other's mothers, Terri with my mum, who had come over to visit from England, and me with Terri's mom, Joyce, who was not only the genetic source

288

of Terri's beauty but also a person who helped teach me the benefits of spirituality and inner calm. Joyce was a very special person and I was blessed to know her.

As Terri worked hard in the studio and time took her away from me again, I returned to rocking the clubs and, sadly, to my wicked, wicked ways.

1983 was racing to a close and people were out in droves, trying to get their partying in before the clubs took a hiatus over Christmas. Mr. J's was particularly crowded that night. The capacity was around 450 and at least 600 were crammed inside with another 100 waiting outside in the parking lot. By the time I entered the club around 10pm the energy was electric. There was a huge cheer as the house DJ, Hot Toddy, introduced me. He handed me the microphone and I welcomed everyone to the club, threw out a few t-shirts and bellowed a guttural "Kay—Rock" that mimicked the jingles that ran on the station.

I slipped quickly behind the turntables and pulled the vinyl from my leather record company shoulder bag. The brown bag held maybe forty albums and twelve-inches, enough to supplement the club's collection.

I was playing a two-hour set so I went immediately into a series of crowd-pleasers— New Order, Depeche Mode, Thomas Dolby, The Cure. The place was rocking. It was a DJ's dream. The club was so jammed that you couldn't empty the floor if you tried, there was nowhere to go. And I had no intention of allowing even one person to stop dancing. This was a KROQ party after all, damn it! I clearly recall doing a beat-on-beat segue between Soft Cell's "Sex Dwarf" and B-Movie's "Nowhere Girl" when the Pink Fairy arrived.

RICHARD BLADE
KROQ/MV3 TV

In the DJ booth at Mr. J's

How to describe him? He looked like the topper to a five-year-old's birthday cake, if that particular five-year-old had a fixation for six-foot-tall men dressed head to toe in pink spandex with a set of lace fairy wings with wire supports protruding from their back.

He was standing at the entrance to the DJ booth and as soon as he got my attention (which, in that outfit, was pretty quick!) he waved his pink magic wand at me three times with a great flourish.

I laughed at this pastel apparition and grabbed the mic. "Looks like someone's got a singing telegram! Anyone expecting a pink fairy?"

I dipped the music for a second and the crowd stopped dancing and took in the crazy sight in front of them. The Pink Fairy gestured for the mic so I held it out to him.

"The message is for you!" He half sang, half spoke into the microphone.

"Okay," I said, "let's hear it."

"Not in here," came the sugary reply. He gestured to the stairs with his wand. "Up there."

I laughed again and yelled into the mic, "Who wants to check it out with me?"

I nodded to Hot Toddy to take back control of the decks for a couple of minutes and jumped down from the DJ booth.

I had not come alone to the club that night. With me was Peter Facer, the music coordinator of *MV3*, and my former co-host, Karen Scott.

Karen and I had begun a secretive affair a couple of months before and only Peter knew about it. Mr. J's had sent a limo for me that night as the club was so far from my apartment and I had to be up so early the next day for my morning show, so I invited Peter and Karen to join me. Plus I had planned that the night would end with Karen staying over at my place.

"Come on, this will be a blast," I said. "A singing telegram dressed like the sugar plum fairy. Crazy!"

Peter, always cautious, gave me a quick, "Careful, Mr. Fun." (his nickname for me) "You never know."

I'd been in a few skirmishes outside clubs and still carried a four-inch scar on my right wrist from that particularly nasty encounter in Denmark eight years before but I didn't think this Pink Fairy was anything to be concerned about. I didn't realize that Peter was right. I was about to be hurt a lot worse than any angry biker with a broken bottle had ever hurt me.

I bounded up the steep, carpeted stairs two at a time, not because I was excited about the message that was waiting – it was after all, in my mind, probably just a fan wanting to say thanks for the music. I was moving quickly because I hate leaving the DJ booth for even a minute when I'm playing. I might be known as a radio presenter or a sometime TV host but look inside me and you'll find a club DJ who loves getting a crowd on the floor and keeping them dancing.

Ironically the only other time in my entire career that I left the booth in mid-set was that first time I met Terri. Now, all these months later, unknown to me, that same girl was causing me to leave the DJ booth once again, but this time my exit would mark the end of our relationship and hurl both of us into nearly a decade of romantic distress.

It was cold outside in the parking lot that night. It was late November and there was a definite chill in the air. And it had been so hot in the club that even if we had stepped into a sauna it would have seemed cooler than that packed dance hall. I saw Karen shiver and pulled her in close. She slipped her arm around my waist and held me tight. I kissed her gently on her lips. Now there were nearly 200 people surrounding Karen, Peter and me that had followed us up from Mr. J's.

"Okay, Sugar Plum. Sing me your telegram," I said.

"I don't have it. It's up there!"

He pointed his wand into the clear night sky. There, maybe 500 feet above our heads, a small fixed-wing aircraft was circling. On cue it lit up. The plane was sky-writing a message across its wings. It was short, to the point, and horrific. On most other nights I would have welcomed those seven words with unbridled joy, but I knew, I just knew, what was going to happen as I read the message.

I'M READY TO JUMP. MARRY ME. TERRI

Have you ever been in a situation when the world stops? Perhaps during the first milliseconds of a car crash or when those feelings pulse through your entire body as you put the phone down after receiving word that a loved one has passed away? Nothing exists but the moment that you are caught in and the awful realization that you cannot do anything about it. You have lost control and there is no way to get it back. That's how I felt as I turned to the pink messenger of doom.

"Please, just tell me she's not here," I begged.

He grinned happily, unaware of the sentence he was bringing down upon the two of us. "She's over there," he giggled.

It took an eternity for me to force myself to turn my head in the direction he was pointing. I felt Karen kissing my cheek as I turned.

Terri's yellow Cadillac was parked just forty feet away. She had seen everything. Her eyes met mine through the car's windshield. Karen kissed me again. The car door opened slightly and Terri started to get out.

My God. She was wearing the wedding dress she had worn in the video for "Masquerade"! Was it going to be tonight? Did she have an officiant lined up, waiting, or were we going to shoot off to Vegas, get married and race straight back, barely making it in time for the morning radio show?

That was the spontaneous Terri I loved. Like the time we woke up on a Sunday morning after the kind of night that they write songs about and I wanted to take her to a fancy brunch. She said she had nothing appropriate with her to wear so I laughed and said I would buy her a dress. I tossed her a bath towel and told her to put that on for now and get out of bed.

We drove to the Galleria (totally!) and walked around the mall through a stunned crowd as the DJ and the nearly naked rock star shopped for brunch-worthy attire to replace the barely-there towel that she wore so well.

That laughter was gone now. Terri took one step, then doubled-over as tears exploded from those gorgeous eyes.

I turned to Peter and barked, "Take Karen back in the car. I'll find my own way home. Go!"

Peter scooped Karen up in his arms and ran with her to the waiting limo. I turned and pushed through the confused crowd. If I can just make it to Terri . . . I sprinted towards her as fast as I could run. Her door slammed shut when I was just a few feet away from my love.

I was banging on her window as she started the car. I could see her hunched forward over the wheel as the tears flowed down her face and sobbing racked her body. I hit the window again.

"I love you," I yelled.

She looked up at me with a huge emptiness in her eyes and dropped the car into gear.

"I love you!" I pleaded again.

She turned her head away and jammed her foot down on the accelerator. It was the last time I would see her for more than seven years.

The limo was gone and Terri was gone. I stood there in the parking lot stunned. As Terri's tail-lights disappeared into the darkness they took my dreams with them. The crowd knew something big had happened but weren't sure what exactly. Overhead, the plane continued to mock me as it circled with its message of a never-to-be future still scrolling across its wings and lighting the night sky.

A buzz went through the group. "Was that Terri Nunn from Berlin?" I could only nod. It was hard to form words.

I continued to stare in the direction that Terri had driven off. I realized that this was a major turning point in my life. It marked a chapter that would never be written, a destiny that would never be fulfilled.

There was a deep secret we had between us that I have never revealed to anyone until now and all these years later as I type these words to share it with you, that moment still resonates through me.

Months before, I had gone over to Terri's apartment to pick her up for another memorable date but almost immediately that evening became more unforgettable than I could have imagined. As soon as I arrived Terri asked me to sit down and then quietly explained that a few days before she had found out she was pregnant with our child and didn't know how to tell me.

She had thought carefully about the options and everything that was happening with us, then made the decision to end the unplanned pregnancy.

"I did it this morning. I'm sorry I didn't tell you first. I hope you're okay with it?"

I stood up, pulled her into me and held her tight. "Are you all right?" I asked.

"Yeah, I'm fine. A little sad."

I was lost for words. This was a lot to take in all at once. I had never thought of having children because I had been so focused on pursuing my dreams but now, holding Terri, I felt such a great loss sweep over me as my mind raced through scenarios of the two of us growing old together as the parents of our loved child.

"We'll have plenty of time to have another," she told me. "After all of this (our careers) is established."

But for once she was wrong. We had no more time. There would never be another child for either of us. And it was entirely my fault. Terri was blameless. She had wanted to make our relationship work even as both of our careers skyrocketed.

This girl had fought for me, had battled one-on-one with no less than David Geffen, who had called her into his office and ordered her to stop dating me because I was a radio DJ and that could be bad for her career. But Terri didn't flinch. This diminutive girl went toe-to-toe and faced down the billionaire mogul and told him to go ahead and drop her from the label, Geffen, if he wanted, but she was not giving up on me.

It was too much. Tears began to form. I remember saying to someone, "Tell Toddy I'll be down in a minute." I wandered aimlessly across the parking lot until I crumbled to my knees behind a van and cried like a newborn baby for what could have been. And above, the plane continued to blink out its message of a promise that would never be fulfilled.

I'M READY TO JUMP. MARRY ME. TERRI.

Eight months later Berlin's second album *Lovelife* was released. In the liner notes Terri dedicated it to Joyce, her wonderful mother, and to me. The biggest hit on that album, "No More Words," contains the lines:

"You're telling me you love me, but you're looking away.
No more words, no more promises."

VIDEO (nearly) KILLED THE RADIO STAR

As 1983 drew to a close I was not in the best place. In a little more than twelve months I had not only lost my father, but a great love, Terri Nunn, who I could not get out of thoughts no matter how hard I tried, and my two TV shows, *MV3* and *MV Network,* which had fallen apart and been taken off the air.

Slowly things began to look up when I was approached by Mick Kennedy, who ironically had previously worked with Steve Poole and helped create *MV3.* Now Mick was prepping to launch a weekly music and interview show across Southern California called *L.A. Music Guide.* The format was perfect for me and I signed the deal with Mick, Larry Namer and Dick Brooks and the series was set to debut that winter on multiple cable systems covering more than 400,000 viewers.

Less than a month later a producer from Japan contacted me about shooting a series of commercials for them playing a DJ called Mr. Doughnut. I wasn't quite sure how they picked me for that as doughnuts were definitely not a part of my diet but I was more than happy to cooperate and be their spokesperson.

They had me draw out a layout of a radio booth and then gave me the shooting schedule for the following week to film six commercials. When I showed up to the studio I was stunned that my chicken-scratch drawings had come to life and their custom-built studio looked more authentic than KROQ's real on-air booth.

Shooting Mr. Doughnut commercials for Japan

We shot for fourteen hours non-stop and I think they were pleased with the results as they signed me for a second campaign to air over Christmas.

The company came back to me and offered me another sponsorship to be a spokesman for cigarettes in Japan. I thanked them but turned it down flat. One thing I refuse to do is endorse a product that's known to kill, so cigarettes were out for me. Mr. Doughnut was one thing, but Mr. Smoker? Never!

At the beginning of November I was asked to go to the headquarters of KCBS in Los Angeles. The program director there, Mary Kellogg, had seen some of the footage from the ill-fated CBS network show, *MV Network*, and asked if I would like to host a year-end special for them called *CBS Music Video Countdown*.

We met in her office at KCBS and hit it off immediately. Mary wanted me to be very hands-on with the project and asked if I knew anyone who could help with the videos, both obtaining them and clearing the rights. Did I know someone! One phone call and Peter Facer and I were working together again. The boys were back in town.

We came up with a format to spotlight the year's top twelve albums and created a set that featured the album covers blown up to a four foot by four foot size and printed on glass. That way we could hang them and hit them from behind with a backlight and I could walk between the glowing covers talking about the bands and introducing the videos.

The two-hour show aired the last week of December 1983 on CBS. Mary was thrilled by the huge overnight ratings the countdown achieved and without hesitation offered me a contract to do a second retrospective for them the following year.

It seemed my budding TV career was getting back on track; the big question was how to maintain this momentum. I met with Peter and suggested that we start producing our own video shows and get financial backers to underwrite them. I had been signed by an amazing agent, Eric Gold, and he said that if I came up with the programming concepts he'd find the investors.

I sat with Peter at a coffee shop in Los Feliz and we spent four hours hashing out ideas for a show on the back of a napkin. We came up with a thirty-minute weekly program that would be heavy on interviews and shot on location. We would cut the interviews with the latest music videos and try and use our editing techniques to match the concept of the video itself; if it was letterboxed then we would shoot in that format, if it was in black and white then we would go monochrome, if it was filmed at the beach or at night then that's how we would shoot the interviews and my host wrap-arounds.

Peter and me on the set of our second CBS Music Video Countdown

It was an ambitious format but Peter and I knew we could do it. We set ourselves a deadline to shoot and edit the pilot and Peter got to work calling the record companies.

We picked a day in early January 1984 to shoot the interviews for the pilot. Peter had found out that a number of groups and artists were in Los Angeles that week and had booked five interviews in one day. It was the craziest, most impossible schedule imaginable.

We hired a three person crew to work with us: one for camera, one for sound and one for lighting. We met with them ahead of the shoot and explained that we were going to be running all day and into the night. Peter and I would help carry the equipment. Spare batteries were a must as there would be no time for recharging and backup gear was a necessity in case anything failed during the shoot. I brought several changes of clothes with me so we could make it look as though the footage were shot over multiple days and rented a van so we could all travel together and not get separated by the notoriously bad LA traffic. At 9am that morning we all met up in Hollywood.

Our first stop was a hotel on Wilshire Boulevard where we interviewed Boy George and Culture Club. I knew Boy from the radio interviews I'd done with him months before and we slipped back into the rhythm we'd had together on mic instantly. Boy was funny, articulate and played to the camera. He was everything that an interviewer could hope for, the perfect guest.

Then we hustled our gear into the van and met up with a British rockabilly band called Roman Holliday. They had two hits, "Stand By" and "Don't Try to Stop It." That second song's video was shot as if they were on tour in a van so that's how we filmed the video with them in the van. That way we could cut back and forth from the clip and make it look as if the interview were actually a part of the video itself.

Next it was the turn of The Gap Band, who were having huge success with "Party Train." That video was shot at Venice Beach so naturally that became the setting for our interview as it matched the video footage perfectly. After we wrapped with The Gap Band I shot a series of host intros there with an eclectic crowd on roller-blades, along with beach babes and body-builders to complete the fun visuals.

There was still no stopping for Peter, me or the crew. We grabbed the gear, raced back across town to Sunset Blvd. to do an interview with Nick Heyward from Haircut 100, who was having a solo hit with a single, "Blue Hat for a Blue Day." Nick was gracious and talked not only about his current music but went back to the days of Haircut 100 which allowed us to air "Love Plus One" and "Boy Meets Girl."

Our final interview of the day was at 9pm, outside on the rooftop deck of Le Parc Hotel in Beverly Hills with my friends in Spandau Ballet. Their manager, Steve Dagger, knew how important this was for us and made sure all five of the band were there. It was a cold night and in the footage you can see our breath freezing in the chilly night air.

With Boy George *With Nick Heyward*

We finished the shoot and were back at our cars in Hollywood around 1a.m. the next morning. It had been total madness attempting to do what we did but somehow we pulled it off. It was guerilla TV-making at its finest. They said it couldn't be done so we went ahead and did it anyway.

For the next two weeks we edited the pilot and while doing that Peter and I realized we had so much footage that maybe there were other things we could use it for. We kept that in the back of our minds as we locked picture on our demo tape and got ready to try to sell the series.

With the pilot complete it was my turn to get on the phone. My first call was to KTLA channel 5. They aired Casey Kasem's video countdown on Saturday mornings so I knew they had a good understanding of what video shows were all about. Within fifteen minutes of leaving a message for the program director of the station, David Simon, I received a call back.

David was a fan of my radio show and was happy to meet with me, so two days later Peter and I walked into David's office at Tribune Broadcasting in Hollywood and after a few minutes of pleasantries slipped the VHS of *VideoBeat* into David's tape machine.

The seven-minute demo flew by and even as I ejected the tape I heard David saying, "How about if I give you the Saturday morning 10am slot? You can be the lead-in for Casey."

It sounded great to us and David explained he'd have his programming department draw up the contract.

"I'd like you to start mid-March. I'll get you the exact date," he said. "We'll start with a four-episode commitment. We'll be going into ratings sweeps. Can you be ready by then?"

No problem, we told him, and we left his office in a daze.

Peter and I didn't speak until we were away from the building and out-side on Sunset Boulevard. Then we turned to each other and screamed. We'd done the impossible. We'd sold the show "in the room." That's the stuff of Hollywood legend. Normally you receive a polite, "Oh, I really like it. Let's see if we can find a place for it. I'll call you." And then you hear nothing. Zilch. Silence.

The rule is that in Hollywood no one ever says yes or no. Everything is "really good" and "Let's talk soon." Which is code for "Get the fuck out of my office." In Hollywood you can die of encouragement. But we had walked away with a deal. This was almost unheard of.

We'd dreamt up the concept, we'd shot the show and now we'd sold it. And as we walked back to our cars filled with euphoria little did I know my problems were just beginning.

As executive producer, host and director of *VideoBeat* I was wearing a lot of hats. I met with Eric Gold, my agent, and told him the good news and now it was his job to put the awkward little bits together, like finding the money to do the show and a place to partner with to shoot and edit it.

Eric brought in a major video facility in Hollywood to be the produc-tion house for *VideoBeat* and found a small, independent record company who wanted to underwrite the funding of the show, depending on the budget.

Eric, Peter and I crunched the numbers, and I do mean crunched. The video facility wanted $4,000 an episode for which they would provide two days of editing and access to camera crews. We would also bring a lot of our acts to shoot at their facility so they could use that to advertise their services and offset their costs.

Peter would book all the artists, obtain clearances for the videos and be the line producer for the shoots, both in studio and on location. I would write the show, host it and direct it. Peter and I would both be there for the edit sessions. It was a lot for us to do but it meant we could keep the costs way down. Our salaries would be $1,000 each per episode. With a $500 pad for unexpected costs we came up with the incredibly low cost of $6,500 to deliver a thirty-minute TV show. The investor agreed and we were ready to rock.

The word was in all the trade magazines that Richard Blade had sold a show to Tribune broadcasting and very quickly other stations were coming to me. KCOP channel 13 asked if there was any way I could produce a one-off special for them on their leap-year night, Wednesday, February 29.

Peter and I had a lot of footage left over from our crazy day of shooting the *VideoBeat* pilot, plus I had a huge event coming up with the hottest band in the world, Duran Duran, so I knew we could do something spectacular. I signed to produce and host a two-hour special called *SuperStars of Video* and to match the name I sat down with Peter to line up an all-star cast.

What KCOP forgot to tell us was that they wanted us on the air on February 29 because America—and the world's—number-one TV show at that time, *Dynasty*, was airing a very special episode to follow the previous week's cliff-hanger ending which had Fallon Carrington hit by a car. "Is Fallon dead?" screamed all the newspapers, "Tune in and find out Wednesday, February 29!" That was the competition that *SuperStars of Video* was facing. But amazingly enough, even though we had our asses handed to us in the "adult" ratings we were number one with teens and number two with 18–24-year-old viewers. As a result KCOP was thrilled, and unknown to anyone at that time, across town at KHJ channel 9, the former home of *MV3*, they saw the numbers and began making their own plans.

With SuperStars of Video done we returned our attention to polishing VideoBeat and making it the very best it could be. We were elated when it debuted on KTLA Channel 5 on Saturday, March 17, 1984, to huge ratings. We more than doubled the previous show's audience and gave *Casey Kasem's America's Top 10* its biggest lead-in ever and its highest ratings in eighteen months. The following Monday Casey had a magnum of Dom Perignon champagne sent to my apartment with a wonderful thank you note.

Our second show on March 24 was rated even higher and set a record for the time slot. David Simon called me into his office and gave me a revised contract. It was no longer for just four episodes; it was for a full twenty-six week commitment with the station having the option to renew for another twenty-six weeks. *VideoBeat* was locked in for an entire year! The trade magazines reported:

KTLA has ordered up a 26-week run for "Video Beat" the Saturday morning music vid show, which the station initially had commissioned for four weeks. KROQ DJ Richard Blade hosts and coproduces.

Finally, someone has done more than just string video clips together

Blade Rocker productions

in conjunction with CCR Video and Lick'Um Productions
present

SuperStars of Video

THE NEXT GENERATION OF VIDEO SHOWS
Featuring interviews with
DURAN DURAN   BOY GEORGE
Spandau Ballet, Toni Basil, Berlin and Nick Heyward

Hosted by Richard Blade

AIRING TONIGHT
8:00 - 10:00 P.M.   KCOP Channel 13

*Special thanks to Suzanne Horenstein, Bill Frank
Eric Gold and John Collins/New Image*

Look out for more unique music video programming from Blade Rocker

It was so exciting to read that in the press, but who knew that just a couple of weeks later I would regret signing that deal as I watched my bank account empty.

I was still on the high from the new *VideoBeat* deal when I received a call from a woman named Barbara Joachim. She asked if we could meet as she was producing a TV show and wanted to talk to me about hosting it.

I met with Barbara and her husband, Larry, at their favorite restaurant at the Beverly Hilton Hotel. At first they came across as a very strange couple. Barbara smoked incessantly and wore her dark hair in a bob cut with a severe fringe across her forehead; Larry was short and bald and sported a very bad attempt at a comb-over. His high-pitched voice and raucous laugh completed the illusion that he was actually the cartoon character Mr. Magoo come to life.

As I talked with them I came to the realization that appearances aside these were two of the nicest people I had ever met and when they started their good-natured bickering with each other, back and forth, it was all I could do not to laugh out loud.

Larry and Barbara had made their money in the film business doing overseas distribution for low-budget movies such as *Cannibal Holocaust* and the Jim Kelly series of Karate films. They had sold several movies to KHJ channel 9 and in return the general manager there, Chuck Velona, had approached them to produce a daily video show for him. Chuck had seen the huge ratings that *MV3* had brought his station and wanted to continue that success. But this time he wanted reliable producers who could keep the show on the air so he approached the Joachims and asked them to bring me in as the host.

The show would air Monday through Friday at 5pm and for the purpose of saving money we would shoot ten episodes back-to-back live to tape every other week at a studio in San Diego. It would be a single twelve-hour shooting day and the tape operator would roll in the videos as I introduced them—no editing and hopefully no screw ups—all in real time. Could I do that? I said I could and we made the deal.

At the end of our very successful business meal, Barbara wondered if I might know someone who was good at obtaining videos and getting the legal clearances to show them. It was exactly the same question that Mary Kellogg had asked me at CBS six months before. I gave Barbara the same answer. I did know someone!

The next day I waited until Peter and I had finished cutting the latest episode of *VideoBeat*. As we walked out of the edit bay I asked Peter to sit with me in the reception area of the video facility. The late-afternoon sun filtered through the big glass doors as we talked and I told Peter of my meeting the night before. Then I got to the crux of it.

"So here's the deal. I want you to join me on this. We'll be back on channel 9 five days a week doing what we do best, a video show."

The color drained from Peter's face as memories of the drugs, guns and disrespect to the artists on the *MV3* set flooded back to him. He jumped to his feet.

"I can't do it, Mr. Fun, I just can't. It was terrible last time. I'm not going through that again."

"But these are great people, Peter. They are real producers," I implored.

"No, I'm not going to do it!"

Peter ran for the door and sprinted into the parking lot as if video demons from hell were on his tail.

Shit! My best friend and producing partner was running away from me in panic. I got to my feet and sprinted after him. I caught up with Peter just as he turned and began his dash down Santa Monica Boulevard. I had no choice so I rugby tackled him and we both went down hard onto the sidewalk.

RICHARD BLADE IS BACK! YOUR FAVORITE VIDEO DJ NOW HOSTS VIDEO ONE WEEKDAYS 5pm KHJ 9

"Get off me, Mr. Fun. I'm not going back," he yelled.

"Peter, Peter! Listen. They're not Poole. You'll like them. We're working directly with the station. It's not like last time. I promise."

"I almost went back to selling ice cream after *MV3*, Mr. Fun. It was crazy for me," said Peter, but he was calming down a little.

"I know. You took so much of it. But this is different. Real producers, a real show and real checks that won't bounce."

Peter was starting to listen now.

"You're my buddy, Peter. Let's do this together. And any problems and we both leave. Okay?"

"Okay. I'll meet with them. But if I don't like them I'm not doing it."

"Fair enough. I'll go with that," I confirmed.

"Excuse me," said a voice. "Are you guys all right?"

That's when Peter and I realized we were still on top of each other in a pile of scuffed knees and elbows on the sidewalk at the intersection of Santa Monica and Cahuenga.

"We're fine, thanks," I assured the voice. I looked at Peter, "We should get up. We've got a new show to do."

Video One went on the air on April 9, 1984, with me as the host. Unlike *MV3* it was primarily videos but Peter and I kept pushing Larry and Barbara to spend a little more money and start shooting interviews for the show. It was something that they promised they'd keep in mind.

By the end of April our two video shows were making waves in California and the record companies were flocking to us asking if we could play their label's videos and interview their artists. Finally I seemed to be in a sweet spot until I went to deposit the funding check to cover *VideoBeat*'s sixth week of production.

I knew the manager of the Bank of America branch in Sherman Oaks well. Sarah was a lovely girl and was always a pleasure to deal with. I would go directly to her desk to make my deposits and withdrawals, and once the business was done we would talk about music and concerts. That's what I thought was going to happen today but instead I was in for a major shock.

I handed Sarah the *VideoBeat* funding check for $6,500 and she casually ran it as we talked. Then she stopped speaking and stared at her computer screen. She typed in a few numbers and looked again. I could see she was concerned. She scrolled down a little and tried to take in what she was seeing.

"Hang on a second, I'll be right back," she said. Sarah got up and walked over to another bank officer who followed her back to her desk and studied at Sarah's screen with her.

"There's no doubt what it says," stated the officer conclusively.

Sarah looked again at her screen and then at me. I'd never seen her eyes so sad.

"There's a problem with this check," she said.

I shook my head, "Don't tell me it's no good!" Visions of *MV3* began to float through my head.

"It's not just that," Sarah answered hesitantly. "It's . . . got an FBI hold on it. It's been flagged for suspicion of embezzlement and money laundering."

She took a breath. "If you want to come around to my side you can see the note on my computer that came up when I ran the check. It's requesting that we have the depositor remain here at the bank until the authorities arrive."

I read the warning and advisement. Sarah wasn't lying and unfortunately I was the depositor the authorities were referring to! It also said about freezing the account.

"Is that my account that they are talking about?" I asked in total disbelief.

"Yes. We can't make you stay here but if you leave we have to put a hold on your account until we are told we can lift it. That might be a few days if all goes well. If you stay we can keep your account liquid."

"But I haven't done anything. I was just depositing the check I was given." I was starting to get anxious.

"Unfortunately that check links you to the investigation. I'm sure once they talk to you it'll be fine. If you want to wait you can sit in my office. I'm so sorry."

So was I. This was something I had to take care of now, so I waited in the back office reading and re-reading the *Los Angeles Times* until a little over an hour and a half later two federal officers arrived.

They asked me a series of questions regarding the check, my business and my relationship with the person and company who issued the check. They went through my bank records and saw that the previous five checks had been deposited and cleared. They also noted the checks I'd issued from BladeRocker to the video company and to myself and Peter for salary that backed up my story.

"Well, it all checks out," the first officer said. "It looks like you are a victim too. We have all your contacts; if we need any further information from you we'll be in touch. Thank you for your cooperation. You are free to go."

"So what's the deal? What did they do wrong?" I asked.

"We can't comment on an ongoing investigation but you have been very helpful," said the other officer.

And just like that, after only five weeks, the funding ran out for *Video-Beat*. I went to the investor's office but it was shuttered and over the next few months I read about pending legal action against the person who had been underwriting *VideoBeat*. We were small potatoes compared with some of the other questionable activities they had been up to.

But my problem was either finding the cash to keep *VideoBeat* on the air or pull it off and risk a lawsuit from Tribune Broadcasting. I had signed a contract to deliver fifty-two original shows and with only five paid for, I now had to come up with the money myself to fund the remaining forty-seven. At $6,500 an episode that meant I had to find over $300,000. I didn't have anything close to that.

The first thing I did was cut my salary to zero. Peter reduced his to $500 and I convinced the video company to reduce their weekly costs to $2,000. Now it was a little more manageable but it still meant it would take all of my salary from *Video One* and most of my money from KROQ to keep the show afloat. Only one thing to do, and that's up the number of club gigs I was doing.

This was tough because to be on time at the station to do my morning show I had to be up by 4:40 in the morning. With the clubs keeping me out until 1a.m. it meant barely three hours of sleep a night. But when you're pushed into a corner you have two choices, give up or come out swinging, and I hadn't come to America to give up.

Video One and VideoBeat logos

While Eric Gold hustled the streets looking for another sponsor—hopefully one who wasn't the target of an FBI investigation this time—I started picking up some outside television work to replenish my bleeding bank account.

Paramount enlisted me as a reporter for their new afternoon talk show *America* hosted by Sarah Purcell of *Real People* and ESPN hired me to cover a series of skateboard events for Vision Sports.

In September of 1984, with almost $70,000 of expenses paid out of my own pocket, Eric found a new sponsor for *VideoBeat*. I happily signed the deal and my financial hemorrhaging ceased.

KTLA offered to renew VideoBeat's contract for a second year. I felt like Peter at this point and wanted to run for the door but instead our new investor was happy to keep the money coming so we accepted the twelve month extension with Tribune Broadcasting and VideoBeat continued through to April of 1986 with 104 successful, but financially challenging, episodes.

Our hard-working, underpaid VideoBeat crew

RADIO GAGA

Ramondo and Blade were flying high. The two of us just clicked together on the radio. Ramondo's dry American wit and precise timing matched with my British enthusiasm and music knowledge worked well with the listeners and in just a few months we had hit number one in the ratings in virtually all of KROQ's key demographics.

We were friends off the air as well. We both had similar experiences in radio, paying our dues and coming up through the smaller markets. Raymond's last gig prior to KROQ was in San Diego at the rock station KPRI and just like me he had fallen into an open spot on KROQ.

Raymond was very supportive of my outside TV adventures. He would often come to the shoots and show up at the TV set in Burbank and a number of times I was able to get him on camera doing segments. Our live audience loved him and within just a few weeks he starting dating one of our *MV3* dancers, Pam.

Our morning show had a team of characters who appeared on the air with us including Rhonda Kramer, our flirtatious traffic reporter, and two surf reporters—this was Southern California after all—Rockin' Fig and the Poorman. But we still had no budget!

We had been together for four months and with Christmas rapidly approaching we were being inundated with thousands of Christmas cards sent in to us from fans. Many would enclose a stamped addressed envelope asking if we could mail a picture of Ramondo and Blade back to them just as I had done with my photograph for the listeners in my first days at the station.

We asked the management if they would pay for a few thousand cards to send to our fans and were laughed out of the office. That got me pissed.

We borrowed a camera and had Quay Hays snap a couple of pictures as we stood in the corner by his desk. I had the photos developed and made into a Christmas postcard that would fit into the stamped addressed envelopes and spent hours lickin' and stickin' them.

It cost us a little money but it was worth every cent. Those cards were going to the kids who listened to us every day and loved *their* station. We knew that they would treasure anything with KROQ on it. We were building loyalty, one card at a time.

KROQ was notorious for being cheap. Our salaries were miniscule and while every other morning show in LA had a producer, a writer and a talent booker Raymond and I only had each other. But we made it work and fortunately because of our mammoth ratings every record company, movie studio and TV station would come to us and ask to have their stars appear on our show.

And it wasn't just the TV stations and press agents pushing to get their clients on the air with us, they also wanted to use our growing popularity and name recognition to promote their shows, newspapers, and magazines by booking Ramondo and the Blade to boost their ratings and sell copies.

Suddenly it was Raymond and I who were in demand which took us by surprise. There were times we would look at each other and think, *Holy shit!*

We were featured in the *Los Angeles Times, Daily News, LA Weekly, BAM Magazine, The Press Telegraph*—virtually every publication in Southern California came after us. Then we got a call from *Playgirl* magazine.

This was big. It was national and international but we said yes—except I insisted that there be no nudity. Four months after the shoot the magazine came out with Kurt Russell on the cover and for the next few weeks Raymond and I would be met at all our gigs by fans clutching the magazine and wanting us to sign it. I have to admit it was a little disturbing to have a fifteen-year-old girl approach you with a *Playgirl* in her hand asking for an autograph.

The main thing that differentiated us, and the rest of KROQ's airstaff, from every other station in the market was the music. We played what nobody else would play and we played it first.

Music was defined and pigeon-holed by its categories; you had top 40, rock, oldies, hip-hop etc. but in Southern California a new genre was born, K-Rock music. Everyone called it that. We owned certain bands: Duran Duran, The Cure, The Smiths, New Order, Depeche Mode, The Police, Tears for Fears, Talking Heads, Missing Persons, Berlin, Oingo Boingo. If you went to a record store and bought an album from one of those groups, and many more, you were buying K-Rock music. It was a phenomenon.

KROQ became an adjective. And it was everywhere. Clubs all over LA and Orange County staged "KROQ nights," meaning that was the music you would hear if you went there that evening. No other station in America had that kind of influence or following and the record companies knew it.

In 1983 Adam Ant had a huge hit with his debut solo single "Goody Two Shoes." To build on his chart success Adam embarked on a five-month tour of the United States. At many of his dates he had a little-known Australian band opening for him. In fact the group was so new that no one knew how to say their name correctly so all the newspaper ads read "INXS, pronounced in-excess."

Their record label, Atco, saw the huge potential in the band and promoted them hard, so when they came to town at the end of March they pushed to have them on *MV3* and KROQ. I talked with Raymond and agreed to both.

For the *MV3* TV shoot the record company persuaded me to interview lead guitarist Tim Farriss and singer Michael Hutchence at the LA Zoo in front of the kangaroo enclosure. They wanted all my viewers to be sure to know that INXS were from Australia, the home of Men at Work. It sounded cheesy but I loved to take the show out on location so I went along with it.

*With Michael Hutchence and Tim Farriss
for a TV shoot at the LA Zoo*

The next morning Michael and Tim came on the Ramondo and Blade morning show for their radio interview. They were both tired and dragging a little and that made Ramondo think they didn't want to be with us at KROQ.

"I guess we got you out of bed too early," said Ramondo.

"No, mate," replied Tim, "We wanted to be here today."

"Seriously?" laughed Ramondo. "Then you're the only ones! No one wants to come to Pasadena at seven in the morning!"

"It is early," agreed Michael, "but it was important for us to be here."

"Why, did you want to check out the Rose Parade route?"

"I don't know what that is, but we wanted to see what K-Rock was like," explained Tim.

It was my turn to be doubtful. "Right. We're the number-one tourist attraction in California right after Disneyland."

Everybody laughed. I continued, "I bet you never even heard of us until the record execs dragged you out of bed this morning."

"That's where you're wrong, mate," said Michael. "We know all about you in Australia."

"What?" asked Raymond. "They can barely hear us in Irvine, never mind Australia."

"Yeah," said Tim, "but if you're in music then you know that to make it in America you have to be played on KROQ first."

Michael caught Raymond and me looking at each other in disbelief.

"Tim's right," agreed Michael. "We know all about you down under. You're the world-famous K-Rock."

And just like that a slogan was born that over the next year was used side by side with our existing "ROQ of the '80s" and went on to become one of the most recognizable catchphrases in radio and would be featured on every bumper sticker from then on out, "The World-Famous KROQ."

There always seems to be a yin and yang in life and even as the station soared and "Ramondo and Blade in the Morning" hit new ratings heights, cracks started to appear.

Two years prior to my arrival at KROQ Raymond had been running an errand for the station. He was on his motorbike heading to Perkins Palace in Pasadena to drop off advertising copy when he was hit dead on in an intersection. His bike spun off the road and Raymond was flung over the hood of the car but his foot caught in the radiator grill and the jarring impact shattered multiple bones in his leg.

KROQ had no insurance coverage to offer Raymond, and with no money himself he had to settle for his leg being put in a cast and left to heal the best it could. Now, nearly three years later, his limp was becoming worse every day as the still-unhealed, jagged bones ground together causing him excruciating pain.

To deal with this daily agony Raymond tried self-medicating. Unfortunately his medicine came in a six-pack.

As 1983 rolled on Raymond's drinking became worse and worse. Each morning he'd arrive in the studio with a brown bag holding his Budweisers. At first I was at a loss for what to say. He was obviously in pain, and the alcohol wasn't affecting his on-air performance, but I knew it wasn't right. When he moved from twelve ounce cans to sixteen-ouncers it reached the point where I had to do something; I had to step in to help my friend.

I had no medical training so I went to a doctor who had just joined the KROQ team to co-host the weekend show, "Loveline." In truth he hadn't finished his medical training yet and was still a resident but we all called him Dr. Drew.

I explained the situation to Drew the best I could and asked for his advice. Drew told me that with those kind of multiple fractures caused by a traumatic injury being improperly treated for so long there was danger of numerous complications which was probably why Raymond was in such constant pain. When I asked what a worst case scenario was Drew looked at me and said three words, "Worst case? Amputation."

I couldn't bear the thought of my friend, my partner on air, and the man who had willingly shared with me his amazing radio skills and impeccable timing possibly losing his leg. The next day, after our show, I had a serious talk with Raymond. I told him that from now on there would be no alcohol in the control room and if he brought any in there would be trouble.

The next morning Raymond showed up at the station in a shocking state, I had never seen him that bad before. Rather than bring the alcohol into the studio he'd sat in the parking lot out back and drank it, all of it, one sixteen ounce can after another! He was toasted. I couldn't let him on the air like that; it wouldn't have been fair to the station, it wouldn't have been fair to me but most of all it wouldn't have been fair to Raymond.

I grabbed him by the shoulders and walked him outside the small control room into the corridor. He slumped to the ground and went straight to sleep. He stayed like that throughout the duration of the show, even as the staff arrived and the station came to life.

After I got off the air I marched Raymond into Pat Welsh's office and demanded that Raymond be given help. Pat listened intently and to Raymond's and my surprise he promised to take care of it.

That morning marked an end and a beginning.

It was the beginning of Raymond's long battle to recover from that work-related injury that KROQ should have taken care of years before. He first went through a series of operations which required that his leg be broken again, then pinned, reset and cast correctly. After that he was placed in rehab which he embraced with open arms.

But it marked the end of Ramondo and Blade. I was given something I didn't want, a chance to fly solo in the mornings. If I'd had the choice I would have stayed Raymond's partner for my entire radio career. I can think of no kinder, more talented, funnier person to have been blessed to work with. But it was not just a career choice; it was a matter of Raymond's life.

When Raymond returned to the station almost six months later he was a new man: clean, sober and without even a trace of a limp. He was given the afternoon show and a chance to have a real life. I still talk with him often and refer to him as my Obi-Wan Kenobi. But to millions of KROQ listeners he'll always be the anchor of the Ramondo and Blade show.

Ramondo & Blade **KROQ**
ROQ OF THE EIGHTIES
GET ME UP IN THE MORNING **FM 106.7**

HOLLYWOOD SWINGING

What a difference a year makes! In late 1984 I had two hit TV series on the air, *Video One* and *VideoBeat*. In addition I was working on my second Christmas special for KCBS, *Music Video Countdown '84*.

Eric Gold, my long-time agent and good friend, was transitioning from working at an agency to starting his own production company so I needed to find a new agent.

I signed with one of Hollywood's biggest talent agencies, who gave me a pep talk at our initial meeting that "Team Blade" would be out there pushing the studios to bring in all kinds of major projects for me. But I think they must have misplaced my number because it was always me calling them, not vice versa. Very quickly I started missing Eric's hands-on, individual approach. I could feel myself getting hopelessly lost amongst the thousands of clients at that entertainment conglomerate.

It was in October 1984 during my morning show that my phone operator came into the studio and said they had a call for me from a Hollywood producer. My first thought was *Right, Hollywood calling on the request line. Bogus!*

I asked the phone op to get their number and I'd call them back. Two hours later I gave Chuck Russell a buzz and asked what the deal was, expecting to get hit up for concert tickets or a giveaway.

"I'm producing a movie," said Chuck. "We think you'd be perfect for it. Would you like to talk?"

Still thinking this could be a put-on, I referred him to my new agency, thanked him, hung up and promptly forgot about it.

The next week Chuck called back. This time I was off the air and took his call.

"What did you think of the script?" he asked.

I was puzzled. "I didn't see any script."

"I sent it to your agent as you said. I thought you would have received a copy by now."

"Okay, I'll give her a call and find out what's happening. Thanks for following up." I hung up the phone and dialed my agency.

They put me through to my agent and I asked her about getting a script from some guy called Chuck Russell.

"Oh yeah, we got that, but it's so not right for you. Just too big a stretch for what they want you to play," she explained. "We're actually looking at a couple of other major projects right now that you would be much more suited for so just hang tight."

As I put the phone down I was left with the impression that maybe Chuck wanted to cast me as an axe murderer or a child molester or something that was definitely not in my wheelhouse. I put the script out of my thoughts.

Four days later it came screaming right back into my mind when Chuck called again. He was nothing if not persistent.

"What did your agent say?" Chuck asked.

"She read it and said it wasn't right for me, that I couldn't play it."

Chuck was silent for a moment before he spoke. "You should know she sent someone else up for the part, but we really want you. I understand this is a lot to ask," he said, "but could I send you the script to read? I'll have it messengered right now to your house or to KROQ or wherever you want it. Just tell me. I really think you should read it and decide for yourself."

The guy got an A for effort, that's for sure. "Okay, I'll be here at KROQ for about two more hours, then—"

Chuck cut me off, "I know where the studio is. It'll be there in forty minutes. I'll have a runner leave now."

"Okay, I'll look for it." I went to hang up and then thought of something. "Hey Chuck, what part is it that I should be reading?"

There was a smile in his voice as he answered, "You'll know, I promise you'll know."

The script arrived in a brown studio envelope from New World Pictures and as I had a spare hour before I had to head out to the TV studio I sat down in the sales office and began to read through it.

It started in a classroom in Chicago and then on page three cut to a TV studio full of dancers. The host, Gary Woods, runs out and underneath his name was a brief description. This is common for Hollywood; when major characters are first introduced in a script there is nearly always one line explaining to the reader what they look like. For example it might say "Susie Barker, a former model who has not aged well" or "Steven Hardman, a handsome, lean thirty year old who can handle himself." The description for the part Chuck Russell was thinking of for me was shorter and more to the point. It read:

GARY WOODS
(a Richard Blade type)

I was stunned. I read and re-read those four words and almost showed them to the other people in the sales office just to make sure I wasn't imagining things. I reached for the phone to scream at my agent but then thought better of it. Instead I called Chuck.

"Chuck, I got the script. When do you want to meet?"

It turned out that the writer, Amy Spies, was a big fan and had written the part of the DTV host with me in mind and had been pressuring Chuck to get me to join the cast. Chuck and I quickly made a deal and I was signed to appear in my first movie, *Girls Just Want to Have Fun*. But I had one thing to do first.

I drove to Beverly Hills, headed into the agency's offices off of Wilshire and met with my agent. She was all smiles and clichés. According to her she was about to give me the world on a platter. I think I pulled off my best acting performance ever in that office.

"So, that script that was sent in a couple of weeks ago? Did anything come of it?" I inquired innocently.

"No, nothing. Not something we were interested in."

"You didn't send anyone else out for it?" I asked.

"No. I mean it was sent in for you but it just was something that you would have been so wrong for."

"Really?" I reached into my bag and pulled out a photocopy of page three of the script where I had circled "a Richard Blade type" and held it up. "Just how would I have been wrong for that?"

She was at a loss for words. She struggled to speak as I continued.

"And you did send someone out to read for it. The producer told me. It was Mark, right?"

Mark was another of her clients who was also English.

"You were hoping that all they were concerned about was the accent and you wanted him to get the part, not me."

"It's not that, it's . . ." she hesitated so I jumped in. I pointed again to the description.

"Read it out loud to me. Read it," I said.

She shook her head. "I won't do that."

"Then I've got four words I'll say out loud to you. You are fucking fired!"

I threw the paper at her as I got up.

"Put that up on your notice board and tell your bosses that the reason I left was because I wasn't the right type for them!"

With that I stormed out of the office. By the time I reached the street I was smiling from ear to ear. I might not have had an agent any more but at least I was back working on my own terms.

Girls Just Want to Have Fun was a blast to be a part of. We shot on a soundstage in Silverlake, about ten minutes from downtown LA. I was reunited with Sarah Jessica Parker, who I'd worked with in *Square Pegs* and met her boyfriend, Robert Downey Jr., who had an uncredited part in the film as a party-crashing punk. Also in the cast were Helen Hunt, Terry McGovern and Shannon Doherty.

We shot my scenes for "DTV" in two weeks and most of my lines as the DTV host Gary Woods were ad-libbed based on my actual TV hosting with *MV3*. The dance scenes were especially fun as there was a lot of cross-cutting between Sarah, Lee Montgomery and their stunt doubles.

After the film was completed I went on the hunt for a new agent. I finally signed with William Morris, who actually decided that they would hustle to get me out there for auditions and reads. They told me it wouldn't be easy but in all honesty I've never been frightened of hard work and I'd been hustling all my life. Only now, I was doing the Hollywood hustle!

I started to land parts on a number of different episodic TV shows and my first big network appearance was when I played an Australian killer opposite Fred Dryer in his hit detective show *Hunter*.

Hunter set things in motion and a number of parts quickly followed, including that of a lascivious playboy in *Single Bars* with Tony Danza and Paul Michael Glasser, a television personality in *Studio 5-B* which featured Jeffrey Tambor and Kim Myers, an aggressive British customs agent harassing Anthony Geary at Heathrow Airport in *General Hospital*, a DJ on *Throb*, a long-lost brother on *Downtown* with Michael Nouri and Robert Englund, and an adulterous tennis instructor on *Superior Court.*

Playing the psycho killer in Hunter

I was also booked for a number of cameos, guest stars and voice-overs for films which included *Slamdance*, *Crystal Heart* with Tawny Kitaen, *She's Having a Baby* starring Kevin Bacon and the part of "Screamin' Steve" in *Rock'n'Roll High School Forever* with Corey Feldman.

At the beginning of 1986 I read for a major part in a movie called *Spellcaster.* My role was to be the host of a fictitious MTV-like channel that was staging a treasure hunt in an Italian castle and giving away a million dollars to the winner.

My audition was incredibly easy. I just had to act as if I was a TV host. The director, Rafal Zielinski, gave me the part in the room. That's when I found out the movie was actually being filmed on location in Italy at a real castle that Charles Band, the head of Empire Pictures, owned.

I arranged with Barbara and Larry Joachim to pre-shoot a month of *Video One* to cover my time in Italy and asked KROQ for the time off. They reluctantly agreed but only after I said I would take a group of KROQ winners to New York on July 4 of that year for a sponsored prize which in-

cluded dinner at Windows on the World on the 106 floor of the World Trade Center. After that brief trip to the Big Apple the winners flew back to California and I continued on to Italy.

When I arrived I was handed the latest copy of the script and found that my part had been beefed up considerably. Now I was an unscrupulous host who was trying to steal the million dollars for himself while sleeping with all the female contestants. The script changed about a dozen more times during shooting, which is why the film became a mess, but that remained the essence of the flimsy plot.

The other members of the cast included Bunty Bailey, who had just starred in the A-ha video "Take On Me"; Kim Ulrich, a gorgeous soap star from *Days of Our Lives* and Gail O'Grady. But the big thrill for me was the casting of my long-time friend Adam Ant in the role of the supernatural villain, Senor Diablo.

Adam and I spent a lot of time together on and off the set. For the first two weeks we shot at Cinecitta Studios in Rome which had been home to many epics produced by Dino de Laurentiis.

The two of us, the DJ and the rock star, would head into the Eternal City at night to find a small piazza and sit under the stars and talk about

With Adam Ant on and off the set in Italy

Shooting Spellcaster on location in Italy

music and girls as we shared freshly made, home-cooked local pasta. I was so impressed at how relaxed and fluid Adam was in front of the camera; as an actor he was a natural and could pick up on direction in the blink of an eye. It became obvious to all on the set why Adam's videos had become so iconic—he had that charisma that shone right through the camera.

For the final two weeks of shooting we moved outside of Rome to Charlie Band's castle. This was a truly spectacular medieval fortress which featured an armory, a dungeon and was ringed with battlements and watchtowers that commanded an endless view over a breathtaking lake.

As I was now the lead in the picture I was able to pick my shooting schedule, and being used to early mornings, I chose to shoot from 6am until noon. I would then be free for the afternoon and I would head down through the village to the lake and swim for hours along the shoreline. After growing up in and around the ocean, I was not used to swimming in fresh water and found it warm and inviting and each time I would emerge refreshed and ready to go.

Shooting a movie is an unreal situation. You are there to create a celluloid fantasy, but the reality is that while the film is in production you are living in a fantasy world. You are waited on hand and foot. You are spoiled and coddled. You have your own dressing room, an assistant, makeup artist and wardrobe consultant who dresses you. All this creates an environment that you never want to leave. It also produces an intimate atmosphere for the cast and crew as you are bonded together on a mutual quest to hopefully accomplish something great. It's no wonder romances blossom quickly on a movie set. It was no exception for me.

Congratulations
RICHARD BLADE

- **STARRING ROLE in "SPELLCASTER,"** feature film now shooting for Empire Prods.

- **#1 RATED MORNING DRIVE D.J. in LOS ANGELES** among young persons.*

- **HOST OF "VIDEO ONE,"** syndicated TV strip.

- Just completed writing and directing national TV commercial for client Bare Assets.

Special thanks to: everyone at Empire, especially Estelle & Anthony; Ken Roberts; Pat Welsh, Tom McMillan, Rick Carroll & all at KROQ 106.7 FM; Larry & Barbara Joachim; the Bare Assets crew; Andy Friendly; Bill Brummel; Fern Ornstein; Karen Scott ("Bunny"); Pete Segal; Mary Kellogg; Monty Gast; Cliff Brown

and PETER FACER

Exclusive Representation: **WILLIAM MORRIS AGENCY.** XXX

Within days I had started a relationship with a very beautiful girl involved in the movie and we spent much of our free time exploring not only the local sights but also each other. We both knew it was just "a thing" but the romance of being in Italy had kicked in and we enjoyed the *amore e passione* for the duration of the movie shoot.

As we got to the final scenes we all began to realize the ending made no sense at all. Word of how bad the film was becoming reached all the way back to the states and the head of the studio himself, Charles Band, flew out to take over the final two days of shooting but even with his experience the ending was still a confusing mish-mash with no real resolution or payoff.

After getting back to LA we all lost touch and went our separate ways. The movie disappeared into a Hollywood black hole for three years until it suddenly appeared on HBO. That's where I saw it for the first time and was shocked to see I not only had top billing but my name came before the title! That was huge and had it been even a halfway decent film would have been a major stepping stone for my career. Instead it was simply "You were in *that* movie?" as if I should be embarrassed.

But why should I be embarrassed? I did my best, worked with some great people, rekindled my friendship with Adam and had an affair to remember with an incredible girl. To capture the essence of my *Spellcaster* experience it would take, appropriately enough, an Italian phrase—*la dolce vita*.

I'LL FLY FOR YOU

The huge numbers that my morning show on KROQ and *Video One* and *VideoBeat* were achieving were being noticed much further away than Southern California. Getting played on "the ROQ of the '80s" and on my video shows became a top priority for many bands and their record labels.

When Tears for Fears were featured on the cover of the major international trade publication, *Optic Music*, in 1985 they were asked in the interview about how they found success in America.

Orzabal acknowledged the contribution of Los Angeles DJ/VJ Richard Blade in breaking them in the L.A. markets. He concurred with the opinion that Blade had been instrumental in pushing Tears for Fears long before they had any sort of breakthrough in the U.S. Because of Blade's large following through radio station KROQ and his video shows Video One *and* Video Beat *both* The Hurting *and later* Songs from the Big Chair *had a definite edge in Los Angeles. "He (Blade) really picked up on us since 'Mad World,' our first hit single in England," Orzabal says. "That was at the end of 1982 and he's been promoting us for ages and ages. I'd say that he's rather chuffed (happy) that we've got success now."*

Another band from across the Atlantic, Duran Duran's biggest rivals in the UK, were planning an all-out assault on the USA to try and take the pop crown away from the boys from the Rum Runner. And the vehicle that Spandau Ballet planned to use? *Video One* and *VideoBeat*.

Spandau Ballet had scored a massive hit the year before in America (and around the world) with "True" but their follow up, "Gold," had not done as well as they hoped in the US. That is, except for in Los Angeles and in the other markets where *MV3* had aired. In those places the single had gone to the top of the local sales charts.

The band was now getting a consistent buzz from US fans writing to them in England saying they were seeing their videos on *Video One* and *VideoBeat*. We, unlike MTV, were playing older Spandau Ballet videos as well, great cuts like "To Cut a Long Story Short," "Paint Me Down" and "Chant #1" and getting tremendous reaction to them. We were also featuring the songs and videos from their latest album, *Parade*, a release that MTV all but ignored.

Spandau Ballet's manager, Steve Dagger, was very aware of this as he was hands-on with the group and made their success his priority. He was an incredibly intelligent guy and was continually looking for cool and different ways to enhance his clients' success. And Spandau were a lot more than just clients to Steve; they were all boyhood friends who had grown up together in London.

It was Steve who initially was able to book gigs for the band in their early days at London's hip clubs like The Blitz and then orchestrated their launch into the big time with a much hyped performance aboard the battleship HMS Belfast on the Thames River on July 26, 1980. It was a not-so-subtle way of saying "We are here to give battle to all you other groups out there."

Steve also put together the band's publishing and record deals, and Steve, who along with Gary Kemp, had recruited both Tony Hadley and Gary's brother, Martin, into the group.

Steve had said to Gary that they needed someone who looked good to be the lead singer and they both knew Tony from school and to quote Steve, "Tony was the tallest guy in the class and he had a leather jacket and liked Bowie, so Gary said he was in."

Martin was approached when Steve and Gary were in a pub one night planning how the band was going to take over the world. Gary remarked that the group was almost complete; they had the brilliant musician Steve Norman on saxophone and guitars and John Keeble on drums, but they still needed a bass player.

Gary stressed that he "has to be incredibly good-looking. The kind of guy that the ladies will love. But where do we find someone like that?"

Steve was quiet, then noticed Gary's brother, Martin, at the bar with women falling all over him. "How about your brother? The girls love him."

Gary couldn't deny the physical attraction that Martin exuded but he was dubious. "He wouldn't be any good. He can't play the bass. He can't play anything."

Steve's reply was short, and those two words completed Spandau Ballet's lineup—"Teach him."

I had interviewed Spandau a number of times over the years; during their early days they were regular guests on my radio show, one time even serenading a huge crowd of fans that gathered in the KROQ parking lot to see their idols. The band had assembled on the graffiti-covered back-stairs and led the hundreds of kids in a rousing chorus of "True."

With Spandau Ballet on the back steps of KROQ

As I mentioned earlier, I'd also hosted one of their first American TV interviews that chilly night outdoors on the roof of Le Parc Hotel in Beverly Hills, plus I'd spent time with them in London while shooting *MV Network* for CBS, but now thanks to Steve's long distance phone call I was about to become a lot closer to them than ever before.

It was Christmas Day, 1984, and that crazy, topsy-turvy year was just a week away from being over. Karen and I were getting ready to head up to Santa Barbara to visit her family when the phone rang. I picked it up and heard a familiar English voice. I glanced at the clock; it read 1pm, which meant 9pm in the UK.

"Hey, Richard, it's Steve Dagger. How's your Christmas?"

"Steve!" I was always happy to talk with Steve. He's one of those fun people who never hits you with a dumb request or leaves you in a bad mood. "Merry Christmas! How are things in England?"

"Raining, of course. I had an idea and thought it might make a fun Christmas present for you."

"Really? What?" I asked.

"We just booked an Australian tour. It'll be our first time down there. Then we're doing the rest of the world and wrapping it up in the States. We were wondering if you wanted to come on the road with us to Australia."

I didn't have to think twice. "Absolutely. So what's the deal?"

"Here's the thing. It's been more than a year since 'True' and I'm not sure how we're going to do in America, and right now it's crucial that the band makes a statement where you are. All of our dates have sold out already in Europe and Australia. I mean in Sydney we're doing two nights at the Sydney Entertainment Center. The place is massive and we've sold more tickets than Phil Collins for God's sake. We need to let the American kids know that. So maybe if you could come down and talk about it on your radio program and do something on your TV shows, it would get the word out."

My mind was running numbers and unfortunately the dollar signs were big. Too big. "I'd love to, but here's the thing. It would be expensive."

"I know that." Steve had thought this through already. "We'll fly you and a camera crew down. You travel with us for a week, then go back to America and say what you saw. Would that work?"

It was a brilliant idea and I wouldn't go broke doing it.

"I'm in. And depending on when the tickets go on sale for your US tour, I can do a Spandau week leading up to it on *Video One* and *VideoBeat*. That should give you a lot of publicity."

"Perfect." Steve was really excited now. "I'll send you the tour dates and take care of the tickets. You tell me what you need for the camera crew and I'll draw up a budget for that. Don't worry about any ground transportation or hotels; the local promoters will have all that covered."

"I'm on it. Merry Christmas, Steve."

"Happy Christmas, Richard. Hope this was a good present."

We both hung up.

Two days later Peter and I got together to work out the crew I'd need down under. A good cameraman was essential, preferably someone who could use a portable BetaCam because shooting on one-inch tape would be way too cumbersome. We'd also need a great sound person—after all, this was a music act—and a lighting guy who would make sure these five heartthrobs looked great.

We ended up arranging for Bruce Caulk, a cameraman we used in California, to fly out from the States; the sound and lighting crew I would pick up in Australia. It made the most sense financially and even though it wasn't my money, the Spands were my friends and I don't waste a friend's money unnecessarily.

A few weeks later I settled into the comfortable business seat of a Qantas Airlines 747 and readied myself for the seventeen-hour flight ahead.

The next day I touched down in Sydney and as I disembarked I was pulled aside by a uniformed Qantas official who walked me through a special lane at customs and immigration, avoiding all the long lines and tedious paperwork. So this is what it felt like to be a rock star! It was the perfect taste of what was in store for me over the next seven days.

The stretch limo waited patiently outside—obviously immune to the recorded "white zone is for loading and unloading only" announcement which played every twenty seconds with a fun Oz accent. Inside the two Steves were waiting for me—Steve Dagger and Steve Norman.

"Do you mind if we don't go straight to the hotel? We've got a harbor cruise lined up for the boys and figured you'd like to be part of it."

Let me think. Sydney Harbor—the bridge, the Opera House, the beaches. "Let's do it." I said.

Before boarding the boat I pulled a small home video camera from my bag. The cameraman wasn't arriving until tomorrow but just in case I'd brought a little backup—a mini VHS!

The food and drinks flowed non-stop as we cruised one of the most beautiful harbors on the planet. I shot nearly an hour's worth of video and surprisingly the quality came out so well that we were able to use the footage just two weeks later on both of my TV shows. The band was in great spirits and pumped for the opening night of their Australian tour which was now only seventy-two hours away.

As we pulled back into the dock Steve Dagger leaned over to me. "Get a couple of hours sleep. You'll need it. There's a party tonight." He grinned.

It wasn't his usual smile. It was a "'wait until you see what is going to go down" grin. I trusted Steve and couldn't wait.

Steve had arranged with the promoters of the tour—the biggest concert bookers in the southern hemisphere—for the band to have a full schedule each day of press, radio and television, then to relax and party each night at a different club or bar that was taken over just for them.

We pulled up at the club that night in three separate stretch limos. We could have all squeezed into one but Steve Dagger was having none of that; he didn't want an endless parade of bodies pouring from a single vehicle as if they had been packed in like sardines. This was Spandau Ballet's first time in Australia and Steve was making a statement.

The press was waiting outside and flashbulbs exploded frantically as security hustled us into the club. However when I use the word *hustled* I do have to point out that Steve himself led the charge and he wanted to make sure the band was photographed for the morning papers so he deliberately limited how fast the security had us run the gauntlet of cameras. "Hurry slowly—it's an art" he would say later with a laugh.

Once inside the club we stopped dead in our tracks. All six of us, the five Spands and me, were stunned. We had never seen anything like it. It was beautiful. Only Steve Dagger kept going towards the bar. I had worked in clubs around the world but I had never experienced anything close to this.

Apart from the black-outfitted staff we were the only men in the club. Everyone else, maybe a hundred plus people, were female. And not just regular girls, but drop-dead gorgeous women in barely there mini-dresses.

John Keeble expressed out loud what we were all thinking, "Where the fuck is Saint Peter?" But we weren't in Heaven, just Australia at its best!

Steve Dagger walked back over to the six of us who were still rooted in place.

"What is this?" asked Gary.

"The promoters asked me if I had any special requests for you guys, like Van Halen always says 'no brown M&Ms,' so I jokingly said we wanted a party each night of the tour but only models were to be invited. I thought they knew I wasn't serious but they called me this morning and said it was all arranged. They contacted every modeling agency and talent school in the country and gave all the girls a blanket invitation. This is what it's going to be like right across Australia. Have fun guys."

There is an expression "shooting ducks in a barrel." That's what it was like that night. Even though I wasn't one of the band, I was with them and was the "famous TV host from America." And it certainly wasn't a tough sell because all the girls were there for one reason, to meet and hook up with the rock stars. Because of that simple fact the party didn't last long.

Within an hour the three limos were racing back to the hotel—but this time the cars had quite a few more occupants who were all excited females.

As the cars emptied out we took our new friends inside through a crowd of mostly female fans encamped outside the hotel.

John again chirped up, "Holy shit, there's girls everywhere."

Word had gotten out that Spandau was in Sydney and there was only one place to stay at that time if you were in a band, and that was the Sebel Town House, the Oz equivalent of the Sunset Marquis in Hollywood. The fans knew it and that's where they would wait to meet their heroes.

Tony and Martin were not caught up in all the hormone-driven exuberance. Tony was happily married and Martin had brought his girlfriend with him. That just left the three other Spands, plus Steve and me to do our duty as good Englishmen. After all, we couldn't give these Aussie girls the wrong impression.

I should have been jet-lagged that night but somehow the tiredness from crossing the dateline disappeared when my model date and I hit the room. But the next morning came way too quickly.

Steve woke me, and all the band, with a knock on the door. It was 6:20am! The group was booked on a morning TV talk show and had to be up, dressed and at the studio, ready to go on camera by 7:30am. Steve wanted me there to be part of the whole experience and as tired as I was I was happy to oblige; after all, Steve was picking up the entire tab and I had six more nights of supermodels ahead.

This time we all squeezed in one limo. Steve Dagger and John Keeble had not yet gotten in but the rest of us were assembled, tired and quiet. Gary, Steve Norman and I exchanged knowing glances while Tony and Martin sat there, a little sullen. I knew they were good family men but they had to have been thinking a little bit of "what if?" The car door opened and Steve leaned in and looked around.

"Still no sign of John?" asked Steve. We shook our heads. "Hey, Richard, would you run up and get him?" Steve tossed me a key. "He's on the same floor, two doors down from you."

"No problem," I said and bounded out of the car.

I took the elevator to the fourth floor and headed for John's room. "Hey, John," I called out as I opened the door, "Steve needs you in . . ." I had just walked in on John in an extremely delicate position with two models who were obviously going to be very late for their class today.

"I already told Dagger I wasn't doing the interview, dammit!" John yelled across the room at me.

"Got it, buddy," I said and shut the door behind me.

When I returned to the limo the guys greeted me with laughter and a round of applause. Steve had known what was going to happen and shared my embarrassment with the band. But I wasn't pissed. I was laughing with them before the bellman even had time to close the limo's door.

Traveling with a successful rock group is a unique experience. No doors remain closed to you. Drinks are always free—and forced upon you. Someone else invariably picks up the dinner tab and drugs are ever-present. It can be a very bacchanalian existence and it is understandable when you hear of the abuse and overdoses that happen to so many. Fortunately for me, and for most of the guys in Spandau, our drug was the ladies and Steve Dagger had made it easy to score.

I filmed everything that Spandau Ballet did in those first few heady days. We even shot the Aussie film crews filming Spandau! It was the ultimate reality show from Down Under. Spandau is doing an interview with a national paper—we should shoot it. The band is going to appear on Australia's biggest pop TV show *Countdown*—roll tape. It was a wild, never-ending schedule.

The night of the first of their two sold-out shows at the Sydney Entertainment Center was manic. A lot of people were expecting a laid-back performance from Spandau Ballet because, after all, they were famous for their ballads like "True," "I'll Fly for You" and "Round & Round." Instead, under Gary's leadership and powered by John

Spandau Ballet encore on stage in Sydney, Australia

Keeble's powerful drumming, the band rocked from the opening notes and had the crowd of 18,000 on their feet for the entire ninety-minute set.

I had unlimited access to the stage and shot concert footage and 35mm stills from inside the security barricades. At the end of the show as the band linked arms for the final encore Gary gave me a shout out from the stage and a big thumbs-up.

The first thing that Gary said to me in their backstage dressing room after the show was, "How did we do?"

It wasn't a glib question; he really meant it. Gary cared deeply about his band. He wanted Spandau to be great every time they stepped on stage, their shows to be big, and to leave a lasting impression on the Australian kids.

I was happy to tell him, "You rocked it."

He hugged me and grinned. "Just wait until tomorrow night!"

Later that evening the limos ran the gauntlet of press and took us to another club booked out for Spandau and the cream of the Australian modeling industry. By now the word was getting around that these were *the* parties to try to crash and there was a huge mob of wanna-bes outside. The security rushed us into the club and the waiting arms of the nubile Aussie models.

At this point the band had decided that it was crazy not to have a few other guys there just so the parties would last longer and they would have time for at least a couple of post-show drinks, so in addition to the usual record company types about fifty other guys were invited and were inside milling around. But they seemed to disappear as the band entered; after all, the girls were there to meet Spandau Ballet. It's a cliché for our generation but it's so true, models and musicians!

About thirty minutes after we got to the club a mean-looking bouncer who looked big enough to have eaten a kangaroo for breakfast and still have been hungry for a full-grown wallaby at lunchtime approached me.

"You the American TV guy?" the Australian mountain bellowed.

"Yes. That's me," I replied as I got ready to duck.

He growled, "You got a friend outside who wants to come in."

A friend? I didn't have any friends in Sydney. The guy must be mistaken. But then again he was way too big to argue with so I went along with it and answered with a simple okay.

Godzilla led me to the entrance to the club where at least a hundred people and press were all pushing and shoving as they tried to get inside.

There, waiting for me, was a person dressed all in black with a beanie pulled down over his head and dark glasses obscuring his eyes. He saw me and smiled.

"Richard, I heard you were in town at the Sebel. Any chance you could walk me in? I'm trying not to make a fuss here."

It took me a second but then I realized I was talking to probably the most famous man in Australia at the time, a guy I'd been great friends with for the last three years, Michael Hutchence of INXS. He saw my look of recognition and subtly raised a finger to his lips. I glanced around at the Down Under paparazzi herded together and waiting to pounce on any glimpse of a celebrity and instantly understood. If they had any clue as to who I was talking with it would become an insane mob scene of pushing and yelling.

I turned to Goliath and nodded. "He's good."

With that we were shepherded into the club.

Once inside Michael grinned and grabbed my shoulders. "Thanks, mate. So good to see you in Sydney. Found out you were traveling with the band and thought I'd stop by and say hi. Didn't want those bastards outside getting my picture. The press is all over me these days and my girlfriend's very . . . sensitive about that kind of thing."

Michael looked past me and saw the crowd of beautiful girls waiting. Lambs to the slaughter.

"I'm going to get a drink. What do you want?" Michael asked.

Prior to coming to Oz I always thought that Fosters was Australia's most popular beer but I was wrong. In fact the Aussie's have a joke about Fosters. If there are no kids reading this right now I'll share it with you. "Why is Fosters like making love in a canoe? Because it's fucking close to water!"

Not wanting to look like a tourist I opted for the safe choice. "I'll have a pint of 4X, mate."

"I'll get it and be right back."

Michael sauntered over to the bar where two heavenly visions sat talking to each other, their micro minis exposing almost all of their glistening tanned legs. Michael stopped right by them. They looked up at him but his disguise made him unrecognizable so they had little interest. He was not the Spandau Ballet member they were looking for.

Then Michael reached up and I could swear that he moved in slow-motion and that someone, somewhere, turned on a wind machine just for him.

He removed his glasses, slid the beanie off and shook his head side to side so that his long, flowing hair tumbled down around his shoulders and then seemed to blow backwards in that invisible breeze.

Suddenly the anonomous dweeb standing in front of the two models had turned from ugly duckling to swan and transformed into the hottest, sexiest rock star in Australia, if not the world.

Michael leaned into the girls and whispered something softly. Not that he had to say anything, because at this point those girls were toast! They stood up and excitedly followed Michael as he walked back towards me.

He stopped, gave me a hug and as he pulled on his beanie and glasses disguise said, "Thanks, Richard, but I got to go."

I nodded and watched in awe as the superstar left the club with the two women. Less than three minutes and he'd scored the two most smokin' chicks in Sydney. And that, Mom and Dad, is why kids dream of rock'n'roll stardom!

The next morning when I met up with the rest of the guys in the lobby of the Sebel Hotel there was a package waiting for me. It was a case of XXXX and a note that read, "I forgot your beer last night. Thanks again. See you in LA." Michael was always the best.

The seven days and seven unforgettable nights on the road with Spandau in Australia sped by. The flight back to the States seemed quick. I was out cold for at least eight hours—had to put some time back in the sleep bank—and for the remaining time on the plane I did some rough "paper cuts" of what the following week's show on *Video One* and that coming Saturday's *VideoBeat* would look like.

The next two days were nonstop. I was back on the air doing my morning show on KROQ and talking about how amazing Spandau Ballet were live, then running to CCR Video on Santa Monica Blvd. in Hollywood to dub and edit the Australian footage.

We had a deadline. The tickets for the opening nights of Spandau Ballet's US tour were going on sale the following Friday, and we wanted the spectacular footage of their Australian tour to air every day leading up to then. *VideoBeat* was airing first that Saturday and Peter Facer and I worked long hours to put the show together. We dropped it off at KTLA late that Friday afternoon, just making our deadline, and Saturday morning it aired—and it looked fantastic!

Video One's "Spandau Ballet Week Down Under" started that Monday as did the countdown to the on-sale now just four days away. Steve Dagger called me every afternoon from the ongoing tour in Australia—it was morning there, the next day for him—to ask how the buzz was. I had to tell him that virtually every call I was getting on the request lines at KROQ was for Spandau. It was looking good.

In between the radio, my TV shows and the flyers that Avalon Attractions were passing out at all my live gigs, the words *Spandau Ballet* were everywhere in California. We waited anxiously for the on-sale to start Friday at 9am.

Two shows were going on sale simultaneously. The first night of the US tour was in Orange County at Irvine Meadows on Friday, April 19. The second night was at the Universal Amphitheatre the next day, Saturday, April 20.

What the public didn't know was that Steve Dagger was holding another night—Sunday, April 21 at the Universal Amphitheatre—to put on sale over the weekend if by any chance the first night got close to selling out.

I was on the air at KROQ that Friday morning counting down to the on-sale. At 9am I gave a "Spandau Ballet tickets are available now!" and went into "Only When You Leave."

I was readying the first commercial break of the hour at 9:22am when the red line rang. This was the sacred hotline. Only a very few insiders had that number. Steve Dagger was one of them. He was talking as I answered the phone.

"They've gone. They've all gone." he babbled.

Sensing something was wrong I jumped in. "Slow down, Steve. It's okay. What's gone?"

"The tickets, Richard. They've gone. All of them."

I was picturing some kind of ticket heist with armed men making off with the 24,000 tickets, saying, "Budweiser presents Spandau Ballet."

"What do you mean, gone?" I asked.

"All three shows are sold out," Steve answered.

"All *three*?" I was stunned.

"Yes. Irvine blew out 16,000 tickets in seventeen minutes. The Universal sold the first night—6,000 tickets—in six minutes and rolled straight into the second show. Those also went in six minutes. They said it's the fastest sell-out in history at both venues. Thank you so much."

"Hold on, I'm putting you on the air."

As the song faded out I potted up the volume control for Steve and talked to him about the sold-out shows. He promised the fans he would try to add a couple more shows at the end of the tour if the band could find time. Then, ever the promoter and always quick on his feet, he plugged the fact that I was going to be hosting an in-store appearance with Spandau the day before the show at Music Plus Records in Orange County.

He continued with, "Why don't you give a pair of listeners a chance to meet up with you there and bring them backstage to hang out with the guys?"

At Music Plus, April 18, 1985, with the contest winners, Spandau Ballet and my production assistant, Joelle Hood

Boom! Just like that our request lines exploded as I said into the microphone "Okay, caller number 106.7 right now at 1-800-520-1067 joins me backstage with the Spands!"

I told Steve I had to run to the lines and I could hear the smile in his voice as he told me, "We owe you dinner, big time!"

Six weeks later the in-store at Music Plus rolled around and it was frenzied. More than 3,000 kids turned up at three in the afternoon to greet their pop heroes. The band was scheduled for two hours but stayed for four to sign as many albums as possible. I remember one little girl who was crying so hard as she stood in front of Martin that she couldn't speak.

He gallantly got up and hugged her. "It's all right," he said. Waaaaah! She cried even harder because her pin-up was hugging her. Sometimes you just can't win.

The next night was the opening show of the US tour—Irvine Meadows, California. Not an empty seat in the house. Even the lawn was packed. I walked out on stage to introduce the band and for a moment I thought all the monitors were off because I couldn't hear a thing. Then I realized it was because the crowd was so loud.

All I could hear was the chant of "Richard, Richard, Richard." I waited at the center microphone for a second, then asked the question that, had Irvine Meadows not been an outdoor venue, would have brought the roof down. "Any Spandau Ballet fans here?"

I was almost blown off the stage by the roar. Seconds later I introduced the five of them and Tony and I shook hands as we exchanged spots and he took that center mic.

Walking out on stage to introduce Spandau Ballet

The Irvine Meadows' show was a triumph. Spandau came to prove to the American audience they could rock and they did it in spades. After the show Gary asked his usual question of me, "How did we do?"

I think my response was "Awesome," but Gary already knew that. He was pumped and excited.

"I can't wait for tomorrow night, Richard. The Universal Amphitheatre. Everyone's played there—Elvis, Frank Sinatra—and now it's our turn. I promise it'll be a show for the record books."

Ironically, Gary Kemp was right—but not in the way he wanted to be.

That day I DJ'd a special Saturday show on the air at KROQ and had the guys in. The fans turned up in droves, packed the parking lot and spray painted "SPANDAU BALLET" all over the radio station's back wall. I shot the interview for my upcoming TV shows and as the group left the building they couldn't have been in better spirits.

It was a thrilling moment for all involved. It seemed that nothing could stop them from their goal of conquering the USA. Little did anyone know that they were just hours away from that dream becoming a nightmare and encountering a stumbling block that would sideline them from American audiences for the next three decades.

The energy at the Universal Amphitheatre was palpable, both out in the audience and backstage. It was hard to know who was most excited, the fans or the band. I hung with them in the dressing room as I waited for my cue to go up the stairs and out onto the stage.

The show was starting with a three-minute video montage I'd put together from *VideoBeat* of Spandau in Australia. The techs at the Universal Amphitheater had it playing on their two state-of-the-art giant screens either side of the stage.

The stage manager came to get me and as we left the dressing room I heard Gary pumping up the band, much like a coach does to his team before a game. "Don't hold anything back tonight; just go for it out there." Ironic words.

The intro was a rush and the band followed me on stage to a deafening wall of screams. They were firing on all cylinders. I had never seen them so energized. If anything the concert was even better than the night before. Should anyone have had any reservations that Spandau Ballet was a rock band then the sight of Gary Kemp at the front of the stage shredding on his guitar to that sold-out audience would have dispelled those doubts in an instant.

I stood in the pit shooting the show with my SLR camera. About forty minutes in, Steve Norman went into his sax solo and slid across the stage.

But the excitement and energy of the night got to him and he dropped too fast and slid too far and I could see his knee twist out from under him. He dropped the sax for a second as pain shot through his body; then he tried to stand up. He couldn't. His legs gave out from beneath him and he went down again hard.

The band finished the song and Tony, always the great front man, tried to take control of the situation. "Sometimes I guess we rock just a little too hard." His laugh was forced.

John Keeble kept a back beat going as Tony and Gary went over and spoke to Steve Nor-

Tony with the injured Steve Norman on that fateful night

man. He was in obvious pain but wanted to carry on. The two of them helped him up and *bam!* he went down again. I could hear Steve saying, "I'm sorry, guys."

Now Martin joined Tony and Gary and together they hoisted Steve onto Tony's shoulders. Tony might have one of the most beautiful, romantic voices in music but he is a big guy—two inches taller than me and I'm almost six foot three—and he's strong. That strength was put to the test that night because for the next three songs he carried Steve Norman around the stage.

Tony sang and Steve played sax and the show went on as best it could.

The concert finished early, and doctors were waiting backstage as Steve Norman was carried off. The news wasn't good. He'd blown out his knee. It would take surgery and a long recuperation to recover from the injury.

Steve Dagger made the decision quickly. Tomorrow's show had to be cancelled. By the next morning he had pulled the band out of their entire US tour.

It was a setback that would not only rock their status in America but begin friction within the group that by the end of the decade would result in the breakup of the band and a series of contentious lawsuits that would last years and forever taint the relationship of the former best friends.

Steve Dagger told me later that if he knew then what was to happen, he wouldn't have cancelled any of the dates. Instead he would have put Steve Norman in a wheelchair and pushed him out on stage himself at every concert. But he didn't and by the time the eighties came to a close repercussions from that torn knee tore apart the band itself.

WILD BOYS

The British Invasion of new wave music was well underway when Duran Duran brought their 'Rio' tour to North America in June of 1982. It was their second series of shows in the US in less than a year. In September 1981 they had made their first foray into the States when they played clubs, including The Roxy in Los Angeles, but now they were back and headlining in bigger venues.

On July 27, 1982 they wrapped up their American tour at the Greek Theatre in Los Angeles. Even though it was a Tuesday night the buzz around Duran Duran was growing and the 5,800 seats were completely sold out.

Their album *Rio* had been released just two months before. KROQ was the only place on the radio dial in Southern California playing them and none of the other DJs from the station wanted to go out in the middle of the week to introduce the band onstage so as the newbie I was asked to do it. I was actually happy to be given the task as I had been a fan of the band since their self-titled debut release the year before and had added them to the playlist of Z93 in San Luis Obispo when I was program director there.

I had a feeling they would be good live, so I invited my buddy Swedish Egil to join me and together we headed to Hollywood.

The band was excited to go on; it was by far the biggest date in LA they had ever played, and it was the final show of their North American tour and they really wanted to go out in style and make a statement. I received my cue to go out and warm up the crowd, and right after my intro they ran out and owned that stage.

They opened with "Rio", a song that at that time was still mostly unknown to the audience and then segued into "Girls on Film". Now the crowd was getting to its feet and starting to dance. At the midpoint of the show the lights dimmed and they broke into an amazing version of "New Religion" with Simon's voice ringing through the natural valley that The Greek sits in.

I remember turning to Egil and saying, "These guys are the real thing." Duran Duran had it all; amazing songs, great musicianship, awesome stage presence and the kind of good looks that would adorn the bedrooms of tens of millions of teenage girls around the world.

As the concert drew to a close DD rocked into three uptempo tracks back-to-back, "Planet Earth", "Hold Back The Rain" and the cut that features one of the best bass lines in modern music brilliantly played by John Taylor, "Careless Memories".

There was no doubt in the minds of the fans that night that Duran Duran had arrived and had the firepower and raw talent to back up their studio albums with riveting live performances. Both Swedish Egil and I knew that with two great albums under their belt, DD were here to stay.

As soon as their show was finished I sped across town to my own gig at The Roxy. I was pleasantly surprised when an hour into my set Simon Le Bon arrived with a Duran Duran white label twelve inch for me to play.

It was another nineteen months before I was able to cement my relationship with the boys from DD.

In late January, 1984, Michelle Peacock, a promotions executive at Capitol Records, approached me about hosting a special event with Duran Duran. Capitol was planning a worldwide press conference with DD on February 7 at the Magic Castle in Hollywood.

The date was not an accident. It had been deliberately picked because it would be twenty years to the day – February 7, 1964 – that The Beatles had arrived in America, and now, exactly two decades later the Fab Four had new rivals in the States, the Fab Five!

Press from around the globe were invited and the scene was set.

In addition to hosting the press conference, Michelle gave me and Peter Facer exclusive access to film Duran Duran not only onstage but also backstage and during rehearsal; footage that we would air on the upcoming TV shows *SuperStars of Video* and *VideoBeat*.

After rehearsals, waiting for the press conference to start

We spent most of the day with Duran Duran. In the morning we met up with them at their hotel then travelled with them in their limos to the Magic Castle where we did an hour of rehearsal and camera blocking for the press conference. After all that was done it was time to just sit around and wait.

When the press conference finally got under way it was mayhem for the first few minutes. Two hundred reporters fired off a non-stop barrage of flashes that almost blinded us and screamed to get the band's attention.

Finally I had to take the microphone and let the press corps know that if they didn't quiet down Duran Duran would have to leave. After that everything got under control and for the next ninety minutes I called for questions from the invited audience while Simon, Nick, John, Roger and Andy laughed and joked their way through the answers.

The press conference was broadcast live on three continents and elevated Duran Duran to a new level of stardom. The band featured footage of it in their tour move *Sing Blue Silver* and a line of bubblegum cards were

released in Japan featuring the six of us together on stage. It was a pivotal moment for the British invasion in America.

After the ninety-minute press conference we headed backstage. John asked how I had liked it. I only had one word for him, "Wild!"

John laughed and said, "Well I hope you're ready for tonight. Want to come on stage and introduce us?"

I didn't have to even think about my answer, after all Duran Duran was about to play the second of two sold out nights at the Fabulous Forum in Los Angeles, a place where I had been so many times as just a concert goer to see acts like Pat Benatar, The Police and Genesis. Now I was being asked to go onstage and introduce Duran Duran to 16,000 fans.

The word leapt from my mouth – "Yes!"

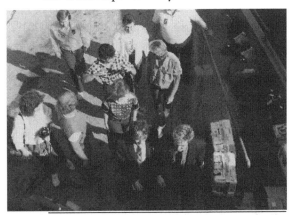

Backstage with Duran Duran for the Feb 7th 1984 concert

It was at that February 7 show at the Fabulous Forum where the comparisons to The Beatles really hit home. When I hit the stage to bring on Duran Duran the wall of sound that erupted from the sold-out audience was deafening. For the band it was ten times louder.

They say that The Beatles at Shea Stadium couldn't hear their own music because their 100 watt VOX amplifiers couldn't compete with the sheer volume of screams coming from the stands. It was the same for Duran Duran.

Even with the latest technology and high-power monitors, the kids unleashed a non-stop wave of adoring squeals and cheers that boomed through the enclosed sports arena. For the first ten minutes, until the audience calmed down a little, Duran Duran played on without being able to hear a single note of their songs.

The next day, to say thank you, Michelle Peacock hand delivered Duran Duran's brand new video 'New Moon on Monday' to world premiere on *Superstars of Video*.

But it was another video that Peter and I received at the end of the year that triggered an amazing series of events for us that culminated with John Taylor of Duran Duran saving our butts!

It was the beginning of December, 1984, when Peter and I were sent a video for *VideoBeat* and *Video One* that was a who's – who of the artists that we played on our shows; Band Aid's "Do They Know It's Christmas." Put together by Bob Geldof and Midge Ure it became a massive hit around the world but Midge told me it was something that almost didn't happen.

In addition to Midge co-writing and producing the song, Bob asked him to help with getting the talent to perform on the record and the first two acts he went after were Sting and Duran Duran. Once he convinced them to come onboard all the other groups fell into place because everybody in music at the time wanted to work with those two superstar acts.

Steve Dagger from Spandau Ballet has the best story about recording "Do They Know It's Christmas."

I was shooting an interview with Spandau when Steve told me, "I was approached to have Spandau Ballet do Band Aid but we had commitments in Europe with interviews and TV shoots so getting to London in time was impossible. But then we heard Duran Duran was doing it so that changed everything and we had to be there."

Steve smiled at the memory, "We really didn't know much about it, the charity aspect of the project, but I made sure the guys got to the recording session. We hired a private jet that flew us into London and then a limo to take us to Sarm Studios in Notting Hill. When we arrived we were shocked. We were the only ones who turned up in a limo! Huge stars like Sting and Wham! had walked there or come on bikes or by taxi to show their support to fight the African famine and here we were, arriving in a big black stretch limo."

Steve laughed as he recalled that day in November, "We were all so tired from gigging the night before. None of us had slept and the band was hung over and just milling around thinking this was some all-star vanity project. And the big thing was when Midge and Bob started the session nobody wanted to be the first to step up and sing, not George (Michael), Sting, Simon, Bono, nobody. It was like 'I'm not going to be bloody first with everybody watching!' So finally Tony steps up and says 'I'll do it' and he became the first person to lay down vocals for 'Do They Know It's Christmas.'"

Steve leaned into me, "But the really funny thing is that during the breaks, Midge went around with a tape machine to get the bands to make a message of encouragement to put on the B side of the record. So he comes up to Steve Norman who hasn't slept for two days and doesn't really have a clue why all these groups and singers are gathered in the studio, and Midge asks him, 'Do you have a message for all the Ethiopian children this Christmas?'"

"Everyone else was saying things like 'The world knows your plight, you haven't been forgotten' or 'Don't worry, children, help and food is on its way,' but Steve who is exhausted and unaware of the terrible famine in Africa and the charity aspect of what they are doing there that morning in the studio sits up and says 'To all the kids in Ethiopia, thanks for buying our records. Sorry we haven't been over on tour to play for you yet but maybe next year Spandau Ballet will be there to rock for you.'"

Steve Dagger grinned, "But despite the confusion we did our part along with Duran Duran and the others and raised a lot of money, like twenty million pounds, to help feed the children, so we're all very proud of that."

The incredible achievement of Band Aid led to one of the most important concert events of all time, Live Aid, and again Duran Duran were a key to its success.

Live Aid was a one-day concert, July 13th, 1985, held in venues across the world and broadcast live on MTV. It featured performances from the Soviet Union, West Germany, Japan, Austria and Australia but its two key venues were Wembley Stadium in London and John F. Kennedy Stadium in Philadelphia.

As soon as Peter and I heard about the mega-concert we knew we had to be there to shoot it for *Video One* and *VideoBeat*, but the problem was MTV and ABC had locked up the exclusive rights to the concert.

But we had an ace-in-the-hole. One of the producers had worked with us at the US Festival and we contacted him and he arranged for press passes to be issued to Peter and me and a small crew. Officially the passes would only allow us into the press tent at JFK Stadium for post-concert interviews but I figured nothing ventured, nothing gained and I found the money for Peter and myself to fly to Philadelphia and hire a camera crew there.

It was a scorching hot July day in Philly and the temperature was sweltering inside the open air stadium where the body heat from almost 100,000 concert goers pushed the mercury ever upwards.

Peter and I met with our two person camera crew – one for camera, one for audio – and the four of us headed inside, proudly displaying our press credentials. Without even slowing down we marched straight past the press area and towards the phalanx of security blocking the access to backstage and the stadium floor. Now was the moment of truth.

Security guards are used to being hassled. Everyone tries to push by them, argue with them, bust out the line "don't you know who I am" – which, by the way, the moment you use it, you've lost because they obviously *don't* know who you are; what security personnel are not used to is people being nice to them. I had put together a plan in my head that often worked for me when I didn't have a backstage pass and now we were going to try and implement it at one of the biggest concerts in history.

I wanted us to be as conspicuous as possible. There was no way we could sneak by these guys so I had us do the exact opposite approach. We would act like we owned the place.

We stopped right in front of the line of security and put our gear down on the ground, almost at the feet of the supervisor in charge. Before any of the uniformed guards could speak I turned to my camera guy for a second and said loudly, "You're sure the new batteries are good? I don't want to have to go all the way back again," - I pointed over my shoulder to the entrance gate, - "to get some more charged ones halfway through the set."

The camera guy nodded his OK.

I turned to the chief security guard in front of us, "This heat is brutal on the camera gear. The batteries drain in less than an hour. If we have to swap out one more camera or mic pack I'm going to go nuts." I smiled knowingly at the guard, "But it's much worse for you. You've been standing out here since we first got here this morning, - what's that, three, four hours ago? I don't know how you do it."

The guard leaned in to confide in me, "You think it's hot now wait until this afternoon. They say it'll be in the nineties."

"Shit!" I said, "It was already pushing eighty when we saw you earlier."

"Yeah," he nodded in agreement, "it got hot early. And humid."

"Well you guys are better men than me. At least we have shade on the stage." I turned to Peter and the crew, "Let's get rolling."

They picked up their gear as I turned back to the guards, "Next time through we'll bring you some water. You're going to need it out here."

The lead guard gestured to an ice chest, "That thing's full with waters."

I smiled. "In that case I'll sneak you some cold beers from the dressing room."

"Now you're talking," he said.

We exchanged friendly nods as the four of us were waved through the assembled guards and onto hallowed ground. We might not have had the proper credentials but we had a smile, a friendly word and we were all determined to get some amazing footage.

PRESS AID

LIVE AID

FEED THE WORLD

JFK STADIUM
July 13, 1985

For the next eight hours things went perfectly. We shot onstage, backstage and throughout the stadium. Politeness, respect and a good attitude got us everywhere, even up into the far reaches of the crowd overlooking the massive stage.

It was a little after 6pm and we had just finished shooting The Cars onstage. Neil Young was up next and he wasn't really one of the artists we played on my TV shows so we decided to take a much needed break. As we moved from the side of the stage a large, gruff man spotted us and stormed up to me. He grabbed the pass from my neck, glanced at it, then threw it back at me in disgust.

"What the fuck are you doing on my stage? You should be in the fuck-

ing tent with the rest of the reporters."

That's when I realized who this was. Standing in front of me, screaming in my face was Bill Graham, the concert impresario

Screenshot from Video One at
Live Aid July 13, 1985

who was putting on Live Aid. His long career was the stuff that legends are made of; he had staged shows for virtually every star in the business from the Grateful Dead in the sixties through to Rod Stewart's latest tour. Here, everyone worked for him and his word was law. He was the sheriff and I was the outlaw who had just ridden into his town and committed a hanging offense.

He stepped up to within one inch of my nose and raged, "Get off my fucking stage right now or I'll break that camera over your fucking back!"

Sticking with my rule of "never argue with security" – especially the people who hire the security and pay them – I nodded silently to Peter and our crew and we turned and shuffled quickly off the stage.

We were done, defeated, humiliated and there were still so many acts to come that we wouldn't be able to shoot.

It was a sad march we made down the stairs and then all the way along behind that massive stage. As we reached the far side of it a familiar face was standing at the other set of stairs leading up to the wings, it was John Taylor from Duran Duran. He saw us heading for the distant exit and called out to us from the steps.

"Richard, you're not leaving are you?" asked John, "I'm just about to go on with Michael and Andy."

"Really?" I said innocently.

"Aren't you going to shoot the set?" John said.

"Of course. We'd love to."

John motioned to the big security guard at the bottom of the stairs, "These guys are with me."

The guard nodded and waved us back up onto that forbidden sta*ge*.

The setup for Live Aid at JFK was so vast that no one on this side of the stage had seen Bill Graham throwing us out. If we stayed here, and if Bill Graham didn't come over to this side – a big *if* – then all would be good and my back would remain unbroken.

John lit a cigarette as he waited for his cue to go on for the first of two

John Taylor waiting to go onstage at Live Aid

performances he played that evening at Live Aid, initially with Power Station and then with Duran Duran.

The security guard who had been assigned to John while he was waiting for his cue somehow attached himself to us for the rest of the night. Maybe he thought that any friends of the bass player in the hottest band in the world at that time, Duran Duran, deserved their own escort, so with him by our side as our protection we continued to shoot the concert until the star studded finale and found ourselves in the surreal situation of standing with Chevy Chase and Mick Jagger watching Hall & Oates perform.

With Peter Facer at Live Aid

It was a day that I'll never forget and one that would have been cut short far too soon if not for the intervention of one of the Wild Boys, my friend, John Taylor.

The next day the weather in Philadelphia broke and sheets of rain sliced down from the dark clouds as thunder shook the skies, but nothing could stop the euphoria that Peter and I were feeling as we headed to the airport. We had shot all the footage we needed for both shows, with enough left over to use in future specials.

I'd bought our tickets on a low budget airline, Tower Air, and as we checked in I asked the counter clerk if they had any room upfront. She checked her monitor and smiled,

"I can seat you upstairs for an extra fifty dollars each."

Fifty bucks to fly first class in "the bubble" of a 747? I couldn't hand over the money quick enough.

As we relaxed in our plush leather seats, enjoying our complimentary drinks and waiting for a break in the storm before we could take off, Peter and I realized we had been present for a moment in history at a concert that had made a global impact. We toasted to our future adventures as the four Rolls Royce engines fired up and the massive plane taxied out onto the rain soaked runway.

MUSIC FOR THE MASSES

The number one question I get? 'Who is your favorite band?' And my answer never varies, Depeche Mode. Maybe one day I should change it up and say "Milli Vanilli" just to shock people, but somehow I don't think that would fly.

Depeche Mode are a band who should never have survived. How many other groups can you think of who have continued on to achieve even more success after their founding member, song writer and musical director left? Particularly when that departure came right on the heels of the release of their very first album, *Speak & Spell*.

They really should have adhered to the industry standard and given up, shook hands with each other and said "Well it was fun while it lasted. Now let's all find another group to play in."

Instead they defied the odds and stayed together. Amazingly after the departure of a musical genius like Vince Clarke they found another equally talented prodigy within the remaining trio, Martin Gore. Martin stepped up and wrote the songs for the second album and a new era for Depeche Mode was under way.

I've always loved the early titles of Depeche Mode's albums; it's almost like they are giving you the linear storyline of the growth of the band. Their first album is *Speak & Spell*, indicating baby steps, what a child would do, learn to speak and spell. With Vince's abrupt exit the picture for success for Depeche Mode was thrown into chaos hence the second album being called *A Broken Frame*.

In late 1982 Alan Wilder joined the band and as a quartet they began rebuilding so the third album's title came naturally, *Construction Time Again*. Alan brought with him an incredible knowledge of electronics and sampling and incorporated it into the band's music and with this new sound Depeche Mode scored two huge international hits, first with "Everything Counts" and then the single "People Are People." The title of their fourth album validated their success, *Some Great Reward*.

But it wasn't the album titles that made DMode my favorite band; it was their music and getting to know the guys themselves.

My first interview with Depeche Mode was in late March, 1983 when they were in town playing a show at the Beverly Theater. Mute Records brought them in on my radio show and then later that day I shot a TV interview with them. After the interview they invited me to their show and we hung out backstage in their dressing room for about an hour. That was the start of a long, ongoing friendship.

TV interview with Depeche Mode

It became a regular occurrence that anytime Depeche Mode was in Los Angeles we would get together. Southern California quickly became their biggest fan base and they would usually wrap up their North American tour in LA with multiple sold out shows, including in the summer of 1986 with two concerts at Irvine Meadows Amphitheatre followed by a sold out show at the Fabulous Forum, playing to a total of more than 50,000 fans in three nights. It was that success that set the scene for their next tour, Music for the Masses, and their most memorable gig ever.

In late March, 1988, Howie Klein from Mute Records arranged a meeting with me at Warner Brothers in Burbank. He and Seymour Stein had been working on an idea for a concert the likes of which had never been done before. They wanted to put a new wave band, a KROQ group, into the legendary Rose Bowl in Pasadena. Only two bands had ever played there before, Big Brother and the Holding Company in 1968 and Journey in 1982. Now the idea was to have these four young guys from Basildon, in the suburbs outside of London, try to fill this cavernous stadium.

Three weeks later we had it all set up. I was broadcasting my show live on the radio from the centerfield of the Rose Bowl when Depeche Mode drove into the stadium in a classic Cadillac convertible. Tuesday, April 26 brought a damp, foggy morning to the Rose Bowl and the seats that filled the sides of the stadium stretched up to the sky, disappearing in the mist. It seemed an impossible task to fill this massive space.

I sensed the nervousness in the band as they piled out of the car and made their way over to me. They were staring up at the endless rows of seats and in their minds running the numbers, - "Just how many tickets do we have to sell to make this place look even half full?"

I went live with Depeche Mode on the radio and talked about the show. I had been told by the record company to expect cameras as the whole event was being filmed for an upcoming documentary.

This was to be the final date of their ongoing Music for the Masses tour. I called Alan Wilder to the microphone because Alan had elected to be the spokesperson for the band.

Alan was a little hesitant at first knowing he was live all across Southern California but quickly settled into his rhythm.

"Good morning to all of our fans listening," Alan said. "We'd like to announce as a special final concert of our world tour that on Saturday, June 18, we'll be playing a concert for the masses here at the Rose Bowl in Pasadena. This will be a very important occasion for us, not only being the largest show we've ever done but also the most prestigious concert we've ever played."

After Alan's official announcement I jumped in to give out the ticket on sale details to the listeners.

"Tickets go on sale this Saturday morning, April 30 at 8am at all Ticketmaster outlets, and it's reserved seating, not festival seating, so get there early for the best tickets."

With the official announcement done we started an impromptu interview on the air which, as always with Depeche Mode, was a lot more fun than work.

After we finished the broadcast we hung out for a while and talked as everyone looked around the Rose Bowl and realized just how huge it was.

"We're going to need the masses to come and fill this place," joked Dave.

Fletch explained it was to be the hundred and first show of their Music for the Masses tour.

"We started last October in…" Fletch looked around for help.

"I think it was Spain," chimed in Alan.

"Yes, Spain. And we were here in December; you were there with us at The Forum, right?" asked Fletch.

"Yeah, great show," I said.

"Well in a few days we go back on the road again here in the US. We have our first gig on Friday in Santa Clara then it's non-stop until we finish the tour here in Los Angeles," said Fletch.

"Kind of a cool setting for the final show of the tour…"

Dave jumped in with a laugh, cutting me off, "The final show of our career if we don't sell this place out!"

I smiled at Dave. "You'll sell this out."

Dave gave me a "we'd better!" look.

I turned to the rest of the band, "When I get back to the studio and talk on the radio about you finishing the tour here at the Rose Bowl," I thought for a second, - 'the hundred and first show' didn't sound cool, "do you have any surprises I should tell the listeners about for concert one oh one?"

Alan looked at me and smiled. "1-0-1? I like it. 101 will be our biggest concert ever so tell them that we don't know about surprises but we promise we'll give everybody the best show we can."

The live broadcast with Depeche Mode January 1988 Rose Bowl

Dave grinned "Tell them to buy tickets and come to our show otherwise it'll just be me and you and the band playing football here."

"101" became a buzz word in Southern California. We knew that Depeche Mode would sell at least 20,000 tickets but in a stadium that holds more than 65,000 people after the stage, screens and sound gear are set up, that number would make the Rose Bowl look empty.

We left Pasadena and I went back to Warner Brothers with the band.

There we met with Howie Klein and we discussed contingency plans such as dividing the stadium in half with temporary fabric walls. That way only 40,000 tickets would have to be sold.

"Only 40,000?" said Dave sarcastically, "That makes me feel a lot better. I just hope 101 isn't the number of people who show up!"

The band left to get ready for the start of the second leg of their US tour and as we only had four days before the tickets went on sale I worked with Howie and Brian Murphy, a very intelligent, hands-on concert promoter with Avalon Attractions, in getting the word out about the concert and the three opening acts.

Everyone on the bill would come from the KROQ playlist. First it would be Wire, a band from England who had a lot of fans in the industry including Robert Smith of The Cure, Paul Weller from The Jam and Depeche Mode themselves. We were playing Wire's latest album *A Bell Is A Cup* and a track from it "Kidney Bingos" was getting a lot of calls, especially at night on Dusty's show.

Next to hit the stage would be Thomas Dolby who is a good friend, a keyboard maestro and a musician who had multiple hits on KROQ with "Europa and the Pirate Twins," "Windpower," "Hyperactive" and, of course, "She Blinded Me With Science."

The last act scheduled to come on before Depeche Mode was Orchestral Maneuvers in the Dark – OMD. They were a fan favorite, had a wealth of hits and if anyone could be counted on to get the crowd going it was Paul and Andy.

The top 40 and rock stations in LA like KIIS and KLOS openly mocked KROQ on the air for attempting to put on a stadium show with a "synthesizer band" like Depeche Mode. Giant arenas were reserved for their acts, the likes of Bruce Springsteen and Michael Jackson. The word on the street was that the "little station" from Pasadena was going to have a major flop on their hands. Depeche Mode had never even had a top-ten hit in America; their highest chart position was number thirteen on the Billboard top forty and that was back in August of 1985 with "People Are People." Their latest single, "Never Let Me Down" had barely scraped into the top 100 before disappearing.

As far as our on-air competitors were concerned, we were bringing a one-hit wonder to town and hoping against hope that we could fill the Rose Bowl. To them it was a costly mistake of colossal proportions. To us it just showed how out of touch with the kids on the street those corporate-driven stations were. They underestimated KROQ, Depeche Mode and their legion of devotees.

When the tickets went on sale that Saturday morning we all waited nervously for the box office report. By the end of the day Brian Murphy called me and said they had sold more than 42,000! Things were suddenly looking good.

Realizing their mistake, the other radio stations immediately stopped their on-air negativity about 101. Instead, on KROQ, we turned the tables and made fun of them saying that their DJs were trying to call in to win tickets from us.

We had exactly seven weeks from the ticket on-sale to the actual concert itself so we did everything we could to hype the show. On my TV show, *Video One*, I put together "Depeche Mode Week" which featured interviews with the band every day. At KROQ we did on-air giveaways and every morning I'd do DMode trivia to win tickets. Now, more than ever, Depeche Mode was locked in as "our band."

Saturday June 18, 1988 was a hot day. It was tropical and humid; very unusual for Southern California. It felt more like Hawaii than Pasadena. The whole day KROQ broadcast live from a booth set up high above the stands in the Rose Bowl. The ticket count was at 62,000 sold, we just

needed another 3,000 gone and it would be a sellout.

Thousands of cars poured into the parking lot and waited, with KROQ blaring out of their radios, for the doors to open at 3pm.

We had a last minute meeting with all of the DJs. We would take it in turns going on stage to introduce the bands and then go back on after their sets to thank them for playing. Right before OMD was scheduled to start the entire air staff would get onstage together to take a shot for the year-end calendar. And finally, after OMD finished, I would be the last on stage to thank everyone for coming and let them know that Depeche Mode would be up in less than fifteen minutes. That would also conclude our live radio broadcast and a tape would roll until DMode started "Pimpf," their intro music. There would be no jock on stage to introduce Depeche Mode; their recorded track would set the scene.

We received word from the box office that all the tickets were gone, 101 was officially sold out and the legendary stadium was jam packed. Everything went perfectly, the bands rocked the crowd and everytime one of our DJs went on stage, - Freddy, Ramondo, Rodney, Jed, Dusty, Poorman, Egil, Spacin' Mason, - the roar could be heard across the Rose Bowl.

At around eight o'clock OMD wrapped their set and it was my turn to go onto that massive stage and address the crowd. The sun had gone down and the lights had just been turned on in the stadium and it was a trip to walk out to center stage in front of that number of people.

I kept my words short; I was as excited to see Depeche Mode as the rest of the crowd and didn't want to waste time. I thanked everybody on behalf of KROQ and told them the greatest band in the world was up next. That got a huge cheer and with a wave I walked off the stage.

I went into the locker rooms below the stage which had been converted into the bands' dressing rooms for the show and told Dave and the guys that the audience was pumped and wished them a fantastic set. I headed back upstairs and towards security, planning to go to my seat.

But something was different. The crowd noise had changed. Instead of the excited buzz that had reverberated for the last few hours there was now yelling and shouting and crashing

While I had been with the band something had happened to alter the mood in the stadium.

A hand grabbed my shoulder from behind and spun me around. It was Brian Murphy.

"Jesus, man, I've been looking for you all over!"

I had never seen Brian like this. He was always so composed, so together. He knew the answer to every question before you even asked it. But now his eyes were wide and his breathing shallow and rapid. I knew there was big trouble going down here at the Rose Bowl.

"The cops are going to close us down, the whole thing," Brian yelled, "They think someone's going to get hurt or killed. You've got to stop it."

"Stop what? How?" I had no clue what Brian was talking about.

"It started up in the stands. Someone threw some popcorn or something. Now everyone is throwing everything. We've got bottles coming down. And there shouldn't be any glass in here at all but somehow there is. The police department are scared that someone is going to get hit with something from up in the stands and get killed. That's over a hundred feet up. A bottle or a can from up there could do a lot of damage."

"Well what can I do?"

"Get on stage now. Tell them to stop throwing shit. I'll send a runner to bring the band up. As soon as the crowd quiets down I'll give you the signal and they'll come straight out. It's the only way we can save the show."

He gave me a push towards the stage. "Go on!"

A little stunned, confused and definitely unprepared, I ran out across the enormous stage to Dave's waiting center microphone. A single spotlight flashed on and lit me up as I stood behind the mic stand. My mind was racing. If I told everyone to stop throwing food I knew what would happen, they would treat me like an annoying school teacher and hurl everything at me. With the stage littered with food, drink and broken glass the concert would be over for sure. But I had to do something.

I took the mic from the stand and walked with it to the front of the stage.

"Are you ready for Depeche Mode?" I shouted into the mic.

The crowd roared back that they were.

"Good, because they are ready for you." There were still some people throwing food; it hadn't stopped but at least I had their attention now.

I had to do something big, I had to bring the show.

I walked the length of the massive stage as I talked. "See all the cameras on stage and out there in the audience?" I pointed to the seven camera crews and boom arms. "They are shooting this concert for a film. And when it comes out everyone will know what you already know, that Depeche Mode are the greatest band in the world!"

A huge cheer came up from the masses.

"In some places in America they don't even know who Depeche Mode are but after tonight they will and you were here and YOU KNEW IT FIRST!"

Now the yells coming from the crowd were deafening. I covered my face with my arm to shield my eyes from the blinding spotlight. I could see the huge audience now. The food fight had stopped and now they were focused on me. I looked to my left, to the wing of the stage. Brian Murphy was there giving me the sign to stretch. The band wasn't there yet, I had to keep going.

"When you drove here today who was listening to the live broadcast on KROQ?"

I already knew the answer but the screams from 65,000 people affirmed it for me.

"To everyone listening at home right now I have a message for you." I was bluffing, our broadcast had concluded already fifteen minutes before, and I just hoped that the crowd in the stadium didn't know that.

"And that message is you should have been here with all these people for a concert that will go down in music history. And this might cost me my FCC license and I might be taken off the radio for saying this live on the air but all of you here tonight," and I gestured to the audience in as big a move as I could so as not to be dwarfed by the gigantic stage, "you knew about Depeche Mode before anybody else because you are so FUCKING HIP!"

The crowd shrieked their approval back to me.

"So everybody here at the Rose Bowl who loves K-ROCK and Depeche Mode make some noise so the listeners stuck in their cars and in their homes can hear what they are missing."

I stretched out my arm and held the mic to the audience as shouts and yells filled the air and shook the Rose Bowl. I glanced over to Brian

Murphy. He was standing with the band and gave me the thumbs up. I pulled the mic back and held it to my mouth.

"But that's enough from me. I think we are all ready for some live music on this stage. I'll talk to you on Monday on K-ROCK. I'm Richard Blade and this, ladies and gentlemen is DEPECHE MODE!"

The lights went down and as I ran off the stage past the band Dave hugged me. Brian had me wait in the wings while the instrumental "Pimpf" played just in case the food fight started back up. I sat on one of four chairs there.

A guy dressed in black sitting in one of the other chairs turned to me and said in a broad Irish accent, "That was a good job you did out there."

"Thanks," I replied to one of my favorite guitarists in the world, the Edge.

The concert got off to a rocking start, the band went straight into "Behind The Wheel" followed by "Strangelove" a combination which had everyone on their feet, dancing. Depeche Mode was there to make a statement and that's what they did. But it was during their third song that something happened that no one at the show would ever forget.

The beautiful, sunny day had turned into a warm, clear night. The stars were shining bright over the Rose Bowl and created the perfect atmosphere for an amazing concert, but as Depeche Mode started into 'Sacred' and Dave sang the words "Sacred, Holy," clouds suddenly rolled in from nowhere and the skies darkened. The atmosphere felt heavy, the feeling became ominous and it was almost as if someone or something were saying "be careful what you're singing about."

Depeche Mode continued with 'Sacred' and as Dave belted out "walking on hallowed ground, but it's my duty, I'm a missionary" a light rain started to fall. Now the crowd was looking up at the threatening sky instead of the stage. As the group segued into "Something to Do" a flash of lightning crackled across the sky above the stadium. The crowd roared in acknowledgement of nature's light show and the following rumble of thunder exacted another cheer.

The band went into their fifth song, "Blasphemous Rumours" and halfway through the lightning abated and the clouds parted and before the song had finished and Dave had sung "God's got a sick sense of humour" the stars were back out and twinkling as if nothing had happened.

But for 65,000 people who experienced that amazing moment it was an eight-minute mystical weather event that will live with them forever.

I said goodbye to Depeche Mode after the show and headed out through the crowded parking lot to find my car. It was crazy outside the Rose Bowl. People were standing everywhere in huge groups, talking; no one wanted to go home. They wanted that night to never end. It was hard to even get through the crowd never mind find your car. That's where I ran into a little kid by himself, a young actor whom I knew from the radio.

Wil Wheaton first found fame in the classic movie *Stand by Me* but now was best known as Wesley Crusher in *Star Trek: The Next Generation*. But Wil looked lost and he just wanted to beam out of there. I approached him and asked if he was okay. These words from his blog say best what happened next.

When the show was over, I couldn't find the car that was supposed to pick me up. It was a little frightening, and I felt like a kid who had been separated from his mom in a crowded department store. Before I could completely panic, though, I saw a familiar face in the mob: KROQ's Richard Blade.

I knew Richard because he was on the air and for several months, after going to school at Paramount in the morning, I'd stop at the KROQ studios in Burbank on my way home to hang out with him. I'm sure I overstayed my welcome, but nobody ever said, "Hey, kid, stop coming around here, you're overstaying your welcome." I wanted to be a KROQ DJ so badly in those days, and the jocks and interns at KROQ were all so fucking cool, I was a total groupie idiot.

Richard was extremely kind and patient with me, though, and when he saw me wandering around the crowd after the concert, he offered to drive me home. So not only did I get to see the greatest concert of my life, I got to end it by getting a ride home with one of my favorite DJs and his girlfriend.

101 set the standard for stadium concerts in the 1980s. It established several records including highest grossing box office for a single show, highest merchandise count per person, and highest food and drink expenditure per person. But business aside it was simply an incredible show. And it wasn't just special for the audience; it was special for the band as well. Dave Gahan said this in a follow-up interview after the show:

It wasn't just an important show for DMode, it was an important show for new music in America. It was like 70,000 people or something, and this was something that we were pretty nervous about doing, playing this big gig. When we actually did the show, it didn't matter. We didn't play particularly good, my voice went, everything went wrong during the gig, like, from what we thought we were doing and what we thought was important about it, but it wasn't. It was, like, the event, it was what was really happening there.

It's hard to describe unless you're standing there, watching it or being a part of it. But I think everybody who was in that concert and was part of it felt that moment. And, you know, I just kind of started, like, blubbing on stage, and trying to cover it up, and still look very macho and do my thing. But I just stood there for a minute, stood on this big kind of riser, and I looked, and at that moment, everybody's arms were, like, waving in the air. And I looked down, and it sounds cheesy, but it just looked like this big field of corn or whatever swaying, and I just stopped. It didn't matter that I was singing or anything, it was just happening.

And I remember afterwards, walking off, and the deflation of, like, "It's over", bang, and then I was like, "ughhh". I wonder if that's ever gonna happen again. And I sat backstage, and my wife was there, Joanne, and I sat in this room, and I remember I just started crying, I don't really know why I was crying, I was happy, sad, everything at the same moment. I remember that, it was a nice moment.

That whole event was just one of those special things, and fortunately we caught it on film. I get these little goosebumps when I watch it, because I remember the experience, it's that euphoric recall that kicks in. A combination of everything: nerves, anxiety, happiness, sadness, the end of it. That was the last show of our tour as well. So, I would say that was one of the most special moments of, I guess, nearly twenty years that we've been together, one we did not know what was going to happen, but it was a beautiful moment.

ALONE AGAIN OR

With Ramondo in rehab I was flying solo on the morning show. It was a tough position to be in. Ken Roberts and Pat Welsh refused to release any extra money to help with the program. That meant I had no producer, no writer, no talent booker, no nothing to assist me. I was literally all alone on the radio in one of the most competitive markets in the world.

My two most important tools were *USA Today,* which gave me capsule reports on what was going on in the news that I could quickly refer to, and my interns whom I increasingly used to put on the air and joke with. I also had Rockin' Fig, Poorman and Rhonda Kramer to banter with. But every day it became increasingly harder to stay fresh.

Amazingly though the ratings went up. I was shocked to see all of the key demographics that we hit number one in. The show remained the talk of the town. A lot of credit for the ratings has

Going solo on KROQ, 1984

to go to my two TV shows. Both *Video One* and *VideoBeat* ran ads for KROQ and the cross-promotion of viewers and listeners certainly did nothing but help.

Doing the morning show alone was a huge responsibility. If the ratings were big from 6am to 10am it tended to lift the rest of the station's broadcast day so as long as I was performing I could get away with anything I wanted to do.

In late May, 1984 I received the brand new single from Frankie Goes to Hollywood a week before its scheduled release date. It was the follow up to their mega-hit "Relax" and I couldn't wait to hear it.

I sliced open the plastic wrap from the twelve inch and talked to the listeners on the air as I slipped it from the sleeve, "It's got a picture of Reagan and Chernenko fighting on the cover."

I looked at the title on the label, "It's called 'Two Tribes – the Annihilation mix' so let's give it a listen together."

I faded it up and was blown away. I love a song that has a *fat* sound with good production. This one had that and so much more. From the spoken intro, "The air attack warning sounds like this…" to the driving rhythm, it was unique. The music seemed to flow from the speakers and envelop the studio in a wash of sonic color. It played for nine minutes and as it faded out the control room felt empty.

"Amazing," I said on the microphone, "I have to play it again."

And I did, over and over for the next hour. The listeners called in non-stop and said how much they loved it. After sixty minutes I went back to regular programming and the hotline rang. I answered and heard a familiar voice.

"It's Rick. I just want to let you know that was one of the best hours of radio I've ever heard. Loved the song and loved your energy. Good job."

After he hung up I realized how fortunate I was. Any other PD would have screamed and yelled at me and probably fired me on the spot but not Rick. For him, if you were making good radio then you were doing your job. His only precondition was if you were going to stray from the music key then make sure it's better than what you would have played. And Rick was secure enough and smart enough to acknowledge when you'd come up with something better than what he'd already planned. Being able to step away from himself and view the station as a listener would was part of his unique magic and contributed to making him the legend he became.

I was burning the candle at not only both ends but in the middle as well. In addition to the radio and TV, my club gigs were out of control and sometimes I would do two appearances in one night and grab barely two hours of sleep on a couch or in a car because I had no time to go home. I think I DJ'd just about every prom or school dance in the Southland and with all this exposure our listenership continued to grow. Some of my gigs were crazy big and I found myself headlining DJ shows at the Hollywood Palladium and at the Pico Rivera Sports Arena.

Pico Rivera Sports Arena and the Hollywood Palladium

I didn't know how long I could keep it going but having worked so hard to get here I didn't want to give it up. I figured as long as I had the strength to get out of bed in the morning and make it to the station then I would keep pushing forward and doing my shows. But a decision to call it quits was almost made for me by Rick Carroll.

Rick disappeared in the spring of 1984 on a bender of immense proportions. We'd only hear from him about once every ten days when he'd ring in with a phone call on the hotline.

"Who's on the air?" he'd ask.

"It's me, Rick. It's Richard."

"Good. What are you playing?"

"A new one from Tones on Tail."

"How is it?"

"It's great. Really uptempo."

"Is Larry doing the music?"

"Yup. Have the music keys right here."

"Okay. Tell everyone I called," and he'd hang up.

It was so sad. One of the most innovative programmers in radio history was caught up in a downward drug spiral. He was a lost soul, trapped in a whirlwind of hurt, holed up in a sleazy motel without even a radio to tune in and hear the station he'd created.

Rick was KROQ. Without him you could feel it starting to unravel.

KROQ needed someone at the helm so once again Pat appointed Freddy Snakeskin as interim program director but it was an impossible job trying to fill Rick's shoes and no one envied Freddy having to try. The word around the hallways was that perhaps this time Rick had pushed the boundaries too far and was gone for good and that KROQ wouldn't give him another chance if he did try to return. It was in this uncertain environment that KIQQ came calling.

Sitting right in the middle of the dial at 100.3 FM, KIQQ had a strong signal and were a mix of top 40 with a token amount of new wave thrown in. But they were getting their butts handed to them consistently by KIIS and KROQ. They wanted that to change and they approached me in the hope that I might be the one to boost their ratings.

Their first proposal was to have me do afternoon drive but after a secret meeting with their PD and general manager at their studios on Sunset they changed their mind and offered me mornings.

Their deal was simple. They would double my salary, give me the money to hire the producer and writer of my choice and put me on a bonus scale based on any ratings increase. As their existing morning show was on death's door a boost in numbers seemed easy to achieve. It was all very hush-hush but then somehow the press found out about it and there were newspaper articles on "Blade leaving KROQ" everywhere.

Pat called me into his office and pleaded with me not to go and explained that while he couldn't match KIQQ's offer he would give me a 50% increase in salary if I'd stay. For me money was never the motivator, it was all about the music and respect. KROQ felt like home and I was already hesitant to split so I used the opportunity to make a deal with Pat. I told him if Rick Carroll came back as program director I would stay with KROQ. Pat agreed to that right away but we both knew the problem was locating Rick and then convincing him to return.

The assignment to find Rick fell upon *Spacin'* Scott Mason. Despite his on-air nickname, Scott was anything but a space cadet. He was a talented engineer and along with Rick and Larry he was responsible for making KROQ the force that it was. If Rick and Larry were the heart and soul of KROQ, then Scott was the backbone. He was the one who kept us on the air, made sure our transmitter functioned and actually went to Washington D.C. in person to battle the FCC face to face when our license was challenged.

I got on very well with Scott but we did have our occasional run-ins when I pushed the limits. At the beginning of 1984 when we were solely vinyl and tape, I brought in a CD player to the KROQ studio and plugged it into the console where our reel to reel machine was connected. Then I played "Synchronicity" by The Police on the air.

I proudly announced, "For the first time ever on KROQ I'm going to play a song from a CD. Let me know if it sounds better than vinyl. This is Sting, Andy and Stewart on K- Rock!"

The hotline rang instantly. It was Scott and he was in full panic mode.

"What are you doing? You can't broadcast a CD!" he yelled.

"Why not?" I asked.

"Because it gives off a square sine wave, that's why."

"And what does that do? Is it like a death ray? Will everyone tuned to the radio die?"

"No. But it doesn't transmit correctly."

"So can you hear it? How does it sound?"

Scott paused and listened for a second, "Actually it sounds really good." he said.

"Awesome," I replied, "because I've got "Rio" cued up on CD and that's on next."

"Nooooo..." said Scott as I hung up on him.

Six weeks later he installed CD players in both the on air studio and the production room.

Now Scott was tasked to find Rick and he went at it full force. Scott approached all of Rick's friends to find any leads as to where Rick might be found and eventually located him in Orange County. He drove down that day and sat with Rick for a while and persuaded him to come back and start over.

Rick took Scott's advice and returned to us with a new attitude and focused on not only the music but also on himself and trying to stay clean. I knew with him back in control, KROQ would continue to be the most influential music station in America.

The press reported on the entire situation, from KIQQ's offer to Rick's return and it became a running soap opera for several weeks in the trade publications and newspapers. On May 20, 1984 the LA Times printed the following;

'The rumor mills have been working overtime with the news that KROQ's Richard Blade, rock radio's answer to Simon Le Bon, is leaving the station to take over the morning-drive deejay post at rival KIQQ.....with Rick Carrol's return to the KROQ helm, Blade says he's now 'reconsidering everything.'

"KIQQ made a very generous offer." Blade explained. "But Rick's return is a very important factor for me, because I really have an enormous amount of respect and trust for his musical judgement and I think KROQ had floundered without him."

BAM Magazine also picked up on the buzz;

Popular KROQ DJ Richard Blade was leaving that station to take over the morning slot at KIQQ, but now it appears that Blade is considering staying at the ROQ since programmer Rick Carroll is now back at the helm. Stay tuned.

Excited at what now lay ahead I passed on KIQQ's offer and happily stayed at KROQ despite the fact it remained just me on the morning show.

Sadly just a few months after his return Rick started to relapse and again we felt his hand slip from the tiller. The irony was that most of the drugs that Rick was getting came from the record company promo people who hoped that Rick's weakness for cocaine would help get their music played on KROQ. What they didn't think through was that Rick and KROQ were virtually the only avenue to break their new acts.

It was a known fact that if we added a song to our playlist then within two weeks more than 200 other stations across America would also add that track because they all followed what KROQ did on air so closely. This could pave the way to landing a spot on MTV and the song breaking out and becoming a national and even international hit. So getting it on KROQ was their number one priority and the drugs that flowed into the station arrived in staggering quantities.

All those eagerly-offered drugs were destroying Rick, but without Rick there would be no avenue to get their music played. The promo guys put that consideration out of their minds because that was long-term. All they wanted was "this record on KROQ, right now." It was "full speed ahead and damn the torpedoes."

But this time the torpedoes hit quickly and Rick again left the station. His role became limited to "consultant" and when in 1986 Infinity Broadcasting offered Ken Roberts the biggest cash sum in history to buy a radio station, 45 million dollars for the station that he'd paid $2 million for just a decade before, we knew that Rick's role would be, at best, diminished even further.

During all this uncertainty, in November 1986, another station came to me and asked me to move across-town and work for them, the legendary KMET.

However that station was now a shadow of its former self and was barely surviving in the ratings. The firm hand of their previous PD who had mocked me was long gone and it seemed like their current programming staff didn't have a clue how to adapt to the rapidly changing world of rock.

I met with their latest PD and he told me that KMET was still the music powerhouse in LA and what an honor it would be to work there. As I looked around this failing station I wondered about his questionable grasp on reality.

He told me he wanted to make the morning show *hipper* and expand from straight ahead rock to incorporate new music.

"But not too much new wave or punk," he qualified.

So right off the bat I was being given limitations by someone who obviously had no clue as to what either new wave, punk or hip was or how the listening audience related to it. No wonder KMET had fallen so low.

Plus I had a strange feeling about that meeting; nothing seemed right. The money they were offering was great but there was something that didn't sit well with me. Even though KROQ was now in a state of flux with new owners getting ready to come onboard I decided I would rather remain at KROQ and take my chances there than go against my gut and leave for a financial reward.

I turned KMET down, a station that just four years earlier I would have given anything to have worked at, and returned to the morning show on KROQ.

Two months later the news hit the press that KMET was changing format. They were firing all of their DJs, going to a smooth jazz mix and even dropping their famed call letters to become KTWV – The Wave. Had I made the move it would have marked a sudden end to my career.

There were only two possible scenarios as to what had happened. Either their owners had hoped that if I'd had joined KMET their ratings would have had a rapid resurgence and the rocker would have come roaring back or they had (more likely) already planned on the format change and simply wanted to take one last swipe at the station and the morning guy that had helped cause their demise. The fact that it would possibly destroy my career and devastate me personally didn't bother the corporate suits one bit – in fact they were probably hoping to do exactly that in retribution for their failure.

So on February 14, 1987, the Mighty Met said goodbye forever and that little station in Pasadena at 106.7 on the dial became the giant killer.

Later that year KROQ moved studios from that tiny building on Los Robles to a glistening high rise in Burbank, situated in the hub of all the media buildings. From our ninth floor windows we could gaze out of the control room and see Disney, NBC, Warner Brothers and Dick Clark Productions. We were now physically right in the middle of the entertainment world but spiritually that's where we had always been because wherever KROQ was, that became the center of the action. As our jingle said 'K-R-O-Q, it's totally hip, it's the only thing happening.'

The move didn't make us any better. Battling the old, unreliable gear in those cramped, tired spaces above Uniform Circus had forced us to be creative. It reminded us every day we were the outsiders, the renegade station that didn't fit in and we used that feeling to fuel our on-air fire.

Now we had equipment that didn't fail, printed music logs that were generated by computer rather than hand-written by Larry and Rick, and vending machines in case we were hungry or thirsty. But for everything that was gained we lost the thing that was most vital to KROQ and had distinguished us from everyone else in radio, our freedom.

Our new general manager called a jock meeting and told us that as of that day forward all "jock choices" were gone. No longer could we bring in a record we had found or been turned onto and just play it on the air and discover it together with our listeners. Now it would be the sole responsibility of the music director to determine what made our playlist.

If somehow we managed to find a song that they had "overlooked" we should give it to the music director to listen to first and then, and only then, they would decide whether or not it should be on the radio.

I was stunned. Memories of all the songs that my father had sent to me that ended up becoming huge hits came flooding back. Did this mean that many great artists that Jed or Freddy or Dusty or I might have championed would now be overlooked and never break big? If this had been the doctrine in '82 and '83 would that have meant that groups like Tears for Fears, Pet Shop Boys or The Smiths would have gone unheard? It was sadly very possible.

Moments that could never have happened on any other station were now gone forever, such as the time Jed was given the new Oingo Boingo album from Danny Elfman himself and then asked the listeners to choose which track he should play first. They had to decide after he dropped the needle on each cut one by one and let just five seconds of music play before he lifted the tonearm from the vinyl and put it down in the middle of the next track. It was crazy, unprofessional and brilliant. You just had to keep listening to find out what would be chosen.

Our new GM continued with his announcements. He put on a song, New Order's "Blue Monday," the biggest selling twelve-inch single in history, and let the opening drum beats that we all knew so well play for twenty seconds. Then he stopped the track.

"That's what we don't want to play. We're no longer looking to be a radio station that's known for electronic dance music. KROQ is going in a rock direction. We want to put guitars ahead of synthesizers."

I was sick to my stomach. We had never differentiated guitars from synths before. For us there was just good music and bad music. Turn on my show and you would be as likely to hear The Alarm, Simple Minds, U2 or Midnight Oil as you would Gary Numan, Depeche Mode, Ultravox or OMD. We had a fight on our hands that we probably couldn't win but I knew that a number of us would rally and do everything we could to keep the original KROQ flag flying.

It was a tough battle and we all tried to not let it affect our sound on-air. We remained as irreverent and unpredictable as possible, but with my music freedom stifled I needed help and thought that taking the show a little more off-center might work. Hoping to get that vibe, our surf reporter, and the host of *Loveline*, the Poorman, joined me as my partner on the morning show.

The two of us made a strange pair, the Englishman known for his music choices and the California beachbum famous for farting into the microphone but the audience loved it. To the listener tuning in it seemed like scripted comedy that "Blade and the Poorman" were always irritated with each other. But we were a real life odd couple and unfortunately that was the truth both on the air and off.

When we weren't doing the show we never saw each other socially or hung out, and the pretaped 'bits' that I would put together in the production room for the next day's show usually didn't go as planned because we had not spent any time together going over just how they should work. He was also perpetually late and would often come barging into the studio thirty minutes after the program was already underway and unintentionally interrupt a phone call or interview I was doing.

Just as I was thinking things couldn't get much worse I received the news that Rick Carroll had been admitted to a hospital in west LA and was not expected to recover. I rushed over that afternoon and visited with him as he lay there. He was very sick but totally responsive and happy to get a visitor. We talked for about an hour and I asked if he needed anything. It was devastating to see him that way. I came back again the next day and we talked about music and the state of radio.

I stopped as I was leaving and turned to Rick, "Thank you, man. It all started for me with what you created, Rick. Without you things would have been very different not just for me but for everyone who grew up with KROQ. Who knows what music would be like today if you hadn't been there."

Rick forced a weak smile.

"I'll be back tomorrow, boss," I said as I left.

I never saw Rick again. One of his greatest friends, a true music maven, Mike Jacobs, called and told me that Rick Carroll had passed away peacefully in his hospital bed from AIDS-related pneumonia.

As soon as I found out that terrible news I went on the air and talked tearfully about Rick, what he had meant to music, to radio, to the listeners and to me. Of how he had pushed all of us to be better and how, the next time we heard a song from Duran Duran, The Cure or Sting, to ask ourselves where did we hear them first and where would the artists themselves be without the brilliance of Rick Carroll?

I know the song was written about Ritchie Valens, Buddy Holly and the Big Bopper, but for me Don McLean's words equally apply to July 10, 1989 as 'the day the music died.'

By the end of the summer of 1989 I was done. Rick was gone and I was unhappy doing the morning show I once loved and cherished. I kept thinking back to those early days, seven years before, when I would race up the metal stairs at the back of the KROQ building with a satchel full of new music, impatient to get on the air and share those unheard records with my listeners.

A vacancy came up for middays and the management, knowing how discontent I had become, asked if I wanted to take it. I didn't have to think twice. Now I could have a normal night's sleep and roll into the station at nine thirty ready for a ten o'clock start. I said yes and left the show.

Just a few months later the Poorman was taken off the breakfast show and replaced by Kevin and Bean who started a new era for the morning program on January 2, 1990. With their arrival the eighties on KROQ officially ended. The big hair, checkerboard Vans, vibrant colors and free sex of the previous decade disappeared and was replaced by plaid shirts, torn jeans, grunge music and the increasing fear of AIDS. I can't help but feel that Kevin and Bean got the raw end of that deal.

CEREMONY

The late eighties might have been a confusing, upsetting time at KROQ but off the air things were different and between late 1987 and the end of 1988 four major things happened that changed my life from there on out.

The first may seem minor but to me it was a revelation. I was now living with my girlfriend, Karen Scott, and she brought up the idea of getting a dog. I wasn't sure at first; I liked dogs but I'd had no real experience with them. My parents didn't want to have an animal in the house when I was a kid so despite my fervent pleas the only pet they let me have was a bunny which I promptly named Thumper. I loved little Thumper but you don't take rabbits for a walk so my animal bonding was limited to carrots and scratches behind her long, black ears.

Karen promised that she had the time to take care of everything so I said to go ahead, she had free rein to get whatever dog she wanted, I didn't really care. She ordered one from a breeder (which I would *never* do again – repeat after me, R-E-S-C-U-E) and four weeks later a tiny little American Eskimo fluffball arrived.

She was so sweet, so little and within days, so sick. We rushed her to the vet who said she had some kind of digestive problem that at her young age could be fatal. We called the breeder who tried to blame us for feeding her the wrong food but we explained that the only thing we had given her was the kibble that had been sent with the little puppy, a two week supply, and we'd only had her five days.

The breeder coldly stated there were no refunds but if we had to put her to sleep we should send a letter from the vet saying they had euthanized her and they'd see about giving us a discount on another dog. They talked as if they were simply replacing a defective tire on a car, not dealing with the life of a helpless living creature.

The poor tiny pup lay on her side, too weak to stand and hadn't eaten for two days. There were specks of blood around her butt and in her urine. She was dying.

I lay next to her on the cold kitchen floor and rubbed her. I held the kibble to her mouth but she wouldn't take it. We soaked it in warm water to make it soft but she still wouldn't eat. My heart began to break. Karen was distraught as well and cried as she called the vet's office to make an appointment to have this little baby dog put to sleep the next day.

We could see how uncomfortable she was and didn't want to move her unnecessarily so rather than leave her alone we brought our chairs into the kitchen and ate our dinner on our laps as she shook and trembled at our feet.

Karen was putting everything away and I was back on the floor saying goodbye to this innocent little puppy when I had a thought.

"Can you give me some of the chicken?" I asked Karen.

"For the dog? You think that's a good idea? She's meant to be on the controlled puppy food," said Karen.

"We're putting her down tomorrow; it can't hurt. And she probably won't eat it anyway. Just a small piece."

Karen handed me some chicken and I tore off thin shreds and held it gently to her tiny brown nose. She sniffed it twice then opened her mouth just a little, put out her tongue and swallowed the chicken.

"She's eating it," I whispered to Karen. I wanted to shout in excitement but I didn't want to scare the puppy.

She took another piece then another. I would have fed her all night but Karen was the voice of reason, "Not too much. Don't make her sick. We know her stomach is bad."

I knew that what Karen was saying was right so we stopped feeding her and just knelt down and stroked her. She tried to raise her head and look at us but she was too weak so she just lay there, enjoying the love.

"She looks like a little angel," said Karen.

"She does," I said "and that's what we should call her, Angel."

*Mum and Angel,
January 1988*

"Honey, we can't give her a name. Not if we're taking her to the vet tomorrow to..." Karen's voice trailed off as she burst into tears.

"If she's eating, she can make it." I put my lips next to Angel's ear and whispered, "I promise you'll have a wonderful life, little Angel. All you have to do is be strong."

The next day she ate three times and by that night she could stand by herself. We did take her in to the vet but happily not to be put to sleep; instead it was to give her a series of medications to clear out the parasites she had picked up at that horrendous puppy mill.

From that day on my given charity became animal rescue organizations and trying to convince people to adopt, not buy, their pets.

Angel became a huge part of our lives and when I told Mum that we had a dog she became a little nervous about coming over and staying with me which she had done for two months every year ever since dad had died.

"What if she doesn't like me and bites me?" she worried.

"Angel won't bite you," I promised, "but she might lick you to death."

When Mum arrived that Christmas she fell instantly in love with that little dog and it thrilled me to see the two of them playing together constantly.

At the beginning of 1988 I decided it was time to go back to school. I'd always loved history and I'll talk endlessly with anyone about the injustice of the Zulu wars, how the roots of the unrest in the Middle East were caused by World War I and Rome's century-long battle with Carthage, but I chose to study American history and I had a special reason for that, I wanted to become an American citizen.

I'd been a permanent resident – a green card holder – for more than a decade but now I figured it was time to really become a part of the country that had been so good to me and that I called home. As part of the requirements to become a US citizen you have to take an exam on US history so for six weeks I took a comprehensive class at LA's Valley College.

I wrote extensive notes, asked questions, read and re-read the textbooks and finally figured I had it all down. I knew how many branches of government there are (three), how many amendments there were to the constitution (26 were ratified by 1988), and all the Presidents, their terms and key dates in the continuing history of the United States of America.

My papers were submitted and approved, my appointment made and off I went to the Federal Building in Los Angeles.

I was nervous walking inside as memories came flooding back of my experiences there in December of 1976 but this time it was different. I was here, I was legal, and even if I failed the exam I'd still have my green card. But I was sweating a little when I stood at the window and was given the exam paper. I had to get a least six out of ten correct. I knew they were multiple choice so I had a one-in-four shot, but had I studied enough? All I could do was give it my best.

I turned the paper over and looked at question one. I was shocked.

Why does the flag have fifty stars?
One for each state
One for each Senator
One for each amendment
One for each original colony

Seriously? That was the question? I answered and moved on to question two:

When do we celebrate Independence Day?
January 1
April 15
July 4
Second Tuesday in November

So here I am equipped to answer questions on the Louisiana Purchase (1803), the second British/American War (1812) and the Alamo (1836) and I'm being asked about July 4? I felt like requesting a harder test paper but I shut up and marked down the remaining eight finishing with:

If the elected President can no longer serve, who then becomes President?
The Speaker of the House
The Vice President
The Chief Justice
The Postmaster General

I'm not sure if I can recall my final score on the test, Oh yes I do– TEN! I think that if I'd missed even one I would have surrendered my green card there and then and left the country in disgrace.

With the exam out of the way a second appointment was made for the swearing-in ceremony. This was held in the Convention Center in downtown LA and scheduled for November 30, 1988. It was quite spectacular and filled with emotion. More than 4,000 people were crammed into the massive room which featured two huge video screens playing Lee Greenwood's 'Proud to be an American". As the Stars and Stripes fluttered in the wind and eagles soared into the firmament it was hard not to be moved, especially for a kid coming from a little town in England.

With 1988 being a year of changes my next goal was to get back into SCUBA diving. Although I had certifications with BSAC through the RAF, I wanted to brush up on my skills so I convinced Karen to join me and we both took a PADI diving course.

Having gone through my initial dive training with the military this was a piece of cake. We were presented with no nightmare scenarios where the instructor would swim up behind you, turn off your air and rip off your mask, instead it was all real world situations involving buoyancy, equalization and breath control. I loved it.

Karen and I immediately continued on and took our advanced course, but that wasn't enough for me. I took a rescue diver course with the guy who wrote the book on it, Dennis Graver, and then persuaded Karen to let me go to the Florida Keys for ten days and study to become a Divemaster.

I realized how much I had missed the ocean and I remembered that boy in Torquay who made his own wetsuits and dreamed that one day he'd be diving in warm, clear water. I made a promise to myself that eventually this was what I'd do, quit the business and move somewhere to teach diving. There would be no money in it; it's not a lucrative enterprise. In fact there's a long-standing joke that the way you end up with a million dollars teaching diving is by starting with two million, but money isn't everything. My father had shown me that. I'd seen the future in that cold mortuary and it is inescapable, so we have to live every day, enjoy our lives and not just chase the almighty dollar.

When I returned from Florida Karen asked how had been.

"Great." I replied. "I signed up for an Instructor Development Course."

For the next eighteen months every spare moment I had, and every vacation I took was spent diving as I ramped up my studies and immersed myself completing technical courses in Santa Monica, Hawaii, Grand Cayman and the Great Barrier Reef.

PADI offered a professional pathway so I started to climb that ladder, one rung at a time to the top. First I passed my IDC exams and received an Instructor ranking, then it was on to become a Master SCUBA Diver Trainer with specialties in deep diving, underwater navigation and boat diving. Next I enrolled in a series of medical courses and was certified as a Medic First Aid Instructor, then an IDC Staff Instructor which allowed me to help certify future instructors and finally on to becoming a Master Instructor. I looked at my diplomas and my certification cards and knew that they held a gateway to an opportunity that would be waiting for me one day.

I had one more ceremony in store for 1988; marriage.

In March of that year I asked Karen to marry me. There was no hesitation or doubt from either of us that this would happen. We had dated since *MV3* went off the air and for the past year I had turned over a new leaf and not strayed from her once. And why should I? Karen was wonderful. She had started as the pretty girl next door but had grown into a beautiful woman. She was stunning to look at and a talented actress. She had appeared in TV series like *The Love Boat*, *Perfect Strangers*, *The Larry Sanders Show* and many more. She was constantly being sent out for auditions and usually getting callbacks, Hollywood's way of saying "we like you."

And for all her good looks she didn't mind getting messy when it came to sports; she'd join me on the slopes in a snowstorm or jump into murky water in the hope of a fun dive. I like that. I've never been one for prissy people. Who cares about your hair, "let's get wet" is my motto.

Karen and I tied the knot in Santa Barbara on September 11, 1988. My mother was there but not my brother. I had asked Stephen to be my best man and he readily agreed but two days before the wedding there was no sign of him.

Mum made excuses that he was busy writing another book and meeting with his publisher, but unless his publisher had opened a branch office in a nearby pub then that story was bullshit. The truth was Stephen's alcoholism was

Karen with Angel

getting worse and worse. It was causing major problems between his girlfriend and their two kids back in London and now had left me hanging in the lurch in California.

My second choice for best man was a no-brainer; Peter Facer. Peter stepped in at the last minute with no reservations or conditions. He stood by my side that day just as we had stood together so many times over the years. The programs for the service had already been printed so we had to slip a note inside each of them explaining that Peter was replacing Stephen.

I joked with Karen that it was like going to a play on Broadway and when you sit down you find out the lead actor is off that evening because of the note in your playbill that says "For tonight's performance…" She didn't think it was funny when I suggested that the printing on our inserted note should read, "Today the part of the best man will be played by Peter Facer."

Nonetheless it was a beautiful ceremony but I knew that my mother's heart was breaking that her two boys weren't up there together in matching tuxedoes. That would have made her so proud.

WAITING FOR THE NIGHT

It all started innocently enough. Howie Klein from Sire Records called me in late January 1990 and asked me to come over to see him at Warner Brothers as he had the new single from Depeche Mode for me. Howie's offices were literally less than 200 yards from the KROQ studios in Burbank and I would often go over there to meet with Howie's artists, everyone from Erasure to Morrissey, but nine times out of ten the subject matter would turn to Depeche Mode.

After I finished my mid-day show I wandered into the Warner Brothers building which was nicknamed "the Ski Lodge" due to the wood paneling and steeply sloping roof, and sat down in Howie's office. Howie handed me the new DMode single that wouldn't be released for another week. It had a cool blue cover and an interesting title, "Enjoy the Silence." I told Howie I would debut it on my show the next day.

Even though the new management at KROQ was now very restrictive with the station's playlist there were certain artists that they knew I had special friendships with which gave me access to their music ahead of anyone else and they *allowed* me to put those records on without having to get them pre-approved or researched first. The list included Duran Duran, Pet Shop Boys, New Order, The Cure, Moz and, of course, Depeche Mode.

"Enjoy the Silence" was to be the second release from their upcoming album *Violator*. The first single, "Personal Jesus," had come out five months before at the end of August, 1989, and quickly broke all of Warner Brothers' existing sales records and become the biggest selling twelve-inch single in the label's history. The buzz around Depeche Mode was now huge and that was the real reason that Howie called me in to his office that day, to work out ways to capitalize on it and take the group to the next level.

"I want to make a statement with the band. I want to do something that everyone, everywhere will be talking about," Howie said.

"So not just a free concert or a showcase?" I asked.

"No, something big, really big."

"That's hard," I said. "The Rose Bowl was massive. You can't get much bigger than that."

"Yes," agreed Howie, "but it was a concert and if you were there it meant something, but if you read about it you say 'I wish I had gone' but it's still just a show you missed. That's why we put out the DVD. For this I want to do something different."

"That rules out a rooftop performance because The Beatles then U2 did that, and a day-long Depeche Mode takeover of KROQ would only mean something to our listeners here in Southern California," I said.

"Yes, and that would be no big deal to the press. It's a big statement I'm looking for," said Howie.

"To get the press involved there has to be something going on, something like a car chase or a bank robbery or a riot," I was thinking out loud.

Howie sat up. Something had occurred to him. "How many people would come to see Depeche Mode if they did an in-store?"

"A record signing?" I asked.

Howie nodded.

"That would be nuts. You couldn't do it. I did one with Billy Idol about six years ago at Music Plus in Hollywood and more than 2,000 people showed up and it got crazy. With Depeche now? No. It would be out of control."

"But hopefully in a good way, right?" asked Howie.

"Yeah. I mean it's not like DMode fans are heavy-metal rockers who get into fights. They just want to see their heroes. I mean if 70,000 paid to see them at the Rose Bowl just how many would come to get a chance to actually meet them and shake their hands and get a picture with them for free? Too many. They would have to close the streets down where they were doing it."

"And if they did that...?" said Howie.

I realized where he was going with this, "Then the press and TV would have to come out to see what was going on," I paused as I took it in, "and right there you would have your statement – *British band closes down LA streets.*"

"Then that's what we'll do." Howie grinned. "Don't mention this to anyone. Let me put this together with the guys and we'll get it going. This will be fun."

Over the next two weeks and several more meetings, everything was locked into place. The worldwide release date for *Violator* was set as March 19, 1990, and the in-store appearance and signing for the band was locked in for Tuesday, March 20 at The Wherehouse record store on Beverly and La Cienega. I would do the broadcast live on KROQ starting at 8pm with the band joining me there and the doors opening one hour later at 9pm. We kept everything under wraps until one week before when Andy Fletcher and Alan Wilder came onto my show on March 12 and broke the news.

"In studio with me are Andy Fletcher and Alan Wilder from Depeche Mode to help me with this special announcement. In just over one week you can meet the band when they do an in-store appearance at The Wherehouse at The Beverly Center on Tuesday March 20. We've been keeping this a secret until right now," I announced.

Fletch laughed, "You've certainly been hinting about it a lot!"

"Yes," I said, "everyone wanted to know what you were going to do to mark the release of *Violator*. Alan, do you have any tips for the fans who want to come down to meet you?"

Alan nodded, "We've done in-stores before and this works best. We'll only sign one thing per fan to keep the people moving through because hopefully they'll be a good turnout."

Fletch jumped in, "We hope there will be!"

"You'll start the signing at nine o'clock. How long are you planning to stay?" I asked.

"Maybe all night." joked Alan. "We're having our sleeping bags taken down there for us."

With the word out the excitement spread amongst the Depeche Mode fans like wildfire.

People drove in from as far away as Arizona and Colorado to be there and the lines started forming outside The Wherehouse as early as Sunday afternoon in anticipation of the signing. By mid-day on Tuesday the

20 more than 7,000 people were waiting in a line that stretched six city blocks. And that was just the beginning.

For the rest of the afternoon thousands of cars carrying devoted fans poured into the area. The intersection of Beverly and La Cienega became so congested that special traffic police were brought in and detours had to be posted. It quickly became the top story on all the afternoon newscasts

who sent their remote camera trucks down to cover the rapidly growing crowds.

By 7pm four of the streets in the area had to be closed down to all traffic and the newsreaders were reporting that the number of fans present numbered over 15,000 but that there were still more flooding in on foot to avoid the road closures.

I was already there and inside The Wherehouse with Scott Mason who was running the technical side of the live broadcast. It was impossible to walk outside of the store without getting mobbed, and looking through the plate glass windows at all the antennas of the multiple TV trucks parked in the now-closed street I realized that the plan Howie and I had made was succeeding beyond either of our dreams.

When I went live on the air at 8pm Scott handed me a note. The word from the police was that the number of people in line was now being estimated in excess of 17,000 and that a tactical alert had been issued. This meant that police from various departments across the city were being rushed to the scene, including fifty mounted police and three helicopters, to control the ever-growing crowd.

Depeche Mode arrived at 8:15 and entered unseen through the high-rise parking lot and the loading entrance behind the store. They had seen the helicopters above, both the police and the news choppers, and couldn't believe how huge the event had become. They were excited and nervous.

Just before we opened the door the word on the police scanner was that the line of fans now stretched over fifteen city blocks and every street in the area was being closed down and a secure perimeter established. I looked at the band and we all knew that this could get out of control very quickly.

I went on the radio and made a final plea to the fans.

"We are about to open the doors here at The Wherehouse. Please remain calm and orderly and everyone will get to meet the band. I know many of the thousands waiting in line have a radio with them and are listening right now so please spread the word; Depeche Mode have no time limit. They will stay as long as it takes to meet all of you and sign something for you. But please do not push or shove or cause any trouble because the police are here and we are told they will have zero tolerance for that." I could see the security moving to the twin doors.

"Here we go. We are opening the doors. Depeche Mode are here to meet the fans so let's keep this mellow and all have a good time."

With Depeche Mode, hosting The Wherehouse instore March 20, 1990

With those words the doors were opened and the first of the almost 20,000 fans who had been waiting for the night to fall to meet their heroes were ushered inside.

The first ten minutes went perfectly; security let in a steady stream of fans who were thrilled to be standing there with their favorite band and to get something signed, but then the people waiting outside starting doing the math in their head. Four people a minute, 20,000 fans in line.....that would take 5,000 minutes or more than three and a half days for everyone to get through. That's when the pushing and the screaming started.

Chaos during the first seconds of The Wherehouse riot

We felt the vibe change even inside of the store. The head of security immediately took charge.

"Close the doors now!" he commanded.

It was easier said than done. Hundreds of kids rushed forward and tried to force the doors open even as the burly guards struggled against them. Record company reps and store employees raced to the door to aid the overwhelmed security personnel. I jumped on the radio and pleaded for everyone to remain calm. Outside the temporary barricades were toppled as the fans surged towards The Wherehouse doors, and now sirens and searchlights mixed with screams and yells.

The head of security yelled at his men inside who were battling at the doors, "I want the band out of sight now. NOW!"

Four guards manhandled Dave, Alan, Fletch and Martin to their feet and half-lifted, half-carried them to the office at the rear of the store. His hope was that if the fans couldn't see Depeche Mode through the huge windows that they would calm down. It was a good idea but unfortunately it didn't work.

Police continued to line the streets after the instore

Outside the huge crowd began pounding on the windows to try to get Depeche Mode to come back out and now there was real fear that the floor-to- ceiling sheets of plate glass would shatter and people could get seriously hurt.   Seeing the situation rapidly spinning out of control more than one hundred riot police lowered their visors, lifted their Plexiglas shields and marched side by side in two unbroken lines that stretched across the street like a Roman legion assembled for battle against a warring tribe.

Fans climbed trees and scrambled up lamp posts to avoid the approaching ranks of police but most were driven back without a fight. With the street clear the limo carrying Depeche Mode sped out of the closed parking lot and raced away into the darkness.

It was two hours before anyone inside The Wherehouse was allowed to leave and when we did it looked like a war zone with police on watch in the middle of the still-closed streets and circling helicopters illuminating the menacing scene with their two-million candlepower Nightsuns.

For the next few days I was in the eye of the storm as Warner Brothers, Sire Records, Depeche Mode, myself and KROQ were all accused of instigating a riot. I was on TV every day that week as the station's spokesman (and fall guy!) and finally had to defend myself and KROQ against Councilman Zev Yaroslavsky who wanted to initiate a major lawsuit against us.

Throughout the week the guys from Depeche Mode called in to my show to apologize to all the thousands of fans who had waited in line and couldn't get in. We all met up at Howie's office and we came up with an idea to hopefully make things right with everyone who had been there but had not been able to meet the band. Depeche Mode would put out an album for those disappointed fans and it would be distributed through The Wherehouse stores across Southern California and by KROQ. Flood would produce one side and I was asked to produce the other side. I was stunned. Produce an album side for Depeche Mode? That was beyond my wildest dreams.

As I went to work on the production in the studio, The Wherehouse stepped up and put an end to the threats of lawsuits from the city by paying $25,000 for any cleanup involved. The most important thing was that no one had been hurt. As I'd said to Howie more than two months before, Depeche Mode fans aren't the type to start any violence.

In early May I finished my production on the album *Depeche Mode....* *The Wherehouse 3/20/90* and 50,000 were pressed and distributed across the southland to make sure all the upset fans received a copy. Having my

name as producer on an official Depeche Mode release remains one of my proudest achievements.

With all of the resulting publicity for Depeche Mode generated by the news media around the globe, *Violator* became DMode's biggest album to date entering Billboard's Top 10 in its first week of release. I asked Dave on the radio about this new success in America and this is what he told me:

"There's a lot of people that want to talk to us now, but Depeche Mode as a group has the same policies; it doesn't matter how big we get, we're going to have the same attitude to what we do. You know, we care about what we do, and we're not going to just change anything in the way we do things. The people that have got us where we are so far we won't forget."

Dave was true to his word. He didn't forget. Two months later they flew me and Scott Mason out to Florida to cover the start of the World Violation tour live on the radio and when Depeche Mode wrapped up their North American dates with a sold-out concert at Dodger stadium in

Dodger stadium August 5th, 1990 before and during World Violation

Onstage introducing the final date of US World Violation tour

393

Los Angeles on August 5, 1990 the band invited me to come onstage and introduce them on that swelteringly hot August night in front of fifty-five thousand fans.

LIVING ON VIDEO

As the '80s raced by I found myself doing more and more television. *Video One* had become a staple of afternoon viewing in Southern California and when after more than 700 episodes, Channel 9 decided to move away from music programming in favor of syndicated reruns, the show was immediately snapped up by KDOC in Anaheim and continued without even a one-day break in its programs.

In early 1987 I received a call from Larry Namer who I had worked with several years before on *LA Music Guide*. Larry was in the planning stages to launch a new 24-hour cable network that was based around films, celebrities and everything Hollywood. It was to be called *Movietime* and would feature hosts introducing clips and previews and interviewing the stars.

"Think of it as MTV for movies," said Larry.

I understood the concept right away and along with Larry's partner, Alan Mruvka, reached a deal to be one of the on-camera hosts.

The channel launched on July 31, 1987, and the original team of hosts were all there to meet the press; Greg Kinnear, Katie Wagner, Julie Moran, Marc DeCarlo and me.

With Larry Namer and Greg Kinnear at Movietime launch, 1987

Movietime originated out of a one-story brick building on Santa Monica Boulevard in Hollywood that barely had room for the two studios, three edit bays and cramped office space it housed. We shot almost around the clock and as the network rapidly added cable outlets and millions of subscribers the five of us would travel all over the country to cover movies that were in production rather than relying simply on trailers provided by the Hollywood studios.

Competition between us was fierce as to who was assigned to interview which star and we would have friendly battles over everyone from Tom Cruise to Michelle Pfeiffer.

When in October 1988 I was asked to host *Movietime*'s very first live broadcast, the premier of U2's concert film *Rattle and Hum* at Grauman's Chinese Theater in Hollywood, I jumped on it. Not only would it be a flagship event for us but it meant I would get to spend some time with arguably the biggest rock band in the world and interview them live on camera. The word quickly came in that they were planning to perform two songs live outside the theater for the throngs who would be gathered there to see them and I knew this would be a huge night for me and for *Movietime*.

The broadcast went without a hitch and it became just the first of many live events that *Movietime* would do over the next two years.

Movietime became a real force in Hollywood and needed to increase its staff quickly. Charles Segars, one of the senior producers at the network, asked if I knew of any other good, available producers who would want to join us as the channel expanded. It took me two phone calls and one meeting, and

Interviewing U2 live on Movietime 1988

once again Peter Facer and I were working together.

As the fledgling network grew by leaps and bounds it attracted interest from outside sources and in late 1989 was purchased by Time Warner who decided on a major restructuring and relaunch of the channel. So on June 1st, 1990, E! Entertainment Television was born. Sadly I wasn't a part of it.

Two days before the switchover all of the on-camera talent, except for Greg Kinnear who was picked to host a show called *Talk Soup*, were called into the office and let go. It was a shock but I wasn't too upset. It had been a great three years helping build the network and I'd learned a lot about live TV. It would have been nice to have been a part of E! but just as they moved on, so did I.

An early version of *Fox Sports West* was starting up and they asked me if I would be a commentator on their pro snowboard tour. My knowledge of the sport was limited to two things; you did it in the snow and you had a board strapped to your feet. The people at Fox weren't bothered by that; I'd be the straight man moving the action along while all the technical calls would be handled by a rotating group of snowboard champions who could point out a backside alley-oop or an off-the-lip720 as they happened in the half-pipe.

For the next four winters I flew to the greatest ski resorts in North America to cover the tour. Every weekend from December through early

April I would board a plane at LAX and jet off to Vail, Baker, Taos, Park City, Hunter, Bachelor, Steamboat etc… to commentate on the action on the slopes. I used the opportunity to take lessons and found myself loving being out on the mountains.

I would fly back on Sunday evenings after the contests were wrapped and several times found myself caught in major storms and unable to make my flight. Sometimes I would sleep at the airport hoping for a break in the weather and would hop on the earliest flight the next morning to get back to SoCal in time for my radio show. I never once missed being on the air though I had many close calls including racing ninety miles in a tiny rental car through driving snow to get to Seattle after finding that my original departure airport in Bellingham was completely closed down for all flights for a minimum of twenty-four hours due to hazardous conditions. Speeding south into that blinding blizzard was one of the scariest and stupidest things I have ever done but fortunately I was just about the only fool out in those conditions so I had the icy roads all to myself.

Snowboarding wasn't the only sport to come calling. Also in 1990 I had another call that I welcomed with open arms.

I was getting off the air and checking my messages when I saw I had one that was asking for a call back as they wanted to talk to me about diving. I recognized the number, 1-800-729-7234; it was the number for PADI – the Professional Association of Dive Instructors. I'd used it many times on my way up to becoming an instructor. I was puzzled, my dues were up to date and I had only been teaching a few private lessons and didn't think I'd committed any violations of standards so why did they want to speak with me?

I returned Frank Palazzi's call and had a really intriguing conversation.

"You wanted to speak with me?" I asked.

"Yes," said Frank. "Who are you certified with? We've been hearing you talk about diving on the radio but we can't find you in our data base."

"I'm with you, with PADI. You've just been looking under the wrong name. I'm certified as Richard Sheppard, not Richard Blade."

"That's great. Are you Open Water?"

I laughed. Open Water is the very first level of certification for new divers. "No," I said, "I'm a Master SCUBA Diver Trainer and just starting my IDC Staff."

Frank paused for a second and then I heard him say away from the phone, "He's a PADI instructor!" Then Frank came back on the line. "Look," he said, "I'm here at PADI headquarters in Orange County and I think we may have a very interesting proposition for you. Can we set a time to meet up?"

I learned a lot at that meeting. I already knew PADI was the world's largest dive organization responsible for more than 85% of all the dive certifications globally but now they were looking to up their already high standards. They had the innovative idea to allow all their new students to take a video course to supplement their classroom, pool and ocean training, and they asked me if I would narrate the six hour course.

They chose me because they wanted someone who was a diver and because the course would be released in every English speaking country around the globe they didn't want too distinct of an accent. After fourteen years in America mine didn't sound like I was right off the boat, and being a little less obvious they felt it would play well in places like Australia, New Zealand, Canada and South Africa as well as the UK and the US.

The recording sessions lasted more than three weeks in total and were intense. Because it was an educational course dealing with life-support equipment and potentially precarious situations every read had to be checked by not only the technical team for accuracy but also by lawyers for potential litigation liabilities. Finally it was completed and the tapes were released and received universal acclaim from dive shops worldwide as being

*Shooting for PADI
in Kona, Hawaii*

revolutionary in aiding not only the instructors but in assisting the students in learning about diving.

The PADI execs were ecstatic about the response and went full steam ahead with phase two of their plans, putting all of their courses on video. This time I was to be not only the narrator but also the on-camera instructor.

Over the next three years we shot videos for deep diving, buoyancy, rescue, navigation, medic first aid, boat diving, night diving and many more in locations around the world from Grand Cayman to Catalina, from Bonaire to Hawaii.

It really forced me to refine my skills as a diver and instructor and that was a challenge I welcomed. And the more time I spent walking the decks of a boat, setting up gear and leading dives the more it convinced me that one day I should make this a career.

Diving, and teaching diving, made me feel alive and in touch with nature. It became almost transcendental. One of the single most memorable moments of my life occurred while we were shooting in Grand Cayman. We were filming a buoyancy control video and I was asked to hover in thirty feet of water in the center of a large school of yellowtails, none of us moving as we remained stationary above the same spot of coral on a dive site appropriately named Aquarium. Frank and his team got the shots of me they needed and returned to the surface, but with plenty of air left and being well within the no- decompression limits I remained below with the schooling fish. I can honestly say I have never been more relaxed than I was in those moments.

I floated, completely still, in the center of the school of perhaps 2,000 fish. The longer I stayed there, the more they seemed to accept my presence until I began to feel I was one of them. As they moved slightly in light current so did I; the almost unnoticeable side-to-side motion of their tails I matched exactly with a tiny fluttering of my fins as we all remained bonded together above that colorful reef. After perhaps ten minutes I became so attuned to nature and the environment that my mind began to play tricks with me and I couldn't be sure if I was a man thinking he was a fish or a fish dreaming of being a man. It was an amazing out-of-body sensation and one that I treasure. To this day I can close my eyes and return to that moment instantly. In doing so a feeling of tranquility floods over me and my entire body relaxes. When I go to the doctor for a physical and he straps the blood pressure monitor on my arm I close my eyes and return to the center of that school hovering in the clear, calm, warm water. And almost instantly my pulse drops way down to as low as thirty-eight beats per minute.

It was while hovering above that reef that I finally made my decision that one day I would do this full-time; move to where the water was warm and clear and try and instill my love of the ocean in others. I didn't know where or when or how but from that day on I knew I would do it.

I had one big favor to ask of PADI. I wanted them to change the name on my instructor card. When I taught the occasional private lesson I found that the students wanted "Richard Blade" showing as their instructor on their certification card. Right now it read "Richard Sheppard."

The lawyers at PADI said it was impossible as it was a legal document accepted globally but I asked if there was any way they could make an exception or find a loophole. Apparently my pleas were heard because a solution was found and two weeks later I received a new instructor card reading *Richard Blade Sheppard*. It was the first and only time PADI allowed an alteration such as this but I was so pleased and so were the students I certified from then on out.

I taught Scott Mason and Jed the Fish how to dive and got them their PADI 'C cards', and as word got out over the radio about my diving from the other DJs I started putting together *KROQ'n'Dive* trips to Catalina. These were long weekends which involved me leading KROQ listeners who wanted to try SCUBA on a resort course and then certifying a group of new divers. The weekend would also include me DJing a Saturday night party at a club in Avalon.

We were expecting perhaps twenty-five people to sign up for the three days; within twenty-four hours of announcing the trip KROQ had sold 400 tickets. I had to tell them that they couldn't sell anymore – it would be an impossible number to handle otherwise.

I went to City Scuba and had David Leach supply a number of instructors and divemasters to work with me so that we could conform to PADI's strict standards. I certified more than one hundred people in three days and took more than a hundred and eighty others on introductory dives.

I felt bad for anyone who was going to Catalina that weekend who wasn't on the trip with us as KROQ took over the entire island including the number one dive site there, Casino Point. I think there were more

KROQ'n'Dive in Catalina with my phone op, Michelle

K-Rock divers in the waters of the marine park than there were fish.

In addition to the diving and the on-camera work for the instructional videos, I started to write again. I had sold a script to a company in Hollywood in 1987 called "We're with the Band" about two teenage girls who accidentally find themselves on the road with their favorite boy band. They paid me well for the screenplay but sadly it was never made.

I wrote several more scripts over the years all of which got me meetings with producers who "loved" the writing and concepts but then they never called me back, the typical Hollywood BS of never giving you a straight answer.

In 1998 I was watching a new series on the UPN network called *7 Days*. It was a time travel show about a clandestine government agency that had discovered a way to send their man, Frank Parker, back seven days to save the world from the disaster of the week. Being a sci-fi fan I loved the show but after just three episodes I noticed there was a gaping plot problem with the concept; if Frank was going back just one week to the same timeline then why didn't he meet himself?

Just for fun I mapped out an idea explaining exactly why he never had that encounter using parallel timelines and then a temporal rift that allowed the two Franks to interact. As I looked at it I realized that not only did it work but it made for a great episode so I called Paramount and after a lot of running around with secretaries on the phone I was put through to Chris Crowe, the creator and executive producer of the show.

I told him I loved *7 Days* and explained the problem I'd spotted.

"We are very aware of that," said Chris. "It's a grey area we don't address."

"Well I have the solution," I said.

Chris's response was simple. He would meet me at a very expensive restaurant in West Hollywood, the Palm, and if I did have the answer he would pick up the tab but if not then the bill would be all mine. I told him to bring his credit card because he'd need it and two days later we got together. Before we had even ordered Chris bought my concept and invited me to be a part of the writers' meetings at their office in North Hollywood. For the next two years I bounced ideas for shows off the writers and helped tweak existing episode concepts.

As season two was coming to a close I brought an idea to one of the meetings that everyone, including the executives at Paramount, loved. It was a story of Frank falling in love with a female scientist whom he'd been sent back to save. But in saving her she would unwittingly cause the death of billions. It left our hero with a terrible decision; let three quarters of the planet perish or allow the only woman he had ever loved to die.

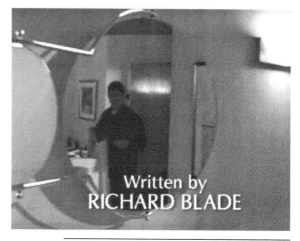

7 Days screenshot

The finished script was so well received it was picked to become the second season finale. I named the episode "The Cure" and had the beautiful scientist's lab located inside "Depeche Pharmaceuticals." I figured that while I had the chance I would get the names of two of my favorite bands on network television.

---◇---

FRIENDS OF MINE

Part One – SUEDEHEAD

My on-again off-again friendship with Morrissey began in 1986. I'd just been signed by Andy Friendly to be one of the hosts of a network show on CBS called *The Rock'n'Roll Evening News* along with Steve Kmetkco and Eleanor Mondale. The show was to premiere on September 6, 1986 and featured live performances and recorded pieces that highlighted the biggest acts in music. It was all set to become a hip version of *Entertainment Tonight*, but instead of movies and TV we were all about rock'n'roll.

At our planning meeting for the premiere show I suggested that we interview The Smiths who were currently on tour in North America. That idea received a resounding *yes* from everyone so the band's management was contacted and a date and location was set in stone. We would be doing the interview with Morrissey and The Smiths at the site of their concert in San Diego, August 29.

We started off early that Friday morning. It was the beginning of the long Labor Day weekend and we knew traffic would be horrendous on our 140 mile drive. With the network camera crew leading the way in their van, I followed behind and we began our drive down the 5 freeway to San Diego.

We arrived in plenty of time to shoot the soundcheck and following that we set up in a room backstage which we dressed and lit in preparation for the interview. With everything in place we sat and waited. And waited.

Some of the crowd waiting for Morrissey, Friday February 9th, 1990

Ninety minutes later we received word that Morrissey wasn't up for doing the interview after all and the whole thing was scraped. The expensive union crew was dismissed and as great as the concert was that night I couldn't fully enjoy it knowing what we had missed out on.

Two weeks later *The Rock'n'Roll Evening News* premiered on 130 stations and I did a piece on The Smiths and their importance to modern music using footage from the soundcheck and a two minute standup that I wrote. I couldn't help thinking how much bigger and better it would have been for both us and The Smiths if only Morrissey had followed through with that arranged on-camera interview.

Almost four years later Morrissey more than made up for it.

At the beginning of February, 1990, Howie Klein called from Morrissey's record company and said that Moz wanted to come into the station and do an interview with me. I was thrilled, but also a little nervous that he might cancel again. Howie assured me that he would make sure that the interview happened so we immediately went on the air and started promoting it.

When February 9 rolled around there was a huge crowd of fans surrounding the KROQ building. They carried signs expressing their love along with pictures and album covers for Morrissey to autograph. Many had been there overnight to be close to the entrance so they wouldn't miss their chance to glimpse their favorite singer.

As Morrissey's car pulled up to the building, Moz saw the mob of fans waiting for him, but instead of sliding back in his seat, remaining concealed and being driven into the comparative safety of the underground parking lot, Morrissey asked the driver to stop and he got out and met the kids, taking pictures with them and walking through the crowd, saying hi.

A lot of people ask me what is the best interview I've ever done. My answer is always the same. The most fun to interview is Boy George, the hardest is Bono or Sting as many times they come across as far too serious, but the best, by far, is Morrissey.

Moz is intelligent, quick, and often very humorous. And he doesn't suffer fools lightly. When you are sitting with Morrissey you had better be prepared and bring your A game; if not, he will rip you to pieces, but if you do your homework and preparation you will be rewarded by an incredible verbal tennis game from someone who is justifiably known as a wordsmith.

Our interview was scheduled for twenty minutes but that Friday as we went back and forth about his career, the way his fans loved him, his songwriting process, etc.., it became obvious that both of us were enjoying it so much that the clock on the wall was ignored and Morrissey stayed in the studio with me going one-on-one for more than an hour and a half.

When the interview wrapped up we both knew that something very special had just occurred. All across Southern California hundreds of thousands of fans had made their own personal recording of the

In studio with Morrissey 2/9/90

407

interview on cassette and a limited-edition CD of the Morrissey interview was released. It was a moment in time that lives on.

A few months later I was hosting a Morrissey look-a-like contest at Fashions Nightclub in Redondo Beach. The commercials for that Saturday evening ran every day on the radio and on the Thursday before the big night I received a call from Howie saying Morrissey was in town and had heard the ads on my show. What shocked me was that instead of being mad, Morrissey asked if he could join me at Fashions that night and judge the contest.

Of course I said yes without hesitation. The only caveat was that I keep it secret and not announce it on the air. That was no problem and we put the wheels in motion.

That Saturday Fashions was even more packed than usual. The club was located underneath Redondo Beach's famed harbor pier and the only way in and out was down a single, wide staircase.

As Morrissey arrived and joined me in the DJ booth, Fashions was pumping. At least forty other Morrisseys were in the house all ready for their big moment on stage which would be coming up in a couple of hours, around midnight.

There was a constant ebb and flow of dancers making their way through the crowd to the DJ booth to make requests. When they saw Morrissey standing with me they inevitably nodded their heads in approval and made comments like "Good job, you look just like him" or "You're one of the best here tonight."

Slowly a buzz began to develop in the club; you could feel it growing. Now it wasn't just the dance floor that was packed; the area in front of the DJ booth had a large crowd standing, staring at the two of us.

Every time Morrissey would give his fans a shy wave through the low Perspex surround that ringed the booth they would wave back then turn to each other with a "Do you think that could be....?"

Moz and I talked and agreed I had to say something. I picked up the microphone and flipped it on.

"Hope you're having a good time so far tonight here at Fashions. Thanks to everyone who came dressed up as Morrissey. It's going to be a fantastic contest." I paused for a second. "If you all promise to stay cool I'll let you in on a secret. Who out there can be cool?"

I held the mic out and 500 people yelled back, "We can!"

I glanced at Moz and he nodded in approval. I continued on the mic, "Okay, cool people. We have a special judge for our look-a-like contest tonight. Remember, you are all cool, because this," I pointed to the famous singer from Manchester standing next to me, "is Morrissey!"

A hush dropped over the crowd and I had never heard Fashions so silent, not even during the early evening hours when the club was still closed and the only people inside were me and the bartenders. Amazingly everyone was being cool – for exactly one second!

Then a roar erupted. The crowd pushed forward as one and a tsunami of bodies surged at the DJ booth, shattering the Perspex surround and everywhere there were hands and arms reaching in, grabbing, pulling. The two security guards by the booth were overwhelmed and Morrissey leapt to the rear of the DJ area in an attempt to find shelter among the vinyl albums and record crates.

Two more security guards rushed downstairs from the door and together managed to hold back the crowds. Lance, the owner of Fashions, knew it would be impossible to get Morrissey up the stairs and out of the club so he yelled to the security, "Take him to my office now."

The four burly guards encircled Moz and shoved their way through the crowd to the comparative safety of the windowless office. A few minutes later I joined them there. There was a constant hammering on the door from desperate fans while we talked.

We came up with a plan. I would start the look-a-like contest right away and hopefully that would distract enough people for a couple of minutes that they would be able to safely get Morrissey extricated from the office and out of the club.

Morrissey and I exchanged glances right before I squeezed my way out of the door and back into the crowd; for all the chaos and mayhem we were actually both having fun.

The diversion worked and by the time the contest was over and the number-one Morrissey wannabe was crowned the real article was safely on his way, virtually unscathed, heading north back to his place in West Hollywood.

Just over a year later, Morrissey and I would be thrown together again after another crazy mob situation, this one at Pauley Pavilion on November 1, 1991.

Morrissey was on the road on tour supporting his brilliant *Kill Uncle* album and decided to do a special show at UCLA. Normally Moz would play –and sell out – venues like the Hollywood Bowl or the Forum, but on that night he decided on a much more intimate show on an indoor basketball court at Westwood's famed university campus.

The packed crowd had been on their feet since the opening number, "November Spawned A Monster," an ironic choice to start with considering the date and what happened, and as Morrissey tore into the ninth song of his set, "We Hate It When Our Friends Become Successful," he was feeling the love from his fans and said into the microphone "Get up out of your seats and come on down here." Unwittingly it was an invitation to unleash the Gods of Chaos.

The crowd yelled their approval and heaved forward, overturning the folding chairs that had been placed on the floor of the basketball court and trampling others as they charged the stage. Morrissey was visibly upset and rushed into the back of Pauley Pavilion for his own safety. Riot police and paramedics were called and in all, forty-eight people were injured.

Morrissey called me on the air the next day to say how sorry he was about the incident. The concert had been going so well up to that point and he had been overcome by the energy from the fans. Over the years so many had made their way onto the stage to hug him and give him flowers but never anything like this. He was truly shaken by what had occurred and distraught that anyone might have been hurt.

Five months prior to the ill-fated Pauley Pavilion show, Morrissey and I spent an unforgettable evening together at the Capitol Records building in Hollywood.

Morrissey wanted to do something special for his fans in Southern California so he came up with the idea of putting together a special EP for his followers there. He contacted me at KROQ and said that the plan was that he and his band - Spencer Cobrin, Boz Boorer, Alain Whyte and Gary Day - would go into the studio at Capitol and record three tracks for the CD. He then wanted me to go on the air the next day and talk about the experience of being in-studio with Morrissey and produce a segment to be included on the CD that would feature listeners sharing their thoughts and feelings with me on Morrissey.

Scott Mason and I arrived at Capitol Records around 7:30 on that Monday evening of June 3, 1991. Scott made sure all the gear was hooked up correctly including multiple DAT machines for backup, and the very talented Ian Horne was on hand to mix the set. The amazing thing about that night was that as the band played, Ian would mix it live to tape. There would be no re-dos, overdubs and inserts; it had been decided that what went onto the CD would be exactly what they played and laid down on tape that night.

Morrissey and his band had come ready to rock and after a ninety-minute rehearsal and practice session they played the three songs live, "There's A place In Hell For Me And My Friends," "My Love Life" and "Sing Your Life," as Ian worked the mixing board and Scott recorded the session.

When everything was done, we all hung out for about an hour afterwards, talking and slowly coming down from a natural high. None of us were in a hurry to leave; we knew that this had been a once-in-a-lifetime night that had just happened for us in the same Hollywood studio where legendary acts like Sinatra and the Beach Boys had recorded their own timeless music.

After hearing the three tracks the record company knew they had something special on their hands and changed their plans on how they were going to release the CD. Instead of it being limited to Southern California it became an official Sire/Reprise worldwide release and a part of Morrissey's catalogue

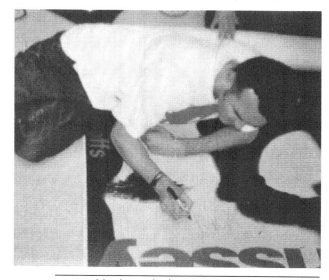

Morrissey signing a poster to commemorate the recording session

nationally and internationally complete with my eight-minute produced feature on it. And the live version of "Sing Your Life," recorded that night, became the definitive version of the song for radio stations around the world.

---◇---

Part Two – NEVER TEAR US APART

How I miss Michael Hutchence. In many ways, of all the musicians and performers I was privileged to know over the years, I would have to say Michael was the epitome of the ultimate rock star. He had it all. The voice, the looks, the moves, the talent, the song writing ability and most of all, that rare, intangible thing – the charisma. When he walked onto a stage or into a room, he owned it and all eyes followed him. It was like he wove a magic spell and transfixed the audience with his presence.

Understandably women found Michael's charms irresistible. I often joked that if you were to come home and find your wife in bed with Michael that instead of breaking into a furious rage you would completely understand and simply say, "I'll leave you two alone for an hour." To which the wife would probably reply, "Could you make that two hours, honey?"

I first met Michael on Thursday, March 31, 1983 when I was scheduled to introduce INXS on stage at their show with Adam Ant at Raincross Square in Riverside, California. All the attention was focused on Adam at the time but I was curious about INXS. I was playing their video "The One Thing" on my TV show and thought they would be worth checking out.

Hanging backstage with them before the concert I was swept up in the sheer energy that this band of brothers had. Technically only three of them were brothers - Jon, Tim and Andrew - but all six of them felt like they shared the same blood. They were excited to be in America and were eager to make their mark here.

After I brought them on stage I watched their performance and all I could think of as Michael strutted, danced, sang and won over the fans who had flocked to the hall primarily to see Adam, was that it was like seeing a young Mick Jagger in the early days of The Rolling Stones. He was that good.

Over the next three days Michael and Tim spent a lot of time with me as we did radio interviews and TV shoots. They had no walls or reservations about them and we became fast friends.

With Tim and Michael in the Video One studio, 1985

Two months later I waited with them backstage at the US Festival as they wiped the sweat from their bodies after battling both the huge crowd and the nearly one hundred degree heat. They were tired and exhausted but thrilled. It was the biggest show they had played to date.

Over the next few years I would always get a call from Michael when he was coming to town and we would go for drinks and talk about the next step for INXS.

As INXS got bigger and bigger Michael didn't change. He remained that excited young Aussie I first met and was always happy to join me at the station or on *Video One* or *VideoBeat* for INXS week.

Just two months after the above picture was taken I was with Michael in Sydney when he turned up to meet me at one of Spandau Ballet's infamous parties.

One of my biggest regrets in music is that I was unable to make it to London for the INXS concert at Wembley Stadium on July 13, 1991. I already had commitments for a TV shoot in Los Angeles and had to tell Michael I couldn't accept his invitation and come to England for the show. I knew it was an important milestone for the band to sell out a legendary arena like Wembley which exactly six years before to the day, had been the UK home to Live Aid on July 13, 1985, and Michael wanted his friends and family there to see their triumphant show in front of 75,000 fans.

The band knew how significant this concert would be for them and had it recorded and filmed, and released it on album and video as *Live, Baby, Live*.

Less than two years later in March of 1993 Michael called and asked if I could help with the promotion of an upcoming show they were planning at Barker Hangar in Santa Monica for their "Get Out of the House" tour. I was happy to do it and Michael suggested that as it was being held in an airplane hangar we should make a statement and fly in together in a helicopter and meet the press as it would look great on camera.

We left from Van Nuys airport early in the morning and soared over Mulholland Drive and the Sepulveda Pass before touching down for the live broadcast in Santa Monica. After we concluded the radio show we boarded the helicopter again and flew back to the valley.

Michael was 100% right with his idea for getting the word out for the concert. When the tickets for the show went on sale all 4,000 were gone in just three minutes. It was a chopper ride that definitely paid off.

With Michael at Barker Hangar, March 1993

In July 1997 the band was touring to promote their latest album *Elegantly Wasted*. They reached out to me about doing some kind of a special performance for their fans in California. I suggested to Michael that they do a pre-show party outside of the Greek Theater before their scheduled concert on July 11, 1997. Michael loved the idea and we set it up and broadcast the live event as a special "Richard Blade's Flashback Lunch with INXS."

July 11, 1997

416

After the show Krista and I had lunch with Michael behind the Greek and we talked for nearly two hours about his recent month-long trip to Bali, his hiking in the hills there and the time he spent with the monks in the mountains. He was looking forward to the band's upcoming shows in the US and Europe in just a few months. He laughed, joked and was in great spirits.

Just four months later, on November 22, 1997 I received a call from Australia. I thought it was Michael, but tragically it wasn't; instead it was about Michael. He had been found dead in a hotel room in Sydney. I couldn't believe it. This vital, wonderful man was dead at the age of thirty-seven.

The coroner ruled Michael's death a suicide. I don't believe it and neither do many others close to him. I think it was a terrible accident. But whatever it was the world was robbed of a great performer and I lost a dear friend with a precious heart.

Part Three – BEING BORING

Who are the nicest guys in music? The answer to that is simple, Neil Tennant and Chris Lowe. The two guys make up the Pet Shop Boys, the single most successful music duo in British history, but you would have no idea at the scope of their success by talking with them. They are down to earth, open and unreserved, and just fun to be with.

I fell in love with their first single "West End Girls" in April 1984. It was the Bobby O mix and I played it every night in the clubs and every day on my radio show. No other stations in Los Angeles were playing it but for me it just worked and I thought it sounded amazing on the air. And it's crazy who else happened to hear it. These are Neil Tennant's own words that he sent me:

Richard Blade was one of the first supporters of Pet Shop Boys on the radio anywhere. In 1984 we had released our first single, "West End Girls", and seen it get a little airplay in the UK, become a minor hit in Belgium and France and then apparently sink without trace.

Months later our then manager, Tom Watkins, flew to LA on a business trip for the design company he also ran. Getting into a cab at LAX he was aston-ished to hear "West End Girls" on the car radio and asked the driver which station it was. "KROQ" came the answer and the DJ was an Englishman called Richard Blade.

Tom was so excited that when he arrived at his hotel he phoned up Richard Blade and was not only put though to him but told that "West End Girls" was his "Pick of the Week" at the station and then interviewed live by Richard on the radio.

Through the support of Richard, the ground was laid for "West End Girls" and Pet Shop Boys to achieve mainstream success in the USA when the song was later released in a different version.

On our first visit to LA in 1986 we appeared on Richard's radio show and attended a massive record-signing in Westwood where thousands of listeners mobbed us and we signed autographs for hours with Richard beside us. A few weeks later "West End Girls" was number one in the USA and our album was in the Top Ten.

What Neil fails to mention in his modesty was that the Pet Shop Boys were scheduled to be at Music Plus in Westwood for ninety minutes to sign autographs. When they saw how long the line was they told their management and record company that they wouldn't leave until everyone got a signature. They stayed for more than five hours, something that won them the love and loyalty of every person there.

It wasn't just at record stores where Pet Shop Boys met their fans. In

1986 they came with me to my gig at the massive club where I DJ'd every Friday, the Florentine Gardens. That night I brought them onstage and they were mobbed by nearly 2,000 people who'd come to dance but instead used the opportunity to meet this incredible duo from England.

*With Neil Tennant
in 1985*

While they were in Los Angeles, Chris and Neil shot the video for "Suburbia" and invited me down to the filming in East LA. We covered the making of the video for *Video One* and the guys were surprised at just how many fans they had in the rough inner city.

In 1986 with the success of their first two albums the Pet Shop Boys were pushed to go on tour. I asked Chris and Neil in an interview about playing live and Chris said that they hadn't done it yet because they were frightened that they'd end up being boring on stage. Neil was working on a theatrical production to back up their onstage show but it proved way too expensive and was shelved.

It wasn't until 1989 that the Pet Shop Boys were able to stage the tour that they had dreamed of and it contained all of the immense, colorful elements that the two of them had conceived three years before. The tour earned them great reviews and made the Pet Shop Boys a must-see live act.

Krista and I with Neil and Chris on the Nightlife tour, 1999

Every time Chris and Neil come to town I always get together with the two of them both for fun and for work at their concerts and on the radio. Often Krista and I will join them for lunch where they show up in their regular clothes then catch up with them backstage at night while they are in full costume. Whatever they are wearing or wherever you meet with them, they remain the nicest guys to hang out with.

Part Four – YOUNG GUNS

George Michael. That name conjures up so many different images to so many different people. I have many words that describe my thoughts of George; star, talent, voice, performer, writer, giver, friend, but the one that sticks in my mind the most is metamorphosis.

I first met George in late January 1983. I had been playing Wham!'s debut single "Wham Rap!" for several months on the radio and was now into their latest release "Young Guns." Wham! were in LA hoping to promote their record and get some American success with it. So far, outside of KROQ, they hadn't had much recognition. MTV didn't know what to make of these white boys from England wearing leather jackets and trying to rap and Top 40 radio was having none of it. Rick Dees said famously "The day KIIS FM plays Wham! is the day we sign off the air." So when George and Andrew sat across from me that morning they knew they were in the only friendly spot in town.

George was nineteen at the time and Andrew had just turned twenty, and as much as they wanted to be pop stars they were first and foremost two young guns having a paid working holiday in America.

Our on-air interview went great. A lot of listeners already knew the songs from hearing them on KROQ and seeing them on my new TV show, *MV3*, so they were excited to call in and talk with the two lads. George and Andrew joked with the callers and were absolutely at ease on the air. They had nowhere else to go and they sounded so good on the radio that I asked them to stay a little longer.

I went into a commercial set and the first ad that played (I made sure it was first) was for my gig that night at the 321 Club in Santa Monica. After it finished playing and the next spot ran I noticed George and Andrew whispering to each other.

"What's up guys?" I asked.

George looked a little embarrassed when he asked, "We were just wondering how much it is to get into that club?"

I laughed, "For you?" They nodded.

"Don't worry; if you want to come I'll put you on the guest list."

George smiled and then looked at Andrew doubtfully.

Andrew took a breath, "Could we get a couple more people in with us? We're here with…"

I cut him off, "Pepsi and Shirlie?"

They grinned and I could see I had guessed correctly.

"That's fine," I said. "I see them in the videos all the time. It would be great to have them there. I'll even take care of your drink tab."

That night the four of them turned up in their best all-leather Wham! outfits. I set them up at the bar, which I know was wrong as they were all underage but my flawed logic justified it by saying that as they were from the UK and the drinking age there was eighteen it was OK, and I told them to come up to the DJ booth whenever they were ready to say hi to the crowd.

About thirty minutes later they all appeared and I faded down the music and chatted with them on the microphone. They talked to the kids in the club for about a minute then I put on the promo twelve-inch I had of "Young Guns."

As it played, George flashed a glance at the other three, then leaned in to me, "Could we sing along to it?"

I thought that was a great idea so I stopped the vinyl and told the crowd what was happening. I grabbed an extra XLR cable so the mic was now able to reach the dance floor and the four of them readied to bust into their moves.

I restarted the song and right there in Santa Monica Wham! played their first ever US show to an audience of enraptured club-goers.

After the song finished I yelled to George – I had to yell, he had my microphone – "Want another?"

"Wham Rap?" he suggested.

I said yes and put the single on and the four kids from London showed the LA crowd just how it was done.

At the end of my DJ set I joined them at the bar.

"Did you have a good time?" I asked.

"Great," answered George. "You don't have any other club gigs coming up do you?"

With Wham! on MV3

I did, and that next night Wham! performed their second American gig ever with me at Dillons in Westwood.

Wham! had one more day in Los Angeles and I brought them down to *MV3*. Sadly we weren't set up for a live performance but instead we did a really fun ten-minute on-camera interview.

Before the four of them left they made a special point to say thank you to me for spending so much time with them when so few other media outlets were showing any interest. It was my pleasure and zero problem. After all I was already playing them on the radio and on TV so why wouldn't I, and they had been so great with the listeners at the clubs. But George never forgot.

Ten months later Wham! was making it big and I was the one asking George for the favor.

MV3 had gone off the air and I was working on a new show that would shoot its pilot in Britain, *MV Network*. But CBS was demanding big

Shooting with George and Andrew in London 1983

425

names. I called George and asked him if he could find time in their jammed schedule to shoot with us in London and he didn't think twice. His reply was quick and simple, "yes!"

Wham! was rapidly becoming one of the biggest pop groups in the world but George continued his friendship. He was developing into a major star in his own right but he never forgot his roots. Even though he would be shooting shows and interviews for Dick Clark and for Friday Night Videos he always found time to do my radio show and then sit down for a TV interview.

Wham! November 1984 with the release of Make It Big

In early April 1985 I received a call at home from George. He had just been told that Wham! was up for best New Video Artist at the American Video Awards that were being televised live from Los Angeles. He knew this would be huge for Wham! but that there was no way they could be there as they had just been invited to be the first western pop band to perform in the People's Republic of China.

George wanted to know if I could do him a favor. Would I go on his behalf and if Wham! won to accept the award for them? Of course I said yes and on that night in April 1985 I was thrilled when Wham! won and I heard my name announced and I ran on stage to accept it from Grace Jones, Jack Wagner and Lorenzo Lamas on national TV.

Over the years I stayed in contact with George and we would meet often and not just for work. Despite being one of the biggest solo stars in the world he remained a huge music fan, and we hung out and watched Morrissey at the Fabulous Forum on June 2, 1991, the same venue that George himself had headlined and sold out three nights at with his *Faith* tour less than three years before in October, 1988.

Accepting for Wham! at the American Video Awards 1985

So my word for George, metamorphosis, comes from watching him transform from being that nervous, fun-loving kid, to becoming one of the biggest, most exciting performers on the planet. He truly was a miracle of nature, that little caterpillar who emerges from his cocoon to evolve into a beautiful butterfly. His voice, his talent and his songs helped change pop music but inside he remained the same; a loyal and honest friend.

POLICY OF TRUTH

On the subject of friends, there are two that I cannot avoid mentioning. Neither knew each other but they did have one deadly connection.

One of the prime rules of journalism is that a journalist shouldn't interfere with the story. The reason being that any interaction they have with the subject will change the outcome and therefore bias the reporting. I've never understood that. Why not try and change things for the better if you can? Have you ever watched the reports coming in of starving chil-dren in Africa and screamed at the TV, "Just give them some food!"? But instead the camera moves on leaving the child to its hunger and misery.

I'm not a journalist. I'm a DJ. I'm allowed to interfere if it makes a difference. I didn't once, and a friend died. After that I vowed, "never again." And when, in August 1995, I was given a second chance to make a difference, I did so even though my job was threatened and lawyers were woken out of their beds at 6am to shut me down. This time I refused to remain simply a passive observer. The life of a good friend and the fate of the biggest electronic band in history hinged on what was I was about to do early that Thursday morning.

There were, of course, many times when all I could do was report the story. I was on the air when John Lennon was brutally murdered outside his New York cooperative on Dec 8, 1980. I was a DJ at the hard rock station Magic 98 in Bakersfield and it didn't take me a second to pull off the Zep track that was playing and cut in to break the tragic news. For the rest of the night the station paid tribute with all Beatles and Lennon cuts interspersed by sobbing calls from distraught listeners.

Other tragedies would fall upon me to bring to my audience. Less than four months later I broke the news about President Reagan being shot by a crazed, Jodie Foster-obsessed assassin. Then on January 28, 1986 it was my somber duty to inform Southern California that the Challenger had exploded less than a minute after liftoff. I had few words to describe that moment. I left it to David Bowie to speak for me. I played three songs back to back from that icon that seemed to fit the moment, "Space Oddity," "Ashes to Ashes" and "Heroes."

My personal involvement in public tragedies began innocently enough with the first TV show I hosted, *MV3*. I got to know a lot of the acts that appeared on the show. Many became close friends.

One of those was Jeffrey Spry, the lead singer of the California band, Felony. Jeffrey, along with his brother, Joe, had been trying to make it in the music world for years. I had never met anyone who wanted to be a rock star more than Jeffrey. He loved the attention and the spotlight. If Freddie Mercury and Adam Ant had had a child together, that offspring would have looked like Jeffrey.

He played on the good looks and camp feel he possessed and accentuated them with his spandex pants, flowing shirts and leopard print jackets. Those clothes, coupled with his long hair and high cheekbones made him every kid's idea of what a rock star should look like. In fact, I'm sure that's how his finished look came about. He probably stared in the mirror and asked himself that exact question, "What should a rock star look like?" And out popped the fully-formed Jeffrey Spry, lead singer of Felony.

When I asked Jeffrey to appear on *MV3* it was as though he had won the lottery. He was in studio at KROQ guesting on the morning show with Ramondo and me. The radio station was already playing Felony's first single, "The Fanatic," and Jeffrey could always be counted upon to show up at a station event to perform. Bikini contest – Felony was there! In-store appearance – what time does it start? Club gig – when should I go on? And to be completely honest, we loved having Jeffrey, Joe and the band at our radio shows. They were great with our listeners and would sign autographs all day long. But a shot on TV – that was another story!

Ramondo and I were hyping a clothing store appearance we would be making together that weekend and sure enough Jeffrey volunteered to come down to Seal Beach with us and say hi to the fans. As we played his single on the air I mentioned to him off mic that I had just signed to do a

TV show that was starting in January. We were going to be on broadcast television in LA, San Francisco, San Diego, Chicago, Detroit, Atlanta, St Louis and more than thirty other cities. Jeffrey literally hugged me and said two words, "I'm there!" For the rest of the radio interview that morning Jeffrey was distracted. His mind was already on his television performance and the lights, camera, action! that awaited him.

Three weeks later Jeffrey, Joe and the rest of the band arrived early at the Burbank soundstage for their performance on *MV3*. I was wearing a cut-off Felony t-shirt in their honor, an outfit that I liked so much that I wore it at a multitude of gigs thereafter and in fact it appeared in a number of publicity shots and newspaper articles over the next year. And every time that shirt would appear in a 'Richard Blade' interview, Jeffrey would call me the next day to give me a big thank you.

Felony rocked *MV3*. They came to play and did just that. There was a live audience of more than a hundred teenage dancers who jammed up against the stage as the band tore into "The Fanatic." They sang along with Jeffrey and knew all the words because of the song's popularity on KROQ. On the chorus which featured the line "chasing limousines" they almost drowned out the lead vocal. Felony was a hit.

The massive TV lights were roasting Jeffrey who was dressed in a head-to-toe leather outfit, scarf and white high-heeled boots, but he didn't want to slow down or blow the moment. They willingly reshot "The Fanatic" a second time to give us extra camera angles to edit from and then performed their next single "What a Way to Go." Even an hour into the shoot Jeffrey still kept the energy up and worked the crowd, shaking hands with his fans and chatting with the girls between takes. Backstage, after we wrapped, Jeffrey came into my dressing room and cried, "This is the best day of my life." And that was no show business B.S., he meant it.

At a club gig with Jeffrey Spry of Felony

That performance on *MV3* led to a lot of good things for Felony including a tour and an appearance on Dick Clark's *American Bandstand*. "The Fanatic" also ended up on the *Valley Girl* soundtrack. Jeffrey LOVED it all. He worked the success as much as he could and for the next year he probably came to at least half of my live appearances. Every time he brought with him a big smile and a new story 'from the road'.

We started playing a couple more songs from Felony on KROQ over the next eighteen months including "Vigilante" and then "Gladiator School" but neither took off. Jeffrey stopped coming to my gigs as much and then dropped off the radar completely. Apparently this rapid fall from grace was taking a toll on both Jeffrey and the band, and behind the scenes even the relationship with his brother was becoming strained.

I would only hear from Jeffrey a couple of times a year over the next decade. He'd always make a point to phone me on my birthday, and occasionally there would be the late night call saying he was working on new music and that it was going to be bigger than "The Fanatic." I'd tell him to get me a copy when it was ready and would wish him well. I didn't realize that one day he would do just that and the repercussions it would have.

March 1992. *MV3* was becoming a distant memory as we moved into this grunge-powered decade. I was keeping the '80s alive on KROQ with Richard Blade's Flashback Lunch but many of the acts that had seemed so important back in the day were rapidly being forgotten by today's radio audience who were being fed a constant diet of Nirvana and Pearl Jam. The '80's revival had not yet started and groups from A Flock of Seagulls through to Spandau Ballet called it a day. It was into this hostile environment that Jeffrey reappeared.

I was finishing my show when Margie, who was working the front desk, called back to the studio and said I had someone waiting upfront to see me. I remember it vividly. I was getting ready to phone my mum in England to talk with her before it got too late – the time difference of eight hours often made it hard – and she was going through a tough time back in the UK; my Dad's birthday was rapidly approaching and it would soon be the ten-year anniversary of when he had passed away so unexpectedly. I was making sure to speak to her every day that week, to let her know she wasn't truly alone. I delayed the call to find out who was waiting for me and because of that I missed talking to her.

I went out to our station lobby and instantly recognized who was waiting for me there – Jeffrey Spry! I hadn't seen him in more than seven years but he looked exactly the same. He was even wearing the leather outfit that he'd worn on *MV3*, complete with the scarf and boots. I almost wanted to search the office for the time machine he'd arrived in.

"Great to see you, Richard. I drove all the way from Vegas to give you this. I've got new music." He proudly held up a cassette.

I knew what the next words would be before they tumbled out of his mouth. "It's better than 'The Fanatic.'"

I smiled and led him back to one of our production rooms to listen to it. The next three minutes were some of the most uncomfortable of my life.

Jeffrey's new song was bad. I mean to the point it was almost unlistenable. Nothing about it worked. Not the lyrics, the music and least of all, the vocals. When the cassette finished and the torture ended, the inevitable question was asked, "What do you think?"

I've been in that uncomfortable situation many times, when an artist asks you for your opinion of their work. Prior to this, the one that stuck in my mind the most was when I was with *Movietime* and battled with fellow host Greg Kinnear for the honor of being flown down to the Florida Keys to cover the world premiere of the latest 007 movie, *Licence To Kill*.

Being a huge Bond fan I pushed hard until I got the gig and ended up sitting next to Timothy Dalton for the screening. I was so excited that I couldn't wait for the film to begin, and when Monty Norman's "Dum Da

Da Dum" theme finally started and the gun-barrel logo appeared on the screen I had to pinch myself to realize that I was really watching a Bond movie sitting next to 007 himself.

However the film didn't live up to my high expectations and when the lights finally came back on and Dalton, Timothy Dalton, turned to me and said, "So what did you think of it?" all I could come up with was something like "It was in focus the whole time." Now here I was in-studio facing my long-time friend, Jeffrey Spry, and he was asking the same question. I had to tell him the truth.

"I don't think it's right for the station at the moment."

Boom. Unknown to me that statement made me judge, jury and executioner. And just like that the sentence was passed. Sadly it was the truth. KROQ was struggling to cope with the way music was changing and had deliberately – and in my opinion, mistakenly - pulled away from anything that sounded remotely '80s. Only a few bands that had emerged during the previous decade were still on the KROQ playlist (outside of my Flashback Lunch) and that list was very rock based.

Apart from Depeche Mode, Duran Duran, New Order and The Cure, the only '80's groups that appeared in regular rotation were Red Hot Chili Peppers, Jane's Addiction, Guns'N'Roses and Nine Inch Nails. There was no place for Felony on that playlist.

"Are you sure? Maybe one play?" pleaded Jeffrey.

"Leave it with me. I'll make copies and give one to Lewis (our music director) and one to Rodney (Bingenheimer). Maybe they can find a spot for it."

Jeffrey wasn't a stupid man. He knew what that meant. He took one more shot.

"How about on your Flashback Lunch?"

"Jeffrey," I said, "it's new music. It's not a Flashback."

"I know. But I guess I'm a Flashback, right?"

"Yeah," I was really sad for him, "and I'll play 'The Fanatic' for you tomorrow. People still love that song. And they love you. I'll give you a shoutout on the air."

"Okay. I get it. Thanks for taking the time to listen." He got up from the swivel chair in production and headed for the heavy soundproof door.

I stood up with him. "Maybe you can bring in another song in a few months?" I said hopefully.

Jeffrey shook his head even as he said, "Maybe."

The rest of our conversation was a blur as I walked him to the elevator. The final glimpse I had of my friend who so loved his brief romance with stardom was as he stepped into the elevator, his scarf trailing behind him. Normally he would have looked back, waved and said something like "See you at the next gig." But there was none of that today. Jeffrey had already decided where his next gig was going to be. He stood there silently as the elevator doors closed on him.

Was there something I should have said differently? Given him false encouragement perhaps? I've asked myself that a thousand times since and I'm asking myself again as I type this. Maybe I could have invited him down to my Friday night gig at The Palace in Hollywood and had him walk on stage with me in front of more than a thousand fans. Would that moment back in the spotlight have changed anything? I don't know.

Five days later, on March 10, 1992, I was on the phone with Mum. It was my dad's birthday and I was comforting Mum – and she comforting me – on his loss. It was at that moment that I was interrupted by another call. On the line was Joe Spry, Jeffrey's brother. He was calling to tell me the tragic news. His brother, my friend, Jeffrey Spry, was dead. He had shot himself the day before, leaving behind his wife, Tamara, and their children.

I offered some meaningless words of consolation and returned to the call with my mother. Somehow I got through the conversation with her and hung up. I clicked on the "On Air" light in the production room so no one could walk in on me and leaned back in the chair. The world was spinning. Had I contributed to this person's death? Was this the price of ambition? I resolved that day that if ever there was another time that I was put in the position of being able to do something and help a friend who was in dire straits then I would do everything I could to intervene and change the course of events for the better. I didn't realize I would have the chance to do just that only three years later.

It happened while Kevin and Bean were on vacation. LA's top-rated morning team was taking a few days off. I loved Kevin and Bean and even though they had replaced me on the KROQ morning show I had no hard feelings towards them.

Listeners would – and continue to – come up to me and say that my morning show was much better than Kevin and Bean's but in all honesty

With Depeche Mode's Dave Gahan in studio and assistant Michelle Gonzalez.

I have to disagree. Kevin and Bean, in addition to achieving monster ratings, produced amazing talent that sprang from their program including Ralph Garman, Adam Carolla and Jimmy Kimmel. So whenever I would be asked to fill in for Kevin and Bean I was always proud to do so.

The morning of August 17, 1995 started off quietly as most Thursdays do. The excitement of the weekend was still a day away and there wasn't the frantic feel of the listeners on the phone desperate to get their requests played. Not to say the lines weren't busy. They were and had been all week.

My assistant, Michelle Gonzalez, was outside the studio in the hallway finding great calls for me to either take live on the air or tape for playback later. I had gotten into the practice of recording everything and thanks to the advent of digital technology and hard drives I was able to edit and playback calls within literally a minute.

I was just starting a classic feature of mine, Bogus Entertainment, where the listener has to guess which one of four showbiz stories I've made up to fool them, when Michelle rushed into the studio. She had a caller on the line who claimed to be a paramedic who had just treated Dave Gahan for multiple lacerations on his wrists and had him admitted to the Cedars-Sinai emergency room in critical condition. I dropped into a song and talked with the paramedic off the air. He sounded genuine.

I was a Medic First Aid Instructor, something I picked up while taking my SCUBA diving instructor's course, and everything this guy said sounded spot on, from where he picked Dave up to how he treated his wounds and how he was transported to the hospital's ER for treatment.

I was upset and pissed. Dave had been in a downward spiral for the past two years and it didn't seem like anything had been done to help him. No interventions or rehab. And now he could be about to die. But I had to make sure it was true before saying anything.

I got the number and called Cedars-Sinai. I asked for Emergency and the operator put me through to the admitting desk.

I knew there would be restrictions on the release of information so as soon as my call was answered I led off with, "I think my brother's just been admitted into your hospital. My name's Stephen Gahan. His name is Dave Gahan. He's English. How is he?" I waited while the admission's nurse pulled his file.

"We don't have too much right now. It looks like he's stable. He's in ICU."

"I was told he cut his wrists. Is that correct?"

There was a pause as she checked. "Yes. Multiple lacerations on both wrists."

"Damn," I said. "It was self-inflicted, right?"

Another pause. "At this moment, that's how it seems." Pause. "Everything points to that. We have the admission written up as an attempted suicide. He can't have any visitors until he clears the ICU. That may be a few hours."

"Is he going to be okay?"

"We hope so. He has lost a lot of blood but he has the best doctors anywhere taking care of him now."

In Florida with Dave Gahan, Scott Mason and Martin Gore
https://www.youtube.com/watch?v=C6DJdb33a6s
A link to Dave drunk-dialing me twice in one night!

"Okay. Thank you for your help." I hung up the phone. I looked at Michelle who'd heard the whole call. I added one word to the conversation. "Shit!"

Dave was a great friend of mine. We'd known each other since 1983 and done many things together. Dave had invited me on the road with Depeche Mode, had me introduce them at a multitude of their live shows, featured me in the band's movie *101*, helped me put together the infamous Wherehouse in-store for the *Violator* release, flown me and Scott Mason out to Florida to host their press-conference for the *Songs of Faith & Devotion* album, and even drunk-dialed me dozens of times from around the world when he needed a friend to talk to.

I slipped on my headphones, opened the microphone and faded down the music. I took a deep breath because I realized the implications of what I was about to do; I was going to break the news to the world that one of the most important artists in the history of modern rock and a good friend, had tried to end his own life.

"I hate to be the bearer of bad news," I spoke into the mic, "but I just found out something really disturbing. Dave Gahan, lead singer of Depeche Mode, tried to kill himself this morning by slashing his wrists. He was rushed to hospital less than thirty minutes ago. I just spoke with the nurse who admitted him and she thinks he'll be okay but he's currently in the intensive care unit. Send out positive thoughts. We are all hoping for the best for him and DMode. Keep it on KROQ and we'll keep you updated. Here's "Never Let Me Down" for Dave on K-Rock. Stay strong, my friend."

I hit play and music flooded the airwaves.

Michelle and I worked the phones. It was all tears and well-wishes. As the song ended I began playing back calls. I did a quick recap of the situation on the air and went into a seminal song by Depeche Mode that deals with suicide, "Blasphemous Rumours." It was during that track about a 16-year-old girl, bored with life, when the hotline rang.

I had been waiting for its ominous red light to start flashing. It would almost definitely be our program director, Kevin Weatherly, asking why I had deviated from the format. An understandable question as it was the second DM track in a row a little before seven in the morning. I answered with a not-so-cheerful "Good morning". An unfamiliar voice (at least over the phone) responded.

"Who is this?" asked the voice.

"Who are you calling?" I replied. Occasionally listeners got the hotline number and you did not want to encourage them. This line was strictly for business.

"I'm calling whoever is on the air right now at K- Rock."

"Well, that would be me."

"Richard Blade, right?" the voice asked.

"Yup. Who is this?"

He told me his name. I recognized it instantly. I'd met him a number of times, both at the record label and here at the station. He was a diminutive little know-it-all who thought himself superior to everyone. He had the attitude that he was doing you a favor just by breathing the same air that you were. The dweeb continued.

"What the hell have you been saying on the air?"

That was an easy answer. "That Dave Gahan tried to commit suicide. That he's in ICU at Cedars fighting for his life."

"That's bullshit!" the dweeb yelled down the phone. "Stop saying that immediately. You need to go on the air right now and take it back."

"That's not going to happen." I was getting pissed. A record company minion was not going to dictate to me, especially not at a moment like this. "I'm going to play Depeche Mode all morning until everybody knows."

"I'm going to get you fired for spreading lies."

"Do it. I'm not going to stop. Hold on." I placed him on hold and clicked the mic live on air. I leant forward and talked into it, knowing that he would hear every word while he was on hold.

I continued with the story of Dave's attempted suicide and as I talked a thought crossed my mind of something that had happened the previous year to a huge artist on the same label that this self-centered turd worked with. And then I remembered Jeffrey Spry and my complete inability to save him. It was a perfect storm of guilt, retribution and an insider's knowledge that swept over me. I decided to run with it, knowing that this quite possibly might be my last show ever on any radio station on the planet if I was wrong, but if I was right then I had the chance to help save Dave.

"I just got a call from one of the big wigs at the record label that works with Depeche Mode." I said. "He wants me to stop talking about Dave's suicide attempt. He doesn't want me to tell you that he slashed his wrists and he's in intensive care and that the hospital still doesn't know if he'll pull through. I know what he wants to do. He wants to hush it all up and make it seem like an accident. That way he doesn't have to worry about Dave getting clean or getting mad and then maybe leaving the label."

I could imagine the record geek screaming down the phone as my voice played to him on hold.

"He is more worried about collecting Depeche Mode's publishing money than saving Dave's life. Just over a year ago another artist had an *accidental* overdose in Italy from a combination of aspirin and sleeping tablets. We were told to say on the radio that it was a fluke, a mistake, not to make a big deal of it. But it wasn't true. It had been a full-on suicide attempt, a cry for help. But it was covered up rather than getting that artist help. And what happened? Less than five weeks later that same artist went missing and it took the record company goons two days to locate him after an 'exhaustive search.' And where did they finally find him? With his head blown off, dead on the floor of his own apartment in Seattle. Some search! They hadn't even bothered looking for him where he lived! The artist's name was Kurt Cobain, and that's what they let happen to him."

I paused and let the 'dead air' speak for me before I continued, "I'm not going to let that same thing happen to Dave. He's been a friend for too long and given us all too much over the years to let him make the same mistake. This idiot from the record label can threaten me all he wants but I'm not going to stop saying this. Let's get Dave the help he needs before it's too late." I started "Policy of Truth."

With the song playing I went back to the phone. "Yes?" I asked.

I think the reply included several choice curse words. The gist of the rest of his hurried words was that I was about to lose my job and that I had had improper sexual relations with my mum. He hung up.

I watched the hotline and waited. Less than sixty seconds went by and it flashed red. I answered on the first ring. It was Gene Sandbloom, assistant program director. The record company goon had called him and read him the riot act but Gene, ever cool, wanted my side of the story. I told Gene everything that had gone down since the very first call with the paramedic. He was quiet for a moment, thinking before he spoke. Gene is a good guy and loves musicians and artists like I do. He was concise and to the point.

"If you are sure, really sure, run with it. But if you're wrong it won't just be your job, it'll be all our jobs and the station's license."

Wow. That was putting a lot of responsibility on my shoulders. KROQ was the most important rock station in America. Its broadcast license was now worth over six hundred million dollars. No pressure there! This would not be a good day to fuck up.

I jumped on the mic and recapped the story again. I told the listeners that they could send their well-wishes to Dave addressed to me at the radio station and I would keep the Depeche Mode music going all morning. I wished Dave strength and started a 1981 classic "New Life." By now the hotline was blazing again. The slimy record company exec was back with another threat.

"Lawyers are on their way over with a cease and desist notice. Plus if you say one more word about this on the air we will sue you personally for everything from slander to interfering with free commerce."

My voice might have sounded calm but inside I was Scared with a capital S! I had to play the only card that I had. "You know we record all our incoming calls, correct?"

"Yeah, of course I know that."

"Well, I have you on tape threatening me."

"So? I'm just protecting our artist."

"You're protecting the record company's money. I also have this on tape," I hit playback and both calls – the initial paramedic's and my call to Cedars-Sinai, went down the line to his ears only.

"So how will that sound when I play your threatening calls to me on the air saying that this never happened and then the paramedic's call and the comments from the admission's nurse confirming that it did and that you are the one who is deliberately lying?"

Silence.

"So send over the lawyers. I'll read their cease and desist notices live on the air to the listeners then play all the calls again, including yours. Let's see who becomes the scapegoat then and loses their job." The line went dead as the record company exec slammed the phone down on me.

Michelle smiled at me. We dropped from Def Con 5 to Def Con 3. The lawyers never showed up but the reporters did. Everyone from the *Los Angeles Times* to *USA Today* filed in. Even Britain's *Daily Express* and *Melody Maker* sent people over to interview me and get the scoop on Dave's condition. Within hours the record company was forced to go public with the news that Dave had tried to kill himself and that pending a 72-hour suicide watch they promised they would be getting him help.

I was mentally and physically drained when I got off the air at 10am but I didn't leave the station until after 2pm. Camera crews from all the television news services turned up to get the inside story on what had happened. It was mayhem at KROQ with reporters pushing and shoving and cameras and lighting equipment piled up in the hallways, but with each interview I felt that perhaps Dave was a little closer to getting the assistance he needed. Certainly any future cries for help would not go ignored.

As I drove home hours later, alone in my car, I felt that something had been achieved that day. That I had actually been able to help a friend. My past failure to intervene had taught me that sometimes you just have to step up and act. I said a little prayer that Jeffrey Spry, the kid from Fresno who so wanted to be a rockstar, was watching and that wherever he was he knew that he had been a major part of saving the life of one of the most important figures in modern music.

After Dave was released from his suicide watch I took him four mailbags full of cards from our listeners wishing him well and sending him love. Dave looked me in the eyes and said "I heard what you did for me. Thank you." He hugged me tight before I left.

I remain good friends with Dave Gahan, Martin Gore and Andy Fletcher and see them at virtually every Depeche Mode show. They send me Christmas cards every year.

LOSING MY RELIGION

Ask any KROQ kid who grew up with the station from its early days in Pasadena and they'll tell you that the nineties were a time of change for 106.7.

Gone was the unpredictable, loose and crazy element that had come across so clearly on the air and it was replaced by a smoother, more corporate approach. The music changed too. The fun feel that new wave had ushered in was replaced by the doom and gloom of grunge. No one knows exactly when the eighties began; was it with The Ramones at the CBGBs, the Sex Pistols swearing on live TV or Duran Duran running through the jungles of Sri Lanka? But we all know the moment when the eighties ended. It was the day Kurt Cobain picked up his guitar and lit into the opening riff of 'Smells Like Teen Spirit.'

In 1991 I was doing middays at KROQ. Andy Schuon had been appointed program director and Lewis Largent, as his music director, was using his talented ear to find and add grunge to the playlist as quickly as it came across his desk. For them the Seattle sound was what was happening and the eighties music that had built KROQ had become a lead weight pulling it down. As almost a joke they decided that for the Memorial Day weekend they would program three days of nothing but eighties music and then possibly use that as an excuse to remove it entirely from the rotation at the station and start with a clean slate. However sometimes things don't go quite as planned.

The listeners' reaction to the eighties weekend was very different to what was expected. Instead of the previous decade's music coming across on the radio as being 'old' and 'burned out' the station was bombarded with overwhelmingly positive phone calls about how much they loved hearing it and asking when we were going to do the next one. Andy and Lewis were a little shocked at the response and asked if I could meet with them about the feedback. They both viewed me as *Mr. 80s* which coming from them in the spirit they meant it was a bit of a put-down but I didn't care; I'd survived much worse insults.

We sat down behind closed doors in Andy's corner office and the gist of the meeting was that the station needed to use this listener outpouring as an opportunity to create somewhere to put (I got the impression they meant "dump") all these eighties bands. Andy and I might have very different tastes in music, but he has one of the best minds for promotions that I've ever encountered or worked with and as we talked an idea was developed.

KROQ already had a noticeable bump in the ratings during my show around noon when people were off for their lunch break so why not play all the eighties music there for the maximum number of people to hear? That way they could get the majority of it off of the regular playlist while still letting the loyal listeners know that KROQ had not entirely lost touch with its roots.

The only problem was coming up with a catchy name, and one that separated KROQ from all those "oldies" that would be played. That was the last thing the programming department at the station wanted at the time, to be associated with the past and the eighties. I thought the solution was obvious and I was happy to be identified with the decade that had given me so much. On that day, in Andy's office, Richard Blade's Flashback Lunch was born.

Though the rest of the air-staff initially thought of the show as a short-lived novelty feature I refused to see it that way. To me it was insane that the station was dismissing its own heritage as disposable and wanted to turn away from the very music that had made us great. These were bands that were forever associated with KROQ and we were willing to throw that legacy away? As far as I was concerned that wasn't going to happen. Even if everybody else at KROQ viewed Richard Blade's Flashback Lunch as a place the eighties went to die, for me it was a chance to showcase how unique that music really was and how it could hold its own against any of the grunge that was being released.

I decided I would give it my all and try to make it the most vibrant, exciting show on the dial, and rather than mock the songs and the bands, I would treat them as if they were as important today as when we first discovered them.

I worked on a number of ideas to enhance the show, to make it stand out from the rest of the day's programming; I contacted all the artists and groups directly and had them cut IDs and promos for me and every day I featured interviews, both live and recorded, tour information, birthdays, anniversaries of important releases and any new music they were putting out. Suddenly I was not the only one excited about this; the feedback from the bands was immediate. They were thrilled to have a place on the radio dial where they were still played and respected and during the first week of my show's debut we had Howard Jones, Dave Wakeling of The English Beat and Boy George in studio plus phone calls from Depeche Mode and Bernard Sumner of New Order.

Instead of the Flashback Lunch being a graveyard for eighties music it became a celebration of the previous decade and people tuned in in droves.

It was an instant hit and now KROQ had three huge ratings winners in three distinct time slots; Kevin and Bean every morning, Richard Blade's Flashback Lunch in the middle of the day and Loveline every night. It was a salesperson's dream come true and soon we not only had sold-out commercial sets booked months ahead but sponsors squeezed in at the open and close of the show.

Ironically none of the three highest rated programs on KROQ were about nineties music; Kevin and Bean were a fun, raucous morning show which was mostly talk and humor, Loveline featured teenage sexual problems, while on the Flashback Lunch I took everyone back to the days of Aqua Net and Kajagoogoo.

Richard Blade's Flashback Lunch continued to grow in popularity and within months was the number-one show in its timeslot in many of our key demos. Andy added a weekend version of it to the KROQ line-up, Richard Blade's Flashback Sundays which lead into Rodney Bingenheimer's Sunday night show. I loved seeing Rodney every week as I had nothing but respect and admiration for him.

Rodney is a legendary DJ in the music world and had been responsible for breaking so many groups and artists on his radio show from the Go-Gos in 1981 through to Oasis in 1992. He loved music and his reputation for being able to find new, upcoming artists was unmatched. I felt that the two of us, back-to-back on a Sunday night, made a great combination and it gave the listeners tuning in as their weekend came to a close a comforting glimpse back to the KROQ they had grown up with.

Word started to appear in the trade publications such as *Radio & Records*, *Hits* and *Billboard* that all across America radio stations were launching their own version of Richard Blade's Flashback Lunch. The name was different of course, "the Retro Lunch Bag" or "the Midday Time Machine" but they were direct copies of what we had started. Andy and I both regretted not trademarking that particular radio format and then syndicating it as it quickly spread to more than 400 stations coast-to-coast.

The impact that the Flashback Lunch was having was quickly noticed by the record companies and I was contacted by Carl Caprioglio in 1993 to put out an album on Oglio Records through Sony/EMI called *Richard Blade's Flashback Favorites*. It was to be a one-off project released locally and that was okay with me.

Richard Blade's Flashback Favorites series Volumes 1 – 6

Over the next three months I compiled a list of artists and rare tracks to put on the CD and cassette and set to work on the liner notes. When it was released it went straight to the top of the best seller list throughout LA and Orange County. After seeing it hit #1 Sony and EMI immediately changed their marketing strategy and Oglio Records re-released the album on a national level. Within just weeks it had sold more than a hundred thousand copies!

We signed a new deal and five more *Richard Blade Flashback Favorites* albums followed to complete the series. It always makes me smile when I walk into a club or visit another radio station and see that they have all six of my albums. And from that first release onwards, at every gig I play someone inevitably comes up with one of those CDs for me to sign.

KROQ continued to soar and with Andy Schuon's guidance responsible for keeping us in the top five in the ratings and generating huge sales revenue for the station he quite rightly became very much in demand and within a few months was lured away from radio to head up MTV in New York. Andy knew he would need a great music director for MTV so he took Lewis with him plus a former intern and part-timer from KROQ, Kennedy, to appear on camera. A new program director was needed and quickly. Thankfully the spotlight fell on exactly the right person to lead KROQ through the coming years, Kevin Weatherly.

I've been blessed to work with some incredible talents over the years in radio, TV and film; Ramondo, Mark Driscoll, Sarah Jessica Parker, Larry Groves, Greg Kinnear, Jimmy Kimmel and the creator of KROQ, Rick Carroll, and I have to add to that list, Kevin Weatherly. I think Kevin is the rightful heir to KROQ that Rick himself would have anointed had he lived.

Unlike most new program directors, Kevin didn't come in thinking he knew everything and acting like an axe man cutting the existing staff and replacing them with his own people for no good reason. Instead he arrived at the station wanting to learn, to absorb what KROQ was and what made it great before making changes. Kevin learned what Morrissey, Depeche Mode and New Order meant to KROQ and to our listeners even as he tried to work out where they would fit in with the influx of groups like Pearl Jam, Alice In Chains and Soundgarden.

Having said that I felt that Kevin didn't 'get me' personally. I don't think he ever understood why the eighties remained so popular and why people tuned into my show in such numbers. I think his focus was to push KROQ forward into the future, embrace the new music and trends in rock and keep the station cutting-edge. That is a very understandable position for a hip radio programmer but it did ignore the fact of the station's inescapable heritage and the impact it had on millions of kids who had grown up with it during the previous decade and viewed KROQ as almost a beloved family member who was there for them during the good times and the bad. To those "KROQ kids" we were the friend they could turn to, to rely on, when no one else "got them." Around the world, but especially in Southern California, it could never be forgotten that the eighties were a unique time in music and KROQ had been its number-one champion.

Initially dismissed as disposable pop, virtually everyone, myself included, thought at the time that the songs would have no shelf life. Only one person knew better, Rick Carroll. He said to me as far back as 1985, "Richard, one day they'll be stations everywhere playing nothing but KROQ music."

I thought he was nuts, but as usual as in all matters of music, Rick was 100% right.

Kevin was always really civil to me and no one could ask for a more loyal boss but still, the vibe I picked up was that I was like a distinguishing facial birthmark and that as much as you'd like to cut it off and get rid of it you just can't because everyone would notice it was gone. I was the one keeping the eighties alive on KROQ and pulling huge ratings doing it. But every day when I came in to do my show there was a feeling in the air that I was, ironically, a square peg that no longer fit into KROQ's round hole. After all those years and all that work I now felt uncomfortable in the place that had become my home, my KROQ.

KROQ had been my church, my religion, for so many years but now with the foundation gone it was crumbling down around me. But surprisingly at this point in time it didn't bother me. My father's death had shown me life is fleeting and not to be concerned with petty matters and with that knowledge burning inside I knew I had already glimpsed my future on that reef in Grand Cayman and it was not KROQ.

I was tempted to leave in 1995 and just head into the sunset but I was very aware that if I did that then eighties music on KROQ would depart with me and that would start an inevitable snowball effect across radio in

America and all those great artists and their music would be lost, perhaps forever. That would be a tragedy.

For young kids getting into music in the nineties I felt they had to hear Joy Division, Siouxsie, Gen X, the Specials and so many others to really appreciate how modern music had evolved. KROQ without the eighties would become a wasteland. It would have been like a regular rock station ignoring The Beatles, The Who, The Stones or Zep. It would just be wrong.

The irony was that I was actually a huge fan of a different kind of music that was emerging at the same time as grunge; electronic dance music.

I loved 808 State, Basement Jaxx, the Chemical Brothers, Front 242, Nitzer Ebb, Crystal Method, Snap! and Moby. I pushed hard to get their music on KROQ but was told there was no place for it.

I would find instrumental tracks from those acts and many others and use them as talkover beds on the Flashback Lunch just to give them some kind of exposure on the radio, and every day throughout the nineties I would close my show with Orbital and their song 'Halcyon' (which I loved so much I also used as a chapter title in this book.)

I took Front 242's "Headhunter" to our production director, John Frost, and suggested making a KROQ jingle from it. John, who is beyond brilliant at what he does, conjured up something that surpassed all of my expectations and a classic KROQ ID was born mixing the break from 'Headhunter' into a chant crying out for "forty minutes, forty minutes, forty minutes of non-stop K –Rock." I still think that to this day that it is one of the best radio jingles ever produced.

For all the unspoken tension that might have existed between us I found Kevin to be a great person and phenomenal at finding the next great act in rock music. There could have been no one better than "KW" as we called him to helm KROQ. And through all my time with Kevin we only had one major run-in and that was during the fallout from a tragic Friday night in 1996.

DEATH OF A DISCO DANCER

Even with my radio shows and TV gigs I still made time to play in the clubs. Those early days driving back and forth across Europe and building my own mobile disco consoles have never left me. If you were to scratch the surface off this radio personality you would find a club DJ waiting to get behind the turntables.

One of my all-time favorite places to spin anywhere on the planet is The Palace in Hollywood. Located across from Capitol records, the home of The Beatles, Beach Boys and Duran Duran, and just yards from the intersection of Hollywood and Vine, it was a legendary nightclub and it had certainly earned its status.

The Palace has a history stretching back to 1927 and had been home to iconic performers who held court there with long-running shows, both live and on television, including Jerry Lewis, Bing Crosby, Lawrence Welk, Lucille Ball and Frank Sinatra. America's most influential punk group, The Ramones, chose The Palace to be the location of their final show and its Art Noveau architecture both inside and out has been featured in many movies. I was continually in awe of the fact that I was given the opportunity to play at the same venue as those superstars. But even with all those amazing talents that walked that hallowed stage at The Palace, I had the privilege to hold the record for longest residency of them all.

From 1991 onwards The Palace was mine every Friday night. And even though I would play music for the packed crowds and then go onstage to entertain the audience much like the legends who had preceded me over the decades before, that night I had something happen at my show that none of those phenomenal acts ever experienced; I had a fan die in my arms.

The Palace had become a much-needed source of comfort and support for me over the past couple of years because in January of 1993 I had come home from my radio show to an empty house. My wife was gone.

At first there was nothing to suggest there was anything unusual. No note, no angry phone call. Normally I would have assumed that Karen was just out shopping or picking up groceries. But something didn't seem right. Even little Angel felt the different vibe and looked at me as if things were amiss.

I searched our bedroom and saw that a few of her clothes were gone along with a suitcase. I was starting to panic. For some reason she had just left.

I looked all around the house and in my little office I noticed that my checkbook and papers weren't in their usual place. Plus they weren't in order; they had been gone through. Then in the trash in the spare room I found a receipt dated that morning, from a copy shop just a few blocks away on Ventura Boulevard. Had someone made copies of all our bank accounts or was I just being paranoid? My world felt like it was spinning out of control and my breathing became shallow and rapid, I could barely think because of a pounding deep inside my skull and it seemed like my head would explode.

Karen and I had a good marriage. We rarely, if ever, argued. We travelled together extensively and always had a good time. And from the day I said those two words, "I do," I had put my cheating ways aside and not even looked twice at another woman. I took my vows seriously. But now she had for some reason walked out.

I racked my brain as to why. A few days before we'd had an in-depth talk about her career. She was about to hit thirty on February 14, a Valentine's Day baby, and as an actress in age-sensitive Hollywood that was an unwelcome milestone. It was becoming tougher for her now to land parts because her competition was the hottest new eighteen-year-olds in the country just off the bus to Tinsel Town. But she had proved time and time again that she was up to the task, with terrific guest star roles in huge shows such as *Seinfeld* and starring in a just-released movie, *Dangerous Curves*.

In between the roles however she would often come home from her latest audition in a sad mood, feeling that she was missing out on her chance to finally get that breakthrough part and land the lead role in a TV series. I tried to be the rock that she could lean on just as my father had been Mum's support but obviously I hadn't done enough. Even with all her talent, Hollywood was slowly beating her down and, unknown to me, our marriage with it.

We hadn't really talked about kids until that previous night and when the topic came up I dismissed it as "not being ready; maybe now, maybe ever." My reasoning was that if we had children it would completely change everything for us. I was not willing to be a part-time dad. I would want to be there for my kids 100% just as my father had been for me. That would mean giving up my gigs and so many side projects and I just wasn't ready to do that, but for me that would be the only way I would even consider starting a family, so that I could be the best father possible for them.

Karen hadn't seemed upset as we discussed the situation but could that have been it? Had my comments triggered feelings inside her that she didn't express to me? With her landmark birthday approaching, had children suddenly become a priority and had I just inadvertently dashed her dreams of becoming a mother? Whatever the reason, something had caused her to leave and I was totally blindsided by it.

I called Karen's sister who reluctantly told me that Karen needed "some time" and was with her mother and asked me not to call, that she didn't want to talk and she would reach out to me when she was ready. Her words confirmed my worst fears and as I hung up I fell to the floor and tears exploded from my eyes as my body shook uncontrollably. I rolled back and forth on the carpet convinced of the inevitability of what was going to happen.

It had been many years and many women since I'd left a great love whom I'd never forgotten, Terri Nunn, for Karen and now I was on the verge of losing everything I had ever worked for. All I could hear, roaring through my mind, was the word *divorce* and those were seven letters that were strangers to me. I grew up in a happy household. My parents had married for life and never once even came close to splitting up. But here I was, after just four years, on the brink of a failed marriage. I was rocked to my core. This was not something petty, this was life-changing and I had never been so low.

Was it a combination of events, was it because I'd changed so many things about myself to try and make this marriage work or was it because it was so unexpected? Whatever it was it hit me like a ton of bricks and the silence of that empty house, once so full of love and laughter, screamed at me. If I had been so wrong about this then perhaps I was wrong about everything?

I desperately needed someone to talk to so I called Peter but all I got was his answering machine mocking me. I felt so lost and alone and I found myself falling into a deep, dark abyss. It was like nothing I'd ever experienced before. If my life could turn so bad, so quickly, then what terrible thing would happen next? And what was the point of this? What was the point of anything? At that moment, in fearing losing everything, I lost myself.

I went into the bedroom and took out the twenty-gauge pump shotgun that I'd bought to have in the house for Karen to use for protection during the nights I was gone at my gigs. I was not a fan of guns but figured my wife needed something and a handgun has to be aimed and the bullet needs to hit its target to be effective. A shotgun with its loud discharge and wide scattershot field is much better in a dark, chaotic situation. Just point it roughly in the right direction and you'll probably hit what you aiming at.

I took the gun and loaded a single shell into the chamber and pumped it. I thought for a moment about what this would do to my beloved mother but she still had Stephen and my pain was so great. And this would be easier than having to tell her I was a failure at one of life's most important relationships.

My jeans were wet from my tears and I took a final look at the house that I knew the lawyers would inevitably take from me. It was all too much to bear. I raised the gun and steeled myself for the hot blast when I heard a cry.

Sitting just feet from me was Angel. She had her head back and was howling in distress. I had heard her howl many times before when Karen and I would tease her with our own "little wolf" calls that we'd make just so she would join in with us to be part of the pack. It was so cute and we loved to do it with her. But this was a different howl. It was like her heart was breaking too. If a dog can scream in anguish then this is what Angel was doing.

I lowered the gun and Angel took a few steps to me and lay down across my feet. She looked up at me with her chocolate brown eyes that said "take me with you," then lowered her head in a motion of surrender as if she should go first.

Hurt her? How could I do that? Then how could I leave this poor, defenseless creature who only wanted love? If I was gone how long would she be alone in the house before she would be found? And who would take care of this innocent animal?

I realized that for the first time in my life I was being a coward, wanting to run away from a tough situation, just to make the pain stop. I had never done that before and it had taken my beautiful Angel to show me my weakness and fear.

I ejected the shell and put the gun away. Bring on whatever might come, take from me what you will; I would face it the way I had done everything in my life so far, by meeting it head on. After all I had failed in love before; the only real difference here was that we had signed a contract that now might require lawyers to be undone. And everything can be replaced, even my house, it was only stuff. But there was one thing I promised myself that I would never give up in the legal battle ahead.

I reached down and petted Angel, "Whatever happens, baby girl, you're staying with me."

Ten days later Karen returned. I was right about what caused her to leave, she had been upset by our conversation about work and children and needed time away. We tried to work things out, to put it behind us and even went to a marriage counselor, but there was no violence, or drinking or abuse for them to address. From the outside we seemed to have a great marriage, a perfect couple, but for us it was never the same.

In June of 1993 things came to a head when Karen returned from six days away in Aruba with her sister, her husband and their new baby. Who started what is a matter of conjecture but within minutes I said quite simply, "I'm getting a divorce," and within three days I moved out to an apartment in Burbank just blocks from KROQ.

When the staff at the radio station found out about our pending divorce they were stunned. The DJ who followed me on the air, Tami Heide, reacted like she had been punched and had to sit down when she heard the news.

"My God," she said, "if you two couldn't make it then there's no hope for anyone."

I was saddened by everything that went down. Karen was a wonderful girl, a talented actress and a good wife but something had happened between us and whose fault it was I still don't know. The only thing that was certain was the divorce severed our relationship for good and Karen never wanted to see me or talk to me again. That is something I regret as I treasured our friendship as much as I treasured our actual marriage.

The lawyers did their work and ended up being the ones that came out ahead as they usually do, but I walked away a single man once again, and I retained possession of the one thing that meant the most to me, my little Eskie, Angel.

My first thought now that I was single was to find Terri and see if she was willing to give me another chance. Sadly for me, but hopefully happily for her, she was married and that meant I couldn't even think of suggesting anything with her. I might be a scoundrel but I respect sacred institutions like marriage. So instead I went on a tear.

I started working out like a mad man, put on nearly ten pounds of muscle and began dating every beautiful girl I ran into. I was almost insane in trying to put my failed marriage behind me and had one night stands with actresses, soap stars, strippers, waitresses, models, you name it. It was a wild time but I was lost and needed to find myself again,

The Palace became a haven for me and a great place to meet girls. They would all come there because it was Richard Blade night so I had an almost unfair advantage. One Friday in late 1995 I noticed a particularly gorgeous girl dancing her heart out on the floor and whirling like a dervish as I played "You Spin Me Round."

I called her up to the booth but she wasn't interested in me. Instead she tried to set me up with her friend, Susanne. She was cute but now I had my mind on someone else.

My wild dancer was back the next week and again I made a point to speak to her but this time instead of summoning her to the booth like some monarch granting her an audience I came down to the floor and chatted with her. Maybe that was the trick because we just clicked that night and we laughed together and danced. I found out her name was Krista and we made plans to meet outside of the club and go for dinner.

Krista was awesome. So much fun to be with and just down to earth and happy to stay in, kick back and watch TV. There was no pressure from her to always have to go out and be seen around town. Her favorite thing was to put on comfies and cuddle on the couch. Plus she loved Angel and Angel loved her. The two of them bonded instantly and it was so cute to watch that little fur ball follow Krista around the house. I only had one problem with her.

Krista was only nineteen years old. I was twice her age. It didn't bother her but as we were starting to get serious I was concerned for the future. I met her parents and immediately saw where she got her fantastic personality. Dyle and Lonnie Henderson were incredible people and so down to earth. We laughed, shared beers and enjoyed each other's company.

I took Dyle to the side and had a man-to-man talk with him.

"I know I'm a lot older than your daughter but…" I hesitated, "but there's nothing I can do about that and we really like each other."

Dyle nodded, "As long as you don't hurt her I'm fine with it. I'd rather her be with a good man like you than some idiot who is the same age as her."

And just like that, Dyle cleared the air and the Henderson family gave us their approval to continue our relationship.

Krista had come with me to The Palace on Friday November 29, 1996. She was living with me now and had thought that this might be the last night she would be going out before getting our home ready for the holiday season and her big twenty-first birthday coming up on December 20.

The Palace was particularly packed that night and being the first weekend after Thanksgiving everyone was there ready to party. It was a little after midnight and I was getting ready to head out of the DJ booth and make my way to the stage to start a series of contests and giveaways that had been a feature of my Friday nights at The Palace for the past five years.

I slammed into House of Pain's "Jump Around" which all the regulars knew was the signal that the contests were about to begin and as I turned to leave the raised booth I saw a guy dressed in a red plaid shirt step up onto the balcony rail.

The balcony was at the same height as the DJ booth, about fourteen-feet above the dance floor. It was always a great vantage point to see the stage. It held about 400 people who normally watched the action from their seats. But this person wasn't sitting.

He moved so fast there was no warning, nothing anyone could do or say. He stepped up to the balcony rail and without hesitation did a swan dive from it, his arms outstretched to his sides and plunged head first to the floor.

I pushed Krista and everyone else in the booth out of the way and took the spiral staircase down three steps at a time. I jammed through the stunned crowd, my mind racing. I had been teaching Medic First Aid for more than five years and a dozen scenarios flashed through my mind; Head, neck or back trauma; stabilize but do not move the patient for risk of aggravating the injury. Broken arm or leg; bind and stabilize until it can be X-rayed and placed in a cast. Rib fracture; check for signs of punctures or internal bleeding, have the victim remain still until a stretcher can be brought in. Remember the ABCs - Airway, Breathing, Circulation. Introduce yourself with the first responder's greeting, "My name is Richard. I'm medically trained. I'm here to help you." and get his name so you can have him answer you and keep him responsive.

Like a series of flip cards all those thoughts went through me in less than a second, but as I reached the fallen victim I saw something that my years of training had not prepared me for.

Kevin Fowler lay there, face up, in a rapidly spreading pool of his own blood. The top of his skull was crushed in and split open from the impact. It looked like the back of his head was also broken open also but it was hard to tell because of how he lay. He was breathing but just barely.

Blood was pouring from his mouth which suggested a puncturing of his lungs. This meant that should his heart stop beating, CPR would be impossible because of the probable existing lung damage and the obvious trauma to his spine and ribcage. Chest compressions would only aggravate his injuries. This was beyond the scope of anything that could be done in the field; it would take a miracle to save him even if he were in a well-equipped ICU rather than lying on the floor of a crowded dance club. All that could be done would be to prevent him from being hurt any further by the crowd and getting paramedics here as quickly as possible to transport him to the expert care of a hospital.

The Palace security and Krista were with me now and I called out instructions to them.

"Keep everyone back ten feet so he has air. Krista, call 911 and get paramedics here. Tell the operator that there is major impact trauma to the head, back and lungs." I pointed to the side exit and then to security, "Keep a path to that exit open and unobstructed and have one of your guys wait outside and as soon as the ambulance arrives bring them in that way as it'll be a lot quicker."

I turned back to the fallen disco dancer and knelt beside him. I spoke continuously and reassuringly to him hoping to ward off shock. "We've got people coming to help you. They'll be here soon. It's going to be OK. They'll patch you up and everything will be good."

His eyes locked on mine as I lied to him, "Don't worry about anything it's all going to be taken care of."

His gaze didn't move from mine as he violently coughed twice and blood flew from his mouth. He convulsed for a moment, then his whole body seemed to sag and slowly his pupils glazed over as the life fled from his eyes. I was the last person he saw on this earth.

A few minutes later the paramedics arrived and took the twenty-year old's body out on a gurney.

I got to my feet and walked silently through the crowd to my dressing room backstage. My hands were covered in his blood, my jeans soaked through from where I'd been kneeling by the dying boy and my face was stained with streaks of red.

I stood at the sink and scrubbed and scrubbed as though the very act of getting clean would bring him back. I gazed hopelessly in the mirror and prayed to myself that nothing like this would ever happen again. Little did I know that not only would my prayers go unanswered, but that this young boy was just the first of three people who over the next six years would die in my arms as I held them.

All the local papers and news channels carried the following report.

December 1, 1996

A 20-year-old man apparently jumped to his death early Saturday at a Hollywood nightclub, police said. Kevin Fowler was dancing at the Palace in the 1700 block of North Vine Street when he dove from a second-story balcony into the crowd below, sometime before 12:30 am Los Angeles police Officer Mike Partain said Fowler, who lived in the Los Angeles area, suffered head and neck injuries and died at the scene.

Kevin Weatherly was furious when he heard the news and called me into his office that Monday morning before my show.

"We're taking The Palace off the air and you are to do no more gigs there. It's over," he yelled.

I understood his anger but it was misdirected and I stood up to him.

"You can't do that," I answered forcefully. "The Palace did nothing wrong. Their security were on top of the whole situation. It was no one's fault but the kid who decided to jump. It was a tragedy but The Palace wasn't responsible for it." I was not going to back down; after all, I was the one who watched the boy die. "If someone died in a car wreck driving to a KROQ show would you stop putting on concerts and cancel the Weenie Roast or Acoustic Christmas? No, you wouldn't and no one would expect you to." I took a breath. "The owners are reaching out to his family and in respect to the kid are going to be dark this coming Friday. There's nothing else they can humanly do."

Kevin thought for a second and I knew he was fearing a lawsuit coming at KROQ. "Okay, if that's all there is," he said, "but one thing you should know. You're not bigger than the radio station. Lose KROQ and you lose everything. It'll all go away and you'll have nothing."

I have immense respect for KW but his words ripped me apart inside. All I had tried to do was save that boy's life and the memory of his fading gaze would haunt me forever. And to stand there and hear my job threatened and be told I had nothing else going for me in my life after all the work I had done and the experiences I'd had over the years shook me to the core and dispelled any doubts that I might have had in my mind about my importance to the station.

I pulled myself together and said simply, "I have to get on the air."

I left Kevin's office and went into the control room. I sat there trying to regain my composure, to bring the show for the listeners. As my opening song played I picked up the phone and called Krista. She answered on the first ring.

"You okay?" she asked.

"Yeah," I said. She could tell from my voice I wasn't. "Tonight, when I get home let's start making plans."

"For what?"

"For getting out of here. For leaving LA. That is if you want to go with me," I said.

"I'll go anywhere with you," she said without hesitation. "Where are you thinking?"

"How does the Caribbean sound?"

CARIBBEAN BLUE

I had chosen the Caribbean over Hawaii because of the fact it had less restrictions for bringing in animals. We had Angel and now the sweetest kitty, Soxy, and there was no way on earth that Krista and I would put them through six months of quarantine. So Hawaii, as perfect a paradise as it might be for us humans, was out.

Plus I knew the Caribbean well. I had travelled there extensively, not only while shooting the PADI videos but also for vacations. I loved its kick-back vibe, its beautiful weather and its warm, inviting ocean. But being there for a week or so is a very different thing to living there.

Krista and I sat down that night and started with a list of places that wouldn't work for us. Jamaica was the first we eliminated. It's a gorgeous island with an amazing history but outside of the major resorts it's dangerous. I'd seen the armed guards protecting the entrances to the massive hotel complexes and knew that if it took an Uzi to keep tourists safe then that was not a place for us.

Honduras, Belize and the outer islands of the Bahamas were crossed from our list due to lack of infrastructure, and Grand Cayman, the Virgin Isles and Turks & Caicos were struck off as potentials as tit was too expensive to buy a home and live there.

We also needed an island which had a major airport so friends and family could fly in and visit us, and we could leave to fly back to see Krista's parents in LA and my mum in England. I had visited one island that had all of that and more.

In 1989 Karen and I took a cruise of the Caribbean and visited six islands. One of them was St. Maarten. From the moment we disembarked at Great Bay in Philipsburg I felt relaxed. We rented a car and drove from the Dutch side up to Orient Bay in the French territory. There we played in the breaking waves and snorkeled the clear water. We grabbed a baguette in a small bakery and I was happy to have the opportunity to practice my very rusty schoolboy French.

Krista listened as I talked about the island and I could feel her excitement growing. Before we went to sleep we had our plans in place. I would put in for a vacation request and take a week off in February and we'd fly to St. Maarten and check it out together. If we both liked it, then just maybe that might be the place for us.

It had been a cold, overcast morning when we departed LAX but we found California's missing sun waiting for us when we touched down at Princess Juliana Airport in St. Maarten. It was picture-perfect weather, everything that you would hope for from a tropical paradise; a warm breeze, whispering palm trees, unending blue skies broken up by a few puffy white clouds that only served to highlight the incredible azure color and a sun that beamed down erasing any chill from your body.

We were staying on the French side at a boutique hotel on Orient Beach

and within two days had decided that we were going to move to the island. We made up our minds that quickly; Krista was always up for a new adventure, for a fresh horizon and I could hear my father's voice inside of me telling me "Life is short, my boy, make sure you live it."

With Krista in the Caribbean

A little research took us to a realtor on the Dutch side. There it was much easier to buy and sell property and obtain residency than in the French territories. They took us to see a dozen homes but one that hit us instantly was a villa high on a hill overlooking Simpson Bay. It had a million dollar view for a price that was barely one third of that. It was currently rented out and had a long-term tenant living in it which was perfect for us as we had a lot of planning to do before our move.

The house did need some work so we took photos, put an offer in and flew back to the States as we waited to hear the news. Two days later we received the phone call we had been waiting for; the villa was ours. Now we had to get down to serious business, make our plans for the house and work out exactly when to leave.

One date that kept jumping out to me was the year 2000. It was a new century, a new beginning, a chance to welcome in the second millennium by embracing a new challenge. I love the thrill of the unknown, the prospect of seeing what is around the next bend and discovering new horizons. I have only one fear and that is "Why didn't I?" I was terrified that my life would fly by and that I would wake up one day in a hospital bed, my body turned into a human pincushion of protruding tubes and wires, staring up at a white, tiled ceiling and be lying there thinking "Why didn't I have the courage to pursue my dreams." That idea filled me with dread.

Nearly forty years ago, huddled in his room during a stormy evening in Torquay, a little boy had made a list as the rain pounded against the windows. He wrote:

1. I want to live somewhere sunny
2. I want to swim with the fish in warm water like Jacques Cousteau
3. I want to travel the world
4. I want to be famous
5. I want to be on television like Blue Peter
6. I want to meet my favourite singers
7. I want a beautiful girlfriend
8. I want to be in a movie
9. I want to write a book
10. I want to be brave

I owed that little boy everything and wanted to make his list come true.

How could I let him down? I knew I would be walking away from everything but that gave me an exhilarating feeling of freedom, to throw off what you know and to begin again. It would be too easy to stay.

Orson Welles had said that Los Angeles was like a comfortable chair; that once he sat down in it, it took him twenty-five years to get up. If I left in 2000 then I would have beaten Orson Welles by one year.

And the big news was that Y2K would be the end of the world as we know it due to a calendar glitch within everyone's computers. Trains would stop running, planes would fall from the skies, and satellites would tumble from orbit. I knew that was nonsense but I thought it would be appropriate that Y2K would mark the end of one world for me and the beginning of another for the two of us.

Krista and I flew to St. Maarten several times in the next three years. We measured the house and bought new fixtures, cabinets, countertops, TVs; virtually everything for it would be new and we had it ordered and ready to be shipped out with us.

My dream was to teach SCUBA and make it a very special "white gloves" service. It would be small and cater to a clientele that didn't want to be shuttled onto big boats with lots of divers but instead could have a boat all to themselves and be whisked off to pristine reefs and uncrowded dive sites.

We researched boats and decided on a twenty-eight foot WorldCat. We took her out for a test run in San Diego Bay and she was perfect. We arranged to have her put in storage and shipped to the island when we were ready, and thought of the perfect name for her, *Living the Dream*.

We needed to make one final visit to the island to be sure everything would be ready for us the next year, so in July 1999 we flew out to meet with the government authorities and finish up the filing of our business license and residency papers. The realtor who sold us the villa heard we were on island and contacted us and asked if we wanted to go out on his cigarette boat. I had only seen power boats like that on the opening titles of *Miami Vice* so we jumped at the opportunity to experience a genuine open water racer. I wish we had turned it down.

The afternoon started brilliantly. We sped across St. Maarten's huge lagoon and out through the bridge at Marigot into the calm channel separating St. Maarten and Anguilla. The realtor gunned the boat's 600 horsepower engine and in the smooth waters of the lee of the island we hit almost seventy knots. We felt like we were flying fish as the boat grabbed air and shot over the small waves.

We anchored off of a tiny island called Pinel and waded ashore to eat lobster and freshly baked loaves of French bread from a tiny restaurant that looked like it had been put together by Gilligan's band of castaways. Krista had a glass of wine and I stuck with water. Unseen by us our captain was downing the local rum in quantities that would keep a distillery in business for a year.

As the sun began its descent towards the ocean we swam back out to the boat, climbed aboard and raced back around the island. Within minutes we were approaching Marigot and the captain cut the engines as we prepared to glide under the low bridge that marked one of the two entrances to the lagoon. As we passed under the concrete bridge he dropped the gears into neutral and opened up the engines to full throttle. The roar from the massive twin inboard motors was amplified by the base of the low bridge above us and the reverberations shook the air.

"I *love* that sound!" he yelled, his speech slurred.

Once through the French-side bridge he gunned the engines again and now we were hitting speeds of fifty to sixty knots as we flew across the lagoon's still waters.

We could see the dock ahead of us as we raced by Maho and towards Simpson Bay and on our right the concrete and steel bridge that was raised twice a day to allow the billionaires' mega-yachts to sail into the shelter of the lagoon. Then it happened.

For whatever reason, whether it was he wanted to hear the engine's roar once again or just for the insane thrill of it, he suddenly wrenched the wheel hard to the starboard. The boat lurched to the right and went up on its side but being designed for racing it didn't tip over as most other boats would have. It would have been better if it had, because now, as it straightened out, we were hurtling straight at the reinforced bridge.

There were six of us onboard when he lost control and rammed into the massive concrete supporting pillar. I was sitting at the very back on the long padded engine covers that took up almost a third of the length of the boat. I grabbed a line and held on as the front of the boat disintegrated from the impact and a large piece of fiberglass came flying back and hit me square in the face. Antonio, who was sitting next to me was not as

lucky. He was hurled from the boat and his arm was sliced open by the rocky embankment.

With the entire bow gone the boat swung wildly in the water and came to a dead stop high on the rocks under the bridge.

The smell of diesel fumes filled the air and I could hear Krista calling my name.

I pushed forward through the haze and found her extracting herself from beneath two people.

"Oh my God, are you okay?" she asked frantically as she saw the blood pouring from my nose.

"It's nothing. Just a little blood. How about you?"

"Good. I'm fine too," she said as her left arm hung limply at her side. She was almost in shock and wasn't yet feeling the excruciating pain of her major fracture.

Two of the other passengers started to cry out in agony. One had broken their leg, and the other, the driver's girlfriend who had been next to him as he piloted the boat in a drunken haze to its sad end, had by far the worst injuries including a broken hip, broken ribs and a concussion where her head had hit the boat's mahogany console.

Only one person on the boat escaped without a scratch, the captain. All the alcohol in his system had made him go limp at the moment of impact and while the rest of us were flung around he collapsed back into his seat.

Two ambulances rushed us to hospital. Krista was X-rayed, treated, given painkillers and medication and her arm was put in a cast. Thank goodness St. Maarten has a great healthcare system; our total bill was a little less than $250.

The next day I was waiting at the so-called captain's real estate office when he returned there after spending the night in jail. I handed him the bill. At that moment I wished it were more, a lot more.

He looked at it and then at me. "You're leaving today, right? I'll mail it to you in the States."

I had warned Krista before I walked into his office that day that if he gave me any bullshit there would be trouble. I didn't say anything; I just grabbed his throat and slammed him against the wall. Then I spoke.

"You nearly killed my Krista. Give me the money now or I'll do to you what you did to her and break your fucking arm." I released my grip and watched as he scurried to his desk and pulled out the money.

"Here's three hundred," he said.

I took it silently and left. It if he was expecting change he was sorely disappointed.

That afternoon, with a bright blue cast on her broken arm, Krista and I boarded the plane back to Los Angeles. The next time we would be at that Caribbean airport we would be arriving as residents.

GOODBYE, GOODBYE

The date was set. We would leave Los Angeles, our friends and Krista's family on May 5, 2000. We would drive across the country to Miami and take a plane to St. Maarten from there. We didn't want to fly all the way because we wanted to put the minimum strain on our ever-growing pack of fur babies. We now had three; in addition to Angel and Soxy, Krista had rescued a puppy mix - part Lab, part Collie, all adorable - and named her Zoey. They would be a lot happier with us, in the car, on a four-day drive than they would be taking their chances in the hold of a plane for five and a half hours.

In anticipation of the drive and the kind of car we'd need on the island I traded in my Lexus and bought a Mitsubishi Montero SUV. It wasn't glamorous but we weren't moving to impress people; we were moving to leave behind the jackets and heels needed for dinners out in Los Angeles and instead live in shorts and flip-flops while we ate at beach bars.

I contacted a realtor in LA and we quietly put our house on the market. We insisted that as part of the deal the buyer couldn't take possession until May 6, 2000. To our shock it sold before even the first open house. They had staged a day when all the real estate agents caravan around together to see new properties before they appear on the MLS. During that closed showing one of the agents broke with protocol and put in a secretive call to his client, a soap star from *Days of our Lives,* who drove straight over and bought it on the spot.

If there had been any doubts about our move they were gone now. The house that had been a warm, loving home for Krista and me for the last three years was no longer ours. The die was cast.

The only people who knew about our pending move were my mum in England and Krista's parents. The time was rapidly approaching to break the news that we were leaving. Krista and I talked it through and decided that I would give everyone two months' notice. That would give them time to replace me.

I had a lot of goodbyes to make. In addition to KROQ I was walking away from four TV shows. *7 Days* had just been renewed for a third season by Paramount and the second season finale that I had written was currently shooting in Canada and wouldn't even air until the middle of May. By the time it premiered we would be long gone and watching it in St. Maarten.

I'd also taken over Casey Kasem's TV show, *America's Top 10 Videos* which aired in my old *VideoBeat* time slot on KTLA Channel 5 and around the country. In addition to that I was the host of two TV shows for Europe, *Music, Games and Videos* and *Inside Hollywood*. It was a lot of money to leave behind but I knew I had to break out of those golden handcuffs if I really wanted to live the next stage of the life I'd dreamed of.

After I said my farewells to the world of TV it was time to face KROQ and bid adieu after eighteen great years.

Krista and I had talked about what was certain to happen. I would give my two months' notice and everyone would be sad but that would be the end of it right there. I wouldn't be allowed back on the air to say goodbye to my beloved listeners; DJs never are. The reason is because if they are leaving then they could say anything or do anything without fear of retribution and a station can't risk that. Give your notice and the response is inevitably, "Thanks, now unplug your headphones and don't let the door hit you in the ass on the way out." I was 100% prepared for that reaction and with that mindset I walked into Trip Reeb's office to tell KROQ's GM I was done.

I sat at his desk and slid a picture of our house in St. Maarten across to him. He looked at it and smiled.

"Nice place," he said. "Your next vacation?"

"No, I'm moving there."

Trip looked puzzled. "Can you explain that to me?"

"Yeah," I said, "Krista and I bought it three years ago with the plan to move there when it was time," I sighed as I looked at Trip. "It's time."

Trip took a moment before he spoke. "So you're leaving KROQ?" he asked.

"That's why I'm here, to give you my notice."

Trip got to his feet. "Wait, let me get Kevin." He rushed out and appeared seconds later with KW. Kevin looked stunned.

"You're leaving?" he said incredulously.

"I am. You know how much I love diving. And I've done everything I've ever wanted to do here at K-Rock and in LA. It's time for something new."

"So you're not going to another station?" asked Kevin.

"There is no other station. KROQ is it for me. And we might have our differences in music, Kevin, but as far as I'm concerned you and Rick Carroll are the two greatest programming talents in the history of American radio. And you Trip, as the big boss, have been amazing to work for, but I want to try something new while I'm still young enough to sling tanks and drive a boat."

Trip looked at Kevin and then back at me. "You know, I envy you. What do you think, Kevin?"

"Have you said anything about this on the air?" Kevin wanted to know.

I shook my head, "Nothing."

"And when are you planning to leave?"

"Two months. The end of April. After eighteen years I wanted to give you time."

"Okay, here's what we'll do. Don't tell anyone and on Monday I'll have a meeting with Kevin and Bean and we'll work out how to position this and when to break the news."

Kevin's words were shocking me. "So you want me back on the air on Monday?"

"Monday? Isn't it your turn to work a Saturday shift tomorrow?"

Kevin's loyalty to his staff was legendary but this was staggering. I was lost for words as KW continued.

"I'll let Lisa and Gene know about this and have them start working on a going-away party for you, a huge farewell concert for you and your fans," Kevin grinned. "It might end up even bigger than the Weenie Roast, who knows?"

That was the single most amazing thing about KROQ, its people. Behind the scenes they were honest, trustworthy and caring. We might have had disagreements about bands, music, genres, but we had each other's backs. In the end Kevin Weatherly proved to be not just a musical genius but also a true friend.

When I arrived home that afternoon Krista greeted me with a warm, soothing cup of tea. She was quiet and subdued, waiting to hear my sad news of being kicked out of KROQ.

"How did it go, honey?" she said softly.

"They want me to work out my notice. All of it. They're giving me a going-away party on the air."

"You're kidding!" she exclaimed in disbelief.

"No, it's the truth," I grinned. "I guess you'll be doing all the packing by yourself."

IT'S THE END OF THE WORLD
AS WE KNOW IT
(And I Feel Fine)

I was really nervous as to if anyone would actually show up for the going-away party that KROQ was throwing for me. It was happening Friday April 28, 2000 exactly two months to the day after I'd handed in my notice and ironically the station had decided on my home away from home, The Palace, as the venue for the massive farewell show.

It would start at 6am with Kevin and Bean broadcasting live then roll into a series of performances which included Billy Idol, Dramarama, Save Ferris, Berlin, The English Beat, Tears for Fears and John Taylor of Duran Duran. It would wrap up at one in the afternoon with my final Flashback Lunch.

I knew it was an awesome lineup but it was a Friday morning and people had to work and I was dreading walking into a half-empty building and having to feign excitement. I expressed my concerns to Krista as we drove into Hollywood that damp, overcast morning. She was my comfort as always and said, "Don't worry; I'll be there for you."

As we exited the freeway on Vine we had to slam on our brakes to avoid rear-ending all the cars backed up on the off ramp. They were there trying to get to The Palace as well!

The line of people snaked all the way up Vine Street and then along Yucca. It was crazy.

We parked in the Capitol Records parking lot and as I crossed the street I was greeted by cheers and yells. Right then I knew how emotional today would be for me.

Inside, the 1,500 person venue was already jammed to capacity. All those people waiting outside sadly wouldn't be getting in. I took Gene Sandbloom, the assistant PD, aside and told him that as soon as there was a break I wanted to go out and walk the line to say thank you and goodbye to everyone who was waiting and to take pictures with them. We set that up but first I had to go on the air with the morning show and get everyone ready for the concert ahead.

The performances were incredible. To have Billy Idol and John Taylor singing to me was beyond belief, and when Terri Nunn took to the stage and talked about our love affair and sang "Take My Breath Away" I think we all cried.

John Easdale from Dramarama actually changed the words to one of his hits, "What Are We Gonna Do?" from:

"It's April 21 and everybody knows today is Earth Day," to

"It's April 28 and everybody knows today is Richard's last day."

Cheers and applause greeted his new lyrics and I was so touched John would do that for me.

KROQ had lined up some surprises for me as well; my longtime buddy, Dave Gahan from Depeche Mode, phoned in and his call was pumped over the PA for all to hear. He wished me well and thanked me for all my love and support over the years and joked that if I was quitting then maybe Depeche Mode should break up as well. We all, myself included, screamed "NO!"

That was followed by a call from Robert Smith of The Cure who said goodbye and wondered who would play "Just Like Heaven" after I was gone.

Carl Caprioglio from Oglio records came on stage and presented me with a framed set of the six *Richard Blade Flashback Favorites* CDs in honor of the hundreds of thousands of copies sold and my dear friend, Rodney Bingenheimer, showed up to wish me well.

For me, the biggest tears of the day came when Curt Smith performed "Mad World" and dedicated it to me. He had no idea of the significance of that song and what it had meant to me at such a devastating moment in my life, but with every word he sang I felt my father standing there, his arm around my shoulder supporting me, and I knew that as hard as it was leaving all of this, it was the right thing to do. Nothing in nature stays the same; it either grows or decays. It was time for me to try and grow again.

With the performances over I started my final Flashback Lunch to wrap everything up and say farewell to my eighteen wonderful, unforgettable years at the world's greatest radio station with the best, most loyal listeners anywhere on the planet. But I had one final surprise left and this time it was from me to the audience. It was how I wanted to go out.

At 12:52pm I was ready with my last two songs. I'd already played thirteen records that were special to me and my listeners; songs from The Smiths, New Order, The Pet Shop Boys, INXS, Duran Duran, The Cure, Berlin, Depeche Mode and others; but now it was time to put it all behind me, that amazing music that had helped me build a career.

I knew that hundreds of thousands of people would be wondering just which tracks would be the last I would ever play on KROQ. I'd put a lot of thought into it and had not come up with my decision lightly. I turned the microphone on. My voice trembled from the conflict of emotions seething through my body and mind.

"Well this is it, my last songs on my last day on the World Famous KROQ," I said. "I wanted to choose one song for all of you and one song for Krista and me. The first is for you, every single one of you incredible people who have listened to and grown up with KROQ and with me over the years. I started here as a kid and I never thought of this as a job, to me it was a gift. I was as much a fan of the station as everyone out there and there hasn't been a day of my life during the past eighteen years that I haven't considered it a privilege and an honor to be able to sit here and play this fantastic music for all of us."

I stopped for a moment as I was choking up. Then I pulled myself together and continued.

"Neither song I'm going to play has ever been on KROQ before but I figured I can get away with it because what are they going to do, fire me?" I laughed, "But it's the lyrics and haunting vocals that made me choose the first one, because I know that even though I'm moving far from here to start a new life in another country there will be moments when I hear a song or the warm wind blows in a certain way and I'll be transported back to those early days at that little station in Pasadena when I would sprint across the parking lot and up those old metal stairs two at a time, racing to get on the air and play something brand-new for you that we could all discover together; and it's those magical moments that bonded all of us like family and those precious memories that will make me miss you like the deserts miss the rain."

I hit *play* and the remix of Everything But The Girl's "Missing" went out over the KROQ airwaves for the first time.

I was crying as the song finished but I had my final goodbye to say.

"I'm sorry I'm a little upset but this means a lot to me, you all mean a lot to me. I've worked with some incredible talents here at KROQ over the years and I want to thank all of them for their help, inspiration and friendship. Thank you, Trip Reeb, our General Manager, for being a great guy and thank you to the two single greatest programmers in radio history, Rick Carroll for having the vision and starting it all and to Kevin Weatherly, the most loyal boss there is, for rescuing KROQ when it desperately needed help and for building it all the way back up; without you two this station would not be around today." I took a deep breath, this was it.

"But this story that began for me when I huddled with my friends around a little transistor radio listening to new music booming in from pirate radio stations off of the coast of England ends now as I am again surrounded by friends as we tune in together to America's greatest radio station. I made a promise to a ten-year-old boy and I have to keep it. He bequeathed me a list of things to do and wanted me to check them off for him one by one when they were done and that's the real reason I'm leaving. I've done just about everything else on that list except for one that he wrote where he said he dreamed of one day living like Jacques Cousteau and swimming with the fish and diving every day in warm, clear water."

I took a breath and readied my final words to my beloved listeners.

"I was that ten-year-old boy. That's why for the past decade I've studied and trained and taken diving classes to become an instructor just to get ready for this day. That's why I certified so many of you on our KROQ'n'Dive trips. And now I'm moving to the Caribbean where Krista and I can teach fulltime in that welcoming, turquoise ocean and share with others our love of the environment and this planet. So if ever you're in the Caribbean watch out for an English dive instructor who is cranking Depeche Mode on his boat. We can talk music and swap memories of the World Famous K-Rock. And if you want to find me just look for a place where the sun is shining and the weather is sweet and I'll be there, waiting for you."

With that I started Bob Marley's "Sun is Shining" (the Funkstar's Club Mix), unplugged my headphones and left the KROQ studios forever.

SUN IS SHINING

We sat and waited on the American Airlines flight from Miami to St. Maarten with our faces pressed against the window. We had told the stewardesses and the pilot that we had two dogs coming onboard (we had our kitty, little Soxy, in the cabin with us) and if we didn't get the word that they were safely on the plane then we were getting off. From our seats we could see the conveyor belt moving the suitcases, one after another, up from the open truck and onto the plane. Then, with the last of the luggage loaded, the truck drove off. And no doggies!

Krista and I both got up but were stopped by the stewardess. She wasn't angry but was smiling.

"I just heard they are coming. They wanted to load them last so they don't get too hot in the hold while we sit here on the tarmac," she whispered as if she were confiding in us. "I have dogs myself."

Almost on cue the first of the two hard plastic cages started up the ramp. The front of the cage faced towards us and we could see Angel's face looking out. She was smiling as if she was enjoying the ride. Krista and I had tears in our eyes and hugged. The stewardess brought us both a glass of champagne. "I told you it would be fine," she said.

Our first two months in St. Maarten flew by. We were staying in a little condo below our house on Pelican Hill as the contractors worked on it. By the end of June we had moved in. It was everything we wanted. I felt like my mum and dad must have when they had bought number 22 almost forty years before; Krista and I had found our home.

We were also planning our wedding. I had proposed to Krista in front of her entire family the previous Thanksgiving. I dropped to one knee, pulled out a ring and asked if she would marry me. The family cheered and applauded and Krista's answer went down in Henderson history. For all the love and romance at that table, the waiting turkey smelt so good that Krista replied simply, "Yes, but now let's eat!"

Our wedding date was set for November 1, 2000. Family members would stay with us at our house, and we had rented a villa called Witen-blauw – 'white and blue' - for our friends on the beach in Simpson Bay. My mother would be unable to come as she was having heart problems so I flew over to England to see her for a week in July. To keep Krista company while I was gone her father, Dyle, flew out to St. Maarten to stay with her.

Krista and I had deliberately moved to St. Maarten in the summer months because that was low season. I wanted time to get to know all the reefs, dive sites and safe harbors before starting up our dive business. My rationale was by the time the Caribbean moved into high season in December we would be settled in, married and I would have a good working knowledge of the best places to take our dive guests.

Sunset from our house overlooking Simpson Bay

I took the boat out and dove most days. I had my tanks filled at a near-by shop in Simpson Bay called Dive Safaris. To fill a SCUBA tank you need to show your C (certification) card. They saw mine and noted I was a Master Instructor, I think the only person that qualified on the island, and I was good to go.

In early August Krista and I were shopping when my phone rang. It was Whitney Keough, one half of the husband and wife team that owned and ran Dive Safaris. She told me that one of her instructors, Chuck, had just had a heart attack. Was I available to teach a resort class that afternoon? Two hours later I was onboard Living Waters with Whitney's husband, Bobby, captaining the boat as we headed to Little Bay.

The introductory class went perfectly and all the new divers had fun and signed up for a certification course and more dives. On the trip back Bobby said that the four of us should get together for dinner. That night over Indian food a lifelong friendship was born and I was given an offer I couldn't refuse, come and work for Dive Safaris.

This would be perfect. I could dive every day on their boats and just use mine for fun, and anytime I wanted to spin off my own business I could. I asked when they wanted me to start and Whitney answered with a grin, "Can you be on the dock by seven tomorrow?"

Krista came out on that first dive with me and was there to witness the scariest, most challenging open water experience of my life.

We were on a bigger boat that day, Many Waters, and heading for a reef called Fishbowl. Nicholas, who hailed from Sweden, would be leading the dive as he was very familiar with the site and I would act as the safety diver backing him up. I knew something was wrong as soon as we hooked on to the buoy marking the site. As we pulled the buoy's line up and attached it to our forward cleat I felt the boat surge backwards and then pull hard as the slack line tightened. There was a very strong surface current running.

Because of the current we threw out our longest safety rope behind the boat, a one-hundred-yard float line that divers can hold on to when they surface and are waiting to come back onboard, and with everything in place Nicholas started his briefing.

The divers would enter the water one at a time. There was a weighted line by the dive step that the divers would hold on to and use to help make their descent. This would take them down thirty feet. They would then swim the remaining fifteen feet to the bottom. There they would wait until we were all gathered and then the dive would commence.

I took Nicholas to the side and pointed out my concerns with the current and he told me that he hoped it was just running on the surface and down below at fifty feet, broken up by the raised profile of the reef, it would be a lot less strong. We would start the dive and make the final decision when we were in the water.

We all made it down, but during the descent you had to hold tightly to the weighted line to avoid being swept away. The bubbles from our regulators streamed almost horizontally away from us instead of rising to the surface. This was an extremely powerful current and it was not looking good.

We all met at the bottom, checked air and gave ourselves the divers' 'OK' then Nicholas began the dive correctly, heading first into the current and around the coral heads. But it was almost impossible to make any headway and we had to 'crawl' on the bottom, grabbing for handholds just to stop from blowing backwards. After five minutes we had moved less than ten feet from where we had started. Even underwater you could hear everyone breathing hard from their exertion.

Nicholas turned to me, caught my eye and made a big X with his arms against his chest. He was "Xing" the dive. It was over - too strenuous, too difficult and too unsafe. He was making the right call.

Krista went up first to let our boat crew know what was happening and to get them ready for the early return of the group. Sixty seconds later Nicholas followed to assist the divers as they broke the surface. I stayed below as safety diver and last man down to send the tourists up in their buddy pairs.

The current had gotten even stronger and was running way too fast now to send more than two divers at a time up the line because the rapidly moving water made your body act like a sail and with any more than two people on the line the combined force of the current against them would do what seemed impossible, lift them and that weighted fifty-pound rope all the way out of the water as they were pushed backwards and up by the ripping flow of water racing from the Atlantic into the Caribbean.

Within eight minutes almost everyone was up safely and I was down to the last two divers. It was a husband and wife that I'd talked to earlier on the boat. She weighed barely one hundred pounds whereas he was over three hundred. They were both certified and had told us when they filled out their dive forms that they had a lot of experience.

I had us positioned so we were about twenty feet upcurrent of the weighted line so that when we started our swim up to it, fifteen feet above our heads, the current would actually assist in taking us straight to it.

I smiled with my eyes through my mask and gave them the OK sign. The big guy shook his head in distress and pointed to his heart. He made a desperate pounding motion with his hand.

I kicked over to him and as he wasn't wearing a wetsuit when I placed my hand against his chest I could clearly feel his heart racing. I guesstimated that his heart rate had to have been 140 or above. I pushed my hands in and out to give him the sign to breathe more slowly and I checked his air. To my horror he was down to less than 700 pounds. He had sucked down more than three-quarters of his air in barely fourteen minutes and not let me know as any competent diver should. His SCUBA tank was nearly empty. With this current roaring around us having him try and share my air would be nearly impossible and in his almost panicked state, unsafe. I had to get him up, and quickly.

I signaled for his wife to stay kneeling on the bottom and wait for me, grabbed the strap of his buoyancy compensator vest (BCD) and swam him up to the weighted descent line. I wrapped his hand firmly around it and held up my hand to his mask and showed him a grip sign meaning "hold on to the rope."

I dropped back down to get his wife, gave her an OK and we started up to join her husband on the line and then head to the surface together. We were about six feet away from him when he let go!

Instantly the current grabbed him and he tumbled away from the line and the boat. I tightened my grip on his wife's vest - I sure as hell wasn't going to lose her as well - and went after him. It was the beginning of a mad, crazy ride.

He was doing nothing to try to fight the current, he was just dead weight, spinning helplessly in the racing water as it swept him away thirty-five feet below the surface. Normally I could have caught up with him in seconds but there was nothing normal about today; plus I was dragging his wife which slowed me down.

I kicked and kicked and was close to him now, but a quick glance up to the surface showed I was already halfway down the length of the floating safety line, which meant we were already fifty yards from the boat in just seconds. If I couldn't get the three of us to the surface before we passed the end of the float line then the situation would be dire indeed.

I reached out and grabbed the waist strap of his BCD and now with his wife in one hand and this behemoth in my other I kicked hard upwards. But they weren't helping. They both hung there motionless, not swimming, not kicking. I'd seen this many times before. For whatever reason, in a tough situation, a distressed diver will shut down and allow their instructor or rescuer to do all the work.

Under any other circumstance I would have made a fluttering sign with two fingers on my hand meaning *kick* but both my hands were full. I couldn't let them go; this was life and death now. I had to get them up even without their help. I kicked as hard as I could and my legs started to cramp under the strain of pulling the 450 pounds of inert divers upwards.

I heard that sergeant major's voice ringing in my head from nearly thirty years before, "It won't always be easy. You do what you have to do to get through it." He was right and at that moment I blessed him for instilling that military discipline in me. We were going to get through it; there was no other alternative. So I pushed the pain aside and kicked and kicked and powered us up.

Now we were just feet from the surface but I could see the orange float at the end of the line rapidly approaching. We had to get on that line, or we would be swept away from the boat and from safety. I swam the three of us right into it, released my grip on the lady for a second and threw my arm over the line and once again grabbed her BCD. At least we had made it to the line and we were on the surface.

All three of us were spun around by the current and were now forced horizontal as the raging water continued its attempt to tear us away from the boat. The flow was so fast and strong that the ripping water was forming waves that broke over our heads.

I needed to speak, to let them know what to do, and most importantly, what not to do. I spit out my regulator and screamed to them, "DO NOT TAKE YOUR REGULATORS OUT. HOLD THE LINE. DO NOT LET GO!"

Shocked by my yelling right in their faces they did as instructed. I coughed saltwater out of my mouth and said forcefully to the woman, "You go first. Pull your way up the line to the boat. Do not let go and do not take the regulator out of your mouth until you are seated on the boat. The crew will help you get out of the water."

I kept my eyes locked on her as she slowly inched her way back along that long line against the raging current until she was safely at the boat.

I turned to her husband. "Our turn now. Just a couple of minutes and we're good." I started pulling but he was too tired to do anything but hang on. I could see he was so exhausted he could barely hold on to the rope.

I popped my head under the water to make sure it was clear below and dropped both his nearly thirty-pound weight belt and my ten-pound belt. Now he would be lighter and whatever happened he would not sink. The boat crew saw our plight and attempted to pull us in but with the current pushing against us we were still way too heavy. They had to enlist the passengers to help.

Even with all their combined strength it took nearly six minutes to get us halfway to the boat. I checked the big guy's air. His pressure gauge was now reading less than one hundred pounds. Even on the surface his panicked state was causing him to suck down his air. Unless they could get him on the boat quickly he would run out of air and he was not responsive or cooperative enough to be able to share my tank and use my spare regulator safely.

I was extremely concerned he'd drop his regulator and with the current and wind-driven waves breaking over our faces, he'd quickly start swallowing water and become a serious drowning risk. There was only one way to get him to the boat quicker, and that was without me and my weight increasing the drag on the line.

I got Nicholas's attention and yelled to the boat, "I'm going to let go. Have you got it from here?"

Nicholas raised his arms and gave me a big OK and knowing he was now watching my panicked diver I looked the terrified man in the eyes and told him reassuringly, "Keep your regulator in your mouth and hold on, don't let go. You'll be there on the boat with your wife in no time without my weight on the line."

I clipped two straps from his BCD jacket around the rope and onto the float to secure him in case he did let go, then knowing he would be safe on the line I released my grip and was instantly grabbed by the current and I sailed away, watching the boat disappear in less than a minute. I blew up my six-foot, bright yellow safety sausage and waited as I was dragged helplessly along the western shoreline of the island.

Ten minutes later the prow of Many Waters appeared and I was on-board just a few minutes later. Finding me had been no problem; they just followed the current and looked for my yellow marker.

As I clambered up the dive steps and plunked my relieved butt down on the seat all I could think of was that it had been one hell of an intro-duction to teaching diving in the Caribbean.

The months went on and we settled into the rhythm of island life. No one had any pretentiousness in this land of tank tops and sandals. When we bought a second car, a beat up, scratched, purple Geo Metro for $1,800, instead of getting a "why are you driving *that*?" look that would have greeted us everywhere in LA, people said, "Cool. Can I get a ride?" We loved our life, and so did our doggies, Zoey and Angel, who frolicked on the white sand beaches and at low tide ran across the exposed coral reefs looking for crabs.

Life in the tropics was everything we had hoped it would be. Krista became indispensable to running Dive Safaris while I was on the boats leading three and sometimes four dives a day if we had a night dive sched-uled that evening.

Twice a week we took tourists on a shark feed which was more than I could have dreamed of as we were able to interact freely with one of nature's apex predators and for me it was a gift to be able to help people understand how important conservation is and that we as a species are a much bigger threat to sharks than they are to us.

On every dive, prior to having our divers enter the water I would give a quick briefing about the site, whether it was a wreck or a reef and let them know what they would be seeing and the dive profile; the time and depth. I'd always finish with "any questions?" It was inevitable that at least one person would sheepishly raise their hand and ask either "Are you the guy from the radio?" or "Do you do the PADI videos?" That always made me smile and it would be a big talking point on the boat as we cruised back to the dock after our dive day was complete.

We had just come in from a dive and it was late afternoon. The sun was still fairly high in the sky as I hosed down the boat and cleaned the twin Honda outboards to prevent the saltwater from eating away at the metal parts. I unloaded the SCUBA tanks two by two and lugged them over to the air fill station to get them ready for the next day's dives.

I clamped the fill hoses on the tank stems and opened the valves. The massive compressor began its *thump, thump, thump* as filtered air was forced into the tanks.

As I waited for the gauge to climb to thirty-two hundred psi I looked out at the boat and the sparkling water. A soft trade wind blew in from the lagoon and the warm air caressed my body. I was suddenly filled with such a feeling of contentment. It was as if every force in the universe was saying, "You are where you should be." For all the manual labor I was doing every day - the lifting, the scrubbing, the cleaning - there was nowhere else I would want to be, no person on the planet I would want to change places with.

I had walked away from success to find out if my other childhood dreams could be just as fulfilling and there, in that soothing breeze on the dock, I connected with the hopes of the much younger me and I wondered if on that rainy night in Torquay had that little boy somehow been able to glimpse this future and sense the happiness that waited for us? Did his dreams reach forward to me or was my bliss echoing backwards through time over the decades for him to pick up on and write down on his list to become a self-fulfilling prophecy? Whatever it was I thanked him for it. But within just a few days I would wish that his ten-year-old vision had seen something else and warned me of the terrible tragedy that was about to befall us and shatter our world forever.

SHELLSHOCK

We were just days away from our wedding. Krista and her mother had worked hard with the planning and even though there were only twenty of our closest friends and family invited, Krista had made sure we would all have a great time. The minister was scheduled, the catering chosen and even a steel band booked to accompany us down the aisle that would be marked with shells not flowers.

The dress was simple. Please wear white. And no long pants, just shorts and bare feet. This was the Caribbean and we were being married steps from the beach. Fun, comfort and love was all we wanted for the ceremony and for our friends.

The wedding was set for Wednesday November 1. Krista had chosen mid-week so everyone would have a chance to get there, relax for a while and make a vacation out of it. The first of our guests, my dear friend Ray DeVries, flew in on Friday October 27. It was great to see Ray, he ran a record store in Covina, California and he would bring me the latest songs from Morrissey, DMode and The Cure to play on the radio. And even though those days were behind me now, at any party or event, Ray would always be at the top of my guest list so naturally he was the first to receive and respond to our wedding invite.

The majority of the rest of the guests were flying in the next afternoon, the 28th, which unfortunately coincided with my final teaching day for a class of students. I couldn't let them down, not after having taken them through their classroom, pool and now ocean training so it fell upon Krista to pick everyone up at the airport. I'd only miss about two hours with them and we'd all be together to watch the sunset. At least that's what I thought.

I was driving the boat into Simpson Bay after congratulating my eight happy students on being the newest certified divers in St. Maarten when I saw Bobby and Whitney standing, waiting for me on the dock. Something wasn't right.

As I pulled alongside the dock Bobby leapt on board and yelled at me, "Go home now. I'll take care of her."

I jumped from the boat and raced across the wooden planks. I saw something terrible in Whitney's eyes. She went to speak but couldn't and dropped her head.

It was just over a mile to our house on the hill and I pushed that little Geo Metro to the breaking point getting there in less than two minutes. Ray was waiting for me. There was no sign of anyone else.

"What's happened?" I screamed.

"I'm sorry, buddy. There's been an accident. They're all at the hospital."

I sprinted back down the stairs and sped to the hospital. It was only four miles away but the afternoon traffic was building and despite the fact I drove most of the way on the rough hard shoulder it still took me twenty minutes to get there.

I ran inside and saw Carl Harmon, a good friend and one of our guests.

"What's happening, Carl? No one's told me anything."

Carl shook his head, "It's Krista's mom. Something's happened to her. She's in intensive care."

"Show me," I said.

I was taken into a small room and a horror show was waiting for me. I was expecting blood from a fall, a broken arm or leg, or perhaps a dozen stitches in her forehead, but not this. This was impossible.

Krista was sitting there with her father and as soon as she saw me she burst into hysterical tears. She was inconsolable. She got to her feet and buried her beautiful face in my chest and cried so hard that no words could come out. I looked at Dyle and he could only shake his head.

Lonnie lay there on the table, a drip was inserted in her left arm and a pulse monitor was attached to her finger. The steady *beep, beep, beep* that came from the LCD display marking her heartbeat was the only sound in the room apart from Krista's sobs.

Lonnie had only been on island for less than three hours. How had this happened? A doctor came in and took me outside to explain.

Apparently Lonnie was fine when she arrived at our house. She changed into shorts and was sitting at the edge of our pool, her feet in the water having a beer, a Carib, when she suddenly started to act strangely. Her arms went limp and her body sagged.

Krista and her dad put Lonnie in the guest bedroom where it was cool and dark and called the paramedics. They arrived quickly and assessed the situation. They thought Lonnie was probably exhausted from the flight, and the sun and heat had caused an adverse reaction. They advised keeping her in the room with the air conditioner on and letting her rest.

Relieved at the thought that it was merely fatigue, everyone left her undisturbed to recover. Around an hour later there was a huge crashing sound from Lonnie's room. Krista ran inside and found her mother on the floor writhing in the throes of a seizure. Krista put her hand in her mom's mouth and yelled out for her friends to call for an ambulance.

In minutes the paramedics had returned and rushed Lonnie to the hospital.

The doctor looked at me and said, "It's not good. It was a grand mal seizure and it seems to have done some damage. How much we aren't sure. We have her on anti-seizure medication now and hopefully that will help."

I went back inside the room and Lonnie now had her eyes open and was trying to talk with Krista, but she was very weak.

"Get better, Mom. We need you for the wedding," said Krista.

It was hard for Lonnie to form words but she managed to say, "I will, don't worry. I love you."

We sat with her for a couple of hours but then were asked to leave so she could sleep.

Dinner that night was memorable only because of the conversation. It was all about poor Lonnie and what had happened. Dyle sat there, silent. You could see in his eyes he was lost, not knowing what to do with his wife in hospital. Krista tried to pick up the mood but we were all too aware of how she was crying inside.

We woke early the morning of October 29. Krista called the hospital right away and asked how her mother was. Instead of hearing a comforting phrase like 'she's doing fine', the orderly paused as he checked Lonnie's file, then said the words you never want to hear, "Let me get the doctor for you."

Krista waited an eternity on the phone and her eyes opened wider than I'd ever seen them before as the doctor gave her the news. After listening all she said was, "We'll be right there."

The three of us, Dyle, Krista and I, raced to the hospital. The doctor led us to Lonnie's room.

She still lay in bed but now she was in a coma and hooked up to a ventilator; an EKG machine was attached to her chest and six electrodes circled her head. I noticed that her chest rose and fell in conjunction with the hiss of the ventilator. That's when I realized she was no longer breathing for herself; the machine was breathing for her.

The medication hadn't worked. During the night Lonnie had suffered a series of grand mal seizures, several of which were centered in her brain. Her heart had stopped and the doctors had resuscitated her twice. Now she was being kept alive only because she was on full life support. It was the worst news possible that we could have received.

The doctor asked us to step outside and presented us with two options.

"Lonnie Henderson is alive only because of the machines that she is connected to. Her brain and motor functions are almost non-existent. You have to make a choice. We can keep her on the machines indefinitely until her body starts to reject them which could be a couple of days, a week or even several months or we can turn the machines off." He shook his head sadly. "That's all that can be done."

"Can't we fly her back to America for treatment?" pleaded Krista.

"I'm afraid that without all the machines she wouldn't even make it to the airport. This is exactly the same treatment that she would be given in the USA. It is what has happened to her body that is the problem, not any lack of the right medical equipment or medication."

Dyle sat there silently as Krista spoke again with a question I knew she dreaded asking.

"Is there any way she could get better? Anything at all that could be done?"

The doctor shook his head, "No. I'm so sorry. The grand mal seizures were so severe that she has no chance at coming back from them." He took a beat as if this was consolation, "And she would never be the same if she did."

We all sat there silent in total disbelief, caught up in a waking nightmare.

"Let me know what you decide." The doctor got up and left us alone.

I reached out and held Dyle and Krista's hands.

"You two have to make this decision. She's your wife and your mother. I'll support whatever you say," I told them.

No one spoke for ten minutes, instead tears were our words.

The doctor returned and sat down with us.

"I have an idea," he said. "I can only imagine how hard this must be so perhaps this will help. If we turn the machines off she will stop breathing right away and will be gone almost as soon as we push the button. I can see why you don't want to do that. There is a way we can give Lonnie a chance and she can live or…" He was hesitant to say the word, "die on her own terms."

We were all ears, finally something positive, no matter how small.

"I can give her a massive shot of adrenalin to restart her heart and then we disconnect the life support. If she is strong enough her heart will continue to beat on its own."

"And if she's not?" asked Krista.

"Well, most likely she isn't. And so her heart will slowly fail as the adrenalin wears off and she will pass away peacefully."

Krista's eyes welled up with tears.

"But she will go on her own terms when her body says it is time, not because a machine is turned off. Then you will know it was inevitable and not something you chose."

Dyle nodded and Krista put her hands in her face before saying, "Okay, if that's the only way. Then we should do that."

The doctor got to his feet, "I'll attend to it and let you know when."

Within minutes an orderly with a small cart appeared and wheeled it into Lonnie's room. The doctor followed and knowing what was about to happen the three of us held hands and wept.

The doctor came back out and stood with us. "It's done," he said. "I've given her the shot and removed her from life support."

How my beloved Krista was holding it together I don't know. She looked up at the doctor, "So is she…?"

"No, not yet," he replied softly. "She is unconscious and unresponsive but her heart is beating strongly right now. How long that will last I can't say. You can go in and be with her if you like."

Krista shook her head, "I can't."

The doctor left us and we sat outside of Lonnie's room as she fought for life.

After less than a minute I stood up.

"I can't leave her alone. I'm going to sit with Lonnie. Do you want to come in with me?" I asked.

Krista and Dyle shook their heads. The shock was too much for them to confront this. I understood and went into the room alone.

Beep, beep, beep called out the heart-rate monitor which was the only piece of equipment left attached to Lonnie. It was an Oximeter, a small, unobtrusive device that was clipped to her finger. It displayed her oxygen level and heart rate. It was reading sixty beats per minute. That was good, a strong resting heartbeat.

With all the hoses, wires and endotracheal tube removed and the respirator turned off, Lonnie looked at peace as she lay there.

I sat next to her, put my hand on hers and started talking. I knew from my Medic First Aid training that hearing is usually the last thing to go which is why you never talk about an unconscious patient's condition in front of them lest you trigger a bad reaction or even cause shock. I spoke out loud and told Lonnie what a wonderful mother she was, what an amazing wife to Dyle and how much Krista loved her. I thanked her for all the planning she had done with Krista in preparing for our wedding and the wonderful engagement party she had thrown for us months before in Los Angeles.

I leant forward and kissed her gently on the check and told her how lucky I was to know her and that she should hang on and be strong as I so wanted her as my mother-in-law and that we had many wonderful times ahead.

The *beep, beep, beep* had changed now. It had fallen to fifty one beats per minute. The adrenalin was wearing off.

For the next forty minutes I stroked Lonnie's hand and held her gently as I talked about everything we had shared together, of driving to see her parents in Oceanside, of picnicking on the infield of Santa Anita racetrack, of Molly, her lovely little dog. But most of all I told her again and again how much Krista loved her.

It had been nearly an hour and Lonnie's heartbeat had fallen to twenty-one beats per minute and had been holding there for a long time when the door opened a fraction. It was Krista.

"I wanted to see if you're oaky?" she asked as she leaned in a little, trying not to look into that frightening room that was destroying her life.

"I'm fine. Come in and tell your mother you love her."

"I can't," said Krista as she avoided my eyes.

"Yes, you can. She's been waiting for you."

Krista pushed the door open and stepped in.

"Tell her you love her," I said.

Krista stood by her dying mother and said simply, "I love you."

"Honey, she can hear you but she can't see. Tell her who you are and what's happening."

Krista steeled herself and leant in close to Lonnie. "Mom, everyone's here for our wedding. I couldn't have done it without you. I love you so much."

I mouthed to Krista, "Say your name."

Krista understood, "It's Krista, Mom. I love you I always will."

She reached out for Lonnie and as their two hands touched the heart meter changed. It sounded one continuous droning tone as the display fell to zero and a single flat line displayed on the screen.

"No!" Krista exclaimed.

I was stunned, but I realized what had happened. "She was waiting for you. She wouldn't go without you!" I said.

I rushed around to Krista and held her shaking body tightly in my arms as we watched her mother leave our world. Lonnie was forty-seven years old.

Now instead of holding a wedding we were planning a funeral.

WHITE WEDDING

We broke the news to our shocked friends when we returned to our house on Pelican Hill. They were shaken at what had happened but we told them that we would be taking care of everything concerning Lonnie and that they should try and enjoy their days in the Caribbean. The wedding was cancelled of course but they had the oceanfront villa we'd rented for them and they travelled all this way so they should make the most of it.

Dyle and Krista were understandably beaten down by the events of the past eighteen hours so it fell on me to pick up the slack. I called the minister, the steel band and the caterer and explained what had happened and that there would be no wedding. Then I had to start with the funeral arrangements.

Lonnie had wanted to be cremated and that's when I found out that crematoriums are rare in the Caribbean. We would have to have her flown to Puerto Rico and then her ashes returned to us. Dyle and Krista didn't need to be bothered with that so I took care of it.

There was one more thing still to do. One last couple, Steven and Brooke, were due in late that Sunday afternoon. Steven's work schedule hadn't allowed them to travel with the main group and so they had no idea what they were flying in to. At around two in the afternoon I received a call from them; they were at Miami airport excitedly waiting for their connection.

I had to throw a damper on their enthusiasm as I explained everything that had occurred and told them the wedding was off but to please come and have fun without us. Steven was quiet as he thought of his response.

"Look, you can't cancel the wedding. Lonnie planned it for a year with Krista. It's the wedding she wanted for the two of you. How would she feel knowing that something she did stopped the two of you from getting married? You have to go ahead with it."

It was my turn to be silent. Steven was correct. I loved Krista and was going to marry her anyway; we just thought it would now have to be pushed to sometime in the future. But why not do it the way Lonnie had wanted, and hold the wedding in her honor?

I told Steven he was right and I'd see him and Brooke in a few hours. Now I had to explain this to Krista and Dyle, and then get back on the phone with the minister, the steel band and the caterer.

Wednesday November 1 rolled around far too quickly. The minutiae of the final wedding plans fell on Krista. That morning the three of us, Krista, Dyle and I drove to Princess Juliana Airport to extend Dyle's stay in St. Maarten. Krista, ever the loving daughter, didn't want her father returning to an empty house until he was strong enough and ready to face that loneliness.

As we stood at the counter I saw the American Airlines agent being given a special package from a baggage handler. I overheard their first few words and knew instantly what it was.

I turned to Krista, "Don't ask why, just take your dad and go outside for two minutes, then come back in, okay?"

With everything that had happened Krista went along with my request without question and led her father outside. I said "excuse me" to our ticket agent and stepped to the next counter.

"Are those Lonnie Henderson's ashes?" I asked.

The clerk nodded.

"Okay. I'll be back for them later. Please don't say anything now; that's her daughter and husband outside."

Once Dyle's ticketing was taken care of we left.

Two hours later I returned and collected Lonnie's remains. I drove back to Pelican with our wedding cake and Krista's mother's ashes in my car.

The wedding was the best of times, the worst of times. Krista looked beautiful and set a place for her mother at our table. Lonnie and her love for Krista were mentioned in every toast. The sunset, instead of the usual reds and oranges, turned the sky a spectacular shade of gold. Under any other circumstances you would have written home and said how amazing the day had been, but these were no ordinary times.

Lonnie's place setting – Mom

With the wedding done and our friends back in California we struggled to return to island life. Krista was promoted to running the Dive Safaris office in Simpson Bay which she took to and excelled at. High season arrived and Dive Safaris became the most popular dive company on St. Maarten and had contracts with all the major hotels and cruise lines that docked at the island including Disney and Carnival.

In low season Krista and I travelled extensively and I would fly back to England four times a year to see my mum and spend time with her.

In early September, 2001, we decided to take a big trip. We would fly Dyle with us to England, stay with Mum for a while then Dyle, Krista and I would fly to the south of France to vacation in one of our favorite places on the planet, Villfranche-Sur-Mer.

We had a wonderful time in Torquay at number 22 and early on a sunny Tuesday morning we headed up to Heathrow Airport in London.

We dropped off the rental car and hopped on the airport shuttle. The driver turned to us, "You Americans?" We nodded.

"Just came through on the news that a little plane flew into one of your skyscrapers. Let's hope your pilot is a bit better than that one was."

We arrived at the terminal and waited in line for boarding passes. Two ladies behind us were talking.

"I heard another plane just crashed into one of those big buildings."

I turned to the TV monitors that play throughout Heathrow. They were all tuned to CNN as usual. As I looked up all the monitors went blank, every one of them. They had been turned off deliberately. Something was very wrong.

"If two planes have crashed into buildings then it's not an accident," I said to Krista.

We went to the gate and waited for our 3:45pm flight to Nice, France. Everyone was buzzing that something major was going on, but what?

The British Airways lounge was right across from our gate and the three of us walked over.

"We need to come in and see what's happening," I said.

The pretty agent behind the counter smiled back at me and slipped into her well-rehearsed speech, "I'm sorry, sir; unless you have British Airways club membership privileges then you can't come in."

I slammed down our three American passports on her counter.

"Are you telling me that you will not let three Americans in to see what is happening in their country right now?" I was furious.

She obviously knew the real story that was unfolding and just waved us inside.

As we walked into the first-class lounge we saw a giant projection screen dominating the room. A hundred people were crowded around it in disbelief. The twin towers of the World Trade Center were burning. I could see that the 106 floor of the north tour, where I had taken the KROQ winners to Windows on the World restaurant fifteen years before, was now totally engulfed in flames. I glanced at my watch. It was almost three, which would be 10am in New York. As I looked back at the screen the south tower disintegrated and dropped straight down more than one thousand feet. Everyone in that private lounge screamed out loud.

We were the second to last plane to take off from Heathrow before the airport was closed. Our flight took thirty minutes longer than scheduled as air traffic control diverted us over the ocean rather than allowing us fly across France and possibly be used in an attack on Paris. No one knew what was happening in the world anymore.

I went to the bathroom and spoke to the stewardess who told me that there were reports that all across America planes were being shot down and there had been attacks on cities everywhere.

A tank and two armored vehicles were waiting for our plane as we touched down in Nice. Instead of being greeted with croissants we were met with automatic weapons. We all knew the world had changed that day and not for the better.

The headlines of the French newspapers reflected that. Le Jour printed, quite simply, *L'apocalypse* while the biggest newspaper in the country, Le Monde, featured a long article about the terrible day entitled *Nous sommes tous Americains* – We are all Americans.

It was eerie to be so far away when your country is bleeding.

A week later we returned to St. Maarten and even in that Caribbean nation things had changed. It was sad to think of the effect that just a few evil people can have on billions.

Krista and I continued to love our life on that little island. Every day we would go off to work together, Krista to take care of the shop and me to run the dives. It was paradise and everything I'd hoped for.

The local police approached us and asked if we could train their helicopter crews in water safety and open ocean survival.

I jumped at the chance, having learned a little of that from the Royal Air Force while at college.

I drew up a basic course for the flyers who spent so much of their time in the air over water and I trained them for three long days and one night, figuring that accidents don't only happen when the sun is shining. We ran surface techniques, entanglement and underwater egress using a sunken fishing boat in Simpson Bay as our stand in for a downed helicopter's cockpit.

Teaching the course was fun, challenging and strenuous but I would do it again in a second.

With our flight crew trainees in St Maarten, November 2001

LOVE & PRIDE

In between my visits back to England to see my mum I would call her every other day. She would often ask me to tell her again about Ville-franche Sur-Mer. Finally I asked about her fascination with that wonderful little seaside village. She told me that in all her journeys to Europe with Dad they had never made it to the south of France even though they had both dreamed of going there. The closest they had gotten was when they visited me in Spain in 1975.

Since Dad had died I'd taken Mum on many trips; we'd been to Hawaii, Cancun, Playa Del Carmen, the Florida Keys, Paris, Switzerland, Lake Tahoe and the Bahamas. By the time I hung up I had convinced Mum that I would take her to Villefranche for my birthday that coming May.

She was looking very frail when I picked her up from number 22. The National Health Service had issued her a wheelchair which she hated to use as she had been such a great walker but now it was her only option.

We made the best of it and had a wonderful time, just the two of us, exploring the restaurants, harbors and castles around Villefranche. We drove along the coast visiting Nice and Monaco and then into Italy where we ate pasta and drank red wine together dining outside in a centuries-old piazza, laughing and applauding the opera singers who serenaded us at our table. And all the while I knew it would be our last trip together.

Krista was in LA staying with her dad while I was in Europe with Mum. After our vacation came to its end far too quickly I dropped Mum back off in Torquay then flew out to California to join Krista for a few days before we returned to St. Maarten.

Knowing I was going to be in LA I made an appointment to have some much-needed dental work done and it was while I was burying my fingernails into the arms of the dentist's chair in Burbank suffering through a filling replacement that the receptionist rushed in and interrupted the oral torture.

"I'm sorry, but I have an urgent call for Richard," she said.

My heart dropped instantly. This was the worst kind of déjà vu. I had been here before when Katy raced into the production room at KROQ with that other terrible call in 1982.

Tragically, my premonition was right. It was Krista with news I didn't want to hear. The heart flap that mum had had installed two years before had detached and she was in heart failure. She had been rushed to hospital but the doctors had determined that there was little they could do; the flap couldn't be reattached because she was too weak to survive the invasive operation. Her heart was enlarged and she wasn't expected to make it through the night.

I told Krista to book me on the next flight to England and I ran out of the dentist's office with a hole in my tooth crying out for a porcelain filling and my mouth still numb from the anesthesia.

My only thought was trying to get over to see Mum before she died. I hadn't had a chance to say goodbye to Dad, maybe this time I would be able to make it there and be with her before she passed away to tell my beloved mother how much she meant to me.

The ten hour flight seemed to take an eternity and when I picked up a rental car at Heathrow I hammered south at ridiculous speeds. This time the motorways were dry and the 200 miles flew by in just over two hours.

I had no time to look for parking so I left the car in a tow-away zone at Torbay Hospital and sprinted up the stairs to the cardiac ward on the third floor. It was a little after six o'clock and the shifts were changing, the night nurses just arriving and getting ready to take over their duties. Because of that there was no one at the desk to help me.

I was praying I wasn't too late as I ran through the wards that were still so familiar to me having changed little since my days of volunteering at the hospital radio service there all those years ago. I spotted a nurse in front of me and called out, "Mary Sheppard? Do you know where Mary Sheppard is?"

Before she could answer a little voice that I'd known all my life said the most welcome words I'd ever heard, "I'm over here, my love."

My mother, my dear, lovely, cherished Mum, was sitting up in her bed sipping a cup of tea.

She smiled and asked, "Would you like a cup? I can have one sent up. And do sit down, you look quite exhausted."

Mum never respected the oddsmakers. They had said she would be dead in less that twenty-four hours but this strong little lady who'd worked on city transportation during the height of the blitz of WW II to "do her bit" in the war effort wasn't going to go easily. But a great attitude and inherent toughness isn't enough to fight the ravages of time. The doctor told me quite emphatically that she would not be leaving the hospital and the end was coming sooner rather than later.

I spent every minute with Mum for the next week. They moved her to a private room and brought in a chair for me and then, after two days, when they saw I wasn't leaving, a rollaway bed.

My last day arrived. I had to go back to L.A. I awoke early so I could make it to London in time to get the 11am non-stop to Los Angeles. I reached forward to Mum and said my goodbyes and told her how much she had meant to me and to Dad. I hugged her frail body gently and as I pulled away she smiled.

"How I ever gave birth to such a great big thing as you I'll never know."

We both laughed, and I gave mum a little wave goodbye.

"Be careful, my son. And remember, I'll always love you."

Tears poured from my eyes as I gunned the car out onto the Newton Road, heading north to Heathrow. I knew I would never see Mum again.

The sun was rising as I sped over the bridge that spanned the River Teign. A low, early-morning mist hung over the estuary as small fishing boats appeared through the fog and headed out into the channel in hopes of returning with full nets as they had done for centuries.

I had grown up with this river, this countryside, and I was as familiar with it as I was with the back of my hand. It had always been like this, unchanged and untouched by time. But it would never be the same for me again because I had always known it with my mother alive, an unseen but very present part of it. The next time I would cross this bridge she would be gone and to me that loss would mean more than if all those little wooden trawlers ceased to exist and the very river itself dried up.

I slammed on my brakes and swerved over to the hard shoulder. I smashed the steering wheel with my fist over and over again in frustration. I was running away and leaving my mother to die alone. What part of being brave is that? How could I possibly leave when the person who gave me life, who filled me with love, needed me most?

I spun the wheel and crossed the grass center divider. The sign ahead said "Torquay 8km." I would be back there in ten minutes.

Mum looked up as I walked into her room. I could see on her face that she was happy but not surprised.

"I couldn't leave you, Mum. I'm going to stay with you here."

She took my hand and squeezed it gently. "I'm so glad, my love."

Those five words made everything worthwhile. Come what may I would be with my mum until the end.

A week later Krista and Dyle flew over. Mum was starting to go rapidly downhill and it was showing on her face. She perked up when she saw two of her favorite people join me in her hospital room.

"You came all the way from America just to see me? How nice," she said.

The three of us celebrated Mum's birthday in that hospital room. Dyle bought a cake and candles and we sang happy birthday to her. After mum blew out the candles she joked, "There were only four on it. I suppose the hospital wouldn't let you put the right number on because it would be a fire risk."

Mum turned eighty-five that day, June 26, 2002. Three days later Dyle had to fly home and return to work. Krista stayed with me to be by my side, the true, loving, loyal wife.

On July 7 mum started to experience terrible discomfort as her lungs began to fill with fluid. The doctor put her on a morphine drip that knocked her out.

"She'll be like that now until the end. It'll be coming soon." he said.

But still she held on. The greatest generation doesn't go down easily.

On July 9 a dear friend of Mum's, Theresa, who was now living in Chicago, phoned to check on her condition. I told her she was in an induced coma and it would be any time now. Theresa was understandably upset and said to please tell her that she loved her.

I returned to the room, sat on the bed and spoke to my mother, "That was Theresa from Chicago. She just called to say she loves you."

I felt something. My mother had reached out and was squeezing my hand. Then she started to sing,

I heard her sweet little voice repeat the words I had just said to her but with a slight change. Mum was singing "I just called to say I love you."

I looked at Krista in shock. We had been told that the sedation would make her totally unresponsive and that she would never regain consciousness again, but here she was, holding my hand and singing to me just as she had done all her life, and somehow she remembered every word even in her comatose state.

As she sang "I just called to say how much I care" Krista and I joined in and sang the song with her. It was a magical, unforgettable moment.

We were still singing when the doctor walked into the room. He stood there and watched as the three of us sang the Stevie Wonder classic and the dying mother held her son's hand.

After a minute or so Mum stopped singing and the room fell silent again. The doctor took Krista and me outside to speak to us.

"If I hadn't seen that with my own eyes I wouldn't have believed it," he said incredulously. "She has eight times the normal amount of morphine in her to keep her sedated. You could put down two elephants with that much opiate, and yet your mother was singing? That's a first for me."

We went back inside and I lay on the bed with Mum and carefully slid my arm under her neck and around her shoulders to cradle her gently. Krista sat in the corner reading.

Mum and I lay like that for about two hours. I could feel her every breath as I held her. She seemed relaxed, comfortable, at peace.

At two minutes before one in the afternoon of July 9, 2002 she took her final breath and died in my arms. If it had to happen then this was the way we both would have wanted it. She had held me in her arms when she brought me into the world and I was the one holding her when she left it.

That night Krista and I were finally able to take a break from the hospital and decided to grab some much needed food at the pub that had been my haunt as a teenager, The Devon Dumpling. It was just a short distance from Torbay Hospital and as we walked there we passed Kitson Park, the site of so many of my early memories. I started to cry uncontrollably.

I'd had more than a month to prepare for the inevitability of losing Mum and thought I had already run the gamut of emotions. I honestly believed that when that final moment came, as it had just hours before, I would be able to stand resilient and strong, the tears having been shed weeks before, the loss already mentally dealt with. Instead I was hit with a wave of sorrow that wracked my body as an awful feeling of helplessness swept over me. It was there and then, outside that little park that had inspired me to conjure up so many dreams for the future, that the era of my parents and with it, my childhood, finally ended.

Krista reached out, hoping to console me, "I can't believe she's gone. She was such a…" She struggled for the correct word, "…force."

I thought about what had just happened, of everything I'd seen over the last fifty years, losing Dad, losing Lonnie and now losing Mum. It reinforced the perspective on life my father had given me and it made me realize something very important; that of everything I had done in my life up until now, the radio, TV, movies, clubs, concerts, writing, travels, the one thing I was most proud of was not leaving my mother to die alone.

The fact that I had dropped everything and stayed with Mum during her final weeks meant more to me than anything that had come before.

My presence might have been comforting for my mother, but in the end it was me who received the most from it. To know that I had been there with her in those last moments, that I had been able to ease her fears and then experience the passing of the most important person in my life while I held her in my arms meant more than the world to me. It was with those thoughts pulsing through my mind and body that I spoke to Krista.

"Life's short, honey," I sighed. "We have to live it while we can."

Krista nodded in agreement.

"You're going to think I'm crazy saying this, but I think we have to go back," I said.

"Back? Back where?" asked Krista.

"Your dad is in LA. And the rest of your family - Uncle David and Kathy, the girls, Joey, your grandparents. You should be with them while you can. There is no tomorrow, only now."

"But what about St. Maarten? What about your dream?"

"We've done it, we've lived the dream and it was great and I'll cherish it forever. But it won't bring Mum back and it won't buy us any more time with the people we love."

Krista, the most understanding person in the world, grasped what I was trying to say and instead of shooting me down, thought before she spoke, "But we sold everything. You left everything. What would we do if we went back?"

It was my turn to think. Just what would we do? We'd been gone nearly two and a half years. I was probably just a memory now. All my jobs were far behind me. The TV shows were off the air, the radio station had shuffled their line up and was continuing on without me. We'd be going back to nothing. And then I realized how freeing that was, to start again from scratch.

Was I crazy? Could I do it again? I'd gotten a place at Oxford against the odds, I'd found work in Europe when they said it would never happen and I'd done everything I had set out to do in America and more. And now I'd fulfilled that ten-year-old's dream of living like Jacques Cousteau. Maybe it was time to add to that list, to push the boundaries once more and find out where life would lead us.

That night Krista and I decided we would take that chance and embrace the thrill of discovery and the hidden vistas that wait around the next bend. We knew that together we could face anything that was in store for us. We might have no home to return to, no job waiting for us, but for some wild, insane reason that made it all the more exciting. Life is too short not to be lived as an adventure, and we understood that we would have to work hard and bust our butts to try to succeed but wherever that took us or whatever confronted us, we promised ourselves that we would face it head on.

Was I nervous and a little scared? You bet I was, but it's those moments when you don't take the easy path but instead challenge yourself that you become the most alive and attuned to the world around you. Who knows what opportunities might exist if you only dare look for them? But the one thing I was certain of is that given the chance I would once again do my best to bring the show.

TO BE CONTINUED

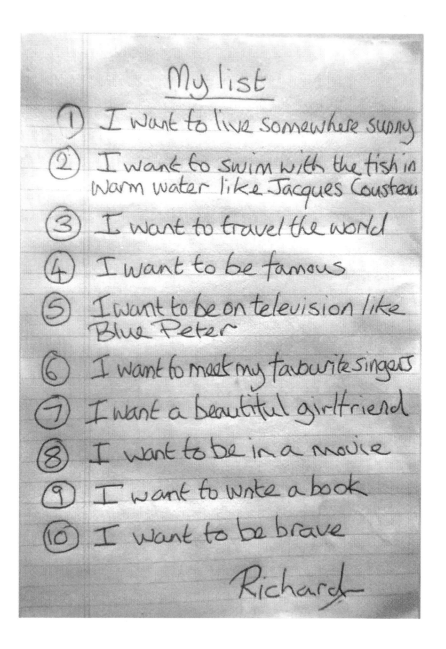

ACKNOWLEDGMENTS

First and foremost I have to thank my mother and father. It's because of them that I grew up to love people and music. I've had many blessings in my life but my parents will always rank number one. To my beloved Krista who put up with me for almost a year as I wrote this book. She encouraged me to put the words on paper (or at least on a hard drive!) despite the fact that quite a few areas of my life were X-rated. And to my furry family who slept at my feet as I tapped out the manuscript on the keyboard.

I wrote the book from my perspective which is why the title, *World In My Eyes,* seemed the perfect fit. I was fortunate to have always taken photos since a young age so that enabled me to piece together the timeline and gave me a lot to draw from and remind me of some of those amazing moments. Other people's memories and opinions might vary from mine but this book is my personal recollection of the events that I was a part of and the people who were important to me. I tried to stay 'in the moment' throughout the book and how everything felt to me as the memories came flooding back. There were many times when I cried and had to walk away from the text on the screen as it became very real to me once again.

Thank you to those who assisted me in recalling those memories and feelings, the good and the bad, that otherwise might have been missed. At the top of that list has to be Peter Facer, who was there by my side for so many of those incredible times and whose notes and photos – several of which are in the book – aided in fleshing out the details. To all the original KROQ crew – I was honored to work with you especially Raymond Bannister, Ramondo, who helped make that little station in Pasadena a monster, Mike Evans whose humor motivated me, Jed the Fish for filling in some of the blanks, Dusty Street for showing me the ropes, Swedish Egil, an early and longtime buddy, April Whitney, and Mike Jacobs who knew Rick and KROQ better than all of us. To Steve Dagger for his memories of Band Aid, our Australian adventures and continuing friendship. Tor Tendon, Rod Wilkins and Zed Bailey who went over our years together in Europe, Neil Tennant for his kind words and reminiscence of the Pet Shop Boys' early days in LA and Martin Gore for his remembrances on my time with Depeche Mode and for letting me use his brilliant song as the title of this book.

I also want to thank all the photographers whose pictures appear in this book. Being a fanboy at heart, I took the majority, but many come from others including Peter Facer, Steven Wayne for the back cover picture, Joel Gelfand the official photographer of KROQ, Lisa Johnson and Bob Sebree. You were there for some pivotal times in music history and your work and talent speaks volumes. If I missed anyone's name I'm sorry, but you do have my gratitude.

Thanks also go out to my late brother, Stephen Sheppard. I wish you could have read this, brother mine. Also the trio behind KROQ, Rick Carroll, Larry Groves and Scott Mason – all sadly missed, Dr. Drew, Jimmy Kimmel, Kevin and Bean, Rodney Bingenheimer, Kevin Weatherly, Lisa Worden, Gene Sandbloom, Rockin' Fig, Rhonda Kramer, Elvira, Michelle Gonzalez who was indispensable, Freddy Snakeskin for your dry wit and the phone call that helped change my life, Andy Schuon, Alan Lawrie, Peter Brown, Baba Bailey, my wonderful cousin, Christine Long, The Northcott family – the best neighbours ever, Bobby and Whitney Keough, Mark Rowlands and Tim Mahoney – the talented duo behind *Towards 2000*, Dave Lawrence, Mark Driscoll, Larry and Barbara Joachim, Eric Gold, Brian Clifford – R.I.P., Mike Frost, John Bennett – who taught me how to ride a bike, Ray DeVries for all the music you brought me, Jon Latta, we miss you every day, Doug 'Sluggo' Roberts, Howie Klein, Jonathan 'Baron' Kessler, Tony Demitriades, JT & SLB, the Kemp Brothers and Spandau Ballet, all the incredible bands, artists, actors and personalities I had the privilege to work with over the years, and to Howard Stern. Howard might not be in this book but his personality and unique ability on the air inspired me to be as truthful as I could and to put it all out there for the world to read. Thanks Howard, listening to you inspires me every day to be better.

To all my listeners, friends and 'fans' (not too comfortable using that word) over the years. Your love and support allowed me to pursue my dreams and avoid getting a real job! And during the last decade it was your repeated entreaties to put my stories down on paper that resulted in this book. Thank you for that, especially everyone in Southern California. Growing up here in the nineteen eighties was a very special experience that few outside of SoCal could ever understand. What a time we all had!

And to all those amazing girls and women that I was fortunate to have known. I reached out to many of them as I wrote the book and asked if they wanted me to change their names. I was shocked when they all said it was OK to go ahead and use their real names. I think of them fondly as

I remember our times together. Katy Manor, an amazing girl, dear friend and what a talent you are on air. Karen Scott, you were a good wife and a great actress, I wish you nothing but love and happiness. Darcy, whenever I hear 'California Girls' I think of you. Taxi, I'm so happy that your life has worked out so well. Your story is one of the few instances in the book where I leave the moment and come up to date to tell the reader where you are today. I felt that you deserved that, you're a very special person.

Finally I have to thank three people. When my publisher first asked me what I wanted to call the book I jokingly said, "Four Deaths, Three Loves, Two Weddings, One Life." The fact that I was lucky enough to have truly loved three such exceptional women in one lifetime blows my mind. Whether I meant as much to them as they did to me I don't know, but they are each irreplaceable milestones in my life.

Thank you Carolyn Wilson for showing me how to love and for being with me all those years at college. My parents loved you too. If you are reading this please reconnect.

Thank you Terri Nunn for the fire you ignited in my heart. Watching you grow as an artist staggered me and filled me with pride. I will never forgive myself for how it ended.

Thank you Krista Sheppard for not just being my wife, but for being my best friend, my confidante, my lover and the person who I can't wait to come home to. You understand my dreams and encourage me to chase them and you are fearless about the future. Whether you're wearing heels or kicking back in 'comfies' I can't believe how lucky I am to have you by my side.

And that does it. For everyone I've forgotten to include, I do apologize but I have to go. Krista has just made me a hot cup of Yorkshire tea and after that's finished the doggies need their walkies. Thanks for joining me on this trip through my stories of old, sharing it with you means more to me than you could ever know.

RICHARD BLADE
BIO

Richard Blade is one of the most popular DJs and entertainers in America. He was born in England and educated at Oxford, and came to the United States in 1976. In the 1980s he was the top-rated morning drive DJ on KROQ, Los Angeles, and the host and director of multiple TV shows including *Video One*, *MV3,* and *VideoBeat.*

He has won many awards, including The Golden Microphone, California's Best DJ and the ADJA Lifetime Achievement Award, and has appeared in numerous feature films and network series. He has also written and produced shows and films for Paramount, Lifetime, and VH1.

Richard, who lives in L.A. with his wife, Krista, and their two dogs and a cat, travels extensively as he continues to DJ live around the world and hosts his daily radio shows on SiriusXM and KCBS.

53833667R00292

Made in the USA
Middletown, DE
01 December 2017